Negotiating with the Enemy

NEGOTIATING WITH THE ENEMY

U.S.-China Talks during the Cold War, 1949–1972

Yafeng Xia

Indiana University Press / *Bloomington and Indianapolis*

This book is a publication of

Indiana University Press
601 North Morton Street
Bloomington, IN 47404-3797 USA

http://iupress.indiana.edu

Telephone orders 800-842-6796
Fax orders 812-855-7931
Orders by e-mail iuporder@indiana.edu

The paper used in this publication meets the minimum requirements of American National Standard for Information Sciences—Permanence of Paper for Printed Library
Materials, ANSI Z39.48-1984.

Manufactured in the United States of America

Library of Congress Cataloging-in-Publication Data

Xia, Yafeng, date
Negotiating with the enemy : U.S.-China talks during the Cold War, 1949–1972 /
Yafeng Xia.
p. cm.
Includes bibliographical references and index.
ISBN 0-253-34758-0 (cloth : alk. paper)
1. United States—Foreign relations—China. 2. China—Foreign relations—United
States. 3. United States—Foreign relations—1945–1989. 4. Negotiation—United
States—History—20th century. 5. Negotiation—China—History—20th century. 6.
Cold War. I. Title: U.S.-China talks during the Cold War, 1949–1972. II. Title.
E183.8.C5X53 2006
327.7305109'04—dc22
2006005790

1 2 3 4 5   11 10 09 08 07 06

Dedicated to

My parents, Xia Changgeng and Lu Xiuhe
My wife, Ma Qianli
My daughter, Xia Hongyi

CONTENTS

ILLUSTRATIONS

Figures

Maps

ACKNOWLEDGMENTS

P ROFESSOR SHU GUANG ZHANG guided my study of modern diplomatic history at the University of Maryland, College Park. As my mentor, Professor Zhang encouraged me to explore U.S-China relations, shared many Chinese documents from his own collection with me, read my manuscript at different stages, and offered extensive comments and suggestions. I am indebted to him. I also wish to thank other professors at the University of Maryland, especially Keith Olson, Jon Sumida, James Gao, Marlene Mayo, Deborah Cai, Arthur Eckstein, Margaret Pearson, George Yaney, and Sandy Cochran, who gave me many useful suggestions during the course of this project.

I would like to extend my appreciation to the Department of History, the Graduate School, and the Institute for Global Chinese Affairs at the University of Maryland for their support. Since I started teaching at Long Island University in 2003, Professor Joram Warmund, my department chair, has served as a source of friendship and unfailing support. The travel grant from the Richard L. Conolly College of Long Island University enabled me to travel to various academic conferences to test my hypotheses and findings.

I am deeply grateful to the following Chinese scholars: Shen Zhihua, Li Danhui, Zhang Baijia, Niu Jun, Zhang Yeliang, Wang Fan, Niu Dayong, Tao Wenzhao, Zhang Qingmin, and Ding Bangquan. They kindly talked with me during my research trip to China in 2002 and guided me to some important Chinese materials. I also benefited from the commentaries of Professors Keith Nelson, James Matray, William Burr, Mitch Lerner, Chen Jian, Xiaobing Li, Qiang Zhai, and Tao Peng, when early versions of several chapters were presented at various conferences.

An earlier version of chapter 8 was published in the spring 2002 issue of the journal *American Review of China Studies*; a shorter version of chapters 6 and

7 was also included in Xiaobing Li and Zuohong Pan, eds., *Taiwan in the Twenty-first Century* (copyright © 2003 by University Press of America, reprinted by permission of University Press of America); and a shorter version of chapter 5 appeared in the June 2005 issue of *Diplomacy and Statecraft.* They have all been substantially revised.

I also owe an intellectual debt to the many scholars from whose works I have drawn. I will let my notes and bibliography serve as partial acknowledgment.

I wish to acknowledge the help of several archivists and librarians at the National Archives, the University of Maryland, and Long Island University, especially Ingrid Wang, Paul Tremblay, and Lisa Burwell. Alisa Yalan-Murphy of Long Island University helped prepare camera-ready maps and photos for the book and offered useful suggestions on jacket design. William Burr of the National Security Archive generously pointed to and shared with me some vital documents. Writing the book in my second language would have been much harder without the encouragement and help of many American friends. Ambassador Gary Matthews, who had a distinguished career in Foreign Service and experiences in negotiating with the Russians, read several chapters and provided unique personal observations on negotiations. Dr. Gerald Bernstein, a neuroscientist by training, but with great interest in East Asian affairs, read every chapter at different stages and provided useful suggestions. Frances Pitlick, Hugh and Colleen Pettis, and Len Lazarick read and edited an early version of the manuscript. I am grateful for their friendship and assistance. Needless to say, any errors or omissions that may be contained in this book are completely my responsibility.

The editors at Indiana University Press deserve great credit for making the entire editorial and production process extremely smooth, particularly Robert J. Sloan, Dawn Ollila, Miki Bird, and Jane Quinet. Carol A. Kennedy did a great job of copyediting, saving me from many inaccuracies and making this a much better book.

This book is dedicated to my parents, Xia Changgeng and Lu Xiuhe, who taught me the importance of history and helped collect many useful Chinese language materials; and to my wife, Ma Qianli, and daughter, Xia Hongyi, who have lived through this whole process and sacrificed holidays and weekends while I was working on this project. I owe a great deal to them. Their love, care, and tolerance have helped me overcome many difficulties and frustrations during the writing of this book. I also thank my brother-in-law Ma Qianshan, who offered generous assistance during my research trip to Beijing in 2002.

YAFENG XIA
Brooklyn, New York
October 2005

ABBREVIATIONS

CCP	Chinese Communist Party
CIA	Central Intelligence Agency
CMC	Central Military Commission (CCP)
CPV	Chinese People's Volunteers
CPR	Chinese People's Republic
DPRK	Democratic People's Republic of Korea (North Korea)
DRV	Democratic Republic of Vietnam (North Vietnam)
GMD	Guomindang (Chinese Nationalist Party)
GRC	Government of the Republic of China
ICRC	International Commission of Red Cross
JCS	Joint Chiefs of Staff
JSPOG	Joint Strategic Plans and Operations Group
NATO	North Atlantic Treaty Organization
NNRC	Neutral Nations Repatriation Commission
NPC	National People's Congress
NSC	National Security Council
PLA	People's Liberation Army
POW	Prisoner of War
PPS	Policy Planning Staff
PRC	People's Republic of China
ROC	Republic of China
ROK	Republic of Korea
SRG	Senior Review Group
UK	United Kingdom
UN	United Nations
UNC	United Nations Command
U.S.	United States
USSR	Union of Soviet Socialist Republics

NOTE ON TRANSLITERATION

CHINESE NAMES AND PLACES are rendered throughout the text in the Hanyu Pinyin system of transliteration. Some names are more familiar to Western readers in their traditional Wade-Giles form. In such cases, the Wade-Giles is given in parentheses after the first use of the Pinyin, e.g., Jiang Jieshi (Chiang Kai-shek) and Zhou Enlai (Chou Enlai).

Negotiating with the Enemy

CHAPTER ONE

Introduction

T HIS BOOK TREATS U.S.-China negotiations from 1949 to 1972. During the heyday of the Cold War, Beijing (Peking) and Washington confronted one another on almost every front, but at the same time, conducted negotiations, open and secret alike. From the perspective of international conflict resolution through communication and negotiation, the decades-long U.S.-China negotiation entailed the unusually complex and contingent dynamics of a de facto diplomatic discourse between the two countries whose differences in fundamental political, strategic, and cultural outlooks were compounded by the conflicts of national interests and political ideology throughout much of the Cold War.[1]

Immediately after taking over Nanjing (Nanking), the capital of the Republic of China, in April 1949, the Chinese Communists anticipated a possible U.S. intervention on behalf of Jiang Jieshi (Chiang Kai-shek) and militarily prepared for the contingency.[2] Yet, to their surprise, John Leighton Stuart, the U.S. ambassador to Nationalist China, stayed at the U.S. embassy in Nanjing after the Communists seized the city and held secret meetings with Huang Hua, a high-level CCP foreign affairs official. They talked about how Washington might deal with a soon to be established new regime. While fighting a "limited war" in Korea, U.S. and Chinese military representatives engaged each other in armistice negotiations from July 1951 to July 1953, first in Kaesong and then in Panmunjom. With no formal diplomatic relations, however, from 1955 to 1970, Chinese and American diplomats held altogether 136 ambassadorial-level talks in Geneva and Warsaw. Before reaching the bilateral "rapprochement" in 1972, Henry Kissinger, President Richard Nixon's assistant for national security affairs, secretly flew to Beijing and talked with Chinese premier Zhou Enlai

China

(Chou Enlai) in July 1971. The secret contacts between the U.S. military attaché at Paris, Vernon A. Walters, and Chinese diplomats, and Kissinger's secret talks with Huang Zhen, the Chinese ambassador in Paris, and Huang Hua, China's first permanent representative to the United Nations in New York, paved the way toward the U.S.-China summit talks in 1972. The historic Mao Zedong (Mao Tse-Tung)–Nixon meeting on February 21 in Beijing marked a transition of the U.S.-China relationship from all-out antagonism to "limited partnership." Exactly what role did the twenty-plus-year talks between the two Cold War adversaries play in shaping U.S.-China relations? There has yet to be a succinct answer.

Previous studies viewed this period of Chinese-American relations primarily through the Cold War lenses of mutual containment, focusing largely on the role of ideological differences, with, however, little attention paid to how the talks fit in the overall puzzle.[3] The few existing studies that deal with U.S.-China negotiations in this period fall into two main categories. The first, mainly by U.S. negotiators and diplomats, narrates their personal experiences and perceptions of Chinese negotiating styles. Admiral C. Turner Joy's diary provides a fairly complete account of his ten-month experience as chief U.S. delegate in the Korean Armistice negotiation.[4] Arthur Dean has written a brief account of his experiences in negotiating with Huang Hua during the post-armistice conference on Korea. Ambassadors U. Alexis Johnson and Jacob D. Beam, who participated in the ambassadorial talks, have written about their roles and experiences in the talks.[5] Richard Nixon, Henry Kissinger, John H. Holdridge, and Vernon Walters, all published their recollections of the negotiations with the Chinese.[6]

A number of studies, largely by Western scholars, also analyze Chinese Communist negotiating styles or behaviors. These include several monographs on the Korean armistice talks.[7] Basing his work mainly on published documents and newspapers, Kenneth T. Young has provided a detailed account of Sino-American ambassadorial talks through 1967. Using documents from *Foreign Relations of the United States*, Steven M. Goldstein has written an article on U.S.-China ambassadorial talks from the American perspective.[8] Having served on the National Security Council, with much experience at operational levels, Richard H. Solomon has produced an authoritative study on Chinese political negotiation with the United States. Originally published by the RAND Corporation, Solomon's analysis has also been included in Hans Binnendijk's *National Negotiating Styles*. In his 1999 published volume *Chinese Negotiating Behavior*, Solomon assessed the "unique" aspects of Chinese negotiating behavior as perceived by the American officials who encountered the Chinese since the 1970s.[9] Alfred D. Wilhelm's study of Chinese negotiation behaviors during the Korean armistice talks and Geneva talks, published in 1994, is also an important addition to the understanding of the PRC's negotiating style and characteristics.[10]

These studies, relying on Western sources in their attempt to analyze the Chinese side, lack comparative and international perspectives. Only an analysis that cross-examines both sides and does so in light of newly available multi-archival records can adequately explain how and why the two powers engaged in such continuous talks, and evaluate how effective they were. This book, therefore, argues that in spite of intense ongoing hostilities, communication and negotiation toward conflict resolution between the two Cold War adversaries were significant and, in the end, fertile. More specifically, it addresses four simple but important questions that remain virtually unanswered by either diplomatic historians or political scientists. First, why did the two antagonists come to the negotiating table, and what kept them talking for more than twenty years? Second, how did they talk over the years, and what dictated negotiation behaviors on both sides? Third, what role did these talks play in shaping the adversarial relationships? Finally, what implications in terms of international conflict resolution did these talks entail over time?

In addressing these questions, the first theme of this study is the demonstration that the two sides shared the motivation to establish and maintain communication links from their early days of confrontation, and yet were constrained by a number of factors from achieving substantial resolution in the bilateral conflicts. To illustrate this theme, this study focuses on analyzing agenda setting, preparation of talking points, and rule making for the meetings, actual bargaining and concessions, rhetoric, and follow-up actions. In addition, the human dimensions such as the negotiators' educational background, personalities, and learning behaviors are also explored to identify those ideological and cultural differences that might give rise to misunderstandings and misperceptions, which precluded agreement. At the same time, how the two sides eventually came to grips with mutual differences and slowly but surely learned to engage each other productively is closely examined.

Around this theme, this study utilizes analytical assumptions of communication and negotiation theories to structure an analysis of Chinese-American diplomatic discourse. It in particular tests Raymond Cohen's assumptions that "a communicatory interaction—the exchange of messages, or proposals, to be more exact—lies at the heart of negotiation, then it follows that negotiation can be considered a special case of communication."[11] This study entails, therefore, four levels of analysis. First, regarding Chinese-American negotiation during this period as a communication process, this study treats the Chinese negotiators as message senders and their U.S. counterparts as message receivers, and vice versa. "For a message to be correctly understood there must be sufficient similarity, if not identity, between the intention of the sender and the meaning attributed by the receiver."[12] It thus assumes that the two governments came to the negotiation table and wanted to solve conflict. To that end, the negotiators were under strict instructions from and monitored by their respective governments.

Second, the negotiators' role went beyond exchanging information; they were to negotiate. Their culture-bound beliefs, values, education, historical consciousness, and mindset may have influenced their negotiation styles and behaviors. The Chinese-American talks constituted both interpersonal communication and cross-cultural interaction. In this regard, this study hopes to test Cohen's hypothesis that culture-bound factors "may hinder relations in general, and on occasion complicate, prolong, and even frustrate particular negotiations where there otherwise exists an identifiable basis for cooperation."[13]

Third, however slowly, communication and negotiation might have improved the adversarial relationship. The long, tedious Chinese-American talks seem to have paved the way toward relationship building and normalization. The key factor seems to be negotiation functioning as a self-learning and a mutual learning process. By the early 1970s, Beijing and Washington seem to have understood each other a great deal better in terms of both policy intention and actual behavior. They might have not been able to overcome their great differences and become "old familiar encounters" had they not kept talking for the previous decades.

Fourth, bilateral talks do not happen just in a vacuum, but within a domestic context to a large extent. Over the two decades, both the U.S. and the PRC experienced enormous changes domestically. The role played by interest groups, media, public opinion, party politics, bureaucratic competition and certainly congressional politics in shaping U.S. China policy presumably affected Washington's intention and behavior regarding the talks.[14] The same thing would be true in China but in a different fashion. China's paramount leader Mao Zedong's anxiety and unrealistic push of China toward socialism and industrialization, and his constant fight to hold "absolute" authority in policymaking over political factionalism within the party, along with the establishment of a bureaucratic government, all should have effects on the U.S.-China talks. To date, how domestic politics played out in Beijing's foreign policymaking has not yet been fully addressed. This study addresses these issues.

The second theme of this study is an answer to a set of more general questions related to international conflict resolution. First, why could two antagonists, such as Washington and Beijing, maintain long, mostly unproductive talks with one another while engaging in all-front confrontation? Second, why did such a phenomenon exist during the Cold War, and what insights can one derive from it in understanding international conflict resolution through talks and communication? To answer these questions, this study presents a fourfold explanation in relation to the existing international relations literature.

First, within the Cold War context, the scope and nature of the international confrontation determined the scope and nature of bilateral talks. During the Cold War, the structure of international politics invariably became polarized. Although the division was accompanied by an immense and escalating arms race in nuclear and conventional weaponry, the struggle between the contesting parties was not always in the form of a real hot general war. George F. Kennan, one of the chief architects of U.S. Cold War strategies, urged Washington to adopt "a long-term, patient but firm and vigilant containment of Russian expansive tendencies."[15] As he later observed, it was almost impossible to achieve "total *military* victory" for either side engaged in the Cold War.[16] Walter Lippmann argued in his 1947 writing that the most rational choice for the U.S. was not to win the Cold War but to take on "a policy of settlement" toward the USSR that "would aim to redress the balance of power." He was the first to point out that negotiation was both necessary and possible during the Cold War.[17] The fact that the U.S. and China were engaged in almost continuous talks for almost twenty-two years reflected this dimension of the Cold War.[18]

Second, the existence and consistence of U.S.-China negotiations hinge largely on how each defines its national interests and perceives external threats within the bilateral context. International relations theorists assume that how political leaders determine national interests is where the foreign and defense policymaking of a nation ought to begin, and threat perception could only come next.[19] In contemporary international politics, especially during the Cold War, policymaking does not necessarily occur in the prescribed sequence. Very often, threat perception comes first, which tends to define and change the scope and nature of national interests. Such a process becomes even more complicated when alliance politics comes into play. While those factors have proven relevant in defining the U.S.-China conflict resolution behaviors,[20] it would be surprising if they had no effect on the two governments' negotiation behavior.

It has been assumed that nation-states, especially weaker and smaller powers, tend to either jump on the bandwagon to advance their own interests or seek allies to balance against the perceived threat; and more important, ideology tends to be weighted much less than balancing.[21] Such an assumption may explain Beijing's negotiation behavior in particular, and may also explain Nixon's eagerness in playing the China card. During the early stage of the talks, Beijing, allied with the Soviet Union—one of the two superpowers—felt less threatened and thus less pressed to resolve its conflict with the United States. Only when China's security situation deteriorated, largely a result of Sino-Soviet split, did Mao become more eager to come to a rapprochement with the United States in the early 1970s. The same logic may explain Nixon's China policy. The increasing Soviet expansion in the late 1960s and early 1970s convinced Nixon that it was in the U.S.'s interest to win China over to its side in containing the Soviet expansion.

Third, as power remains a currency in international politics, the ups and downs of U.S.-China talks had a great deal to do with both sides' comparative advantages,[22] deriving from each other's strategic assets. It is assumed that one can negotiate only from a position of strength and that a win-win situation (often as a result of mutual compromise) can be realized when both sides' comparative advantages are most compatible. It is interesting to note that throughout the 1950s and much of the 1960s, Washington harbored the superpower mentality and was hardly willing to offer any compromise on the major issue (Taiwan) in dispute with Beijing. Only with the nuclear parity between the U.S. and the Soviet Union, and the Vietnam War quagmire where there seemed to be a steadfast decline in U.S. military power and political influence, did Nixon appear more willing and anxious to bring about substantial breakthroughs in the U.S.-China talks. The opposite logic seems to be true with Beijing. Profoundly concerned about its economic, military, and technological weakness in the 1950s, Beijing attached a cautious expectation to the talks, and was very reluctant to move to other issues before any settlement on the Taiwan issue. Only when China became confident in its power status, especially after developing nuclear capability, did Beijing truly believe it could negotiate over and compromise on the substantial issues from a much improved position of strength.

Fourth, the level of development in terms of nation-statehood facilitates and constrains the U.S.-China talks. Any diplomatic discourse and interaction between an established power and a newly emerged nation-state invariably involves vastly different political agendas and diplomatic expectations.[23] The United States as an established power, and especially one of the two superpowers during the Cold War, was in the position to lead and dictate the rules of bilateral and international relations. The "new kid on the block" may either get bullied or be accepted. As a new kid, the PRC was anxious to reach out and be accepted and respected. As an ancient power—"the Central Kingdom"—it had a "rightful place" in the world of nations, and Mao was determined to restore it. The U.S., however, had a superpower mentality during much of the Cold War. Believing in its political, economic, and military superiority, the Americans would have liked to see New China comply with established international norms, and honor "unequal treaties" handed down from the previous regime. When New China's leaders refused to concur, the talks were bound to be fruitless from the outset. During much of the 1950s and 1960s, as the U.S. leaders were not ready to treat China as an equal, the talks were mostly unproductive. Only when Nixon decided personally to go to Beijing and talk with Mao did the Chinese leaders believe that China had attained its rightful place in the universe, and thus was it willing to engage the Americans in resolving substantial issues.

This study is an interdisciplinary effort to *reconcile* theories on international conflict resolution through negotiation and communication with historical evidence. It does not aim at deducing concepts or theories from historical "illustrations." Its main concern is not negotiating styles or behaviors per se. It attempts to depict Chinese-American de facto diplomatic talks in light of detailed historical evidence. The principal database consists of the primary and secondary sources available both in the United States and in China. It also incorporates the newly available archival evidence from the Russian Presidential Archives into analysis.

American documents on the subject are much more abundant and systematically arranged than are the Chinese materials. Government documents, interagency memoranda, intelligence assessments, personal papers, and oral history records from the administrations of Harry Truman through Dwight D. Eisenhower, John F. Kennedy, and Lyndon B. Johnson to Richard Nixon are available at the National Archives, the presidential libraries, and many university manuscript collections. A large amount of materials concerning U.S. China policy in the period under study (1949–1972) has been declassified.[24] The newly declassified documents on Sino-American rapprochement held in the files of the Nixon Presidential Materials Project at the National Archives are especially helpful to our understanding of the negotiation process of the U.S.-China rapprochement. It contains considerable information about Nixon's opening up to China, and how Kissinger and Nixon negotiated with the Chinese leaders.

During the past twenty years, new and reliable materials concerning PRC policy toward the United States from 1949 to 1972 have also become available. These sources fall into five categories. First, a rare and long-awaited opportunity has just come by in regard to PRC foreign archives. In January 2004, the PRC Foreign Ministry declassified ten thousand folders of its diplomatic records for the period from 1949 to 1955. This book makes use of some of these new documents, which include directives and speeches on U.S. China relations and on the Korean War drafted by Zhou Enlai, and the Foreign Ministry's instructions to the Chinese negotiators to the Sino-American ambassadorial talks at Geneva in 1955.

Second, several official collections have been published that cite classified documents including telegrams, correspondences, and minutes of the meetings of the central leadership of the Chinese Communist Party. The Chinese Social Science Publishing House's Dangdai Zhongguo [China today] Series produced several important documentary collections, such as *Dangdai Zhongguo Waijiao* [Contemporary Chinese Diplomacy] in 1988 and *Kangmei Yuanchao Zhanzheng* [The War to Resist U.S. Aggression and Aid Korea] in 1990.[25] Diplomatic History Research Office, PRC Foreign Ministry published *Zhou Enlai Waijiao Huodong Dashiji, 1949–1975* [Chronology of Zhou Enlai's Diplomatic Activities, 1949–1975] in 1993, and the three-volume diplomatic history of the PRC.[26] Division of Central Archives and Manuscripts published *Zhou Enlai Nianpu: 1949–1976* [The Chronicle of Zhou Enlai: 1949–1976] in 1997, *Zhou Enlai Zhuan: 1949–1976* [A Biography of Zhou Enlai: 1949–1976] in 1998, and *Mao Zedong Zhuan: 1949–1976* [A Biography of Mao Zedong: 1949–1976] in 2003.[27] The last five items contain impressive information on U.S.-China contact and negotiations from 1949 to 1972.

Third, several important personal memoirs by those who were involved in decision-making, policy implementation, and actual negotiations at the time have appeared. These include memoirs of such leaders as Marshal Peng Dehuai (commander-in-chief of the Chinese People's Volunteers in Korea and PRC's first defense minister), Hong Xuezhi (deputy commander of the CPV in Korea in charge of logistics), Du Ping (director of the CPV Political Department), and such senior diplomats as Wu Xiuquan (vice foreign minister in charge of East European affairs), Wang Bingnan (Chinese ambassador to Poland and China's first chief negotiator at the Sino-American ambassadorial talks), and Chai Chengwen (one of China's main negotiators at the Korean armistice talks). The Diplomatic History Research Office in PRC's Foreign Ministry compiled the *Xin Zhongguo Waijiao Fengyun* [Winds and Clouds in New China's Diplomacy] and the *Dangdai Zhongguo Shijie Waijiao Shengya* [Diplomatic Careers of Contemporary Chinese Envoys] series. Memoirs in that series include those of diplomats such as Huang Hua, Cao Guisheng, and Wei Dong (the latter two were assistants to Ambassador Huang Zhen at Paris when he held secret talks with Vernon Walters and Henry Kissinger). Other books and articles have come from Han Xu (PRC's minister and ambassador to the U.S. in the late 1970s and 1980s), Wang Guoquan (Wang Bingnan's successor at the Sino-American ambassadorial talks), Xiong Xianghui (a senior intelligence and foreign service officer, one of Zhou Enlai's top aides during U.S-China rapprochement talks in the early 1970's), Luo Yisu (the PRC contact person at the Warsaw talks when ambassador Wang Guoquan was back in China), and Ji Chaozhu (Mao's and Zhou's English interpreter during the 1960s and 1970s).

Fourth, Chinese scholars have also published a number of studies on Sino-American relations of this period. Many of them are well-researched and contain many useful insights; some are based on classified documents and first-person interviews.[28] Most of those articles appeared in *Dangshi Yanjiu Ziliao* [Materials on Party History Research], *Zhonggong Dangshi Yanjiu* [Studies of CCP History], *Zhonggong Dangshi Ziliao* [Materials on CCP History], *Renwu* [Biographical Studies], *Lishi Yanjiu* [Historical Studies], *Dangdai Zhongguo-shi Yanjiu* [Contemporary China History Studies], *Meiguo Yanjiu* [American Studies], and *Bainianchao* [Hundred-year Tide], and similar sources. Making use of the newly declassified PRC diplomatic files, Xu Jingli, a reliable scholar and deputy director of Foreign Ministry Archives, published his *Jiemi Zhongguo Waijiao Dang'an* [Declassifying Chinese Diplomatic Files] in early 2005.[29] This book sheds new lights on the PRC's policy toward the United States in its formative years, especially on such events as Huang Hua–Stuart talks, the Korean Armistice talks, and Sino-U.S. contacts and talks at Geneva in 1955. Gao Wenqian, a former senior CCP official historian now sojourning in the United States, published his *Wannian Zhou Enlai* [Zhou Enlai's Later Years] in 2003.[30] Based on classified party documents and personal interviews with high-level party officials, Gao's work offers new perspectives and insights on how domestic factors affected Mao's decision for rapprochement with the United States.

Fifth, the Division of Central Archives and Manuscripts has published *Jianguo Yilai Mao Zedong Wengao* [Mao Zedong's Manuscripts since the Founding of the PRC]. These are collections of Mao's correspondence with Stalin, Kim Il-sung, Mao's memoranda to other CCP leaders, and his drafted instructions (on behalf of the CCP Central Committee and the Central Military Commission) to field military commanders and regional authorities. *Mao Zedong Waijiao Wenxuan* [Selected Diplomatic Papers of Mao Zedong] focuses on Mao's diplomatic and strategic activities, emphasizing the post-1949 period. *Zhou Enlai Waijiao Wenxuan* [Selected Diplomatic Papers of Zhou Enlai] is a collection of meeting minutes, instructions, policy statements, and speeches related to Zhou's diplomatic activities from 1949 to 1975. The Division of Central Archives and Manuscripts, moreover, has also published selected works of other senior leaders, such as Liu Shaoqi, Zhu De, Chen Yun, Peng Dehuai, Li Xiannian, Wang Jiaxiang, Peng Zhen, and Zhang Wentian, which contain many new and useful materials. With this new information on both the American and Chinese sides, a systematic archival study of Sino-American de facto diplomatic talks during this period becomes possible.

As a study of communication and diplomatic talks conducted between Beijing and Washington for the purpose of resolving the bilateral conflict from 1949 to 1972, several historical cases have been chosen for analysis. They include Huang Hua–Stuart talks in 1949; the Korean armistice negotiation, 1951–53; the Sino-American ambassadorial talks, 1955–70; and U.S.-China rapprochement talks in early 1970s. The story begins with the initial communication in May 1949 between John L. Stuart and Huang Hua, followed by twenty-two years of U.S. containment of the PRC in the form of political isolation, diplomatic non-recognition, and economic sanction and embargo. It ends in February 1972 when Nixon made his historic trip to Beijing, which inaugurated the new relationship between the two formerly antagonistic nations. This was a continuing communication and negotiation process between the United States and Communist China.

Chapter 2 deals with the initial contact between Communist China and the United States in 1949, when Communist troops marched toward nationwide victory and U.S. policy toward Communist China was unsettled. Chapter 3 covers the Korean War armistice negotiations, in which the United States wanted only a cease-fire while the Chinese were interested in a political solution to the larger East Asian problems. Starting with the Geneva Conference of 1954, chapter 4 deals with the U.S.-China ambassadorial talks through the end of the Eisenhower administration, focusing more specifically on how the two came to the negotiating table after the Korean conflict, discussing practical issues (e.g., civilian repatriation and renunciation of force), and finally resolving the crises in Taiwan Strait (1954–55, 1958). Chapter 5 takes on the largely "unproductive" talks during much of the 1960s. It traces the domestic aspects of America's China policy and China's U.S. policy—internal political changes, policy debates, and redefinitions in Beijing and Washington, and how the ambassadorial talks in Warsaw were affected. Chapter 6 discusses how Washington and Beijing, after Nixon took office in early 1969, through both open (the last two sessions of the Warsaw talks in early 1970s) and secret (Pakistani) channels, explored each other's intentions through mutual "signaling" in an attempt to establish high-level talks. Chapter 7 focuses on Kissinger's secret visit to Beijing in July 1971, his open visit in October of the same year, and Alexander Haig's visit in January 1972 in order to arrange a U.S.-China summit. It, in particular, discusses how the talks between Kissinger and Zhou Enlai laid the groundwork for the presidential visit. Chapter 8 treats Nixon's trip to China in February 1972. It examines Nixon's talks with Chinese leaders Mao Zedong and Zhou Enlai. It discusses how the two sides overcame the twenty-two years of suspicion and bilateral hostility and decided to reach reconciliation. Finally, a concluding chapter highlights the implication of these negotiations for managing the relations between the two nations during the turbulent years.

This book examines how a combination of open and secret bilateral communication and de facto diplomatic negotiation can shape and modify an adversarial relationship. Invoking international conflict resolution theories through communication and negotiation and in the light of newly available archival evidence, this study expects to produce four findings. First, in the context of mutual containment, there exists room, however limited, for the antagonists to conduct de facto communications. Second, domestic politics prove to be a crucial actor in determining the scope and nature of negotiations and communications between the U.S. and the PRC, rendering it a difficult but lasting process. Nonetheless, such a process proves to be useful in detecting each other's intentions, settling minor disputes, and eventually paving the way toward real and substantial high-level negotiation. Third, aside from institutional and ideological restraints, individual negotiators can play an important role, and their educational background, negotiation and communication styles, and abilities do matter. Fourth, ethnocentrism, or ignorance of culture-bound factors, such as values, beliefs, and historical consciousness may foster misunderstanding, misjudgment, and misperception of one another, all of which may distract negotiation and protract the ongoing antagonism.

This study will contribute not only to the theoretical discourse on international conflict resolution, but also to the ongoing Cold War international history studies. Specifically, it provides a comprehensive and vigorous examination of the protracted and convoluted process by which China and the United States created a basis for greater understanding and even a degree of cooperation, the appearance of intractable differences notwithstanding.

CHAPTER TWO

Establishing Contact
Huang-Stuart Talks, 1949

T HE YEAR 1949 PROVED pivotal in changing the dynamics of postwar international relations. In 1949, the People's Republic of China replaced the Republic of China, after winning a nationwide victory in the civil war and driving the Nationalist government to Taiwan. The collapse of the Nationalist cause shocked the American public, which had idealized "free China" as a democratic ally and valiant protégé. Now, a Communist China had inevitably extended the Cold War to East Asia. Throughout 1949, policymakers in Washington had to weigh the fear of Communism, particularly the Soviet control of China, against the practical necessity of dealing with the new rulers of China.

For two months in the middle of 1949, American officials saw a seeming opportunity to negotiate with the leadership of the Chinese Communist Party over issues related to the uncertain future of U.S.-China relations. In May and June, Ambassador John L. Stuart met and held a series of talks in Nanjing with Huang Hua, a high-level CCP foreign affairs official. The effort soon proved futile, due in part to the divergence of interests and ideological differences. How did the Stuart-Huang talks become possible? What did the U.S. expect to gain from the talks? What did the CCP expect to achieve from such contact with the United States? How did American officials view the Chinese Communists, and vice versa? What were the major differences that invalidated these contacts? How did this failed contact between the two affect the subsequent CCP-U.S. relations?

I

The unfolding Cold War defined how the initial post–civil war contact between the U.S. and the CCP was to play out. The priority of policymakers in
Washington, confronted with what they saw as the expanding Soviet threat, was
to preserve as much of Europe from Communist control as possible. That
meant, first and foremost, a massive U.S. effort to rebuild the shattered European economy. In 1948, the United States began to send large-scale aid to
Europe under the Marshall Plan. American officials also discussed seriously
with the Europeans a program for mutual security. However, U.S. resources
were "too limited to think in terms of mounting a similar effort" on behalf of
Nationalist China.[1] In the last months of 1948, the CCP's growing military victories forced the U.S. and its allies to prepare for a Communist regime in
China. The fear that China might come to be dominated by a hostile foreign
power increased. The Truman administration was in search of a feasible China
policy, but policymakers in Washington were uncertain of what direction CCP
policy toward the United States would be heading. It is interesting to note that
when it came to what the U.S. could realistically do, available and feasible options were limited.

Secretary of State George C. Marshall and his advisers were convinced that
Communist control of China would have adverse effects on American interests
there and on the world balance of power. Notwithstanding this view, Marshall
was determined to avoid a commitment to provide Jiang Jieshi's Nationalist
government with the means to victory because they feared the burden on the
United States would be too large and too long, "of uncertain magnitude and
indefinite duration."[2] Marshall was acutely aware of the burgeoning demand
for U.S. resources in Western Europe and the possible need to send U.S. troops
to Greece, Italy, or Palestine. Direct intervention in China on Jiang's behalf was
ruled out on the ground that the weakness of Jiang's regime precluded success.
George Kennan, director of the State Department's Policy Planning Staff, had
similar views. Kennan had a low estimate of China's importance in the Cold
War. In February 1948, he counseled ending American commitments to Jiang,
thereby boosting Philippine and Japanese security by using troops and other resources that had been committed to Nationalist China.[3]

The Marshall-Kennan "consensus" on China seems to have dominated a
National Security Council meeting in March 1948 when America's China
policy was discussed. The NSC believed that the Soviet objective in Asia was
to establish influence over China first, then over Southeast Asia, and finally
over the whole Asia-Pacific area. Council members pointed out that for the
Soviets, China was militarily significant "because of its (a) geographical position and (b) tremendous man power." They agreed that "China's propinquity
to Southeast Asia means that if the Chinese Communists take over all China,

they would in turn probably strengthen Communist movements in Indochina, Burma, and areas further south."[4]

The council members then considered four possible U.S. courses of action in support of the modest immediate goal of saving at least part of China from Communist domination. First, the United States could refrain from providing any more economic and military assistance to Nationalist China. This action would most likely lead to Nationalist collapse and the Communist consolidation of power. Such a policy would anger friends of the Nationalists and run counter to popular sentiment in America, which favored some form of U.S. commitment to Jiang. The second option, the opposite policy, was to assure all the economic and military help needed to secure Nationalist victory. American aid on such a scale might also precipitate large deliveries of Soviet equipment to the CCP, perhaps even leading to general war.

The third and fourth options were moderate proposals. Defense Department representatives James Forrestal, Kenneth Royall, John Sullivan, and W. Stuart Symington favored furnishing "limited economic and military assistance to the National Government of China." Secretary Marshall and Arthur Hill from the National Security Resources Board voiced objections to this approach and urged instead that the United States grant *only* "limited economic help." The political-military division was not great, but it reflected differences of proportion and emphasis. Both groups came to an agreement that China was of secondary strategic importance and that an exhausting American effort there should be avoided. Both claimed that limited aid—whether economic and military or only economic—would at most delay Nationalist defeat but could not possibly guarantee victory, which ultimately depended on the Chinese alone.[5]

President Harry Truman endorsed the State Department's recommendation to grant limited financial aid, enough to slow the rate of economic deterioration and enable the Chinese government to purchase, in either Europe or America, needed arms and supplies. The Republican Congress supported such a policy in April 1948 when it adopted the China Aid Act, appropriating $275 million for agricultural-industrial reconstruction and inflation control and tagged $125 million for military purchases.[6] In view of the Nationalist position, the Aid Act, effective for only one year, was meager and incommensurate with its lofty "goals," mainly, "to maintain the genuine independence and administrative integrity of China and to sustain and strengthen the principles of individual liberty and free institutions in China."[7]

The Truman administration's limited commitment to Jiang's government was also based on its policy to exploit the rift between the Soviet Union and Communist China. Administration officials debated on whether the Chinese Communists were real Communists or Titoists. The Truman administration accepted the argument that a victory for Communists in China would pose no overwhelming threat to American interests—not only because the task of ruling China would absorb the Communists' energies for years to come but also because Mao Zedong and his colleagues were unlikely to defer blindly to Moscow's wishes.[8] Kennan had summed up the prevailing view succinctly for Marshall early in November 1947:

> [There was] no convincing evidence . . . that, even should the Chinese National Government collapse, the Communists could in the foreseeable future assume effective authority over all China and at the same time remain seriously susceptible to Soviet guidance or control in international affairs. Thus while a collapse of the National Government would be deplorable, it probably would not be a catastrophe for American interests in China.[9]

Even before Tito's break with Moscow in the summer of 1948, some American policymakers already believed that "the potential existed for an independent Chinese Communist movement at some indefinite point in the future."[10] State officials believed that even if China became a Communist state, the Kremlin would not necessarily be able to control it or direct it to implement Soviet objectives in Asia in the foreseeable future.[11]

In September 1948, a document prepared by the PPS titled "To Review and Define United States Policy toward China" (PPS/39) argued that China's limited industrial development, its vast social and economic problems, and the poor leadership and training of its army greatly limited the country's potential usefulness as an ally in the event of war, whether aligned with the United States or with Russia. PPS/39 concluded, "we must take into account that for some time to come China will be a chaotic and undependable factor on the Far Eastern scene."[12]

No matter how unimpressed they were by China's military might, Kennan and the Policy Planning Staff believed that Moscow's struggle for the allegiance of the Chinese people was disturbing. A Communist victory in Asia would profoundly embarrass the West. The PPS also recognized that "China is worth having because capture of it would represent an impressive political victory and, more practically, acquisition of a broad human glacis from which to mount a political offensive against the rest of East Asia." Therefore, PPS/39 recommended that the U.S. government "must not become irrevocably committed to any one course of action or any one factor in China." PPS/39 pointed out, "Moscow faces a considerable task in seeking to bring the Chinese Communists under its complete control, if for no other reason than that Mao Tse-tung has been entrenched in power for nearly ten times the length of time that Tito has." PPS/39 argued that ideology was not strong enough to bind foreign Communists to Russia nor was it a substitute for Soviet control of a foreign state's party, secret police, and armed forces.[13]

By the beginning of 1949, there were three decidedly different attitudes toward China in the U.S. government. The first and dominant view stressed disengaging from the Nationalists as gracefully as possible, thereby preserving a position from which to cultivate influence with the CCP. Those who held this view argued that even if the U.S. gave Jiang Jieshi all the economic and military assistance, it was unlikely that his forces could recover from the position in which they found themselves at the beginning of 1949 without U.S. armed intervention.[14]

In the second view, the Defense Department was willing to risk somewhat more generous measures on Jiang's behalf. Admiral William Leahy, chairman of the Joint Chiefs of Staff, recommended in August 1948 increased aid and military support to Jiang, if only to stall the Communists' eventual victory.

In the third way of thinking, some members of Congress, especially the China Lobby[15] — notably Congressman Walter Judd and Senators William Knowland and Patrick McCarran—advocated direct intervention, though usually in a vague manner. They persisted in emphasizing their disenchantment with the administration's policy, and blamed its weakness for China's problems.[16]

By the end of 1948 and early 1949, as China's civil war changed rapidly, the Truman administration agonized over the upcoming CCP victory in China. Washington tried unilaterally to minimize conflict with the emerging Communist-led China in order to draw it away from the USSR, thereby furthering the overriding U.S. objective to minimize Soviet influence in the Far East. What were the feelings of the CCP toward the United States? Were the Chinese Communists going to come to U.S. terms?

II

In late 1948 and early 1949, the course of China's civil war turned in the CCP's favor. The CCP leadership contemplated establishing a new government in China and began to reconsider its relations with Western powers and the Soviet Union. As Washington continued to support the Nationalist regime, Mao Zedong and the CCP leadership were very cautious of the CCP's policies toward the Western powers in general and the United States in particular.

On 1 November 1948, one day before the Communists' entry into Shenyang (Mukden), a major city in Manchuria, the CCP Central Committee cabled the Party's Northeast Bureau regarding its general stand toward Western diplomats. The cable, drafted by Zhou Enlai, provided the following guidelines on Party policy toward foreign agencies and personnel after the Communist takeover. First, foreign banks should not be closed after the liberation of Shenyang as the situation in the Northeast was special. Second, the U.S., British, and Soviet consulates should be protected by troops under martial law, and guarded by police after the lifting of martial law. Under no circumstance should body searches be done on foreign diplomats entering and leaving the consulates. Nor should the consulates be searched. Third, the Northeast Bureau should "consult with Soviet diplomatic personnel (as the CCP was inexperienced in matters of diplomatic practice and international norms)"; but while the opinions of the Soviet should be carefully considered, "[their ideas] should be treated as no more than suggestions, and any matter related to policy should be reported to the Central Committee for instruction before taking action."[17] As a matter of fact, this directive repeated the principles outlined in an earlier document of 7 February 1948, which stated that the CCP local authorities should protect foreign residents and foreign government establishments. If the staff of a foreign consulate contacted the local CCP, "no matter whether this country has recognized our [the CCP's] democratic government or not," they should be received as the country's "diplomatic representatives."[18] These directives seem to indicate that the CCP leadership was willing to conform to general international principles of behavior. At least, it would allow Western diplomats accredited to the Guomindang (Kuomintang) regime to stay on in Communist-controlled areas, and grant them due protection as well.

The CCP, however, seems to have reversed its policies toward the West as it approached a nationwide victory. Shortly after Communist troops took over Shenyang, the CCP leadership initiated a policy of "squeezing out" (*jizou* in Chinese) American and other Western diplomats in the "liberated zone." A Central Committee telegram (drafted by Zhou Enlai) to the party's Northeast Bureau on 10 November maintained that because the British, American, and French governments had not recognized Chinese Communist authorities, the CCP would not grant official status to their diplomats, and ought to treat them as common foreigners without diplomatic immunity. The telegram further instructed the Northern Bureau to take "certain measures" to confine the "freedom of action" of the Western diplomats, so that "they will have to withdraw from Shenyang."[19] On 17 November, Mao instructed Gao Gang,[20] the CCP leader in the Northeast, to act resolutely to force the British, American, and French diplomats out of Shenyang.[21] The following day, Mao authorized the Communists in Shenyang to seize the radio transmitters in Western consulates.[22] When the Americans refused to hand over their radio equipment to Communist authorities, the Chinese Communists, following Soviet advice, placed Angus Ward, the American consul general, and his staff under house detention on 20 November (treated below).[23]

The Soviet Union played an important role in shaping the change of CCP policy toward the Americans in Shenyang.[24] As is well known, the Soviet Union regarded Northeast China as its sphere of influence. With the unfolding of the Chinese civil war, as well as escalation of the Cold War, the Northeast became an area of special interest to the Soviets. Moscow had supported CCP efforts to control the Northeast since early 1946.[25] When Communists entered Shenyang in early November, contacts between CCP officials and Western diplomats remaining in the city, including Angus Ward, raised the Soviets' suspicions. Ivan

V. Kovalev, Stalin's personal representative to the CCP, advised CCP officials to "create trouble" for the Westerners, the Americans in particular.[26]

Mao himself was leaning toward adopting a "revolutionary diplomacy." By late 1948, the CCP was approaching the United States with a set of assumptions with deep historical roots that had been validated by nearly two years of American aid to the GMD and growing Soviet-American global confrontation. To the CCP, the United States had been the principal global supporter of counterrevolution. The immediate concern was that Western diplomats might use their radio transmitters to convey military intelligence to the GMD in the ongoing Chinese civil war.[27] As China's civil war was still under way, the Party's military planners in Manchuria worried that the remaining American diplomats might use their radio transmitter to send information about the PLA's movements south from Manchuria to the Beiping (Peip'ing)-Tianjin area,[28] where a decisive military showdown between the CCP and the GMD would soon unfold. Leading members of the Northeast Bureau concluded that American diplomats were "actively engaged in intelligence-collecting about the PLA."[29] In a report to the Central Committee in November, the bureau claimed that the U.S. consulate in Shenyang had been involved in espionage activities on behalf of the GMD regime.[30] The Party believed that the threat from the U.S. might also take the form of direct military intervention as well as indirect intervention through sabotage, espionage, and political infiltration. It regarded preventing any U.S. intervention or plotting against the CCP as its major task for the time being. Mao warned:

> The China policy of the U.S. imperialists has been changed from the previous sole support of the GMD against the CCP militarily to a double-sided one. That is, on the one hand, the United States government supported the remnant GMD and the local warlord military forces to continue their resistance to the People's Liberation Army; on the other hand, it sent its running dogs to penetrate into the organizations of the revolutionary camp to organize a so-called opposition in order to sabotage the Chinese revolution from within. At the time when the PLA achieves nationwide victory, it may even adopt the method of recognition of the People's Republic in order to acquire legal status to carry out its policy of "sabotage from within."[31]

By this time, the common ground shared by the Americans and the British was to "stay where we are, to have *de facto* relations with the Chinese Communists," by "keeping a foot in the door," that is, maintaining consulates and embassies in the cities taken by the CCP.[32] Washington and London intended to "prevent China from becoming an adjunct of the Soviet Power," and to protect and salvage as much as possible of their interests in China. To achieve these goals, they felt it desirable to maintain flexibility and avoid "irrevocable commitments to any one course of action or to any one faction."[33]

In late 1948 and early 1949 the CCP received information from a number of sources, including the Soviets, that the gist of the U.S. China policy was to "create an effective opposition" within the new government. Washington would recognize Communist China, but in return, the new Chinese government should include an opposition party acceptable to Washington and give the United States the right to station troops in Shanghai and Qingdao. Mao Zedong reacted strongly to these messages. He believed the CCP should be on guard to smash the American conspiracy.[34] Mao warned, "We must pay immediate attention to plots like this, and we must not allow this U.S. imperialist plot to prevail in the new Political Consultative Conference and the coalition government."[35] On 30 December 1948, Mao published his article "To Carry Revolution Throughout to the End." He pointed out that the U.S. China policy already had changed from purely supporting Jiang Jieshi to continuing its aid to the GMD in its military resistance while trying to organize political opposition within the revolutionary ranks. The CCP and the Chinese people must act to foil this American "political program."[36] To prevent Western diplomats and journalists from disturbing the "united front," the Party center decided to "squeeze them out."[37] The "Ward case"[38] was designed to facilitate such a policy.

The events that transpired in Shenyang in November 1948 drove Mao and other CCP leaders to examine the principles underlying the CCP's policy toward the United States in particular and the outside world in general. A Politburo meeting took place on 6–8 January 1949, and the Central Committee's Second Plenary Session followed in early March. It was at these two meetings that Mao further elaborated on the CCP's foreign policy principles. The Party leadership was determined to "make a fresh start [lingqi luzao in Chinese]" in China's external relations. It would "refuse to recognize the legal status of any foreign diplomatic establishments and personnel of the GMD period, refuse to recognize all the treasonable treaties of the GMD period, abolish all imperialist propaganda agencies in China, [and] take immediate control of foreign trade and reform the customs system." It meant that the CCP would unilaterally abolish all existing treaties between China and the West, instead of negotiating to revise the old "unequal treaties." It also meant that the Western countries had to accept the CCP's terms; otherwise, the new regime would sever relations. "To make a fresh start" also required the CCP to "clean the house before entertaining the guests." The CCP leaders concluded that in order to prevent imperialist countries from sabotaging the revolution from within, New China would not establish diplomatic relations with imperialist countries until imperialist privileges, power, and influence in China had been eliminated.[39] Mao put it bluntly later when he said that the Party intended "to force" Western countries to "recognize [Communist] China unconditionally, to abolish [all the] old treaties, and to conclude entirely new treaties."[40] As a Chinese historian has noted: "These measures were aimed not only at completely negating the legitimacy of the GMD government and establishing the independent foreign policy of New China, but also at eliminating the political influence of the United States and preventing American sabotage from within."[41]

It was clear to Mao in early 1949 that the CCP needed to shut Westerners out, especially the Americans, for "a fairly long period of time" in order to "clean the house." This position seemed to be in direct contradiction to what happened in May and June of 1949. Why did the CCP decide to make contact with the U.S.? Was there any change in its perception of the U.S. "imperialism"? What was America's China policy in early 1949?

III

Ten days before Dean Acheson was sworn in as the secretary of state in January 1949, the National Security Council agreed to continue efforts to prevent China from becoming "an adjunct of Soviet power." NSC members also agreed that efforts toward China would be "of lower priority" than efforts where the benefits to American security were "more immediately commensurate" with the expenditure of resources.[42] Truman and Acheson did not relish the prospect of devoting time and attention to a reexamination of American interests in China.[43] As 1949 began, however, they found that China could no longer be ignored, as the Chinese civil war was approaching its final stage and the total collapse of GMD authority on the mainland was imminent. The Americans were confronted by the necessity of dealing with the two Chinese regimes.

Disengaging with Jiang would be seen as a first step. On 3 February, the NSC recommended that the United States suspend shipments of economic and military materials to the GMD. Several days later, however, congressional leaders urged the president not to take any formal action, though they were aware that their colleagues and constituents were willing to have shipments delayed by informal action. Truman accepted the advice. American political leaders feared that a public announcement of the cessation of aid would lead to the immediate collapse of the GMD regime, and they would be held responsible for that.[44]

A few weeks later, Acheson indicated in confidence that he had won the support necessary to end aid to the GMD and to seek an accommodation with the Chinese Communists. He told Ernest Bevin, the British foreign secretary, that Jiang's regime was "washed up," that the Communists now had a free hand in China. The Chinese people were tired of war, and further aid to the GMD would anger them. "We had," he explained to Bevin, "abandoned the idea of supporting the regime and were only extending to June 2 a further 58 million dollars under the China Aid Act." It was difficult to withdraw U.S. backing publicly, but Acheson said, "the extreme supporters of Chiang Kai-shek in Congress were gaining a better appreciation of realities." Most significantly, Acheson promised Bevin, "The U.S. henceforth will pursue a more realistic policy respecting China."[45]

The reason for Acheson's determination to cut off aid to Jiang and to acquiesce in the fall of Taiwan was partly his desire to establish the best possible relationship with Mao's regime. The Communist victory would enhance Soviet influence in China and pose dangers for the United States in the long run. Acheson and his advisers were eager to lessen that influence and to develop among the Chinese Communist leaders a sense that they needed the ties to the West.

The State Department considered trade, recognition, and Chinese representation on the UN Security Council as means of inducement or bargaining chips toward achieving tolerable relations with the Communists. NSC 41, drafted by the State Department in late February 1949, held that it was "in the field of economic relations with China that the United States has available its most effective weapons vis-à-vis a Chinese Communist regime." These weapons were to be used to prevent China from becoming an adjunct of Soviet power.

In order to exploit Communist China's future need for foreign trade, NSC 41 outlined two alternative policies: one was to mobilize "the political and economical power of the Western world to combat openly, through intimidation or direct pressure to a Chinese Communist regime." The State Department rejected this policy because it would help consolidate Communist leadership and force China even more firmly into the Soviet camp; in the worst-case scenario, the regime could forgo Western trade. A hostile policy would also cut off future Sino-Japanese trade.

The State Department preferred a second alternative that gave substance to the "fear and favor" policy. The United States would allow controlled trade between China, the West, and Japan. It would make the Communists "aware of the potential power of the United States, in collaboration with other western powers and SCAP [Supreme Commander for the Allied Powers], to impose severe restriction on trade" if the new government acted hostilely toward the United States. The department called for the establishment of a system of trade controls, which initially embargoed only strategic goods and would indicate "the United States' ability and intention to deal drastically with China's foreign trade if necessary." The hope was that renewed Chinese trade with Japan and the West "might foster serious conflicts between Kremlin and Chinese Communist policy and thereby tend to produce an independent Communist regime."[46]

Reports from the field, from Moscow as well as from offices in China, reinforced American hope for an independent Communist regime. There was evidence of tension between the Soviet and Chinese leaders. John M. Cabot, consul general at Shanghai, sent a number of cables indicating his belief that a Sino-Soviet split was inevitable. The critical question of when might be affected by American policy.[47] He suggested that the U.S. policy should be structured to channel CCP's enmity toward the Soviet Union rather than the

United States. Many American observers in China argued that "most Chinese people felt a natural affinity for Americans."[48]

For a short period in the spring of 1949, Mao and the CCP leadership showed some interest in establishing contacts with the United States. They also wanted to make use of U.S. policy. As the CCP leadership was preparing "militarily and psychologically for possible U.S. intervention," a flexible policy toward the Western powers was designed to avoid Western intervention.[49] Meanwhile, the CCP leadership cautioned against any policy mistakes that might give the United States excuse to respond vigorously. Between March and May, the party center issued a number of instructions to lesser authorities that appropriate measures must be taken to avoid provoking the foreigners in China. On 25 April, Zhou Enlai in particular instructed Deng Xiaoping, who was then in charge of the "Crossing Yangzi Campaign," that the lives and property of the American and British in Nanjing "shall be protected by all means; we should see to it that these foreigners will not be humiliated, and we need not register them."[50] As a Chinese historian has pointed out, "the idea was to avoid a direct confrontation with Western powers and not to give them any pretext to interfere in China's internal affairs."[51]

The flexibility of CCP policy toward the West was also prompted by a suggestion of Stalin to Mao. Early in January, as the Communist-led army was winning decisive victories on the battlefield in the Chinese civil war, the GMD government made a last attempt for a peace settlement through Great Power mediation. At first, Mao rejected the proposal absolutely. With Stalin's advice, Mao changed his mind and agreed in principle to negotiate a political end to the civil war. Mao may have found this technique useful in confusing the enemy so that a possible U.S. military intervention could be delayed or avoided.[52]

In spite of his enduring suspicion of CCP ideological impurity—created by the CCP's attempts to cooperate independently with the United States during and after World War II—in 1949 Stalin believed he could tolerate some degree of CCP-U.S. contact without losing control. Stalin instructed Kovalev on 15 March to convey to the CCP that the Soviet Union had no intention of interfering in CCP's trade with "capitalist countries."[53] In April, Stalin cabled Mao that in order to prevent the United States from dividing China, the CCP should propose to establish diplomatic relations with the United States on the condition that the latter sever its relations with the GMD government. Stalin stated in his cable: "We believe that the democratic government of China should not reject establishing official relations with some capitalist states, including the United States, if these governments officially renounce military, economic, and political support for Chiang Kaishek's Kuomintang government."[54]

Different signals from the U.S. side to the CCP indicated that the American government was also seeking contact with the Chinese Communists. Ambassador Stuart instructed his personal secretary, Philip Fugh, to send a secret letter to the CCP, emphasizing the following two points: (1) The GMD regime had lost the trust of people because of its blind faith in military power. He hoped that the CCP would do its best to win the hearts of the Chinese people. (2) The U.S. hoped that China would be an independent country with political, economic, and cultural freedom.[55] In April, Saul Mills visited North China, at the recommendation of former Vice President Henry A. Wallace. Wallace advocated Soviet-U.S. cooperation after the war. Mills was the former general secretary of the United Association of Industrial Workers, and vice president of the Labor Party of New York. There were political implications behind his trip at this time although he came on the pretext of discussing doing business with the CCP on behalf of ten U.S. companies.[56]

In a telegram to the CCP's General Front-line Committee on 28 April, one week after the Communist takeover of Nanjing, Mao speculated that the United States was now "contacting us through a third person to ask for establishing diplomatic relations with us" and that Great Britain was willing "to do business with us." A Chinese source indicates that the "third party" was General Chen Ming-shu, a pro-Communist "democratic figure," and a longtime friend of Stuart. On 25 and 26 March, Stuart and Chen met secretly twice in Shanghai. Stuart expressed two major concerns regarding the CCP on the part of the United States: "1) that the CCP might ally with the Soviet Union in a confrontation with the United States . . . and 2) that the CCP, after unifying China by force, would relinquish its cooperation with the democratic figures and give up a democratic coalition government." Stuart promised that "if a genuine coalition government committed to peace, independence, democracy and freedom was to be established in China and if the CCP would change its attitude toward the United States by, among other things, putting an end to the anti-American campaign," the United States would be willing to "maintain friendly relations with the CCP and would provide the new government with assistance in New China's economic recovery and reconstruction."[57]

After receiving Chen Ming-shu's report on his meetings with Stuart, Mao and the CCP leadership believed that this indicated that the old U.S. policy of supporting the GMD had failed and the United States was adjusting its China policy. After the CCP had gained undisputable military advantage, its main diplomatic concern was no longer to prevent foreigners from collecting military intelligence. Rather, it now attempted to preclude U.S. military intervention in order to end the civil war as early as possible. Mao stated that "if the United States (and Great Britain) cut off relations with the GMD, we could consider the issue of establishing diplomatic relations with them."[58] On 30 April, Mao, acting in the name of the spokesman of the General Headquarters of the PLA, announced that the CCP would be "willing to consider the establishment of diplomatic relations with foreign countries" if such relations could be "based on equality, mutual benefit, mutual respect for sovereignty and territorial integrity and, first of all, on no help being giving to the GMD reactionaries."[59]

The CCP's desire to have a U.S. connection had been well known even before the outbreak of the Sino-Japanese War in 1937. At the Wayaobao Conference of December 1935, the CCP called for a worldwide popular front against fascism and a united front with pro-Western elements within the GMD against the Japanese aggressors. To this end, the CCP decided to make the necessary compromises and establish relationships with all countries, political parties, factions, and individuals that opposed the Japanese imperialists and their Chinese puppets.[60] In his famous encounter with the American journalist Edgar Snow, Mao called for an international alliance against aggression, war, and fascism—a "united front" against Japanese imperialism by Western democratic, colonial and semi-colonial, and socialist countries.[61]

It was not until the beginning of the Pacific War in December 1942 that the CCP was able to make some official contacts with the United States. In Chongqing, the CCP representative, Zhou Enlai, and his colleagues met regularly with U.S. diplomats such as John C. Vincent, John P. Davies, and John S. Service in 1942 and 1943, reviewing the achievements of the CCP Army, sketching the extent of the CCP-controlled areas, explaining CCP goals and policies, and expressing its willingness to fight under General Joseph Stilwell. He also invited the U.S. government to send official representatives to visit and stay in Yan'an, the CCP capital.[62] The first official American representatives, the U.S. Army Observation Group (known as the Dixie Mission),[63] were sent to station in Yan'an in July 1944. The Party's Central Committee, in its first major foreign policy document (Instructions on Diplomatic Work), heralded the visit as a product of its efforts to develop an international united front and as the beginning of its diplomatic activities.[64] Although the stated purpose of the Dixie Mission was to collect information and coordinate rescue operations for U.S. airmen, the CCP hoped that this would lead to further military cooperation with, and material assistance from, the United States. Zhou Enlai later regarded this event as a milestone in the development of CCP-U.S. relations. As he wrote to Wang Bingnan, "With this channel opened, further contacts will not be difficult. . . . The prospect for subsequent cooperation is boundless."[65]

Mao was equally jubilant. He revised an editorial in *Jiefang Ribao* [Liberation Daily] on 15 August, entitled "Welcome Our Friends the American Military Observers." In Yan'an, Mao, Zhou, and other CCP leaders held many talks with the members of the Dixie mission. In late August, Mao met and talked with John Service, who was then a member of the Dixie Mission, for more than eight hours. In these talks, Mao not only discussed CCP-GMD relations and CCP-U.S. relations, but also China's postwar economic reconstruction. Mao stressed that the CCP attempted to seek U.S. cooperation in its war of resistance against Japan and support for democratic political development in China. He pointed out that postwar China's most urgent need was economic reconstruction. In economic development, "Chinese and American interests are correlated and similar. They fit together, economically and politically. We can and must work together," Mao told Service.[66] Mao also frankly expressed his concern over America's China policy, criticized that the U.S. provided assistance only to Jiang's government, and warned that such a policy would encourage Jiang to head for a civil war in China. The policy analysis elaborated in these talks laid the foundation for CCP's policies toward the United States.[67] Although Service promptly reported Mao's talks to General Stilwell, these reports did not receive due attention from Washington.

The CCP also welcomed Hurley's mediation in the CCP-GMD conflict in 1944 and 1945. When Patrick J. Hurley was appointed as President Franklin Roosevelt's personal representative to China in September 1944, he had three missions. First, to persuade Jiang to appoint General Stilwell as commander of all Chinese forces; second, to study the situation in China and report back to the president on the major factors affecting U.S. support; third, "to help Chiang work out Chinese political problems, such as the relations of the Central Government to the Chinese Communists."[68] With CCP's repeated invitations, Hurley arrived in Yan'an in early November. Mao personally presided over the negotiation with Hurley, which was actually the first of the few negotiations Mao was involved in his lifetime.[69] Hurley soon reached a five-point draft agreement with Mao, which favored the establishment of a coalition government.[70] Mao and the CCP Central Committee were satisfied with the agreement. In his letter to President Roosevelt, Mao stated that "the spirit of this agreement is what we of the Chinese Communist Party and the Chinese people have been striving for the anti-Japanese United Front during the past eight years." He declared, "The people of China and the United States have a traditional and deep-rooted friendship." He appreciated Roosevelt's great efforts and accomplishments, and hoped that "the two great nations will continue to march together for the defeat of the Japanese invaders and the establishment of a lasting world peace and the reconstruction of a democratic China."[71]

After knowing that Jiang firmly rejected the five-point agreement, especially the part concerning the coalition government, Hurley agreed to a three-point plan proposed by Jiang, which compelled the CCP to relinquish its military forces and abandon its base areas in order to earn its legal status. The CCP leaders were truly offended by Hurley's "deceptive abandonment" of the five-point agreement. Nevertheless, in the interest of the common war effort against Japan and of maintaining its existing relationship with Washington, the CCP chose an attitude of restraint and did not criticize Hurley publicly. On 12 December, Mao cabled Wang Ruofei, the CCP representative in Chongqing, asking him to tell Hurley that the CCP had no intention of breaking relations with the United States.[72] In an attempt to sound out U.S. policy and to express its willingness to cooperate, the CCP dispatched a letter to Washington, offering to send an unofficial delegation to the United States. The letter indicated that, if necessary,

Mao or Zhou personally would go to Washington for a meeting with President Roosevelt.[73] Only after Hurley's open declaration in April that the U.S. government would support Jiang's government and would not support any "warlord" or "armed political parties" and the *Amerasia* Incident of 6 June 1945,[74] in which six U.S. diplomats and military personnel, including John Service, were arrested on charges of spying for the Communists, the CCP came to believe that there was a two-line struggle within the U.S. government over its China policy. The CCP started to lash out at Hurley and the mistaken U.S. policy of supporting Jiang's government. The purpose, though, was to force a change in U.S. China policy.[75]

Mao and his associates once again showed considerable enthusiasm in cooperating with the Americans to find a peaceful solution to the CCP-GMD conflict during the Marshall Mission to China in 1945–46.[76] The CCP leadership had noticed President Truman's 15 December 1945 statement, which declared that the United States had decided not to participate directly in China's civil war on Jiang's behalf.[77] They thus decided to take this opportunity to lessen American pressure on the CCP and to force Jiang to "a peaceful reform road." CCP's strategy was "to neutralize the U. S." in the CCP-GMD struggle. Although Marshall's mediation effort failed due to the fundamental differences existing between the CCP and GMD and the intensifying Soviet-U.S. confrontation around the world in general and in East Asia and China in particular, Mao showed considerable respect for Marshall.[78] He never used harsh and emotional words (which he did to Patrick Hurley and John L. Stuart, and other U.S. leaders) when talking about Marshall even when the CCP and the U.S. became very hostile to each other. Zhou Enlai also had extensive exchanges with Marshall and assured him that the CCP policy remained flexible despite its ideological ties with Moscow. He explained, "Of course we will lean to one side. But how far depends on you."[79]

For the Chinese Communists, the question was not whether to lean toward Moscow but to what degree. Even though the CCP was determined to form an alliance with the Soviet Union, this policy did not automatically preclude contact with capitalist countries. As Zhou said, it was "a fond dream of the United States to split China from the Soviet Union." Although it was difficult for New China to form close relations with the United States, Zhou further explained, it could "conduct trade with it."[80] CCP's public statements in April 1949 expressed interest in establishing trade and diplomatic relations with the West, including the United States.[81] Thus, chances for a working relationship with the U.S. seemed to exist. The question was this: Could the CCP and the U.S. overcome their differences?

IV

John Leighton Stuart (1876–1962) served as the U.S. ambassador to China from July 1946 until August 1949. He was born in China in 1876 to missionary parents, and returned to China as a missionary in 1905. He was president of Yanjing (Yenching) University in Beiping (now part of Beijing University), for twenty-seven years before being appointed the U.S. ambassador to China in 1946. It was difficult for Stuart and others of similar background to accept a China hostile to the West as this went contrary to Christian ideals that the mission societies had been propagating for over a century.[82] Before his final departure from China in August 1949, he tried first to support Jiang's successor Li Zongren against the Communists in order to salvage the declining U.S. position.[83] When this scheme failed, he sought to reach some kind of accommodation with the CCP.[84]

After the Communists took over Nanjing, the GMD government fled to Canton. Stuart stayed on in Nanjing. Stuart's persistent goal throughout his ambassadorship was to keep the United States involved in China, and thus protect U.S interests. If Jiang could not resist the Communists, Stuart would try to work with Li Zongren. If Li proved incapable of carrying out the task, he would then like to accommodate the Communists. No matter what happened in China, U.S. interests, which Stuart considered as beneficial to China as well, should be preserved to as great an extent as possible.[85] The State Department had given instructions in December 1948 that, in the event of a Communist entry into Nanjing and the flight of the Nationalist government, Stuart and his embassy were to remain there until the situation was clarified. This decision was reaffirmed in late January 1949, but with no specific instructions as to how long Stuart should stay in Nanjing after the Communist takeover.[86]

Stuart was determined to take his own initiatives. Because of his association with Yanjing University, he personally knew a number of important Communist officials, who were his former students. Fluent in Chinese language and having a long-time devotion to China, Stuart "was eager to try to re-establish what he thought of as the natural understanding which should exist between Americans and Chinese."[87] On 10 March, Stuart sent a dispatch to the State Department requesting authorization to make direct contact with top CCP leaders to discuss outstanding issues between the United States and the CCP. He reasoned that he would like to approach the Communist leaders not only as the official representative of the U.S. government, but also as "one who through long residence here is known to have consistently stood for Chinese national independence and democratic progress as well as for closer American-Chinese relations."

Stuart elaborated the points he would present to the Communist leaders. He would begin his representation by reminding them of the long history of American goodwill and assistance given to the Chinese people. The most recent examples of this American benevolence were President Truman's statements on China in 1945 and 1946 and the dispatch of the Marshall Mission, which, although fruitless, was praiseworthy in its original intentions. Then he would state to them honestly that while the American government recognized fully the right of the Chinese people to choose any form of government they desired, it nevertheless considered the Communist system "a more subtle and sinister form of despotism, the last phase of outmoded domination of the whole by a highly organized minority." Furthermore, as the establishment of such a system in China would result in continued resistance and disorder and would threaten American national interests and world peace, Americans might feel called upon to use every available means "to restore real liberation to the Chinese people." Stuart indicated that he planned to conclude his representation by a statement: "My deep interest in the welfare of the Chinese people, more especially of the students, and my appreciation of any truly democratic and progressive political program inspire me to make this final effort to serve a nation I have learned to love." Stuart assured the department that he would not make his representation in the form of an ultimatum or threat, but as a friendly confession of his desire for a good, mutual relationship. Stuart suggested that if the CCP's response was favorable, then specific steps for the establishment of such a relationship should be undertaken; otherwise, the U.S. should prepare to adopt other courses of action in dealing with the Chinese Communists. Stuart also admitted at the end of this dispatch that he might be "naively visionary" in imagining that he could influence the CCP to adopt a more broadly tolerant policy. However, as the stakes were so high in continuing the present antagonism with the Communists, it was worthwhile for him to approach them.[88]

There were serious doubts in Washington as to the usefulness of lecturing the Chinese Communists on the error of their way. Nevertheless, Dean Acheson replied to Stuart's messages directly on 6 April. He gave permission to Stuart's proposed approach, but also expressed some reservations. First, the substance of Stuart's representation could not but be interpreted by the Communists as a threat of American retaliation if they would not react favorably. Secondly, Acheson challenged Stuart's assumption that the U.S. would use means at its disposal "to restore real liberation to the Chinese people." Acheson informed Stuart that, given the nature of the Chinese situation, "there is little ground for assuming that the U.S. government would at this juncture embark upon a program of all-out military and economic aid for China." Therefore, Acheson wanted Stuart to tone down his representation by simply informing the Communist leaders that if American national security and interests were threatened by developments in China, "the U.S. Government would have to re-examine the Chinese development with a view to adopting a course of action calculated best to serve the interests of the American people and world peace."[89]

On 22 April, when the Communist entry into Nanjing became imminent, the State Department finally decided that Stuart should stay on until Communist authorities were firmly established there, at which time he would return to the United States for consultation. Stuart was to remain behind initially to establish contact with, and gather information from, the Communist authorities and to offer protection to the American community and consular offices in China.[90] Although the State Department's instructions aimed at limited policy obligation, Stuart was pleased with the decision, for it allowed him a period of time to make his last attempt to promote an accommodation between the United States and the CCP.

The CCP leaders were at first puzzled to find Stuart in Nanjing. They soon came to realize that this could serve as an opportunity to explore further America's attitude toward the CCP while making clear the CCP's position. The CCP leaders appointed Huang Hua to be the director of the Foreign Affairs Office under the Nanjing Military Control Commission.[91] The CCP's selection of Huang was well calculated. Huang was a graduate (1936) of Yanjing University, where Stuart had been the president. Huang joined the CCP in the 1930s and later became a prominent official on external affairs. Huang had renewed his acquaintance with Stuart in 1946. His appointment to the post in Nanjing was evidently related to CCP's wish to deal with the Americans. Huang's major task was defined as "taking over the Foreign Ministry of the GMD government and transforming foreign affairs"; it also included "personal contact with Stuart."[92] The CCP's interest in the Huang-Stuart contact was in the first place based on military considerations. As the Chinese civil war was still in progress, the CCP leaders believed that they needed to pay special attention to the possibility of American military intervention, especially during the PLA's march toward Shanghai, the largest port city in China and one of the largest commercial centers in East Asia, "as the U.S. imperialists had deep roots in Shanghai."[93] This concern over direct American intervention was further strengthened by Stalin's advice that the CCP should not exclude "the danger of Anglo-American forces landing in the rear of the main forces of the PLA."[94] The Stuart-Huang contact, in the eyes of CCP leaders, would serve as a practical channel for them to convey messages to and get information from the Americans, thus pinning down the military movement of the Americans through diplomatic activities. Mao therefore instructed Huang Hua that the purpose of his meeting with Stuart was "to detect the intentions of the U.S. government."[95]

The CCP leadership also believed that contact with Stuart offered an opportunity to press Washington to cut off its relations with the GMD and to stop "interfering in China's internal affairs." In a telegram to the CCP Nanjing Municipal Committee on 10 May, Mao set forth a series of guidelines for Huang Hua. He instructed Huang to "listen more and talk less" in his meeting with Stuart. Whenever expressing his own ideas, Huang should follow the tone of the PLA spokesman's April 30 statement. Huang needed to make it clear to Stuart that the meeting between them was informal because diplomatic relations did not exist between the CCP and the United States. Mao asked Huang to be "cordial to Stuart while talking to him if Stuart also demonstrated a cordial attitude," but

Huang should avoid being "too enthusiastic." If Stuart expressed the desire to remain the American ambassador to China, Huang should not rebuff him.⁹⁶

Stuart turned out to be eager to set up communications with Huang. On 6 May Stuart sent over his personal secretary, Philip Fugh, who had been Huang's classmate at Yanjing University, to request a meeting with Huang. Huang met Fugh the next day. Fugh said that Stuart wanted to meet with Huang immediately. When Fugh told Huang that "the U.S. China policy is going to change soon and 'the old President' [Stuart] is helping to make the change," Huang replied that "it is no use for [the Americans] to make empty statements; rather, as the first step, it is necessary for the United States to do more things beneficial to the Chinese people."⁹⁷ When this was reported, Mao was not satisfied with Huang's presentation and criticized him because his reply to Fugh "implied that the U.S. government had done something beneficial to the Chinese people in the past" and that it would "leave the Americans an impression as if the CCP were willing to get American aid." Mao dictated the following principles as Huang's guidelines for discussions with Stuart:

> Our request now is that the United States should stop supporting the GMD, cut off its connections with the GMD remnants, and never try to interfere with China's internal affairs. . . . No foreign country should be allowed to interfere with China's internal affairs. In the past, the United States interfered with China's internal affairs by supporting the GMD in the civil war. This policy should be called off immediately. If the U.S. Government is willing to consider establishing diplomatic relations with us, it should stop all assistance to the GMD and cut off all contact with the remnants of the reactionary GMD forces.⁹⁸

The first meeting between Huang and Stuart went fairly well on 13 May. Stuart seized the opportunity to relate the ideas he proposed in his dispatch of 10 March to the State Department, without mentioning, however, the possibility of the United States' launching a liberation movement to save the Chinese people from Communism. Stuart especially emphasized that, being near the end of his active life (he was now seventy-three years old), his wish for China was "unity, peace, truly democratic government and international goodwill." Huang did not engage in the exchange of lofty statements, but expressed hope that the United States should cease assisting the Nationalists and withdraw its naval vessels from the combat zones near Shanghai and Qingdao. Huang also indicated that the CCP was interested in U.S. recognition of Communist China on terms of equality and mutual benefit, as well as recognition of China's need for commercial and other relationships with foreign countries. In response, Stuart listed several criteria that would have to be met before American recognition of Communist China could be extended. One was that the CCP government should perform its international obligation, meaning respect the treaties handed down from the previous regimes. Another criterion was that the Communist government must have the clear support of its people. Without the fulfillment of these conditions, the United States and other nations could do nothing but wait.[99] Huang refuted Stuart and said that the CCP wanted U.S. recognition on the condition of equality and mutual benefit.[100]

Stuart also told Huang Hua that "there were no American warships beyond Wusong Kou."[101] The CCP leaders were greatly relieved after they learned from Huang Hua's report that American warships in Shanghai had received orders to leave the combat zone. They ordered the PLA units attacking Shanghai to act resolutely against GMD ships staying in the Shanghai port.[102]

The atmosphere, though, became more strained at the second meeting on 6 June. Stuart came away with two definite impressions: (1) that the CCP was anxious to have foreign governments, especially the American, discard the discredited Nationalist government, and (2) that the CCP was very sensitive as to its right to make its own decision in international affairs. Huang also repeated the CCP's desire to establish diplomatic relations with the United States and other nations. If the United States was willing to consider the question of formal relations, Huang noted that the terms that Mao had outlined as the basis for China's dealings with other countries were equality, mutual benefit, and respect for each other's territorial and other sovereign rights. Stuart's response was essentially the same as before. To give some encouragement on the question of recognition, Stuart pointed out that the CCP should take the continued presence of foreign embassies in Nanjing as a "significant" development. Stuart particularly emphasized his and the U.S.'s fear of the CCP's endorsement of the Communist doctrine of world revolution through violence, and explained that such fear had been a considerable factor in forming America's policy toward the CCP.[103]

The next meeting between Huang and Stuart was the most significant and had serious consequences for later CCP-U.S. relations. On 8 June, Fugh came to visit Huang Hua again. He repeated that the United States currently had difficulties in giving any formal answer to the question of its relations with New China, according to his conversation with Stuart. A new American policy would require Stuart's further efforts after his return to the United States. He mentioned to Huang that the undersecretary of state, James E. Webb, had recently cabled Stuart, hoping that Stuart could make a trip to Beiping and meet with Zhou Enlai before his return to the United States. He could also stop by Yanjing University for a visit during the trip. In this way, he could get to know the view of CCP's top leadership, and thus strengthen his argument in America upon his return. Fugh asked Huang to help with the arrangement.[104]

The CCP leaders showed interest in Stuart's request to visit Beiping. They believed that by meeting with Stuart there, they could further test America's policy toward China and, possibly, drive a wedge into the America-led international alliance against Communist China, as the Western powers had formed a "common front" on the issue of nonrecognition of Communist China. From early 1949, American and British officials agreed that trade and recognition provided opportunities for bargaining. The State Department also prepared to cut off all Economic Cooperation Administration operations in Communist-controlled areas to make it "just as difficult for the communists as possible, in order to force orientation to the West."[105] The CCP leaders, however, wanted to handle Stuart's visit very carefully, without creating any illusion of a CCP-American accommodation. After careful consideration, Zhou Enlai arranged for Lu Zhiwei, president of Yanjing University, to write to invite Stuart to Beiping, informing Stuart at the same time through Huang Hua that he could meet top CCP leaders during his Beiping trip.[106] It had been customary throughout the years for Stuart to be in Beiping in June to celebrate his birthday (24 June) and be present at the commencement at Yanjing University. Zhou, in a telegram to the CCP Nanjing Municipal Committee on 30 June, stressed that whether Stuart came to Beiping or not, the CCP "would have no illusion of U.S. imperialism changing its policy." He also wanted to make clear that Stuart's coming to Beiping would not be at the invitation of the CCP. The purpose was to prevent the Americans from using this visit as a "propaganda pretext." Zhou instructed that Stuart could make the trip to Beiping on a special sleeping car with security arrangement, but he was not allowed to fly on a U.S. airplane.[107]

When these exchanges were in progress, Mao once more publicized his own guarded and conditional interest in diplomatic contacts on 15 June. He stressed that the CCP stood ready to discuss relations with anyone "on the basis of the principles of equality, mutual benefits and mutual respect for territorial integrity and sovereignty and on the condition that they would sever relations with the Nationalists." He also expressed his continued interest in resuming and expanding foreign trade.[108]

When Huang called on Stuart on 28 June and informed him that he could visit Beiping and might meet top CCP leaders, Stuart was very pleased. However, he could not decide what to do without receiving explicit approval from the State Department. Stuart was able only to say that while he would enjoy returning to Yanjing, he had not thought it was possible under the circumstances, and that it would be too taxing for "a feeble old man" like him to travel by train. Huang then stated that it would take less than three days to make the trip and that all railway facilities would be put at his disposal. Huang also indicated that if Stuart would insist on flying in his own aircraft, it could also be arranged. (This seems to be not a factual report from Stuart of the conversation with Huang Hua. It is unlikely that Huang would contradict Zhou's instruction.) At the end of the conversation, Stuart still made no firm commitment to the trip.[109]

Stuart knew that he had to convince Washington of the potential consequences of his trip to Beiping. Two days after Huang's notification, Stuart sent a report to the State Department and gave a general outline of the developments concerning this proposed trip up to that time. Then he gave his analysis of the advantages and disadvantages of his making such a trip. On the positive side, it would afford him an opportunity to speak personally to Mao and Zhou regarding U.S. policy, explaining American anxieties over Communist world revolution, and outlining America's desires for China's future. Thus, he might bring back to Washington the most authoritative information regarding the CCP's intentions through such an exchange of ideas with the Communist leaders. Stuart also believed that contact thus made could strengthen more liberal and anti-Soviet elements in the CCP. In short, the trip "would be imaginative, an adventurous indication of U.S. open-minded attitude toward changing political trends in China and would probably have beneficial effects on future Sino-American relations." However, there were also negative consequences to be considered. The trip might embarrass the State Department and provoke criticism at home. The U.S. allies might feel that Washington was first in breaking the united-front policy toward the Chinese Communists. The trip would enhance the prestige, national and international, of Chinese Communists and Mao himself. To offset these, Stuart discussed the desirability of making a similar trip to Guangzhou; but he feared such a double effort might appear to be unwarranted interference in China's internal affairs and would anger the CCP. Stuart finally emphasized that since Mao, Zhou, and Huang were "very much hoping" that he could make the trip and that they were waiting for his reply, he requested the State Department to give him instructions at its earliest convenience.[110]

W. Walton Butterworth, then assistant secretary for Far Eastern affairs, responded negatively. His main concern was domestic reaction, especially from the administration's Republican critics. By mid-1949, Butterworth had become the scapegoat, like John Carter Vincent in 1947, for the American failure in preventing the Communist victory in China. In June, his nomination to the newly created post of assistant secretary of state for Far Eastern affairs had met with complications.[111] In the midst of the Senate's extreme hostility toward the State Department in general and Butterworth in particular, it was no wonder that Butterworth was reluctant to recommend Stuart's trip. Therefore, he suggested that Stuart's visit to Beiping could be made only if Stuart would first fly to Shenyang to arrange the departure of the American consular staff, who had been placed under house arrest by the Communist authorities there for over half a year, and bring Consul General Angus Ward and his wife back in his aircraft. Butterworth felt that this "would make a lot of face for us in Asia and that it would be a justification in eyes of the American public for the visit." But John P. Davies, a specialist in Chinese affairs on the Policy Planning Staff, felt that such a procedure "might well be quite unacceptable to the communists" and ruin the whole purpose of Stuart's trip.[112]

Finally, the whole issue was taken, according to Acheson, to the "highest level" and it was decided that the trip could not be made, mainly because of the

likelihood of an unfavorable domestic reaction. Fearful of a negative outcry on
Capitol Hill and in the press, Truman vetoed Stuart's proposed trip to Beiping.[113] The congressional leaders had been using the "loss of China" to the Communists as a weapon to attack the Truman administration. Truman had already
committed his administration to a gradual disassociation from the GMD, but
objected to any action that would imply eagerness to deal with the CCP. As
president, he feared this trip would jeopardize vital European legislation by an-
tagonizing pro-Jiang members of Congress. He also believed Stuart remained
accredited to the Nationalist regime and could not properly discuss relations
with Communist leaders in Beiping. Truman even wanted Stuart to stop in
Guangzhou to reestablish contact with GMD authorities before he returned to
the United States.[114]

Stuart was notified of the State Department's decision against the trip on 1
July.[115] On 2 July, Philip Fugh informed Huang Hua that Acheson ordered Stuart to make a nonstop rush trip back to Washington before 25 July, and thus
Stuart was not able to visit Beiping for now. Huang told Fugh promptly that
Beiping had responded to Stuart's request to invite him to visit Yanjing University. It was up to Stuart to decide whether he would go or not.[116] Stuart indicated
in his diary that he had already made advance preparations for an intended
Beiping trip. For example, he had alerted friends in Beiping to the possibility of
his arrival.[117] Stuart never informed the State Department of these advance
preparations, possibly fearing the Department's disapproval.

V

When the Stuart-Huang contacts were still underway, Mao outlined China's
foreign policy at the Preparatory Session of the New China Political Consultative Conference in mid-June 1949. He emphasized that New China was
"willing to discuss with any foreign government the establishment of diplomatic relations on the basis of the principles of equality, mutual respect for
territorial integrity and sovereignty."[118] Mao's statement has been taken by
many scholars as an indication that the CCP leadership was willing to reach
an accommodation with the United States.[119] The key, however, was the two
preconditions: to cut relations with the GMD and to treat New China in an
equal and mutually beneficial way. In the same speech, Mao also stressed that
if certain foreign governments wanted to establish relations with New China
they must "sever relations with the Chinese reactionaries, stop conspiring
with them or helping them and adopt an attitude of genuine, not hypocritical,
friendship toward People's China." What was implicit in these words was the
necessity for the Americans to say farewell to the past before they could discuss
establishing relations with New China.[120] Therefore, Mao's statement was no
more than another expression of the CCP's determination not to trade basic

revolutionary principles for the Western countries' recognition of the CCP government.

At the same time that Mao issued the above statement, the CCP escalated their charges against Ward. On 19 June, the CCP alleged through its media that the American consulate general at Shenyang had links with an espionage case directed by an American "Army Liaison Group."[121] The Xinhua News Agency published a lengthy article reporting that "a large American espionage bloc" had been discovered in Shenyang. According to the article, "many pieces of captured evidence show clearly that the so-called Consulate General of the United States at Shenyang and the Army Liaison Groups are in fact American espionage organizations, whose aims were to utilize Japanese special services, as well as Chinese and Mongols, in a plot against the Chinese people and against the Chinese people's revolutionary cause and world peace."[122] On 22 June, Mao instructed the Northeast Bureau not to allow any member of the American consulate to leave Shenyang before the espionage case had been cleared up.[123] Two days later, Mao personally approved an article — "The British and American Diplomacy, an Espionage Diplomacy," prepared by the Xinhua News Agency — calling on the whole party to mobilize to expose the "reactionary nature" of American and British diplomacy, and maintain a high vigilance against it.[124]

To Mao and the CCP leaders, irrespective of the extent to which they believed in this charge, the new accusations against Ward and his colleagues offered an opportunity to further an anti-American mood among the Chinese population and also justified their management of the Ward case.[125] Most important of all, Mao and the CCP leadership used this to send the Americans a clear message: the Chinese Communists did not fear a confrontation with the United States.

The new charge inevitably aggravated the CCP-U.S. relationship. Ambassador Stuart immediately denounced the charge as "too fantastic to merit any comment." He insisted that the Chinese Communists might have leveled such charges in order to distract attention from the fact that they had held the American consul general and his staff incommunicado for the past seven months in violation of international law and custom.[126] The CCP leaders did not take kindly to such assertions. Although Ward asked for an early arrangement to send him and his colleagues home, the Shenyang Military Control Commission declined to respond. No trial was conducted on the alleged espionage charge, and Ward and his colleagues remained under house detention.

Even before he was told that Stuart would not come to Beiping, on 30 June Mao issued his "lean-to-one-side" statement in his article "On People's Democratic Dictatorship." The statement announced that New China would support the Soviet Union in international affairs.[127] Then a CCP delegation led by Liu Shaoqi secretly visited the Soviet Union from late June to August, which proved to be an important step toward the formation of a strategic cooperation between Communist China and the Soviet Union.[128] Nevertheless, in a meeting with Chen Ming-shu in late June, Mao and Zhou explained that "leaning to one side" was a political line. It was wrong to be interpreted as "dependence on others." It must be understood that "our political line is entirely our own." It must be further understood "as regards our national independence there can never be any question of dependence on others." Chen relayed Mao's and Zhou's explanation of the "leaning to one side" policy to Stuart in their meeting on 9 July. Stuart, though, felt very disappointed after his meeting with Chen, believing that there was not any sign from the CCP for improving relations with the United States. U.S. effort to prevent China from becoming "an agent of the Soviets" failed.[129]

By the summer of 1949, Acheson believed that Nationalist China was dead. The Truman administration was under a variety of pressures to establish a more definite policy with respect to China. Administration officials reviewed China policy constantly; they struggled to preserve their freedom to maneuver during the summer and fall, and Acheson knew he needed to meet the concerns of the American people. Thus, the China White Paper was published on 5 August. The purpose of the White Paper was to demonstrate to the American people that the United States had done everything possible to support the Nationalist government and that the responsibility for the reverses suffered by the Nationalist armies in China lay with the Nationalists themselves.[130]

The China White Paper angered the Chinese Communists and provided Mao with fresh material for his anti-American campaign because it denounced the CCP as the agent of the Soviet Union. Mao initiated a nationwide anti-American campaign. He personally wrote five articles criticizing America's China policy from both historical and current perspectives and denounced the United States as the dangerous enemy of the Chinese people.[131] As a Chinese historian has noted, "The United States was depicted as the head of the imperialist camp and all reactionary forces after the Second World War, and as attempting to colonize China."[132] The CCP regarded the United States as the archenemy of the Chinese revolution. Misperception and misapprehension between the CCP and the United States deepened.

The People's Republic of China was formally founded on 1 October 1949. That same afternoon, Zhou Enlai notified foreign governments of the formation of the People's Republic of China. A copy of the notification was sent to "Mr. O. Edmund Clubb"[133] to convey to the U.S. government. Zhou stated in the letter of transmittal that "it is necessary that there be established normal diplomatic relations between the People's Republic of China and all countries of the world."[134] Meanwhile, as a practical step toward building New China's diplomatic framework, the PRC government decided to treat the problem of establishing diplomatic relations with foreign countries with the following distinctions: while relationships with Communist countries could be established without negotiation, diplomatic relations with "nationalist countries" and "capitalist countries" could be formed only after the other countries clarified their attitude toward the GMD regime through the process of negotiation.[135]

The State Department believed that "the announcement of the establishment of the Chinese Communist 'government' would not add any urgency to the question of recognition."[136] On 3 October, a State Department spokesman announced that because the Chinese Communist regime did not promise to "recognize international obligation," the United States would not recognize the regime.[137]

Mao and his fellow CCP leaders, now certain that prospects for an American recognition of Communist China were remote, again emphasized that Communist China would not pursue early diplomatic relations with Western countries. In a speech to cadres of the Foreign Ministry on 8 November, Zhou Enlai made it clear that the CCP's view of the recognition issue had not changed. He stressed that "in order to open [New China's] diplomatic front, we must first distinguish enemies from friends." Therefore, emphasized Zhou, New China needed to "establish brotherly friendship with the Soviet Union and other People's democratic countries," as well as "to be hostile to the imperialists and to oppose them."[138]

Even before Mao acted to transform the "leaning to one side" policy from rhetoric to reality by visiting the Soviet Union in December 1949, the CCP leadership had decided to take further measures to expose the "imperialist nature" of American policy, to strike at the "arrogance" of American attitudes toward China, and to cut off any remaining illusion about a Sino-American accommodation among Chinese people, especially Western-educated intellectuals. On 24 October, Ward and four other consulate staff[139] were arrested by the Shenyang Public Security Bureau on the pretext that Ji Yuheng, a Chinese messenger at the American consulate, had been mistreated and "seriously injured" by Ward.[140] *Dongbei Ribao*, the Shenyang-based Party newspaper, published an editorial on 25 October, declaring that "we Chinese people sternly protest against this violent act and will back up the People's Government in meting out to the criminals headed by Ward legal sanctions due them."[141] Thus, after almost one year of pondering and maneuvering, the CCP was now determined to implement its policy of "squeezing out" Western presence in China. The return to such a policy was mainly due to security concerns. The CCP believed that the Americans remaining in China posed a serious threat to the safety of New China. The Americans, the CCP reasoned, would use their semi-official status to cause political damage and ideological confusion to Chinese people. Thus, Mao decided to dampen the U.S. government's confidence in retaining a presence in China.

The arrest of Ward and his colleagues caused indignation in the United

States. Truman expressed the desire to see if the United States could "get a plane in to bring these people out." He also indicated that the United States should consider blockading coal transportation from ports in northern China to Shanghai.[142] Facing the new tension in Sino-American relations, Acheson announced at a news conference on 16 November that the United States would not consider diplomatic recognition of the Chinese Communist regime until Americans held at Shenyang were released.[143]

The CCP leadership paid little attention to these American threats. One month after his arrest, Ward and his colleagues were tried by a People's Court in Shenyang. On 21 November, they were convicted and sentenced to a year's probation and expelled from China. Ward and his staff left China on 11 December 1949.[144]

Additional disputes soon emerged between Chinese Communists and the United States. In mid-July 1949, as the CCP imposed tighter controls over public media, American news agencies at Beiping, Tianjin (Tientsin), Shanghai, and Hankou (Hankow) were ordered to halt all activities.[145] By the time Ward and his staff were released in December, the Truman administration had virtually abandoned the objective of maintaining an American presence in China. The policy, adopted by the National Security Council in NSC 48/2, and approved by President Truman on 30 December, was to "exploit, through appropriate political, psychological and economic means, any rifts between the Chinese Communists and the USSR and between the Stalinists and other elements in China, while scrupulously avoiding the appearance of intervention." The Truman administration decided to concede China to the Chinese Communists and concentrate on limiting the spread of Communism elsewhere. The emphasis of NSC 48/2 "remained on putting some distance between the United States and the Chinese civil war." The principal focus was "the prevention of the spread of Communism in Asia beyond China."[146] To explore further CCP's Titoist tendency, Truman announced his "United States Policy toward Formosa" on 5 January 1950. He declared that the United States would neither intervene militarily in the Taiwan Straits nor provide military assistance to combatants in the Chinese civil war. Citing the Cairo Declaration and the Open Door policy, Truman stated that Taiwan was part of China and that the United States sought no special privileges on Chinese territory.[147] Truman might have expected that the Chinese Communists would conquer Taiwan and conclude the civil war if the United States did not intervene.

The CCP, unaware of U.S. policy intentions expressed in the classified NSC 48/2, had come to a decision to "squeeze out" all American presence in China in early December 1949.[148] On 6 January 1950, when Mao Zedong was visiting the Soviet Union, the Military Control Commission of Beijing City announced its intention to requisition the former military barracks of the American diplomatic compound in Beijing, which had long been transformed into consulate offices.[149] The Xinhua News Agency, in its report of the requisition, argued that the legal basis for the existence of these barracks was the "unequal" Chinese-American treaty signed by the GMD and the United States in 1943. The new government had announced its determination to abolish these unequal treaties between the old China and the Western powers, leaving no reason for the continued control of these barracks by an "imperialist country." This was a crucial step in enforcing the "complete abolition of all imperialist privileges in China and all unequal treaties imposed on China [by Western powers]."[150] It is obvious that the CCP leadership used this move to repeat the message that the CCP would not yield to pressure from the Americans, even at the risk of provoking a confrontation.

The State Department protested this action by Beijing as being "in violation of long standing treaty rights" and threatened to withdraw all its diplomats from China.[151] But the CCP leaders were not in the least concerned. On 13 January, while in Moscow, Mao cabled Liu Shaoqi, who was in charge of Party affairs during Mao's absence, stating that: "I agree to . . . the requisition of foreign military barracks. We have to prepare for the United States to recall all consulates in China." Several days later, Mao stated in another telegram to Liu: "Withdrawal by the United States of all American diplomats in China is extremely favorable for us."[152] In a statement issued by the official Xinhua News Agency on 18 January, the CCP declared:

> On problems that relate to maintaining the interests of the Chinese people as well as the safeguarding of China's sovereignty, the Chinese people will never follow the will of imperialists. All unequal treaties made by imperialists and their privileges based on aggression should be abolished; whether or not the imperialists withdraw from China, whether or not they will cry out, whether or not they treat us as equals, will have no bearing on the just stand of the Chinese people.[153]

With no prospect of compromise, the U.S. government eventually ordered all American diplomats to withdraw from China. This decision, together with Truman's announcement on 5 January, completed the American disengagement from the Chinese civil war. To the policymakers in Washington, this seemed to be the only rational choice, "of limiting Soviet influence in China without committing American forces to a war on the mainland of Asia."[154]

U.S. policy seemed to be counterproductive. The CCP was seeking an alliance with the Soviet Union to counter the U.S. threat. The Chinese and Soviet leaders signed the Sino-Soviet Treaty of Friendship, Alliance, and Mutual Assistance on 14 February 1950.[155] The Chinese leaders believed that by forming an alliance with the Soviet Union Communist China now occupied a more powerful position in the face of the long-range American threat. On 20 March, Zhou emphasized in an internal address to cadres of the Foreign Ministry that the Sino-Soviet Alliance treaty made it less likely that the United States would start a new war of aggression in East Asia.[156] One month later, in a speech to the sixth session of the Central People's Government Council, Mao further claimed that the victory of the Chinese revolution had "defeated one enemy, the reactionary forces at home." But, the chairman reminded his comrades, "there are still reactionaries in the world, that is, the imperialists outside of China." Therefore, China needed friends. With the making of the Sino-Soviet alliance, Mao emphasized, China's external position had been strengthened. Mao further declared, "If the imperialists prepare to attack us, we already have help."[157] To the Chinese Communists, it seemed that the alliance was the only realistic choice they could make in a world of fierce struggle between socialist and capitalist camps.

American policymakers understood that the Sino-Soviet alliance dealt a serious blow to America's strategic interests in the Far East. The alliance symbolized the failure of "driving a wedge" into Chinese-Soviet relations, a primary State Department objective during the 1949–50 period. As we shall see in the next chapter, the fact that China had now become a close Soviet ally would lead to further escalation of the Sino-American confrontation: China's involvement in the Korean War.

VI

When Huang Hua met Stuart in the hectic months of 1949, neither had a clear idea of the other side's intentions and goals regarding a possible U.S.-China relationship. Both ended up probing, rather blindly, each other's real thinking but producing little, if any, substantive result.

Washington seemed to have overestimated CCP's desire for an immediate official relationship with the U.S. Claiming that the U.S. had traditionally attached great importance to China, Stuart vigorously defended U.S. involvement in the CCP-GMD civil war. It, he believed, was to maintain "the doctrine of the Open Door, respect for the administrative and territorial integrity of China, and opposition to any foreign domination of China." The role of the United States in the civil war had been to encourage a political settlement that would ensure the realization of those principles. American support for the Nationalist government of Jiang Jieshi had grown out of the wartime alliance against Japan, and had been grounded upon the conviction that a strong, democratic, independent China could emerge only under the GMD banner.[158] Now that the CCP was in control of China, Stuart stressed, any relationship with the U.S. would depend on two preliminary conditions: first, the CCP should respect treaties, "to comply with international obligations"; second, the Communist government must have the clear support of its people.

Not anxious to establish any relationship with the West, the CCP leadership instructed Huang to make it clear that unless the United States was willing to sever relations with the GMD and to treat Communist China "fairly," the CCP would not consider having relations with the United States. The CCP leadership seemed to have underestimated the difficulties the Truman administration would face to meet the CCP's preconditions. To fulfill the first one, by cutting off connections with the GMD, would require the complete reversal of the China policy America had followed since the end of World War II. It would be politically impossible for the Democratic administration to accept the new Communist regime as the fanatic McCarthyism was on the rise. As Truman and Acheson were exploring CCP's Titoist tendency in order to "drive a wedge" into CCP-Soviet relations, the unexpected Ward case made any effort to lure the CCP away from Moscow just wishful thinking. On the second CCP condition, the Truman administration was unable to accept the argument that the U.S. had treated China unfairly or unjustly. The Americans could remember only U.S. goodwill toward and assistance to the Chinese people. However, that was not what Mao and his associates had in mind. In Mao's opinion, America's willingness to change its attitude toward China represented a pass-or-fail test for policymakers in Washington, and he simply did not believe that they would pass the test.[159]

How the new regime would establish foreign relations was a pass-or-fail test for the CCP as well. Although adopting a Communist ideology, the CCP leadership under Mao was determined to rid their country of all the "national humiliations" since the 1840s. To restore China's greatness in world affairs constituted the very foundation of the PRC regime and was the aim of the CCP revolution. The CCP was keenly aware of its vulnerability, fearing that any concession to the West and acceptance of unequal treatment would cause serious challenge to the legitimacy of its ruling. The CCP, instead, made a special case by refusing to comply with those "unequal treaties" handed down from the previous regime. They could never compromise between the CCP's devotion to China's independence and the American adherence to "widely accepted international custom and principle."

Neither would the CCP be willing to accept America's "democratic" principles. The U.S. had since WWII attempted to create an effective opposition in China, and hoped that the GMD then and the CCP now would share power with "democratic elements," who harbored illusions of cordial relations with the United States. A coalition government would prove that the PRC had "the clear support of its people." This was unacceptable to the CCP as its leadership regarded those "democratic elements" as "the running dogs of U.S. imperialists."[160] Thus, after the second Huang-Stuart meeting on 6 June, the CCP leadership suddenly became vigilant toward such a U.S. ploy and disillusioned about the U.S. severing its relations with the GMD. It, however, decided to continue the Stuart-Huang contact as it might serve to drive a "wedge" between the

U.S. and the GMD. After Stuart left, Mao and his associates decided to "clean the house," and wait for a fairly long time before they would allow Western diplomatic representations to return to China.

Was there a chance in 1949–1950 for the CCP and the United States to form a working relationship? Historians have been debating on the "lost chance" interpretation for decades.[161] There may have existed room for a modest level of diplomatic and economic relations between Mao's China and the United States early in 1949, and the two sides were moving in that direction by establishing contact with each other.[162] It soon proved wishful thinking. Other than geopolitical factors and domestic politics, different sets of values, beliefs, and historical consciousness, which were reflected during the Stuart-Huang talks, ensured that the talks would lead nowhere. The onset of the Korean War further disrupted any possibility of movement toward normal relations, although Washington and Beijing would soon find that the two would not only fight each other on a foreign soil, but engage in a long and difficult truce negotiation as well.

CHAPTER THREE

Negotiating while Fighting
The Korean Armistice Talks,
1951–53

T HE KOREAN ARMISTICE NEGOTIATIONS, conducted between U.S. military officers representing the UN Command and Chinese and North Korean military personnel, went from 10 July 1951 to 27 July 1953, lasting more than two years. It took altogether 575 meetings before an agreement was reached. During this period, ground actions continued, although more limited in scale than in the first year of the conflict, except for U.S./UN bombing entering its most destructive phase. About 45 percent of American casualties occurred in these two years,[1] and the Chinese, North Korean, and South Korean forces suffered massive losses as well.

Negotiating peace while fighting a war entails the use of two different strategies—diplomatic and military—to pursue the same set of objectives. Diplomacy at the negotiating table is intended to "fool" the enemy into accepting what you could not get at the battleground, while military action is designed to coerce the enemy to give in to your objectives at the negotiating table. How did the fighting affect the talking? How did negotiation affect military action? More importantly, how did the Chinese-American encounters at the negotiating table and in the battlefield shape the general adversarial relationship between the two? How did the armistice negotiations affect subsequent U.S.-China relations?

I

On 25 June 1950, the afternoon of the North Korean attack, the UN Security Council met in response to a U.S. request and passed a resolution. It called for "the immediate cessation of hostilities" and "the authorities in North Korea to withdraw forthwith their armed forces to the 38th parallel."² The UN Security Council Resolution of June 27 asked UN members to give assistance to South Korea in order "to repel the armed attack and to restore international peace and security in the area."³ While supportive of the initial intervention in Korea, America's European allies were keenly aware of its dangers. In a positive sense, it could provide a spark to strengthen the West and deter future Soviet adventurism. But it could also divert U.S. attention and resources from NATO, and the Soviets might move against a highly vulnerable Western Europe. The fighting in Korea could serve as a substitute for World War III, but regional war could easily set off a global conflict. In the latter case, no matter what the eventual outcome was, Europe would be in shambles. While Washington sought to make Korea an affair of the UN, thereby making that relatively new organization a source of international legitimacy, America's allies attempted to use the organization as an instrument to contain U.S. action.

The outbreak of the Korean War changed the Truman administration's overall strategic thinking on the Cold War. China's entry into the war posed a "major threat" to U.S. strategic interests in East Asia and disrupted Washington's effort to search for a working relation with the PRC. Although Europe remained the "vital" interest, Washington could not afford to take China lightly any more. Truman's decision to intervene in Korea and to send the Seventh Fleet to the Taiwan Strait in order to prevent an attack on and from Taiwan was an obvious reverse to the policy that Secretary of State Dean Acheson had announced in January at the National Press Club on the American defense "perimeter" in Asia, which excluded Korea and Taiwan.⁴ The Truman administration now redoubled its effort to contain Communism around the world and was determined to be "tough" with the Chinese Communists as Washington now regarded Beijing as the "trouble-maker" and agent of Soviet expansionism.⁵

The PRC leaders were very much concerned about the outbreak of war in Korea as the Korean crisis presented potential threats to China's physical security and created tremendous internal pressures on Mao and the CCP leadership as the rulers of New China. The PRC leadership were especially concerned over the U.S. decision to send the Seventh Fleet to the Taiwan Strait area. In their view, the crisis was much broader than the Korean conflict itself; its settlement should include such issues as the Taiwan question and the PRC's seat at the UN.⁶ Within this context, on 12 July, Zhou Enlai, Chinese premier and foreign minister, personally drafted five conditions for a "peaceful settlement" of the Korean crisis, including (1) all foreign troops withdraw from Korea; (2) U.S. military forces withdraw from the Taiwan Strait; (3) the Korean issue should be solved by the Korean people themselves; (4) Beijing should take over China's seat at the UN, and Taipei be expelled; and (5) an international conference should be called to discuss the signing of a peace

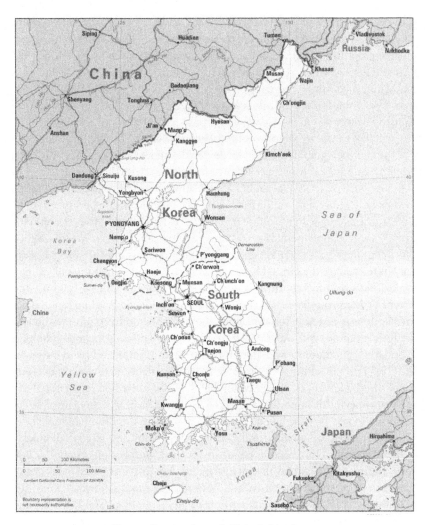

Korean Peninsula and China's Northeast

treaty with Japan.[7] Beijing would repeat these conditions on several occasions in the following two months.

The Inchon landing on 15 September changed the course of the war.[8] The tide soon turned in the UN's favor. The UN forces captured Seoul, the South Korean capital, by late September, and moved across the thirty-eighth parallel and marched deep into North Korea on 8 October as the North Korean resistance gradually collapsed.

Mao and his comrades made the difficult decision to send Chinese troops to Korea in the first half of October.[9] A quarter million Chinese People's "volunteers" entered the war on 19 October. On 25 October, the CPV launched its first campaign in the Unsan area in North Korea, forcing UN troops to retreat from an area close to the Yalu near the Chongchun River.[10] On 25 November, the Chinese forces launched a second offensive attack against UN forces in North Korea and successfully drove enemy forces south of the 38th parallel by Christmas. The Chinese and North Korean troops regained control of nearly all North Korean territory.

The CPV's military victory secured Beijing a favorable position to end the war through negotiation if PRC's leaders so desired. On 5 December 1950, the United Nations established a cease-fire group to deal with the Korean issue. On 11 January 1951, the UN General Assembly approved the five principles drafted by the cease-fire group, calling for a cease-fire in all Korea, to be supervised by a UN commission, with a promise that foreign troops would withdraw gradually from Korea. A supplementary report provided that, after a cease-fire took effect, the General Assembly would organize a conference (among the Soviet Union, the United States, the United Kingdom, and the People's Republic of China), to deal with Korea, Taiwan, PRC representation at the United Nations, and other Far Eastern problems.[11] The UN resolution locked Washington in a political dilemma. As Acheson explained, the Truman administration would lose the Koreans and cause "the fury of the Congress and press" if it chose to support it, and lose "our majority and support in the United Nations" if it did the opposite. The Truman administration made the painful decision to support the resolution "in the fervent hope and belief that the Chinese would reject it."[12]

In retrospect, this resolution should have offered Beijing a very favorable opportunity to end the war had it decided to do so. But the PRC had to defer to Moscow for decision. Advised and instructed by Stalin,[13] China reacted quickly by rebuffing the UN proposal of "cease-fire first, negotiation second." Zhou Enlai claimed on 17 January that an initial cease-fire was simply designed "to give the U.S. troops a breathing space." Zhou's counter-proposal, however, consisted of calling for a seven-power conference to be held in China. The PRC, the permanent members of the Security Council except Republic of China in Taiwan (the U.S., Britain, the Soviet Union, and France), plus India and Egypt, should participate in the conference. The subject matter should include the withdrawal of all foreign forces from Korea, the removal of American protective power from Taiwan, and other Far Eastern issues. PRC membership in the United Nations should be restored on the first day of conference.[14] This was a further indication of how intertwined the Korean and Taiwan problems were for Beijing.

With these tough objectives expressed, however, Beijing showed some sign of flexibility. A few days later, the Chinese elaborated on their position, confirming that the withdrawal of foreign troops would be applied to the Chinese units as well, and that there would be a cease-fire for a limited period prior to negotiation on the large issues. Washington rejected Beijing's position on the ground that no political price should be paid to the aggressor, especially when U.S./UN forces were in a disadvantageous military position.[15]

Only when the U.S./UN military position began to improve as the war stalemated between March and June 1951 would the Truman administration actively contemplate opening negotiations for a cease-fire. When the U.S./UN forces under newly appointed Commander-in-Chief Matthew Ridgway (from April 1951 to May 1952) were able to halt the Chinese offensive and even to counterattack northward in May, Washington thought that the time was ripe for settling the conflict in mid-1951. In his memoir, Dean Acheson expressed his belief that the Communists wished to eliminate U.S. influence from Korea altogether, but "the MacArthur aim of unifying Korea by force entailed costs greater than we were prepared to pay." He continued, "I would regard an armistice, therefore, as something that we must live with for a considerable time and that must be adapted to that end."[16]

The NSC meeting in May 1951 discussed the Korean armistice. NSC 48/5, drafted by the National Security Council, indicated that the U.S. would "seek by political, as distinguished from military means, a solution of the Korean problem which would provide for a united, independent and democratic Korea." It also laid down the following minimum objectives acceptable to the United States for the settlement of the Korean conflict:

1. terminate hostilities under appropriate armistice arrangements;
2. establish the authority of the Republic of Korea over all Korea south of a northern boundary so located as to facilitate, to the maximum extent possible, both administration and military defense, and in no case south of the 38th Parallel;
3. provide for the withdrawal by appropriate stages of non-Korean armed forces from Korea;
4. permit the building of sufficient ROK military power to deter or repel a renewed North Korean aggression.[17]

NSC 48/5 also urged avoidance of escalating hostilities in Korea into a general war. The United States should "seek an acceptable political settlement in Korea that does not jeopardize the U.S. position with respect to the USSR, to Formosa, or to seating Communist China in the UN." In order to guarantee peace after the war, the U.S. would help to build up strong South Korean military units "for continuation of the struggle against Communist forces, and for the organization of a strong barrier to defend the ROK against future aggression."[18]

The Truman administration was eager to end the war on what it considered decent terms—a divided Korea near the 38th parallel, inspection to bar the introduction of more foreign troops, exchange of all prisoners of war, and an ultimate withdrawal of foreign forces.[19] These objectives suggested that Washington was interested more in getting a cease-fire than in having the Korean problem solved once and for all. On 1 June 1951, UN Secretary General Trygve Lie stated that he believed the objectives of the UN resolutions of 25 June and 27 June 1950 had been carried out.[20]

A number of factors also contributed to China's decision to change from offensive to overall defensive action after the spring of 1951. Beijing's war objective was limited. As Mao Zedong had stated in late 1950, its objective was twofold. First, Korea's physical status quo must be restored, meaning that there should be no U.S. or ROK troops north of the 38th parallel. "We would never agree to start an armistice negotiation," Mao explained in his 4 December 1950 instructions to Peng Dehuai, commander of the CPV, "unless the U.S. imperialists withdraw to south of the 38th parallel." He stressed that the Chinese forces would continue to fight until this goal was achieved. Second, Korea's political status quo prior to the outbreak of the war must also be restored. In the same instructions, Mao insisted that China would accept a final settlement of the war only when "the Korean people are allowed to elect their own government under UN supervision with as much Chinese and Soviet participation as possible." To achieve these goals, Mao envisioned that the Chinese forces would "prepare to fight for at least one or a few [more] years."[21]

The failure of a major Communist offensive in late April (the fifth campaign) demonstrated once and for all the inability of CPV's assault to push the well-equipped UN army off the peninsula.[22] As Paul Pillar has argued, "Changes in the perceived possibility of direct achievement may account for changes in the readiness of governments to negotiate."[23] Beijing evidently expected to settle the conflict, although not necessarily to reach a cease-fire only. After the CPV secured their foothold around the 38th parallel, a peace agreement for the restoration of the status quo seemed advisable to Beijing. As acting chief of staff Nie Rongzhen asserted,

> now that we have accomplished the political objective of driving the enemy out of North Korea, [we] should not cross the 38th parallel, [because] restoration of the status quo antebellum would be acceptable to all [the governments] that are involved [in the conflict].[24]

Most of the military strategists in Beijing, Nie recalled later, supported this idea; Mao also concurred. A policy of "keeping on fighting while negotiating a peace [*biantan bianda* in Chinese]" was thus agreed upon by the central leadership.[25] During Kim Il-sung's visit to Beijing on 2 June 1951, Mao and Zhou Enlai persuaded Kim to accept "the restoration of the 38th parallel [as a short-term objective] and phased withdrawal of all foreign troops [from Korea] through negotiations and a political settlement of Korea's future by peaceful means [as long-term goals]."[26] Although he was initially against the armistice negotiations, the North Korean dependence on the Chinese eventually led Kim to agree to negotiations based on an armistice along the 38th parallel.[27]

II

The Truman administration was looking for ways to start negotiations. Fearful of holding them at the UN, where neutrals might propose terms that did not serve U.S. interests, the administration moved to more informal channels. George Kennan, former head of the PPS, was asked to approach Jacob Malik, the Soviet ambassador to the UN.[28] Kennan had worked at the U.S. embassy in the Soviet Union for many years, and was a recognized authority on U.S.-Soviet relations. Although on leave at the Institute for Advanced Study at Princeton University and not currently holding an official position, Kennan could "speak with authority and in confidence for the Government."[29] Kennan was instructed to arrange a meeting with Malik in order to impress on him the dangerous world situation as a result of the Korean War and to make clear the desire of the United States to arrange an armistice or cease-fire. Carrying out his instructions, Kennan met with Malik on 31 May and then again on 5 June. At the second meeting, Malik told Kennan that since the Soviet Union was not a belligerent in Korea, the United States should approach the North Koreans and the Chinese directly. Nothing was then heard from the Soviets for more than two weeks.[30]

On 23 June, Moscow made a surprise move. Malik delivered a speech on a UN radio broadcast in which he said that the Soviet people believed the Korean conflict could be ended. "As a first step discussions should be started between the belligerents for a cease-fire and an armistice providing for the mutual withdrawal of forces from the 38th parallel." Malik, however, said nothing regarding the withdrawal of foreign troops, Taiwan's status, or China's seat at the United Nations.[31]

Malik's words on Korea drew widespread attention in the West. Since early 1951, America's allies, especially Britain, major Commonwealth nations, and some NATO members, had been pushing for an immediate armistice. They did not want victory, only a respectable settlement. A divided Korea, a return to the status quo antebellum at the 38th parallel, would certainly meet their needs.[32] Washington was more cautious, and the State Department issued a statement, remarking blandly, "adequate means for discussing an end to the conflict are available."[33] Only Syngman Rhee, the ROK president, was unhappy with Malik's radio address since he insisted on the unification of Korea under himself.[34] Rhee vowed "hysterically to continue fighting," even without U. S. support.[35]

In a further clarification of this statement, Soviet deputy foreign minister Andrei Gromyko, in a meeting with U.S. ambassador Alan Kirk on 25 June, confirmed to the Truman administration's satisfaction that this was to be a strictly military armistice to be arranged by the opposing military commanders, with no provisions regarding political or territorial matters. The broader issues involving the future of Korea could be discussed following the conclusion of an armistice.[36] Gromyko's statement sounded more positive to Washington. The Truman administration indeed did not want to discuss political issues—PRC's UN seat or Taiwan—with the Chinese and found support for its wishes in a special UN interpretation that negotiations should be limited to military issues. The State Department and the Pentagon also concluded on 28 June that it would be best for the military commanders in the field to arrange a cease-fire. Not only would that avoid the thorny question of negotiating with two governments not recognized by the United States, China and North Korea, but it would also make it easier to exclude more sensitive and tougher political questions from the talks.[37]

Though encouraged by this exchange, Washington still faced the problem of how to commence negotiations. After discussing this matter with General Ridgway, State Department officials drafted a statement and directed Ridgway to broadcast it on 29 June to the Communist commanders in the field. The statement was carefully drafted in order to avoid a sign of weakness on the UNC side or an unacceptable loss of face on the other end.[38] Ridgway was to state:

> I am informed that you may wish a meeting to discuss an armistice providing for the cessation of hostilities and all acts of armed force in Korea, with adequate guarantees for the maintenance of such armistice.
>
> Upon the receipt of word from you that such a meeting is desired I shall be prepared to name my representative. I would also at that time suggest a date at which he could meet with your representative. I propose that such a meeting could take place aboard a Danish hospital ship in Wonsan Harbor.[39]

The statement was carefully crafted to indicate that the Communists had taken the initiative in this matter but not to say that they were suing for peace, thereby avoiding the prestige issue. The statement did not suggest a date, but in order to move the whole matter ahead, it proposed a location, aboard a Danish hospital ship, as meeting place.[40]

Beijing immediately responded. On the first day of July, after Ridgway expressed interest in negotiations, *Renmin Ribao* declared that, while the "Chinese people" had always wanted a peaceful settlement in Korea, "it was not until recently . . . [that] . . . severe blows to the American army . . . [and] . . . the general demands for peace of the peoples of the world " compelled the U.S. government to consider accepting the reasonable peace proposals of Malik.[41] As part of the policy of "keeping on fighting while negotiating peace," the Chinese leadership acquiesced to the Soviet proposal of 23 June, calling for cease-fire talks. Early on 2 July, with Stalin's instruction, Kim Il-sung joined Peng Dehuai, in replying affirmatively to Ridgway's overture.[42] Beijing and Pyongyang replied that they were prepared to confer with Ridgway's representatives but suggested that the two sides meet on 10 July at Kaesong near the thirty-eighth parallel, instead of on the Danish hospital ship.[43] Meanwhile, the CCP Central Committee issued a directive explaining why China decided to participate in the negotiations. It stated:

> [We] have fought for eight months in Korea and forced the enemy to recognize our strength and give up its original plans for [further] aggression so that [we] have safeguarded the security of both the Democratic People's Republic of Korea and the People's Republic of China. These are the direct outcomes of our war to resist America and aid Korea.[44]

Now that the U.S./UN forces "are met with grave difficulties on the battlefield," the CCP documents asserted, "they have to ask for an immediate cease-fire. Therefore, it will benefit both sides to achieve a cessation of hostilities right now."[45]

Coming to the negotiating table, the Chinese had their own agenda. They expected to reach an armistice agreement in order to move on to more difficult political questions. They continually stressed that Malik's offer on 23 June represented only the "first step" toward a peaceful settlement, the implication being that they were hoping for and expecting an expansion on the terms of the discussion.[46] It was clearly going to be an uphill struggle for the Chinese and North Koreans to get additional items onto the agenda now that the Soviets had abandoned the unambiguous reference to the need to withdraw all foreign troops from the country and to the provisions that were of direct political and military interests to the PRC concerning Taiwan.[47]

One day after Ridgway's radio broadcast, Washington advised him on the general policy and objectives of the United States in negotiating a cease-fire with the Communists. Negotiations were under the guidance of Washington. In general, the JCS, the Departments of Defense and State, the National Security Council, and the president participated in the formation and approval of a political-military national policy. Ridgway's channel of communication was the Department of the Army and the JCS. The State Department and the JCS worked out the directives to Ridgway on cease-fire negotiations on 30 June.[48] These directives provided the framework for the American position.[49]

The principal military interests of the United States were to secure a cessation of hostilities, and to ensure that fighting was not resumed, and to protect the security of UN forces. The U.S. feared that the Communists might not want to reach a permanent political settlement in Korea; thus the U.S. political and military leaders advised Ridgway that it was essential to obtain a military agreement that would be acceptable to the United States over an extended period of time. Severely restricting the Far East commander to military matters, they cautioned him against discussing political questions, including, specifically, the disposition of Taiwan, the seating of Communist China in the United Nations, and the 38th parallel. These problems, Washington officials insisted, should be considered at the political level.

To provide flexibility in dealing with the Communists, administration officials held that the U.S. negotiators could adopt initial positions more advantageous than they expected to obtain. At the same time, they should be cautious that a retreat to the minimum acceptable position should remain open. Washington did not want the United States to be accused of bad faith in negotiation.

As for specific details, administration officials felt that a Military Armistice Commission with equal representation from both sides should be established. This commission should have the right of free and unlimited access to all Korea and power to carry out its task of ensuring that the conditions of the armistice were met. Until the commission was prepared to function, the armistice would not become effective. On the battlefield, a demilitarized zone twenty miles wide should be set up based on the positions occupied at the time the truce was signed. For purposes of negotiation, UNC negotiators were advised to demand at the very beginning that the Communist forces withdraw twenty miles or more along the entire front. For the purpose of bargaining, they might agree to some withdrawal of UNC forces. There would be no reinforcement of troops or augmentation of material and equipment except on a one-for-one replacement basis. On the matter of prisoners of war, they would be exchanged as quickly as possible on a similar basis, one for one. In the meantime, representatives of the International Committee of the Red Cross should be permitted to visit all POW camps to render such assistance as they could until the arrangements were completed.[50]

After receiving these instructions, Ridgway delegated the responsibility for the preparation of detailed plans and physical arrangements for the truce talks to the Joint Strategic Plans and Operations Group, headed by Brigadier General Edwin K. Wright.[51] Working closely with this group, Ridgway drafted an agenda and forwarded it to the JCS on 1 July, together with the names of the representatives he had selected to represent the United Nations at the conference table. To head the delegation, he had chosen Vice Admiral C. Turner Joy, commander of U.S. Naval Forces in the Far East and a tough veteran of the Pacific campaigns in World War II. Joy's associates would include Major General Henry I. Hodes, deputy chief of staff of the Eighth Army; Major General Laurence C. Craigie, vice commander of Far East Air Forces; Rear Admiral Arleigh A. Burke, deputy chief of staff of U.S. Naval Forces in the Far East; and Major General Paik Sun Yup, commanding general of ROK I Corps.[52] The State Department turned down Ridgway's request that "his armistice delegation be provided with political advisers."[53] The Chinese would not make such a mistake.

Early in July, the Soviet Union, North Korea, and China agreed that Mao Zedong would lead the negotiation. The three Communist parties would coordinate on major policy issues.[54] The declassified Russian Presidential Archive sources reveal that when Mao asked Stalin to lead the armistice negotiations personally on 30 June, Stalin replied immediately, "It's up to you to lead, Comrade MAO ZEDONG. The most we can give is advice on various questions."[55] When Kim Il-sung asked Stalin for instruction on negotiation issues, Stalin told him, "The Korean government must come to an agreement on the questions raised in the telegram with the Chinese government and together work out the proposals."[56]

The CCP authorities took the negotiations rather seriously. In his telegram to Peng Dehuai and Kim Il-sung on 29 June, Mao requested that "while actively preparing for combat operations . . . you must begin to consider possible issues concerning the truce talks and select appropriate negotiators."[57] On 2 July, he suggested that Deng Hua, deputy commander, and Xie Fang, chief of staff of CPV—both having reputations for being highly intelligent warriors—represent the Chinese forces. He also instructed that Deng and Xie be assisted by a group of hand-picked diplomatic specialists led by Li Kenong, deputy foreign minister and intelligence director of the Central Military Commission, and Qiao Guan-hua, director-general of the International Information Bureau of the Foreign Ministry—two of Zhou Enlai's best aides. Mao himself directed the CPV head-quarters to "arrange a special office for Li and Qiao which should be one or two kilometers [about a half to one mile] away from where the actual meetings take place," so that Li and Qiao could monitor the negotiations closely and be the real leaders on the spot. Mao stressed that "everything must be prepared appro-priately and [you should see to it that] nothing would go wrong."[58] Before Li and Qiao left for Korea, Mao had a lengthy discussion with them, emphasizing that they should treat the coming negotiations as a "political battle" and should al-ways follow the policy lines formulated in Beijing. Mao also ordered them to "carefully form a working team" in order to produce a positive outcome to the talks.[59] "Strive for peace, but do not be afraid of procrastinating. Forcefully strike a counterblow, but also leave some leeway," were the guiding principles, which the CCP Central Committee issued to Communist negotiators.[60]

Deng Hua's assignment to the armistice talks was brief, and largely restricted to delivering short opening statements. His mission ended in October 1951. In assigning Deng Hua to negotiation, the central leadership sent an officer of ap-propriate military rank and political importance to match that of his counter-part, Admiral C. Turner Joy, in expectation that they would expeditiously com-plete the military armistice, the framework of which the Chinese leaders believed had been publicly determined. Like Deng Hua, Xie Fang was an expe-rienced combat commander but with much more experience in negotiation and political maneuvering. Before Xie left CPV headquarters for Kaesong, Peng Dehuai met him and instructed: "Don't let the enemy get anything from the negotiating table that they couldn't get on the battlefield."[61] The UNC chief del-egate, Admiral Joy, considered Xie Fang to be "the *de facto* chief of the entire Communist group of negotiators. . . . [He] rarely spoke from prepared material as Nam Il did invariably. He was the only member of the Communist delegation who seemed to be confident of his position with his Communist superiors in Peking."[62]

Li Kenong was head of the "negotiation steering group" in Korea, whose role derived from an agreement between the Chinese and Korean Communist parties. The North Koreans agreed that this group, which communicated daily with Beijing, would direct the negotiations.[63] Li had been an associate of Zhou Enlai since 1928 and a special assistant to Zhou and Ye Jianying during the Xi'an Incident of 1936. He was head of Communist liaison offices in Shanghai, Nanjing, and Guilin during the War of Resistance against Japan. As a long-time CCP negotiator and intelligence head, Li served as secretary-general in the Peiping Military Coordination Executive Headquarters during the Chinese civil war in the later 1940s. When Mao picked Li Kenong personally in July, Li was seriously ill. Mao could not find a better substitute and insisted that Li lead the "negotiation steering group."[64]

Qiao Guanhua was Li Kenong's deputy in the negotiation. With a doctorate in philosophy from the University of Tübingen in Germany, Qiao was known for his literary and artistic talent and his knowledge of international affairs. As director-general of the International Information Bureau, Qiao had been closely associated with Korean affairs. Confident in Qiao's diplomatic skills, especially as a negotiator, and his linguistic skills (he knew English, German, Japanese, Russian, and French), Zhou sent Qiao to accompany General Wu Xiuquan[65] to the United Nations in November 1950 to present the PRC's charges against the United States for its activities in Korea.[66]

Pyongyang formed a formidable negotiating team as well. Kim Il-sung appointed General Nam Il as the chief negotiator, and Major General Lee Sang Jo as delegate, representing the Korean People's Army. Born in Asiatic Russia of Korean parentage, Nam Il attended military schools in the USSR and had fought in the Soviet Red Army as a captain during World War II. He came to North Korea with the Soviets at the end of the war and was assigned to key posts in the fields of education and propaganda. Shortly before the attack on South Korea in June 1950, Nam Il was transferred to the National Defense Ministry and assigned a top planning post in preparation for the attack. When appointed to head the Communist delegation, Nam Il was then chief of staff of the North Korean People's Army.[67] It is evident that both U.S./UN and PRC/DPRK formed teams of strong and highly skilled personnel.

Kaesong was the ancient capital of Korean dynasties. It was south of the 38th parallel and had been the first town captured by the North Koreans in their offensive a year earlier. Its choice would provide the Communists with a propaganda advantage. Although the Americans were not overtly sensitive to the symbolism, the North Koreans felt strongly that both the Communists' possession of Kaesong and the holding of the armistice talks there were of psychological importance. It was valuable to the North Koreans in improving morale among their disillusioned population with negative implications for the South. The UN Command saw disadvantages in this site. However, it was impossible to find a perfect location on the ground in Korea. Most sites between the front lines would interfere with the fighting, whereas locations to the north or south would present one side or the other with difficulties regarding access and communications, not to mention prestige. The UN Command accepted the Communist counterproposal on a meeting place in the hope of moving quickly toward negotiations.[68]

It is worth noting that both sides tried to employ negotiation as a means to end the war. At the same time, they were well prepared for continued warfare. In his telegram to the CPV in middle June, Mao declared his policy was "to be well prepared for a protracted war, and to end the war through peace negotiation." He was well aware that only when the CPV were able to maintain a superior military position on the battlefield would it possible for them to achieve favorable terms at the negotiating table. After the date and location for the negotiations had been settled, Mao and the CPV commanders in Korea began planning a sixth campaign. In a July 3 telegram to Peng Dehuai and Kim Il-sung, Mao instructed them "to make every effort to increase the personnel of the front line units and especially to replenish them with arms and ammunition."[69] The Russian Presidential sources show that Mao Zedong's decision to go to negotiations in the summer of 1951 was primarily to buy time to reinforce his position on the battlefield. Mao's communications with Stalin in July and August suggested that had he been able to secure satisfactory terms in the negotiations, he may have been willing to conclude an armistice in 1951.[70] However, the documents reveal that Stalin consistently took a "hard line" toward the negotiations, advising Mao that since the Americans had an even greater need to conclude an armistice, the Chinese and North Koreans should "continue to pursue a hard line, not showing haste and not displaying interest in a rapid end to the negotiations."[71] On the American side, the Joint Chiefs of Staff instructed Ridgway to engage in a ground offensive and aggressive sea and air warfare before the actual start of the armistice talks. The purpose was to wipe out as many Communist soldiers as possible and to destroy enemy logistic supply lines. The JCS also requested the UN Command not to launch large-scale offensives while negotiating. Both the UNC and Communist armies contended for battlefield initiatives while their negotiators were negotiating for peace. "Fighting, talking, fighting, talking" characterized the status of the Korean War during this period.[72]

III

The two sides soon agreed to the preliminary meeting of the liaison officers, and on 8 July, the UNC liaison officers, led by Colonel Andrew J. Kinney of the U.S. Air Force, set out from Munsan-ni by helicopter.[73] They landed near Kaesong, where the Communists met and escorted them to the first meeting at the conference table. Zhang Cunshan and Chai Chengwen were the chief Communist liaison officers.[74] Chai was chargé d'affaires and political councilor of the Chinese Embassy in Pyongyang.[75] Fluent in English and well versed in both diplomatic and military affairs, he was well qualified to be the senior liaison officer. Although he was junior to other Chinese military negotiators, his assignment to the talks as a PLA colonel assured equality with his U.S. counterparts, who were all colonels. Chai was later to succeed Xie Fang in 1952 as negotiator for the Communist side.[76]

The initial exchange was formal and without cordiality. The UNC party declined refreshments, and the amenities were quickly gone. As the first order of business, Kinney submitted the list of UNC delegates and requested the names of the Communist representatives. The Chinese and North Korean did not release their list immediately. The UNC delegates rejected the Communists' offer of food, liquor, and cigarettes during the three-hour recess.

Agitated over the UNC delegation's suspicion and arrogance, the Chinese and North Koreans were indeed prepared to fight back and play tough. Before the first actual negotiation on 10 July, Li Kenong chaired a meeting of the Chinese and North Korean negotiators. He emphasized the following points:

1. We should uphold our peace initiatives, and let the whole world know our three principles—cease-fire, establishment of 38th parallel as the demarcation line and withdrawal of all foreign troops from the Korean peninsula.
2. We should pay special attention to security around Kaesong, the negotiation area.
3. Negotiation is "fighting"; it is a "war of words," not a military war. Principle is the most important. While we deal with concrete issues, we can only gain mastery by striking after the enemy has struck. Our negotiators should be very cautious expressing themselves while negotiating.
4. Negotiation is closely related to the situation on the battlefield. Our negotiators should always be aware of this.[77]

These points forged a fighting spirit for the Chinese and North Koreans.

When the first meeting started on 10 July, Admiral Joy attempted to appear tough in his opening address in order to counter the Communist political advantage. He stated quite bluntly that the UNC representatives intended to discuss only military matters relating to Korea and would not consider political or economic subjects. He then presented the UNC's nine-point agenda:

1. Adoption of the agenda.
2. Location of and authority for International Committee of Red Cross representatives to visit prisoners of war camps.
3. Limitation of discussion to purely military matters related to Korea only.

4. Cessation of hostilities and of acts of armed force in Korea under conditions that would assure against resumption of hostilities and acts of armed force in Korea.
5. Agreement on a demilitarized zone across Korea.
6. Composition, authority, and functions of a military armistice commission.
7. Agreement on principles of inspection within Korea by military armistice commission.
8. Composition and functions of these terms.
9. Arrangements pertaining to prisoners of war.[78]

The Chinese/North Korean negotiators proposed an immediate cease-fire, withdrawal of all armed forces to opposite sides of the 38th parallel, supervision of terms, exchange of all prisoners of war, and removal of all non-Korean troops from the peninsula. But Joy pointed out that these were political subjects and thus outside the purview of the negotiations. He refused to be led into any discussion of substantive matters at this time and asked for the Communist agenda.

In the afternoon, Nam presented a much shorter five-point agenda:

1. Adoption of the agenda.
2. Establishment of the 38th parallel as the military demarcation line between the two sides and establishment of a demilitarized zone, as basic conditions for the cessation of hostilities in Korea.
3. Withdrawal of all armed forces of foreign countries from Korea.
4. Concrete arrangements for the realization of cease-fire and armistice in Korea.
5. Arrangements relating to prisoners of war following the armistice.[79]

Joy refused to discuss any specific line of demarcation. He maintained that the UN Command would consider a line of demarcation and a demilitarized zone, but not the 38th parallel as the demarcation line. As for the withdrawal of foreign troops, Joy reiterated that this was a politically substantive question that might be discussed after an armistice was agreed upon. The first subject to be taken up, he said, was the adoption of the agenda. At this point, Joy seemed to dominate the talks.

What Joy offered was far from Beijing's expectation. Mao regarded the armistice talks as the peace negotiation that would settle the Korean conflict. After the talks started on 10 July, he supervised every step taken by the Chinese and the Korean representatives. Every night Nam, Deng, Xie, and Lee Sang Jo would meet with Li Kenong and Qiao, briefing them on the U.S./UN propositions. Li and Qiao would report to Zhou Enlai, who would then immediately relay the information to Mao. Mao's instructions for the next step would go back through Zhou, Li, and Qiao to Nam, Deng, and Xie.[80] In his telegram to the Chinese negotiators on 11 July, Mao ordered that "[we] must insist that all [foreign] forces withdraw."[81] When the U.S./UN representatives refused to put this issue on the agenda, Mao urged the Chinese delegation to press for its inclusion. "We have sufficient reasons to insist on this demand," he wired Chinese negotiators on 17 July. "Since all the foreign troops came to Korea to fight, not to visit, why is it that a cease-fire negotiation is only authorized to discuss the cessation of hostilities but has no authority to talk about withdrawal of all troops?" In his view, there was no reason to exclude this issue in the truce talks. He directed the Chinese negotiators to keep requesting that "the meeting be authorized not only to discuss a cease-fire but to negotiate the withdrawal of [foreign] troops."[82] Simply achieving an armistice agreement was not what Mao had in mind. While editing a proposed response from Kim and Peng to Ridgway, Mao made it very clear that "all misunderstandings over minor issues should be avoided . . . [so as] to guarantee that the negotiation on a peace treaty proceeds smoothly."[83]

Because of the expectation gap, the negotiation was bound to be tortuous. On 15 July at the third plenary meeting, Joy agreed to drop item 3 from the UNC agenda as the Chinese/North Korean side had assured the UNC that only military matters would be discussed at the meetings. As for the visit of ICRC representatives to POW camps, Joy informed the Communists that this could be taken up when the POW issue was under discussion. Thus the UNC dropped two of its nine items at the third meeting. The Chinese/North Korean side, however, clung firmly to the 38th parallel and showed no signs of giving ground.[84]

Negotiations soon centered on the withdrawal of foreign troops from Korea. Joy pointed out that a major consideration of the negotiation was to provide against resumption of hostilities in Korea after a cease-fire and armistice. It was wrong to say that the withdrawal of foreign troops was the basic guarantee against resumption of hostilities in Korea. There had been no foreign forces in Korea in June 1950 when the war broke out. For a long period after the end of the World War II, there was no war in Korea because foreign troops were there. He noted that the withdrawal of foreign troops from Korea was a question to be resolved by the governments that sent them to Korea. Therefore, it was beyond the scope of a military armistice.[85]

Mao and Zhou were concerned about the negotiations. From 10 to 25 July, they made a comprehensive survey of the Korean situation and proposed a counter-proposal on the issue of "the withdrawal of foreign troops from Korea." They came to realize that it was not possible for the Chinese and North Koreans to drive the enemy forces out of the Korean peninsula. They instructed their negotiators not to insist on "the withdrawal of foreign troops from Korea" as an agenda item, and leave the issue for a post-armistice conference.[86]

On 25 July, with Joy refusing to budge after a three-day recess initiated by the Communists, Nam proposed "recommendation to the governments of the countries on both sides" as a new agenda item. This would involve proposals for a post-armistice conference within a specified time "to negotiate on questions of withdrawal by stages of all foreign armed forces from Korea."[87] The next day, the two sides agreed on a five-part agenda:

1. Adoption of agenda.
2. Fixing a military demarcation line between both sides so as to establish a demilitarized zone as a basic condition for a cessation of hostilities in Korea.
3. Concrete arrangement for the realization of a cease-fire and armistice in Korea, including the composition, authority and functions of a supervising organization for carrying out the terms of a cease-fire and armistice.
4. Arrangements relating to prisoners of war.
5. Recommendations to the governments of the countries concerned on both sides.[88]

Joy then proposed that negotiations proceed item by item through the agenda, beginning with item 2. Nam agreed, but reserved the right to propose alternative procedures as circumstances dictated during the course of the talks.[89] After more than two weeks of acrimonious maneuvering, the opposing sides seemed ready to discuss the terms of an armistice.

For nearly four months, from 26 July to 23 November, the two sides quarreled sharply over where to draw a demarcation line. The Chinese/North Korean side, following the agreement reached between Beijing, Pyongyang, and Moscow, proposed that the demarcation line be along the 38th parallel. The U.S./ UN side, however, countered with a line running basically between Pyongyang and Wonsan, about thirty-eight to fifty-three (in some places sixty-eight) kilometers north of the existing front line between the Communist and UN forces, thus demanding more than 12,000 square kilometers of territory still under Communist control.[90]

The Chinese were not going to yield to the United States easily. When the talks did not proceed as Mao had hoped, he came to see that Washington was not yet ready for a peaceful settlement. He believed that only when Washington could no longer afford the war in Korea would it be ready to make peace. He was then determined to stand firm. On 26 July, Mao directed Peng Dehuai to immediately activate the troops "for combat operations" because it was doubtful "whether the enemy truly intends to talk about peace."[91] More importantly, the Chinese would never lay down its arms because of U.S./UN military pressure.

The American negotiators, all military officers, lacking diplomatic experience and mistrusting both diplomacy and compromise, seemed uninterested in bargaining. They wanted to present a position as an immutable principle and then wait for Communist compliance. If the Communists refused to yield, Joy and his associates were eager to terminate negotiations and escalate the war. They had little concern for the Western allies or public opinion at home and often seemed eager to pursue the war.[92] An example of this was Ridgway's oft-repeated requests to Washington for permission to issue ultimatums to the other side demanding immediate agreement if they wished to continue talking. In Washington, administration officials wanted to make sure to "put the onus for a break squarely on the other side."[93]

Following the JCS's instructions to take a strong opening position, Joy had pushed for a demarcation line considerably to the north of the area then occupied by UN forces. Joy argued that there were sea, air, and ground battle zones, and that the UNC had control well north of the parallel on the sea and in the air, so the loss of such superiority should be compensated by additional territory on the ground.[94] The UNC's argument for more territory made little sense to the North Koreans. Nam labeled Joy's arguments "incredible," "naïve and illogical," "one-sided, simple and incorrect." He argued that maintenance of the current battle line by the UNC depended on its air and naval power, which compensated for the Communist advantage in ground forces. Furthermore, since the battle line shifted north and south of the 38th parallel "all the time," present positions did not reflect "military realities." "On the whole," the lines remained in "the region of the 38th parallel," making that point the logical one on which to base an armistice.[95]

To Joy, the Chinese/North Korean negotiators were intractable. But this was an issue of principle, which the Communists were determined to stick to. If the Americans were allowed to win an upper hand in this "serious political struggle," Beijing's leaders believed that Chinese Communist authority at home and its reputation and influence abroad—two main concerns behind China's intervention in Korea—would suffer.[96] When the U.S. threatened to bomb North Korea to force concessions at the negotiating table, it did not seem to soften the Communists.

Not until 16 August did progress begin to be made in breaking this impasse. After subjecting Joy to a sixty-minute harangue on the incorrectness of the UNC position on the line, Nam then said, "I agree . . . to your proposal for forming a subcommittee." The UNC became gradually familiar with this tactic of harangue. The UNC suggestion of referring issues to lower level subdelegations was also a useful tactic, which proved to be the most effective method of resolving intransigence in the talks.[97] The Chinese/North Korean side named Generals Lee and Xie; Joy named General Hodes, and later Admiral Burke, as his representatives. At these meetings the two sides appeared to be more relaxed.[98] On 20 August the Chinese/North Korean side indicated that they were considering substituting the line of contact for the 38th parallel as the final demarcation line.[99]

Before either delegation could act on these promising positions, however, the Chinese/North Korean side called off the talks as a result of the alleged bombing of the conference site. There had in fact been a number of alleged and proven violations of the neutral zone surrounding Kaesong throughout the negotia-

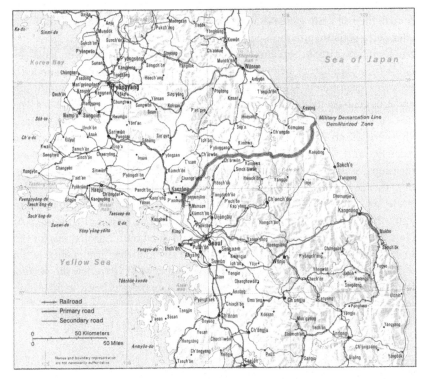

The Korean Peninsula: Demilitarized Zone Area

tions.[100] Mao telegraphed Stalin for advice on 27 August.[101] Stalin agreed with Mao that the UNC should give a satisfactory answer on these incidents. He also encouraged Mao, noting that "the Americans have greater need to continue the negotiations." He advised Mao not to invite representatives of neutral states to participate in the negotiations, as Kim Il-sung proposed. Stalin argued this might give the Americans the impression that the Chinese/North Korean side "has more need quickly to reach an agreement about an armistice than do the Americans."[102]

Peng Dehuai had concluded as early as 24 July that the Americans were unlikely to conclude an armistice under current battlefield conditions. The CPV needed to push enemy forces to south of the 38th parallel. Mao agreed.[103] When the UNC refused to acknowledge "responsibility" for these incidents, the Communists used them as pretexts for suspending the talks and in turn for launching an offensive in order to reclaim territory lost to UNC forces above the 38th parallel in eastern Korea.[104] The UNC also launched a "summer offensive" on 18 August, which lasted till early September.[105] Military conditions did not turn in the CPV's favor.

The two sides did not meet between 22 August and 24 October for several reasons. First, the Communists halted sessions to protest the alleged American violations of the negotiating area (Kaesong). They attempted to use military assault to alter the negotiating situation. Second, since the Western powers were to meet in San Francisco early in September to sign a unilateral peace treaty with Japan, excluding China and the Soviet Union, the Chinese/North Korean side intended to break the armistice talks to affect the San Francisco Conference, which would end American occupation of Japan and be followed by the establishment of a Japanese-American military alliance. As historian William Stueck has contended, "Breaking the armistice talks represented in part a ploy to alarm U.S. allies and jolt Asian neutrals, who might press for a great power conference to resolve outstanding issues in Asia."[106] Third, the United States insisted upon moving the meetings from the Communist-controlled city of Kaesong to Panmunjom, which could be treated as a neutral city.[107] Whether or not the negotiation would move to Panmunjom would soon become a hot and difficult issue. The Russian Presidential Archive sources indicate that Beijing did not want to adjourn negotiations for very long. In Mao's report to Stalin on 27 August, he explained that "if after some period of time the situation will develop so that the enemy wishes to renew the negotiations, then we think that at our own initiative we can propose a way which would lead to a turn in the negotiations and to force the enemy to agree with this."[108]

IV

Alert to the disadvantages of Kaesong, Ridgway was determined to change the negotiation site. On 6 September, in a public message to opposing commanders, Ridgway suggested a meeting of liaison officers to discuss a new site.[109] For more than a month, the two sides haggled over the issue of a new location. The UNC even launched a military offensive to back up its proposal during the last week of September. On 24 October, the Chinese/North Korean negotiators agreed to resume meetings in Panmunjom. Focusing on the content of a truce, this round of talks moved ahead with difficulties. Nam Il and Joy agreed on 25 October to discuss item 2, the demilitarized zone issue, at the sub-delegation level. After some obligatory sparring between sub-delegates over who would first advance a proposal, the UNC presented a map with a four-kilometer demilitarized zone generally following the battle line.[110]

UNC delegates arrive at base camp, Munsan-ni, preparing to resume negotiations in October 1951. From left to right: Rear Admiral Arleigh A. Burke, Vice Admiral C. Turner Joy, and Major General Laurence C. Craigie.
National Archives (111-SC-385641)

Chinese/North Korean delegates leave the conference tent at Panmunjom in November 1951, with Nam Il at the forefront. *National Archives (111-SC-385246).*

The Chinese/North Korean negotiators had originally insisted on the 38th parallel, but now they too were showing some flexibility. They believed although the UNC occupied more land north of 38th parallel than they did south of the parallel, there was more arable land, more natural resources, and more population in the area they held south of the parallel. They would have to return Kaesong to the UN Command had they insisted on the 38th parallel as the demarcation line. It was no disadvantage to accept the line of contact as the demarcation line.[111]

On 31 October, at the seventh sub-delegation meeting since resuming negotiations, the Chinese/North Korean negotiators presented a proposal: a demilitarized zone centered along the battle line. Lee Sang Jo declared: "This new proposal of ours proposes that, apart from the necessary adjustments in a few areas, both sides withdraw two kilometers strictly from the existing contact line, with the area evacuated by both sides as the demilitarized zone."[112] The Communists had accepted the principle of the point of contact determining the line and offered a suggestion of how far to withdraw from that line to create a demilitarized zone.

Washington seemed anxious for quick settlement. The JCS directed the U.S./UN negotiators on 13 November to consider the present line of contact acceptable as a line of demarcation if a full agreement could be reached within a month.[113] The Truman administration was willing to make this small concession and to give up hopes for a line farther north to achieve a prompt armistice. The American negotiators were dismayed and disappointed, believing that this proposal would undercut their earlier firmness, embarrass them, and end their usefulness. There was need for "more steel and less silk," Ridgway bluntly suggested to the JCS. His stand was to insist "on the unchallengeable logic of our position [which] will yield the objectives for which we honorably contend."[114]

The pleas of Ridgway and Joy did not change Washington's position. The State Department and the Pentagon refused to reconsider. Truman and Acheson believed the emerging pattern was based on the evidence through November, which showed that the Communists were willing to compromise substantially, but slowly, to achieve an armistice. China, still consolidating its revolution, could by no means afford the costs of the continuing war, especially because of its increased dependence upon the Soviet Union. North Korea, ravaged by bombings and ground warfare, was also eager to end the conflict. The Truman administration, too, was earnestly seeking a settlement, and had demonstrated willingness to compromise to end the war—ideally by Christmas.

Top Beijing leaders looked forward to a relatively quick end to the war as well. On 14 November 1951, Mao Zedong sent a lengthy telegram to Stalin in which he discussed China's negotiation strategies. The CCP chairman postulated that as the talks resumed, the United States faced increasing domestic and international pressures to reach an armistice in Korea, improving the chance for peace. Beijing's leaders thus believed that China's new strategy of accepting a demarcation line based on the actual line of contact between the two sides had swept away the main barriers on that issue. The fundamental Chinese approach, the telegram emphasized, should be that "it is fine if peace can be reached, but it will not worry us if the war is prolonged."[115] The Russian Presidential Archive sources show that Stalin consistently took a "hard line" toward the negotiations, advising Mao "that the Chinese/Korean side, using flexible tactics in the negotiations, continues to pursue a hard line, not showing haste and not displaying interest in a rapid end to the negotiations."[116] The reason for Stalin's "hard line" policy, as Kathryn Weathersby has suggested, is that "Stalin considered it in the Soviet interests for the war to continue."[117]

Mao did not disagree with Stalin openly, but the heavy burden of the war led him to emphasize the importance of peace. On the same day, Mao and Zhou, with the endorsement of Kim Il-sung, issued instructions to the Chinese/North Korean negotiators:

> We agreed to use the actual line of contact as the demarcation line and an agreement might be reached. On the issue of supervising the armistice, the UNC might insist on unrestricted inspection. We plan to agree to inspection by neutral nations of one or two ports north of the 38th parallel. We plan to include the Soviet Union, India and one Latin American country. If opposed, we may suggest Sweden as a neutral nation. On the POW issue, we propose all-for-all formula. It should not be a hard issue. We have three options for a high-level post-armistice conference. First, a high-level meeting of the two warring sides (China, North Korea, the United States, South Korea); second, a high-level meeting of the Soviet Union, China, the United States, Britain, and North and South Koreas; third, high-level meeting of the Soviet, China, the United States, Britain, France, India, Egypt, North and South Koreas. You may strive for an agreement within this year, but also have to prepare to fight the war for another one year or half year.[118]

The Chinese "negotiation steering group" discussed Mao's instructions on 20 November. The majority believed that if an agreement could be reached on the demarcation line, there was great opportunity to conclude an armistice by the end of the year. Since the enemy had failed to break Chinese defensive lines, there was no reason that an agreement on the demarcation line would not be reached in the near future. Only Qiao Guanhua suggested that the POW issue might be a troublesome issue as he had noticed President Truman's recent statement accusing Chinese troops of killing U.S. POWs in Korea.[119]

On 21 November, the Chinese/North Korean negotiators agreed in principle to the UNC position. The principle was "that the actual line of contact between both sides be made the military demarcation line, and that both sides withdraw two kilometers from this line so as to establish the demarcation zone." More important, the Chinese/North Korean negotiators accepted the UNC insistence

Chinese/North Korean and UNC negotiators discuss "the line of contact" in one session at the sub-delegation level in November 1951. The man at the far left is Chai Chengwen. *National Archives (111-SC-385244).*

on the continuation of hostilities until the conclusion of an armistice.[120] With the ironing out of details over the next two days, staff officers took on the task of determining the actual line of contact. The head of the delegations met on 27 November to ratify the work of their subordinates.[121] More than four and half months after the commencement of talks, the contestants had agreed on an armistice line—provided the remaining issue could be resolved within thirty days. Although the Chinese/North Koreans had been forced to concede on the 38th parallel, they had won on establishing a line of demarcation that lasted until the closing moments of the war. With item 2 finally out of the way, work could now begin on item 3, the setting up of the mechanism to administer the truce.

The two sides had actually made an early effort to resolve differences on item 3. Only a week after discussion on that item began, the Communists accepted the principle of inspection beyond the demilitarized zone. The UNC responded by proposing to move negotiations to the sub-delegation level. Nam quickly agreed.[122] Within two weeks of the beginning of negotiations on item 3, the Chinese/North Korean negotiators agreed to open sub-delegation talks on 11 December on item 4, the prisoners of war issue. On 6 February 1952, concurrent

Chinese/North Korean and UNC liaison officers sign maps showing
Demilitarization Zone in December 1951. *National Archives (111-SC-385715).*

discussions began on the fifth and final item, concerning the "recommendations to the governments of the countries concerned on both sides."

America's thirty-day offer expired shortly after Christmas, but the belligerents
were still far from an agreement. When it was reported that the truce talks might
come to a halt in late December, Mao reiterated his position that "we are not
afraid that the war will be protracted, and we must be prepared for the possibility that [the conflict] will drag on for a considerable length of time before it is
resolved. As long as we are not anxious to end the war, the enemy will be at its
wit's end."[123]

For nearly five months, from late November 1951 until April 1952, the negotiators quarreled about the issues of inspection related to the armistice, including
membership on the commission supervising the armistice, rotation of troops,
and the reconstruction of airfields. By late April, these issues were narrowed to
two—Soviet membership on the supervisory commission, which the United
States resisted, and reconstruction of airfields, which the Communists demanded.[124] To solve the issue, American leaders considered proposing a "package" deal: yielding on the airfields, with the Communists backing down on Soviet membership and also on repatriation of POWs. On 2 May, the Chinese/

North Korean side endorsed part of the package—withdrawal of the Soviet Union from the commission in return for unrestricted reconstruction of airfields.

U.S./UN negotiators pushed for a POW settlement. On 18 December 1951, when the two sides met in a sub-delegation to exchange lists of POWs, the UNC furnished a list of 132,000 names, about 20,000 Chinese and the remainder Koreans, far from the 188,000 missing that the Communists had reported. In response, the Chinese/North Korean side provided a list of only 11,559 names, including 3,198 Americans, which was extremely short of the U.S. claim of 100,000 of its troops as missing in action. The discrepancy was mainly due to Beijing's deliberate policy of releasing the U.S./UN POWs on the battlefield with the intent to dampen enemy morale.[125] At the first discussion of the lists on 22 December, Rear Admiral Ruthven E. Libby, who had replaced Admiral Burke on the UNC negotiating team, explained that 16,000 more prisoners should be classified as ROK citizens, thus not subject to repatriation.[126] Lee Sang Jo immediately protested, arguing that prisoner status should be determined solely on the basis of the uniform worn at the time of capture. Libby counterattacked, arguing that the North Koreans had inducted tens of thousands of captured ROK citizens and soldiers into their army.[127]

The Geneva Conference of 1949 specifically required that all POWs be repatriated regardless of their consent.[128] The problem of POWs now became the chief issue blocking the signing of a truce agreement. The irony was that in July 1951, when armistice negotiations had begun, no one expected that repatriation of POWs would be a big problem. The PRC leaders did not take the POW issue too seriously. In several telegrams to CPV commanders and Chinese negotiators in July 1951, Mao treated the POW issue lightly, believing that after other "important issues" had been resolved, it would be quickly decided that all POWs would be exchanged. Even Truman did not entirely rule out returning POWs on an all-for-all basis (all UN POWs in exchange for all Communist POWs), but he believed that the POW issue should be settled as part of a larger package that included major, unspecified concessions by the enemy. Even more important, he felt it would be morally wrong to force POWs to be repatriated against their will. "He did not want to send back those prisoners who surrendered and have cooperated with us," James Webb commented in October 1951, "because he believes they [would] be immediately done away with."[129] Such an act would be characterized as an open betrayal. The Chinese/North Korean side regarded the POW issue as a political one and was determined to fight to the end. The weapons were Article 118 of the Geneva Convention of 1949 and maltreatment of Communist POWs by the UNC side.[130]

Originally conceived for propaganda and humanitarian purposes as part of the Cold War struggle, the American position on voluntary repatriation was quite unusual. In addition to preempting anticipated domestic criticism, Washington was responding to pressure from South Korea. Political and military leaders in Seoul feared that the more Korean POWs they returned, the more men would be available to serve in the North Korean army, making a renewed conflict more likely. This view was tentative in the summer of 1951, criticized by some U. S. military leaders, challenged briefly by Acheson, and introduced as a bargaining position in negotiations. It ultimately hardened into firm policy when Truman and Acheson endorsed it in February 1952.

By early 1952, Truman and Acheson defined voluntary repatriation as an irrevocable "moral" principle. In so doing, they swept aside or minimized the then skimpy evidence and occasional forecasts that their decisions could mean a stalemate and might significantly prolong the war. Mid-rank CIA, State Department, and Army officials had concluded at a mid-January meeting that the Communists would probably break off negotiations if the United States insisted upon voluntary repatriation. But they recommended that the UNC should insist on this position. "A basic moral principle of political freedom was involved," they reasoned. "To give way on this point now would undermine the whole basis of psychological warfare since neither soldiers nor civilians would defect from Communist rule if they thought they would be returned."[131]

Along these lines, UNC negotiators turned the non-repatriated POWs issue into a hard bargaining chip. The administration instructed UNC negotiators to offer a plan it had worked out according to which the Communists would agree to voluntary repatriation in return for concessions on the rehabilitation of airfields in Korea. As predicted, the Chinese and North Koreans rejected this plan and another one like it that would have deleted restrictions on airfield reconstruction and established a four-member neutral armistice commission in exchange for agreement on voluntary repatriation. They also turned down a proposal to allow prisoners not willing to be repatriated to be removed from the lists of POWs, which would have allowed for the repatriation of the other prisoners without the Communists having agreed to voluntary repatriation.[132]

Nevertheless, the Chinese and North Koreans did agree to have both sides screen POWs in order to determine how many wanted to be repatriated. UNC negotiators told the Chinese and North Koreans that they thought 116,000 would agree to repatriation, and the Chinese/North Korean negotiators indicated that over 100,000 would be acceptable to them. Unfortunately, when the screening of the Chinese and the North Korean POWs was carried out in April, only 70,000 said they wanted to return home. This figure not only surprised Ridgway and Joy, it also startled the Chinese/North Korean negotiators, who charged that the prisoners were being pressured into renouncing repatriation. In response, they suspended the armistice talks for almost a week.[133]

Two factors contributed to the large number of Communist POWs refusing repatriation. Nam accused the Americans of being in league with "the stooges" of Jiang Jieshi and Rhee to coerce POWs into resisting repatriation.[134] As the Americans knew, some of Jiang's troops were actually used as guards in the

Chinese camps, and they established a reign of terror there. Frank Stelle of the PPS had explained in January 1952 that firsthand reports from State Department officers indicated that "the prison camps for Chinese are run by the inmates themselves. The exercise of authority . . . is direct, violent, and brutal, . . . in effect, a reign of terror."[135] The Chinese indicated that many Communist POWs were forced by Jiang's agents to sign non-repatriation "application forms," or they were beaten, even murdered.[136]

The second factor was related to Chinese political culture. Throughout Chinese history, soldiers were required to fight to the last drop of blood. In the Communist army, soldiers were encouraged to fight to the last breath rather than to surrender. Rule number seven of CPV battlefield conduct is "to pledge one's life not to be a POW." It is a great shame and cowardly act to surrender and to be a POW.[137] To be a POW was also a humiliation for the family. Although the procedures the UNC designed were favorable to repatriation, and the UNC publicized a Communist offer of amnesty to all POWs who chose repatriation, many Communist POWs were still afraid of their fate if they chose to return.[138]

When the Chinese/North Korean negotiators returned to the bargaining table at Panmunjom in about a week, they held firmly to the position that anything short of the return of at least 100,000 POWs would be unacceptable to them. By 1 March 1952, the negotiations on item 4 had been narrowed to one issue — voluntary or forced repatriation. The details of the exchange would be easily settled as soon as this principle was decided. But the Chinese/North Korean side gave no sign of weakening their adamant opposition to any form of voluntary repatriation — no matter how it was disguised.

When the UNC side proposed on 13 July to return 83,000 Communist POWs in lieu of 70,000, the Chinese "negotiation steering group" intended to accept the number and reported to Mao.[139] As the fighting dragged on through 1952, the North Koreans increasingly desired to end the war, and they appeared more malleable on the POW issue than did the Chinese. Nevertheless, Mao was clearly anxious to avoid undermining the prestige of the PRC by accepting unfavorable armistice terms.[140] On 14 July, Mao sternly reprimanded the Chinese negotiators, "Your comrades would be too naïve [if you accept the enemy's proposal]. Negotiation is not a matter of numbers. We must agree upon a cease-fire only when political and military situations are favorable to us. To accept the enemy's proposal under pressure means to sign a peace treaty under duress. This is detrimental to us."[141] As Zhou Enlai later explained to Stalin in a conversation in Moscow on 20 August, the Chinese leadership felt that as a matter of principle it could not yield to the Americans on the issue of repatriation of POWs.[142]

It is interesting to note that Washington would follow the same logic in policy thinking. On 8 October, after months of negotiations without any progress and after the Chinese/North Korean negotiators rejected the UNC "final offer" on the POW issue, the UNC chief negotiator, General William K. Harrison (from May 1952 to July 1953), suspended the talks indefinitely.[143] Washington decided, instead, to rely on increased military pressure, mainly the stepped-up bombing of North Korea, to end the war. The UNC launched several offensives to no avail.[144] This was the situation when newly elected President Dwight Eisenhower took office in January 1953. During his presidential campaign, Eisenhower had made it clear that he would never permit the return of POWs against their will. Following his election, he agreed to a statement, made at the Truman administration's behest, backing the White House position on voluntary repatriation and reiterating that there would be no change in that policy once he took office.[145] Although Eisenhower was determined to take new initiatives to end the war, including the possible use of tactical nuclear weapons and utilization of Chinese Nationalist troops, he remained steadfastly committed to the principle of voluntary repatriation. With neither side offering any new proposals to resolve the POW question, the truce tent at Panmunjom stayed empty.

Early in 1953, the Chinese and North Koreans showed more willingness to end the war.[146] Mao Zedong told delegates at the Chinese People's Political Consultative Conference on 7 February, "We want peace. But we are determined to continue fighting together with the North Koreans if the U.S. imperialists do not give up their unreasonable demands and enlarge their aggression." Mao went further and declared, "This is not because we are bellicose. We would like to stop the war and leave those remaining issues for the future. The U.S. imperialists are unwilling to end the war and we have to fight."[147] Zhou Enlai asked Qiao Guanhua to research and find out if the Chinese side should propose resuming the negotiations at Panmunjom. The report, submitted on 19 February suggested: "We'd better maintain the status quo. Wait until the U.S. and the UN are willing to make concessions and take initiatives."[148]

Back in December 1952, the Executive Committee of the League of Red Cross Societies had held a meeting in Geneva and adopted a resolution proposed by the Indian delegate that recommended the exchange of sick and wounded prisoners in advance of a truce. Instructed by the Joint Chiefs of Staff, the UNC commander, General Mark W. Clark, wrote to Kim Il-sung and Peng Dehuai on 22 February 1953 and said that the UNC "remains ready immediately to repatriate those seriously sick and seriously wounded captured personnel who are fit to travel in accordance with provisions of Article 109 of the Geneva Convention."[149]

By the time of Stalin's death on 5 March 1953, Beijing seemed willing to bring the war to an end. The post-Stalin Soviet leadership, headed by Georgy Malenkov, was interested in improving relations with the West. Pursuing what some political observers called the Soviet "peace offensive," fearful that war could escalate into a global conflict, and more confident about its own military capability now that they had their own nuclear arsenal, the new Soviet leaders were eager to end the war in Korea.[150]

With instructions from Moscow,[151] on 28 March, Kim Il-sung and Peng De-huai replied to General Clark. The Chinese and North Koreans agreed to a proposal for exchanges of sick and wounded POWs, called Operation Little Switch.[152] They also proposed to resume the Panmunjom negotiations to solve the POW issue.[153] Paul Pillar has noted, "The imposition of conditions on negotiations can itself be one means of overcoming barriers to the opening of talks, particularly the reluctance to move first for fear of showing weakness."[154] When the UNC broke off the truce talks in October 1952, it announced it would return to Panmunjom only if the Chinese/North Korean side accepted one of its proposals for handling non-repatriated prisoners. In his reply to accepting the proposal, Clark stated that he took as "implicit" in the proposal that the Chinese/North Korean side was prepared to accept one of the UNC plans on the handling of the prisoners or to make some comparable proposal of their own.[155] The UNC considered its condition to have been met without requiring the Communists to admit that it had.

Two days later, Zhou Enlai delivered a radio broadcast in which he offered to have all non-repatriates turned over to a neutral state "so as to ensure a just solution to the question of their repatriation."[156] On 2 April, Zhou Enlai declared at the State Council meeting,

> We couldn't compromise while the U.S. unreasonably insisted on voluntary repatriation. We had to reject their unreasonable demand. Now it is time to solve the problem. We still adhere to all-for-all repatriation and are willing to make a concession in matters of time. We can agree to repatriation of POWs in two steps.[157]

With China no longer insisting on the repatriation of all POWs, it now appeared that the deadlock on the one issue preventing an end to the Korean War had been broken and that a truce or cease-fire was finally at hand. The pace of negotiation at Panmunjom began to pick up. By 12 April, both sides had signed an agreement to exchange sick and wounded prisoners based on the Chinese initiative. On 19 April, the trade of POWs occurred. Talks on the rest of the armistice issues resumed on 25 April.

On 7 May, Nam Il put forward an eight-point plan, the most important components of which were that prisoners would not be moved out of Korea to receive their "explanations"; that the period for persuasion should last not six months but four; and that a five-member Neutral Nations Repatriation Commission be established, consisting of Czechoslovakia, Poland, Sweden, Switzerland, and India. Nam Il also recommended that the future of any prisoners remaining after this time would be discussed at the political conference on Korea already established as part of the armistice agreement.[158] UNC negotiators suggested that changes be made to the eight-point plan, including: unanimity in the voting provisions for the NNRC; India to provide all the troops needed to control the prisoners so as to avoid the presence of Polish and Czech forces behind UN Command lines; and a time limit of only three months for NNRC custody of the prisoners, followed by no more than thirty days during which the future of any remaining prisoners would be considered at the political conference. Most controversially of all, the UNC negotiators proposed that Korean non-repatriates under UNC control should not be handed over to the repatriation commission at all, but should be released in the south of the country as soon as the armistice agreement had been initiated.[159] The Chinese/North Korean negotiators rejected the UNC proposal.

After further military maneuvers, on 8 June, the two sides eventually came to an agreement for releasing non-repatriate POWs from custody within 120 days of an armistice and without their shipment to a third country. After 120 days, the prisoners should be released to civilian status. They also agreed to a five-member Neutral Nations Repatriation Commission, including Czechoslovakia, Poland, Sweden, Switzerland, and India, with a simple majority empowered after an interview process to decide whether or not individual POWs would be repatriated.[160] By 15 June, the military staffs of the two sides had worked out what was supposed to be the final demarcation line.[161]

On 27 July 1953, Harrison and Nam Il signed the completed armistice at Panmunjom without speaking to each other. Twelve hours later, the fighting stopped. Peace in Korea had been achieved.[162] The armistice agreement allowed voluntary repatriation and, in effect, maintained the division of Korea. Ultimately 84,000 POWs (including 6,700 Chinese) chose repatriation, while about 50,000 (including 14,700 Chinese) decided not to return home.[163]

V

While keeping on fighting in Korea, Washington and Beijing were eventually able to produce a truce agreement through negotiations. It was truly a long and difficult process. And, from time to time, it seemed a hopeless effort. However, in the end, both sides managed to stand firm but at the same time adjust their positions and strategies in order to bring about mutually acceptable results. The truce talks proved to be a hard learning process for both.

The culture-and-ideology-driven ignorance of the possible discrepancies and mutual calculation contributed to the protracted truce negotiations as much as to the protracted fighting. At the onset of the negotiations, both sides harbored immensely different expectations, not only about what they could accomplish on the table, but about what the other side should offer. They both were so self-righteous and self-confident that they believed that the other side would come to their terms at the negotiating table.

Although anxious to bring the conflict to "an honorable" end, Washington was faced with a political and strategic paradox. On the one hand, America's

European allies had been seriously concerned about, and indeed opposed to, the U.S. escalating the "wrong war" with a "wrong enemy." To alienate these allies would not only mean the U.S. having to fight alone in Korea, but would render West Europe, America's vital interest, strategically vulnerable to the Soviet threat. On the other hand, America's anti-Communist allies in Asia would welcome an expansion of the conflict in Korea. Moreover, the Truman administration, already being accused of the "loss of China," could not afford to lose more ground to the Communists in Korea. As Rosemary Foot has said, "Sensitivity to public attitudes, to congressional attacks, and to electoral charges that the Democratic administration had been led into a negotiating trap by its 'cunning' enemies, all reinforced the administration's preference for standing firm rather than compromising." Pleas from the State Department for a flexible posture, especially on the issue of repatriating prisoners of war, were not seriously considered at the high level or reflected at the negotiating table. Washington's hard-line posture contributed to the "protracted length of these negotiations."[164]

Mao's burning commitment to restore China to its rightful place as a great power and bitter ideological contention between the two blocs in the early Cold War period contributed to the Communists' adoption of excessively aggressive negotiating tactics in the armistice talks. Negotiation took the form of tit-for-tat. The Chinese/North Korean negotiators believed history was on their side. They used "adversarial" negotiating techniques and regarded negotiation as a zero-sum game. In order not to lose "the people's interests," they were ready to fight in order to gain. They had no hesitation in employing any method calculated to achieve success in the negotiations. Personal acrimony was common among the negotiators, and the two sides waged frequent verbal battles. Regarding the Communists as the "killers of American soldiers," the U.S. negotiators despised the Communist negotiators. The experiences, both at the battleground and negotiating table, added a level of acrimony and deepened mutual suspicions and hostilities that made future talks hard to initiate and made it difficult to achieve substantive results.

The PRC also believed that it benefited diplomatically from the lengthy truce negotiations. China had forced the strongest nation on earth to compromise in Korea and to accept representatives of the PRC as equals at the bargaining table. "The time has gone forever," Peng Dehuai declared in a speech of 12 September 1953, "when the Western powers were able to conquer a country in the East merely by mounting several cannons along the coast."[165] Although the United States did not recognize the PRC officially and the U.S. representatives had acted on behalf of the United Nations when they negotiated and signed the armistice, it was difficult to dismiss the impression that the United States had given Communist China de facto recognition. Although the United States successfully avoided any formal actions that might have legitimized the government of the PRC, including membership in the United Nations, it was clear to the U.S. and all Asian countries that China would inevitably play a great-power role in the future.

Toward the end of the negotiations, both learned so much more about themselves and about each other that they began to adjust their expectations of and attitude toward the talks, although not without setbacks. In deciding to go to the negotiating table in the summer of 1951, the Chinese realized that their demands related to Taiwan and PRC's UN membership were unrealistic and could hardly be met by the U.S. negotiators, and consequently laid aside that portion of the principles outlined earlier in January.[166] Assuming that Communist China would never give up on these demands, Washington continued to resist any discussion that might entail implications over the Taiwan and PRC UN membership issues throughout the negotiations.[167] However, as China and the U.S. probed more into each other's positions, the withdrawal of foreign military forces from Korea, a stated objective of both the United Nations and the PRC, then became the key principle upon which, Beijing believed, the truce negotiation agenda should be based and could be achieved.

China's self-adjustment, slowly but surely, led to a favorable response from the U.S. From the U.S. perspective, the talks would focus only on military matters, not political issues. The U.S. concern was more focused on securing an armistice that could be guaranteed by keeping the balance of military power favorable to the United States. Washington believed that a premature withdrawal of forces would jeopardize the military balance and thus should be rejected. The Chinese at first felt puzzled, as they viewed war only as a violent form of politics. Bringing a halt to the fighting was a common objective, but an armistice would be acceptable to the Chinese only if it paved the way to an acceptable political settlement. Only after considerable bargaining did the Chinese and North Korean negotiators come to realize that it was impossible to drive the UNC forces out of the Korean peninsula. With instructions from Beijing, they again adjusted their positions by dropping "the withdrawal of foreign troops" from the negotiation agenda. Now seeing a real opportunity to get out of the conflict honorably, the Eisenhower administration was ready to yield, by agreeing to an international conference on a political settlement of the Korean problem, by accepting a third party as a hosting country for the non-repatriate POWs, and by coercing South Korea to comply with an armistice.

The truce negotiations, nonetheless, opened the door for Chinese participation in future international diplomacy. At the multilateral level, Beijing was able to participate and play a major role at such important conferences as the Geneva Conference of 1954 and the Bandung Conference in 1955. At the bilateral level, it was the first face-to-face negotiation between the PRC and the U.S.[168] Neither Washington nor Beijing would dismiss altogether the utility of talking to each other in managing the confrontational relationship, no matter how modest the conversation might be.

CHAPTER FOUR

Creating a Special Channel
The Ambassadorial Talks, 1955–60

IN THE IMMEDIATE AFTERMATH of the Korean armistice, both Beijing and Washington seemed inclined to further ease tensions between them. On 7 July 1954, at an enlarged meeting of the CCP Politburo, Mao Zedong observed that "the general international trend reveals that America is quite isolated," and faced difficulties both at home and abroad. "We are no longer able," he added, "to shut our door against outsiders even if we wanted to. Now, things are moving in our favor. We must reach out [to the international arena]."[1] Although defining China as a "major threat" to U.S. security interests in East and Southeast Asia, Washington was under pressure to get U.S. strategic priorities straight by focusing more on Europe, its vital interest. Meanwhile, the Eisenhower administration felt compelled to deal with Communist China in a de facto diplomatic arrangement in order to have unresolved disputes settled, including getting back U.S. citizens detained in China. Without formal diplomatic relations, the two countries agreed to maintain communications through a special mechanism, Sino-American "ambassadorial talks."

From 1955 to 1960, the Chinese and American ambassadors held 102 diplomatic talks, first in Geneva and then in Warsaw. Despite the impasse over the major issue—Taiwan—the ambassadorial talks played an important role in deflecting confrontations and providing a channel for the transmission of information between the two antagonists during those difficult years. Why did these two nations decide to talk after the Korean War? How did the two sides differ in terms of their expectations about and positions on the major issues? Why did the ambassadorial talks fail to lead to more constructive, high-level contacts between Washington and Beijing? Did these talks play any role in managing the confrontational relations?

I

In the spring of 1952, the CCP declared the end of the transitional stage in the economic rebuilding in China and the beginning of a new period of economic expansion.[2] The CCP Central Committee promulgation of the first Five-Year Plan in 1953 amounted to recognition that China needed to avoid armed conflicts such as the Korean War. The CCP policy reorientation brought about a period of intensive internal economic development. During this period, the Chinese leadership adopted a long-term perspective on the country's interests and threats, and focused its resources on the rapid establishment of the socialist system.

Under Mao Zedong's leadership, a new foreign policy was in the making. The changed approach to international relations, developed in 1952 and implemented in 1953, was called "the policy of a peaceful united front," taking as its central tenets the five principles of peaceful coexistence.[3] The primary goal of this policy was the creation of a peaceful environment conducive to China's domestic economic development.[4]

Within this context, the Chinese leaders became more interested in renewing contacts with the West. They came to believe that the threat from the United States was no longer imminent and that Washington had difficulty in reconciling its interests with those of its allies, offering China opportunities for diplomatic maneuvering. Just before the end of the Korean War, speaking at a foreign affairs conference in Beijing on 5 June 1953, Zhou Enlai had pointed out that "the most outstanding international conflict today is that between peace and war" and that Chinese policy was based on "the courage to put into practice peaceful coexistence and peaceful competition among countries with different systems." He added "the U.S. threat of war may . . . deepen its rift with Western Europe and no country in Asia, the Middle East, and North Africa wants to follow it."[5]

The Chinese leaders believed it might even be possible to ease tensions with the United States over many issues. From the Chinese perspective, the existence of the People's Republic of China was a reality and could not be denied. Whether Washington legally recognized the PRC or not, it had to acknowledge reality, and ultimately had to deal with the leadership in Beijing.

The Geneva Conference, held between April and July 1954, provided China with an opportunity to act as a great power in the international community.

Prior to the conference, at a meeting of the Secretariat of the Central Committee on 2 March, Zhou Enlai had pointed out, "We should adopt a policy of active participation in the Geneva Conference and enhance our diplomatic and international activities." China could use this international gathering with major powers to undermine the U.S. policy of "[political] isolation, trade embargo, and military expansion in order to promote relaxation of international tension."[6] Indeed, the PRC leadership attached special importance to this conference, sending a large delegation with over 180 people, headed by Premier and Foreign Minister Zhou Enlai. As Zhou put it, "This is our first real show in the international arena. . . . We have much to learn."[7]

After the end of the Korean War, the Eisenhower administration believed that a Communist China allied with the Soviet Union posed a major threat to U.S. security interests in East Asia and the Pacific. Washington began to equate "Chinese Communists" with "Soviet Russians" as the "major outside threats" to U.S. interests around the world in its overall Cold War strategy. Determined to "hold the line" and assert U.S. leadership, the Eisenhower administration adopted the policies of "massive retaliation" and "brinksmanship" in its confrontation with the Chinese along the Taiwan Strait area. Washington, though reluctantly, had a reason to talk with the Chinese Communists as well. Approximately forty U.S. citizens, who were charged with economic crimes and espionage, had been imprisoned during the last days of the Chinese civil war and the subsequent conflict in Korea. In Geneva in late May, American officials asked Humphrey Trevelyan, the British chargé d'affaires to China, to approach Chinese delegates on the release of those Americans imprisoned in China. The United States also put restrictions on the departure from the U.S. of scientists and students of Chinese nationality (U. Alexis Johnson places the number at less than 175)[8] who were viewed as possessing knowledge that could damage American national security interests, especially after the outbreak of the Korean War.

Seeing this as an opportunity, Zhou Enlai immediately called a meeting to discuss how to exploit the opportunity. He made it clear that China should not refuse to establish contact with the United States. At a time when relations between the two countries were extremely tense, Washington's interest in obtaining the release of imprisoned Americans might lead to the possibility of establishing a channel for contact. Accordingly, the Chinese delegation informed the British chargé d'affaires that, since both China and the United States had sent delegations to the conference, issues involving the two countries should be handled through direct contacts between the two delegations rather than through a third party. Taking the initiative, at a press conference on 27 May the spokesman of the Chinese delegation mentioned "unreasonable detention of Chinese residents and students" by the U.S. government. Nonetheless, he declared that China was willing to hold direct talks with the United States on this issue, implying that China might consider releasing the detained Americans.[9]

For the Chinese, what seemed more important was whether this venture would lead to the establishment of a direct channel of contact with the United States. To prepare for such a possibility, the Chinese delegation held a meeting to anticipate problems that might arise in the talks and to assess U.S. objectives. On 3 June, Zhou Enlai cabled from Geneva to Mao Zedong, Liu Shaoqi,[10] and the CCP Central Committee, reporting that the Chinese delegation had already replied to the British to the effect that China and the United States could meet with the British officials as go-between. "If the United States agreed to the talks, we should meet them in accordance with our established policy and then decide where to hold talks in light of the meeting." During the talks, the Chinese side should "first raise the question of the Chinese students who were prohibited from leaving the United States." At the same time, China should also inform the American side that the Chinese handling of the cases of Americans who had violated Chinese laws would be different from its handling of the cases of other Americans (residing) in China.[11]

While both seemed anxious to talk, U. Alexis Johnson, the American delegation coordinator, met with his PRC counterpart Wang Bingnan four times in June and July. Focused on the issues of detained citizens, these talks achieved little except discussion of the status of each's nationals in the other's country. The PRC pressed for evidence of why its nationals could not leave the United States as they wished, while the Americans sought specific information on the names and the current status (alive, imprisoned, on trial, etc.) of its citizens.[12] On the PRC side, there was a clear preoccupation with issues of sovereignty and mutual equality. Wang denied that American prisoners in China could be treated as ordinary nationals and allowed to leave. Truly sovereign states, he argued, needed not account to others for those who were tried and convicted in accordance with local laws.[13] The United States claimed that Chinese detention of Americans was illegal, but that the U.S. ban on the return of Chinese students to China was consistent with American law. It thus refused to consider the two issues together. In addition, the United States took every precaution to avoid creating the impression that agreeing to enter into talks with Chinese officials in any way constituted U.S. diplomatic recognition of the PRC government.[14] Thus, on 21 June, when Wang suggested a joint communiqué asserting the right of the "'law abiding' nationals and students" of their respective countries to leave and noted that Beijing would designate a "third party" to represent its interests in the United States, the American side broke off the talks.[15] These talks ended on 21 June, but the PRC and the U.S. maintained "sporadic" consul-level talks till mid-1955.[16]

Although the initial talks at Geneva produced few if any significant results, the establishment of official contacts between the two countries was an important move forward in their mutual relations, indeed an ice-breaking effort. Both negotiators actively cultivated a more relaxed and pleasant atmosphere

Chinese and U.S. negotiators Wang Bingnan and U. Alexis Johnson meet in
Geneva in June 1954. *Courtesy China's Archive Press, Beijing.*

Chinese negotiators at the Sino-American ambassadorial talks in Geneva in 1955.
From left to right: Qiu Yingjue, Li Huichuan, Lin Ping, and Wang Bingnan.
Courtesy China's Archive Press, Beijing.

than what had characterized previous Sino-American talks. From the very first meeting, they shook hands and exchanged pleasantries to allay their personal tension and the tension that underlay the talks.[17] However, a diplomatic breakthrough still seemed to be a distant dream.

II

Since the end of the Korean War, the United States had steadily increased its attention to the South China Sea and Taiwan Strait area as Washington's perception of Chinese threats grew. Many U.S. military strategists regarded French defeat at Dienbienphu as the victory of "Communist China." The Chinese leaders held Washington responsible for the mounting tensions in the Taiwan Strait area as they believed that the United States was behind the Nationalist harassment of the mainland. As Washington was eager to increase military assistance to Taiwan to enhance its "deterrence" capability to the mainland, Mao Zedong was especially concerned that the United States "conspired" to sign a mutual defense treaty with Taiwan, which would perpetuate the division of mainland China and Taiwan, similar to the cease-fire in Korea and the Geneva Accords on Vietnam in 1954. In July 1954, the CCP Central Committee decided that China must liberate Taiwan, but it did not call for immediate action. At a Politburo meeting on 5 August 1954, Mao proposed to launch a propaganda campaign for the liberation of Taiwan, the first such campaign against Taiwan in the history of the People's Republic. The PLA artillery bombardment of Jinmen (Quemoy) on 3 September inaugurated the beginning of the Taiwan Strait crisis of 1954–55.[18]

The shelling of Jinmen did not mean that Mao Zedong had given up hope for improving relations with the United States. It seemed that China was practicing "tension" diplomacy, hoping that by China's increasing pressure on Taiwan, Washington would be compelled to reconsider its hostile policy toward the PRC. Mao believed, however, that the two policies were consistent. If the United States continued to expand its cooperation with Taiwan and to support the island's separate sovereignty from mainland China, then U.S.-China relations would further deteriorate, and China would have to adopt even more confrontational policies. As Mao later noted, the relationship between mainland China and Taiwan was different from that between the two Germanys, the two Koreas, or the two Vietnams. China was one of the allies during the Second World War. The lines of partition in Germany, Korea, and Vietnam were drawn through international conferences and embodied in international treaties, whereas the separation of mainland China and Taiwan had never been governed by any international agreement.[19] While signaling to the United States China's preference for peaceful coexistence, Mao used the shelling of Jinmen to demonstrate that China's policy toward Taiwan was unrelenting.

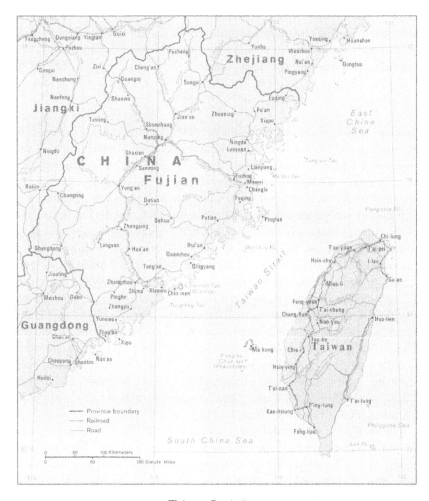

Taiwan Strait Area

The PRC had a limited aim, with no plan to take over Jinmen, much less Taiwan.[20] In a leadership directive on 25 September, the CCP Central Committee observed that the capture of Taiwan was a "long-term and complex struggle," not an immediate objective. "We are not able to liberate Taiwan without a powerful navy and air force and need time to build these up."[21] Mao had no intention to engage directly in an armed conflict with the U.S. over offshore islands at that time. After the successful capture of the island group of Dachen (in Zhejiang province) in February 1955, Mao decided to halt the PLA attack on Jinmen.[22] Having demonstrated its determination to reunify the country, the Chinese government adjusted its policy to reduce the tension. At the Bandung Conference in April 1955, Zhou Enlai was instructed by the top

CCP leadership to declare, "The Chinese government is willing to sit down and talk with the United States regarding the relaxation of tensions in the Far East, and especially in the Taiwan area."[23] Zhou's comment was widely welcomed by at least Asian nations.

The initial American response, drafted by the White House, showed that Washington decided to play hardball in regard to Zhou's offer. The statement insisted that "free China . . . [would have to participate] as an equal in any discussions regarding the area" and that the PRC could show its good intentions by declaring a cease-fire as well as releasing American airmen and "others being held unjustly." The next day, Dulles was more receptive. While the United States would not discuss the "rights" or "claims" of the ROC in its absence, it could certainly discuss a cease-fire or even Beijing's renunciation of force as a way "to satisfy their claim and their ambition."[24]

Seeing some possibilities for opening up negotiations with the United States, Zhou Enlai quickly formulated China's negotiating policy and submitted a report on the Taiwan issue to the CCP Central Committee on 30 April. The report stressed that the Taiwan issue contained two interrelated but substantially different aspects. "The relationship between China and the Jiang Jieshi clique is an internal issue. The relationship between China and the United States is an international issue." The Chinese people's action to "liberate" Taiwan would not result in world tension, just as the liberation of the mainland and the offshore islands did not lead to heightened tension; on the contrary, the completion of China's unification would contribute to world peace. But Zhou warned, U.S. intervention made it likely that an international war could break out at any time in the Taiwan area. Thus, Beijing's current challenge was first to identify ways to ease and eliminate tension in that area. To do so, China and the United States should sit down and negotiate. He further explained that China and the United States were not at war, so there was no question of a cease-fire. The U.S. proposal for a cease-fire was intended to do a deal: Washington wanted to exchange the withdrawal of Jiang Jieshi's troops from Jinmen and Mazu (Matsu) for the Chinese people's abandonment of their demand for, and their action toward, the military takeover of Taiwan. This was something, Zhou insisted, that China absolutely could not agree to under any circumstances. Only when the United States abandoned its aggressive policy and withdrew all its military forces from the Taiwan Strait could China peacefully liberate Taiwan and complete China's reunification. As the United States was anxious to negotiate with China, he suggested, "China should wait and see the outside responses, and then make adequate policy." The CCP Central Committee concurred.[25]

Eisenhower's nuclear saber-rattling during the Taiwan Strait crisis upset America's European and Asian allies, many of whom were afraid of war between Washington and Beijing in the Taiwan Strait area. They made efforts to mediate the Chinese-American confrontation. In March, Krishna Menon, Indian ambassador to the United Nations, traveled to Washington and had a meeting with Secretary of State John Dulles. He suggested to Dulles the importance of "a third party in setting up contact between the U.S. and the PRC."[26] In mid-May, Menon visited Beijing with a plan to mediate the Chinese-American negotiation. In his meeting with Menon, Zhou Enlai emphasized the following three points. First, reducing tensions would require efforts on both sides. If the United States would pressure the GMD to withdraw its troops from Jinmen and Mazu, the PRC would mount no attack on these islands during the withdrawal and take them over peacefully. But this was in no way to suggest that the PRC would agree to Dulles's cease-fire proposal or to abandoning its policy of liberating Taiwan in exchange for U.S. pressure on the GMD "clique" to withdraw from the islands. Nor did it mean that the PRC would recognize the U.S. occupation of Taiwan and the "two-Chinas" arrangement.

Second, Zhou stressed that the PRC and the United States should take measures to ease tensions over other issues. For its part, the United States must do two things: lift the trade embargo against China, and permit the departure of those Chinese students and residents in the United States who wished to return to their motherland. As a reciprocal response, the PRC could do two things as well: on the question of Americans imprisoned in China, including pilots and residents, the PRC was willing to reconsider their case in accordance with Chinese legal procedures, and might release or expel them; the PRC would also permit American groups and individuals friendly to China to visit. Although such permission should be granted on an equitable basis, the PRC was willing to take the first step. The PRC wanted to allow Americans to come to China to see for themselves whether China was friendly toward them or intent on waging war against them.

Third, the PRC was willing to negotiate with the United States and with the GMD authorities over the Taiwan issue. China, however, had no intention of talking to both at the same time because Chinese-American negotiation was international, and its purpose was to persuade the United States to give up intervention and withdraw its troops from Taiwan and the Taiwan Strait area. And the CCP-GMD talk was domestic and should cover both a cease-fire between the China's Central People's Government and GMD authorities and peaceful reunification of China.[27]

While advocating peaceful talks with the United States, China had also begun to formulate new policies toward Taiwan. On 13 May 1955, at the Fifteenth Enlarged Conference of the Standing Committee of the first National People's Congress, Zhou Enlai declared that the Chinese people might adopt two possible ways to liberate Taiwan—through war or through peaceful means—and that the Chinese people would strive toward peaceful means if conditions allowed.[28] This was the first time that Chinese leaders suggested publicly the possibility of a peaceful liberation of Taiwan, and it marked a major change in China's policy. About a year later, at the Third Plenary Session of the first NPC, Zhou went further, expressing wishes to form a third United Front with the GMD in Taiwan.[29]

On 26 May, Zhou Enlai met with the British chargé d'affaires, Humphrey Trevelyan. During their meeting, Zhou further elaborated on China's policy toward negotiation with the United States, claiming that the central theme of Chinese-American negotiations was to reduce and eliminate tension in the Taiwan Strait. As to the specific format of the negotiation, however, the Chinese leaders had not reached a final decision. While China agreed to, and would support, a ten-country conference such as the one proposed by the Soviet Union—the number of participating countries could be greater or fewer—China and the United States could also conduct direct negotiations sponsored by other countries. However, under no circumstances would Beijing agree that the Taiwan authorities should be allowed to attend such an international conference. The Chinese government would not refuse to conduct direct negotiations with the Taiwan authorities; on the contrary, it was willing to do so. Zhou stressed again that there were two ways to solve the Taiwan problem, through peaceful means or through war. If possible, China would try to liberate Taiwan peacefully. The Chinese leaders sought to conduct both international and domestic negotiations, either simultaneously or in any sort of sequence. Zhou also explained that "the two kinds of negotiations were related to each other but should not be lumped together."[30] Beijing thought that it had sent out all the possible signals of its flexibility to the United States.

The United States had been "deliberately" delaying the implementation of China's proposal for direct talks. This was mainly because Dulles's "closed door" approach to the China issue prevailed. There were two schools of thought within the Eisenhower administration over how best to deal with the Chinese.[31] Some, notably Chester Bowles, then ambassador to India and a leading Democrat, believed that China could be weaned from dependence on the Soviet Union through a series of incentives that would "leave the door open." Dulles disagreed. Only through pursuing a "closed door" policy, Dulles believed, would sufficient pressure be exerted on China for it to see merit in altering its "lean to one side" policy.

As the four-power Geneva summit (U.S., USSR, UK, and France) was approaching in July 1955, Dulles was concerned that the Soviets might press for the inclusion of the PRC and the Taiwan issue. Moreover, he believed direct U.S.-China talks were the "minimum needed to preserve [the] de facto cease fire" prevailing in the Taiwan Strait.[32] On 13 July, the United States, under the mediation of Britain, proposed that the Chinese and American sides each send a representative of ambassadorial rank to hold talks in Geneva.[33] The talks would focus on matters of "direct concern" that "did not deal with the rights of third parties" (i.e., Taiwan). It also stated that questions about "citizens in each of our countries" would be discussed and that "further progress" on the question could lead "to discussion of other topics which the Chinese Communists might want to suggest."[34]

Washington's overture seemed promising, offering something Beijing had hoped for. On 25 July 1955, Beijing and Washington announced that the United States and China would hold ambassadorial talks to solve the question of the "repatriation of civilians who desire to return to their respective countries and to facilitate discussions and settlement of certain other practical matters now at issue between both sides."[35] Dulles appointed U. Alexis Johnson, then U.S. ambassador to Czechoslovakia, as chief U.S. representative. Johnson was a career diplomat and had many years of experience working in the Far East since the 1930s. His selection for the job, Johnson recalled later, was "the easiest choice" for Dulles as Johnson had talked with Wang Bingnan during the Geneva Conference and performed well. His selection again was "not provocative" to the PRC and would not incur accusation from the Taiwan lobby, McCarthyites, and the right wing of the Republican Party.[36] Dulles defined the forthcoming talks as "a continuation of the talks held in the last year between representatives of both sides at Geneva."[37]

A day after the 25 July announcement, at his news conference, Dulles outlined the "practical matters" that he wanted the U.S.-China negotiations to cover:

1. Return of American civilians detained in Communist China.
2. Reinforcement of the efforts of the United Nations to secure the return of Americans who became prisoners of war under the United Nations Command in Korea.
3. Precautions against a repetition of such incidents as the shooting down of the Cathay airliner with a loss of American and other lives.
4. The determination of the basic point of whether a cease-fire in the Taiwan area could be arranged and the principle of the non-recourse to force agreed to, or whether it was necessary to prepare for war in that area.[38]

Taking the talks seriously, Dulles personally drafted instructions for the U.S. negotiators. On 23 July, he sent a cable, marked "urgent," to call Ambassador Johnson back to Washington from Prague. Dulles stressed to Johnson that the talks did not imply recognition and would not "prejudice the rights of our ally, the Republic of China." He emphasized that the United States "hope[d] to find out" if the PRC would "accept the concept of a cease-fire" in the Strait as part of a mutual pledge to renounce the use of force other than for self-defense. He did not rule out a future meeting with Zhou Enlai. However, he requested that Johnson hold the talks in secret and make no open announcement on the talks. He also gave permission to Johnson to engage in informal and private social contacts with the chief Chinese negotiator. Johnson was instructed to disclose to the Chinese that if the United States nationals held in China were released, it would facilitate America's "voluntarily adopting a less restrictive policy" on Americans traveling to China. Johnson was also to explain to the Chinese that the U.S.-ROC treaty was defensive and the U.S. would not in any way support a Nationalist invasion of the mainland.[39] According to Ralph Clough, who was adviser to U. Alexis Johnson at the Geneva talks, "Dulles himself went over the instructions line by line, made changes here and there, and approved it."[40]

A 29 July instruction from Dulles to Johnson contained a more formal agenda for the talk. The instructions noted that the first purpose of the meetings was to resolve the issue of repatriation and that Johnson should seek "immediate authorization for U.S. civilians [and members of the military] to return to the U.S." Although he was not "to promise any concessions for their release," he was authorized to mention that their release "might facilitate" a less restrictive policy on U.S. citizens going to the mainland. He was also instructed "at whatever times you deem appropriate," to raise the issue of the United States' desire that the PRC be "prepared to abandon force to achieve its ambitions." He was also told to respond to claims that the Taiwan issue was a domestic matter by contending that any attempt to destabilize divided countries could threaten world peace.[41] It seemed that Dulles's primary focus was how to relieve "the Eisenhower administration's predicament" in the Taiwan Strait area by having the PRC at the negotiating table.[42] It seemed to Dulles that conflict in the Taiwan Strait could be avoided as long as the United States could keep the PRC talking. In a private conversation, Dulles told Johnson that he would be "happy if you (Johnson) are sitting there three months from now."[43]

Beijing attached much more importance to the forthcoming talks than did Washington. The Foreign Ministry set up a "special supervisory group," headed by Zhang Hanfu, vice foreign minister, and Qiao Guanhua, assistant foreign minister—both worked closely with Zhou Enlai—to provide guidance to the Chinese negotiators. Zhang served as director of the group and Qiao was in charge of daily operations.[44] Wang Bingnan, one of PRC's most experienced diplomats, was appointed as China's chief representative. Then serving as China's ambassador to Poland, Wang had been a close assistant of Zhou Enlai since the late 1930s, and had participated in the talks with General Marshall in the 1940s and the Geneva Conferences on Korea and Indochina in 1954. Wang was selected over several other candidates for the job, as Wang later recalled, because he "had experience in maintaining contacts with different types of Americans" and "Premier Zhou knew me and trusted me very much."[45]

However, after receiving the telegram notifying him of his new responsibilities, Wang was concerned over the complexity and difficulty of his new job. As the PRC ambassador to Poland, he had difficult and sluggish communications with Beijing. As part of China's diplomatic practice, any ambassador would have to rely on Zhou's "teachings and direct instructions." He was greatly reassured to learn that a "special supervisory group" had been set up to "devise measures to be taken at the talks." With this talented support structure and with much personal preparation, Ambassador Wang flew to Geneva without having to worry that this "matter of prime importance" would rest solely on his shoulders.[46]

The newly declassified Foreign Ministry files show that the PRC government was prepared to render the talks constructive. In its instructions to the Chinese negotiators, the Foreign Ministry indicated that China's policy at the ambassadorial meetings (at the outset) would be to take initiatives to announce that "China had released eleven convicted American military personnel" before the beginning of the ambassadorial talks. The purpose was to liquidate a U.S. pretext, pressure the Americans in order to solve some concrete issues, and lay a foundation for Sino-American higher-level talks. This would also create an isolated and passive situation for the United States on the issue of Taiwan. To achieve this aim, it instructed the Chinese negotiators to "take a conciliatory attitude." During the course of the talk, "We should respect each other and give attention to courtesy," the Foreign Ministry instructed. The document shows that Beijing anticipated that entering into talks with the United States at the ambassadorial level in Geneva would make the higher-level talks more likely to happen. It planned to propose to hold the higher-level talks at the foreign ministers' level in November of that year. The topic would be "to relax and eliminate Sino-American tension in Taiwan Strait area." The PRC would prefer to hold the foreign ministers' meeting in New Delhi, but would concede to Geneva if necessary.[47]

Beijing was also ready to let its policy orientation be known publicly. On 30 July, Zhou presented a long report, titled "The Present International Situation and China's Foreign Policy," at the second plenary session of the first National People's Congress. He stressed that China needed a peaceful international environment to fulfill its economic reconstruction at home. He pointed out, "We would like to come to normal and friendly relationships with all neutral countries in accordance with the five principles of peaceful coexistence." He made this significant declaration: "There is no war between China and the United States; the peoples of China and the United States are friendly to each other; the Chinese people want no war with the United States, so the question of cease-fire between China and the United States does not arise." He went on to note that, of the two possible ways for the Chinese people to liberate Taiwan — by war or by peaceful means — the Chinese people were ready to use the latter, "conditions permitting" — which meant that the United States should not interfere with such peaceful liberation. He offered to negotiate with "the responsible local authorities of Taiwan to map out concrete steps for its peaceful liberation" and proclaimed that the Chinese people were firmly opposed to any ideas or "plots" of the so-called "two Chinas."[48]

On the eve of the talks, Zhou appeared to be quite optimistic about the prospects of improving relations with the United States. As he told the Indian ambassador to China on 31 July, China hoped the ambassadorial-level talks would pave the way for a foreign-minister-level negotiation, which, he said, could focus on a relaxation of tension in the Taiwan area.[49]

III

The Sino-American ambassadorial talks started on 1 August 1955 in Geneva. In order to create a positive atmosphere for the talks, Ambassador Wang Bingnan first announced that Beijing had released eleven convicted U.S. military personnel on 31 July before the completion of their sentences.[50] The U.S. representative, Ambassador Johnson, welcomed this gesture. The two sides soon reached an agreement on the discussion of two agenda items: (1) return of civilians of both sides to their respective countries and (2) other practical matters at issue between the two sides, such as establishment of diplomatic relations, withdrawal of U.S. forces from Taiwan, development of trade and cultural relations, and UN membership of the PRC.[51]

This proved to be a good start, but did not last long. Wang Bingnan later explained that significant differences on agenda setting and policy objectives existed from the very beginning. The Chinese side held that the talks had to focus on some substantial problems such as the Taiwan issue, arrangements for direct talks between Secretary of State Dulles and Premier Zhou Enlai, and the establishment of cultural ties between the two countries. The United States insisted on repatriating Americans detained in China and demanded that China not resort to force over Taiwan. In the hope of facilitating an amicable and productive session, the Chinese side agreed to discuss the question of the return of the civilians first and then move to other substantial matters.[52]

As Steven Goldstein has observed, "The central difficulty in solving the repatriation issue was apparent almost from the outset: for any settlement to be reached, both sides would have to yield on fundamentally nonnegotiable issues."[53] As a revolutionary regime, the Chinese Communists told the Chinese people that they had restored China's national sovereignty and dignity after a century of Western humiliation. Beijing could not agree to an immediate release or to setting a date for release in response to the U.S. demand as this was regarded as an issue of national sovereignty and dignity.[54] It also insisted on equal treatment for Chinese aliens in the United States and the right, as their international protector, "to entrust [a] third country of [the PRC's] own choice [to] take charge of affairs of nationals [of] each country."[55] This seemed to be the PRC strategy: "play up issue of Chinese nationals in U.S." in order "to steer the talks away from Johnson's objective, the American prisoners."[56] The PRC leaders also feared they would lose a valuable bargaining chip if they released all U.S. prisoners as the Americans might end the talks at the ambassadorial level.

Washington would accept nothing short of the return of all those Americans who wished to leave China, even if they were criminals under PRC law. To get detained Americans back was Washington's primary reason for starting and continuing the talks. To capitulate to such a refusal of a seemingly reasonable demand would surely provoke the Republican right, who wanted immediate release of all Americans in China.[57]

By mid-August the PRC would offer only to announce that the case of some Americans wishing to leave had been "reviewed" and that the rest would be reviewed in the future.[58] Although Johnson proposed the acceptance of the release of some citizens and then a move to other matters, reserving the right to raise the issue again,[59] Dulles was not ready to compromise. He instructed Johnson that it was "essential to hold tenaciously to our basic position on return of all detained nationals as part of any agreement on representation before we proceed to discussion of Item 2 on Agenda."[60] As the PRC side insisted that this was its final offer, the talks seemed to approach a deadlock. Johnson again asked permission to "explore possibility [of] releasing some now and with commitment to release remainder within definite time limit, say three months." Dulles accepted Johnson's proposal but instructed that a word such as "promptly" might be used to define the time frame, "such as two or three months."[61]

Wang responded that decisions would be made according to the nature of each case, but insisted that consideration would also be given to the "state of relations between our two countries."[62] Johnson once again asked Washington to compromise. On 2 September, Dulles agreed, authorizing wording for a settlement through which both sides would recognize the right of nationals to return to their respective countries, and the agreed announcement declared that the two countries had "adopted, and will further adopt appropriate measures so that nationals *expeditiously* [emphasis added] exercise their right to return." Though still dissatisfied, Dulles conceded that he would accept the immediate release of some and release of the rest in a predetermined period, settling for the undefined term "expeditiously."[63] At the fourteenth meeting, on 10 September, the two sides reached an agreement just to that effect.[64] The PRC and the U.S. "invited" India and the United Kingdom to make representations for, and provide funds to, any citizens who "were encountering obstruction in departure."[65] As a result, ten Americans were set free and allowed to leave China via Hong Kong in a few days. The PRC agreed to inform the U.S. through the UK of results of remaining cases.[66]

Beijing reacted rather enthusiastically to the "agreed announcement." The PRC press immediately put out the line that the People's Republic of China would make every effort to improve relations with the United States since a promising start had been made at Geneva. A September 12 *Renmin Ribao* editorial expressed pleasure at the "good beginning," which encouraged conciliation and created an atmosphere of mutual confidence between China and the United States "in the interest of improving relations between the two countries." The editorial expressed the hope that both sides would come to an agreement in the second phase so that the talks could pave the way for further negotiations.[67]

American officials were less vocal and positive than the Chinese about the implication of the first agreement. Washington's aim was to get the remaining Americans back. Deputy Undersecretary of State Robert Murphy used more circumspect language than Beijing had when he stated in a speech that the Geneva talks had "been attended by a certain success."[68] After the "agreed announcement" was being made, Johnson was instructed to limit the frequency of the meetings to twice a week and to narrow their scope to "implementation and details and progress in carrying out [the] agreed announcement." He was not to get into the "substance" of any new agenda items until all Americans had been released. Should the PRC show signs of carrying out the agreement in "good faith," discussions on possible subjects for future talks could begin; otherwise, Johnson was instructed to recess the talks.[69]

U.S. strategy for the second stage of the talk was to use the incomplete implementation of Item 1 to slow the momentum toward consideration of Item 2. It intended to prolong the talks and build "a case for the United States as the aggrieved party."[70] Walter P. McConaughy, director of the Office of Chinese Affairs in the State Department, advised Johnson "to keep him (Wang) so busy reporting on the progress of the departure of the Americans" that he could not raise other issues. Johnson was told not "to get engaged in any discussion of what topics might be accepted for discussion under Item Two."[71]

While Washington was sitting on the talks, Beijing was pressing on. At the first meeting after the "agreed announcement" was signed, the Chinese side proposed two subjects for discussion under the second item: the U.S. economic blockade and embargo imposed on China and preparation for "negotiations at a higher level on easing and elimination of tension in the Taiwan area."[72] Wang Bingnan had repeatedly pointed out during their earlier talks in 1955 that only through talks between foreign ministers could China and the United States address serious problems, such as U.S. withdrawal from Taiwan and the easing of tension in the Taiwan area. The foreign ministers could also discuss establishing cultural exchange programs, trade relations, and other matters.[73]

Reviewing China's position during the second phase of the ambassadorial talks, Wang Bingnan recalled later, "it was impossible for the U.S. to change its China policy at the time." For the Chinese side, "we went directly at the Taiwan question, which was the most difficult, least likely to be resolved, and most emotional." Wang argued that the Chinese side could not avoid the Taiwan issue.[74] Wang also explained why China took a tit-for-tat negotiation approach toward the United States on the Taiwan issue:

In this way we could boost our morale and puncture the U.S. government's arrogance. Having suffered long-term oppression and humiliation at the hands of the Western powers before the founding of the PRC, the people of New China have stood up and should not appear weak again in front of the Western powers. That was the intense emotion the Chinese people had at the time. If we ignored this historical fact and single-mindedly sought for breakthroughs in the talks, we would have sacrificed principle, hurt the feelings of the Chinese people, and even damaged the unprecedented trust the Chinese people had in the government. If that had happened, we would have committed what Chairman Mao called "serious political mistakes."[75]

It was not until late September that Johnson was authorized to agree to a preliminary discussion of future topics. On 27 September, the State Department instructed Johnson to propose that each side be prepared to set aside conflicting claims and declare that they "will not resort to the use of force in the Taiwan area except defensively."[76] Thus, by early October, the "renunciation of use of force in the Taiwan area" had become not only an American priority for the next stage of the talks but a precondition for moving on.[77] Anticipating that the PRC would insist on discussing this issue at a "higher level" (a foreign ministers' meeting), the American side held that the two ambassadors could negotiate the issue adequately in their talks. Meanwhile, Johnson was instructed to keep the repatriation issue on the agenda.[78]

Wang Bingnan refused to keep the repatriation issue alive, arguing once again that it was a closed issue at the nineteenth meeting on 5 October. Wang claimed that the PRC was willing to continue talks on the "tense situation in the Taiwan area," but only at a foreign ministers' meeting. The ambassadorial talks could prepare for such a conference, and moved to a discussion of the economic embargo as the next issue on agenda.[79] The United States continued to insist that the Taiwan issue should be discussed at the ambassadorial level.[80]

From 8 October 1955 to 26 July 1956, thirty-five meetings (more than 25 percent of the total number of sessions) focused primarily on the issue of "renunciation of force." They also proposed six draft agreements—three by each side. For more than six months each side sought a second "agreed announcement," but failed. The repatriation issue still intruded on the talks, but it was mainly a side issue to the discussions of Taiwan, which ended in deadlock.[81]

Washington's position was clear. All three U.S. proposals specified the "Taiwan area" (including the Strait) as well as the right of self-defense, but made no mention of high-level talks. The purpose was to confine the PRC to a commitment to renunciation of force in the Taiwan Strait area. Thus, the U.S. goal of an extended cease-fire in the Taiwan Strait could be reached without compromise.[82]

The PRC drafts also reflected Beijing's two main concerns: to hold a meeting at the foreign ministers' level and to confine the Taiwan question to a purely domestic matter. The first two draft proposals remained within the boundaries defined by these elements. The first draft, proposed at the twenty-third meeting, on 27 October 1955, agreed to hold discussions at the ambassadorial level on the renunciation of force, but without specifying the "Taiwan area." While deliberately excluding Taiwan from the range of international disputes it promised to settle peacefully, it proposed that the "Taiwan issue" should be settled through a conference of foreign ministers. The second draft, proposed at the twenty-eighth meeting, on 1 December, evaded the issue of renunciation of force, although it avoided directly calling for a foreign ministers' meeting. The third draft, proposed at the forty-sixth meeting, on 11 May 1956, combined the first two with a pledge to discuss the renunciation of force in the Taiwan area at the ambassadorial level but on the condition that higher-level talks would follow within two months. The Chinese expected the Americans to pick one. If the United States wanted to discuss Taiwan, there would have to be a foreign ministers' meeting or, as Wang suggested, a meeting with a "presidential representative." If Washington refused, then any announcement would address only the U.S.-China disputes in general.[83] It was politically impossible for the Eisenhower administration to accept such proposals, considering the pressure from Congress and Taiwan.[84]

Beijing found it impossible to reconcile with the U.S. position. Wang Bingnan repeatedly maintained that there was nothing substantial in the American proposals for the PRC. If the PRC was willing to compromise its claim to be a peer sovereign state and agree to a renunciation of force that included both Taiwan and the Strait, it would be equal to accepting the status quo with no assurance that the United States would continue the talks toward a favorable solution on the Taiwan issue. What the American side could offer for now was for Beijing to concede that the civil war had ended short of a total CCP victory, with a part of China still subject to the forces of imperialism.[85] That was unacceptable to Beijing.

The future of the talks was dismal. Faced with a deadlock, Johnson tried to find a way out. He recommended accepting Beijing's December 1 proposal and pledged that both sides simply renounce the use of force in settling disputes. Johnson argued that this would keep the talks going without mentioning a foreign ministers' meeting and would make it difficult for the PRC to "justify" any attack on Taiwan.[86] Dulles was not persuaded. Believing that there was little chance of a breakdown at this point, he instructed Johnson to return to the demand that the repatriation issue be solved before serious discussions of other questions could proceed. Dulles reminded Johnson that one goal of the talks was to keep the PRC at the negotiating table.[87] Johnson could not but follow Dulles's instructions. In response, the PRC publicly charged the United States with stalling. The United States responded in kind.[88]

As the ambassadorial talks became stalemated, the Chinese leaders believed they had developed a better understanding of Washington's real objectives and decided to exert more pressure on the U.S. At the thirty-first meeting, on 22 December 1955, Wang Bingnan threatened "to make public the proceedings of these discussions and leave it to public opinion for judgment."[89] Beijing did take the case to the public through the statement of a Foreign Ministry spokesman on 18 January 1956.[90] The exchange in the press was vigorous, bringing to light much of what had been discussed in previous talks. Beijing was trying to use the international press to justify positions that could not be agreed upon behind closed doors. On 30 January, Zhou Enlai included a long section on the ambassadorial talks in his "Political Report to the Second Session of the Second National Committee of the Chinese People's Political Consultative Conference." He declared that China had been "faithfully complying" with the repatriation agreement, while the U. S. government had not abandoned the use of all kinds of "threats and persecution" to prevent Chinese nationals from returning home. "If the United States Government continues to threaten and persecute them," Zhou claimed, "it must bear full responsibility for wrecking the Agreement."[91] In early March, Beijing issued another press release attacking the United States for its dilatory, noncooperative role in the talks. In rebuttal the State Department accused Beijing of continuing to hold thirteen American citizens as "political hostages"—the first time Washington had employed this sharp term—and for failing even to mention the issue of American repatriation in its statement.[92] In April, Beijing published another explanation of the repatriation issue in an article entitled "The Truth about the Sino-American Talks," accusing the United States of not only failing to carry out the terms of the agreement, but also violating it.[93]

In addition to the repatriation issue, Beijing made public the talks on the Taiwan question and renunciation of force. In June, at the third Plenary Session of the First National People's Congress, Zhou Enlai pointed out that China would not oppose issuing a declaration with the United States on the question of mutual renunciation of the use of force. But "the United States attempted to obtain a declaration that was only in its favor. It wanted to maintain the status quo of U.S. occupation of Taiwan and continue to obstruct the Chinese people's efforts to liberate Taiwan." Zhou explained that when Washington "realized that it could not obtain such a declaration, the United States attempted to indefinitely prolong the talks in order to freeze the status quo of the Taiwan situation. This is the reason why the Sino-American talks have thus far failed."[94]

It is no small wonder that Beijing did not mind allowing the talks to drag on. Briefing the Indian ambassador to China on the Sino-American talks on 14 June, Zhou Enlai said that the United States had two alternatives: to reach an agreement with China or to let the talks drag on. China had the same alternatives: to reach an agreement or to let the talks drag on. China, however, had the freedom to maneuver. If the second alternative served its interests, China would continue to play the game. If it would hurt China's interests, China could refuse to play along at any time. This was China's view on the prospects for Sino-American ambassadorial talks.[95]

When government-to-government relations deadlocked, in mid-1956 Zhou moved to people-to-people diplomacy by offering in August to invite American newsmen to China. From August 1956 to December 1957, the Chinese side put forward successive announcements on the promotion of contacts and cultural exchanges between the two peoples, on giving permission on an equal and reciprocal basis to correspondents of the other side to enter their respective countries for news coverage, and on giving each other judicial assistance.[96] On 5 August 1956, the Chinese government unilaterally announced the lifting of its ban on visits by American journalists. It cabled directly to fifteen U.S. news agencies and invited them to send journalists to China for a month-long visit.[97]

Beijing's people's diplomacy annoyed Dulles, who refused to consider any of China's offers. He directed the State Department to reject all requests for permission to go to China. In the instruction for the fifty-fifth meeting, on 9 August, Johnson was told to inform Wang that Americans would be allowed to travel to the mainland only when all of the prisoners were released. The State Department believed that this would assure that "maximum leverage will be exerted on them to release Americans."[98] The U.S. intention was to block the PRC's people's diplomacy and to keep the focus on the repatriation issue and the renunciation of force.

This turned out to be wishful thinking. The Chinese were not interested in what Dulles had proposed. At the fifty-fifth meeting, Wang raised the embargo question in his opening presentations. He argued for a new approach that would endeavor to address less controversial issues, such as the embargo and cultural exchange, and put aside the larger ones—the repatriation and renunciation issues —that had earlier deadlocked the talks.[99] Dulles was prepared to draw out Beijing's specific complaints about the embargo, apparently reasoning that if pressure from U.S. allies was going to force changes, it might be productive to use the unavoidable changes as a bargaining chip in the talks.[100] Early in July, Dulles had instructed Johnson that he should "lead Wang to disclose just what he had in mind" on the trade embargo, but that there must be a "meaningful agreed announcement by parties renouncing force before trade embargoes can be usefully discussed." Johnson pursued this line throughout the summer.[101]

China, however, continued its people's diplomacy in order to place Dulles on the defensive. On 17 August 1957, *Renmin Ribao* carried an editorial accusing Washington of manipulating the journalist issue. China's people-to-people relations-building effort seemed to have worked. On 22 August, Dulles was compelled to adjust U.S. policy: the State Department announced that the United States would allow twenty-four news agencies to send journalists to China. However, the U.S. government was not going to reciprocate for Chinese journalists. Having scored a big point on the issue, Beijing moved to exploit the advantage. At the seventieth meeting, on 12 September, Wang Bingnan made a journalist-exchange proposal and demanded reciprocity from the United States. Unprepared for China's request, Johnson rejected Wang's proposal.[102]

The talks at Geneva dragged on until the fall of 1957. As Ambassador Johnson was scheduled for a new assignment, the State Department proposed three possible replacement candidates: to appoint a new ambassador to the talks (possibly Karl Rankin, formerly ambassador to the ROC, soon to be transferred to Yugoslavia); to move the talks to Warsaw and designate Ambassador Jacob Beam as the chief U.S. negotiator; or to lower the talks to the first secretary level, with Edwin W. Martin (a frequent participant in the Geneva talks) commuting from London.[103]

Although Johnson supported the option of continuing the talks at the ambassadorial level, he argued that Rankin was not an ideal choice because Beijing perceived him as pro-ROC. The State Department then decided to go with the third plan. In the instruction for the final meeting of the year, Johnson was told to inform Wang that, in the future, Edwin Martin would represent the United States. The State Department specified that the proposal for a change in the level of representation would only come after "a strong statement of U.S. disappointment" with Beijing's posture at the talks. It was essential that Wang "perceive [the] connection" between the PRC posture and Washington's "unwillingness to continue at the ambassadorial level." Believing that Beijing was unlikely to end the talks, Dulles instructed Johnson to leave open the possibility of a future return to the ambassadorial level but to be unyielding should the PRC reject the current proposal or threaten a break.[104]

At the seventy-third meeting, on 12 December 1957, when Johnson informed Wang of the U.S. decision to appoint Edwin Martin to serve as the U.S. representative to the ambassadorial talks, Wang said, "These are ambassadorial talks, and we like Mr. Martin, but can't accept him because he's not an ambassador."[105] Wang was concerned about the U.S. downgrading of the ambassadorial talks. He refused to approve a press announcement that set 9 January 1958 as the date for the next meeting, suggesting instead that the announcement would only note Johnson's transfer and state the talks were "suspended" and that the "procedure for the future talks" would be agreed upon by both sides. In the end, the statement simply said that the seventy-third meeting had taken place and that the date for the next meeting would be pending.[106]

IV

From the early months of 1957, Chinese leaders came to believe that the United States was threatening China by strengthening American military relations with China's eastern and southern neighbors. They thus suspended their efforts to improve U.S.-China relations through negotiation and embarked on a policy of resisting what they called U.S. imperialism. In September 1957, Mao Zedong told a visiting Czechoslovakian congressional delegation that "China's policy toward Western countries was now to fight against them."[107]

In launching the "Great Leap Forward" in 1958, Mao announced that Chinese diplomacy should cast off conservative thinking. Early in the year, Mao had told Marshal Chen Yi, China's new foreign minister, that he had instructed Chinese diplomats to make contact with American officials during the Geneva Conference. This instruction, however, had not been consistent with his usual line of thinking. Now, Mao said, it appeared that his usual line of thinking had proved to be superior: China should vigorously struggle with the Americans policies with no attempt to develop relations with the U.S. government.[108] Chinese policy toward the United States should demonstrate that the Chinese people had truly stood up and that the Chinese people would not forget the long history of imperialist invasion of China. He further argued that China should take advantage of U.S. policies of political containment and economic embargo to close its doors and concentrate on self-reliant socialist development.[109] At an extended Politburo meeting that focused on discussing foreign policy, Mao said, "I said it was all right to make contact with the Americans during the Geneva Conference. In actuality, the Americans were not necessarily willing to deal with us. It is to our advantage to be in an impasse with the United States. . . . The United States would have to recognize us in 101 years."[110] It seemed that Mao was agitated about U.S. policy and decided to take offensive. With Mao's new line of thinking revealed, the Foreign Ministry adjusted its policy in kind. For the time being, China's diplomacy could be summarized as "expose Yugoslavia and consolidate socialism; fight the United States and bring down imperialism; and isolate Japan and win over nationalist countries."[111]

Mao's hardened line of diplomacy was soon put into practice. On 30 June 1958, the PRC issued "Statement on Sino-American Ambassadorial Talks," practically an ultimatum, charging the United States with stalling and giving Washington fifteen days "counting from today" to respond as to whether the talks should resume; or Beijing would "consider . . . that the United States has decided to break off the Sino-American ambassadorial talks."[112]

Since the suspension of the talks in December 1957, Dulles had become impatient with the talks. He was not interested in seeing the talks become a venue for resolving issues in Sino-American relations because of the "trouble" that would result from foreign and domestic political pressures. Although there was "little enthusiasm" in Washington for more talks, they were seen as a useful way "to keep before the world" Beijing's failure to release all prisoners as agreed.[113] At a news conference on 1 July, Dulles replied that the United States would not abide by the fifteen-day ultimatum but would pursue its earlier inquiries about the talks.[114] On 17 July, Ambassador Jacob Beam approached the PRC diplomats in Warsaw, and preparations were made for renewed monthly talks.[115] On 4

August, Beam attempted to arrange with the Chinese Embassy in Warsaw for a meeting with Ambassador Wang on 7 August. When the day came, however, the Chinese Embassy replied that they were not ready and were still waiting for instruction from Beijing.[116] Annoyed at Beijing's stalling, Dulles made an unusually strong public attack on the PRC, claiming that "we will do all that we can to contribute to the passing away of this regime."[117]

On 23 August, the Chinese People's Liberation Army mounted a large-scale shelling of Jinmen, signaling China's decision to adopt a tougher policy toward the United States. Mao's initial assumption was to recover Jinmen by forcing Jiang's force to give up the island through artillery encirclement.[118] Mao estimated that "after a period of shelling, the Nationalists will either withdraw from the two islands [Jinmen and Mazu] or struggle in difficulty. We could then consider and decide whether to land our forces. We shall see as we go."[119] Later the same day, Mao revealed the twofold purpose of the shelling at a meeting of the Politburo Standing Committee: to support the Arab people in their struggle against American imperialism[120] and to determine whether Jinmen and Mazu were included in the U.S.-Taiwan Mutual Defense Treaty. Mao thus made it clear to the central leadership that the decision to shell Jinmen reflected his overall strategic judgment.[121] Mao was also cautious to avoid confronting the U.S. directly. His only concern at the time was whether it was possible to "avoid hitting the Americans" in the Taiwan Strait area.[122] Later when American warships started to escort the Nationalist transport ships, Mao ordered PLA artillery to "aim only at the Nationalists' ships and not to return fire even if fired at by the U.S. ships."[123]

China's military action had two political objectives, to show to the world China's determination to recover Taiwan and to get the Americans to return to the negotiating table. Late in August, Wang Bingnan was recalled to Beijing to report on the ambassadorial talks. Mao Zedong, Liu Shaoqi, and other top Chinese leaders listened to his report.[124] The PRC was busy preparing for the resumption of the ambassadorial talks. At a Politburo meeting on 4 September, Mao proposed that China should make concurrent efforts to resume the ambassadorial talks as part of the struggle in the Taiwan Strait. As Mao told his Politburo colleagues, "There should be scenes of talks and war at the same time."[125] On 6 September, Zhou Enlai issued a statement condemning the serious war provocation by the United States. He stated that since the United States had already appointed an ambassadorial representative and expressed willingness to resolve the Taiwan Strait crisis through peaceful negotiation, China was ready to talk too.[126] On the same day, the United States welcomed China's proposal, an action to which Mao attached great importance. He claimed,

> We fought the campaign, which made the United States willing to talk. The
> United States has opened the door. The situation seems to be no good for

them, and they will feel nervous day in and day out if they don't hold talks with us now. OK, let's talk. For the overall situation, it is better to settle disputes with the United States through talks, or peaceful means, because we are all peace-loving people.[127]

In order to facilitate the talks, Mao specifically instructed Wang Bingnan to pay attention to negotiation styles before his departure for Warsaw. Mao emphasized that the PRC representative should appeal to reasoning when the talks resumed. For example, Wang should tell the American negotiators that the United States was a large country, and so was China. The Chinese mainland had a population of six hundred million, whereas Taiwan's population was less than ten million. This fact could not be changed, nor could it be ignored. It would be foolish for the United States to make an enemy of six hundred million people on the mainland for the sake of relations with fewer than ten million people on Taiwan. Mao told Wang that during the talks "it is necessary to think more, to be modest and prudent, and to be attentive not to use those provocative expressions once used during the Panmunjom talks and not to hurt the national pride of the Americans. The Chinese and Americans are great peoples. Therefore, we should restore good relations."[128] On 13 September, two days before the talks, Mao told Zhou Enlai that "during the first three or four days or the first week of the Warsaw talks, we should do some reconnaissance work. Do not reveal our bottom line. The U.S. side will not reveal its bottom line either. They will conduct some reconnaissance on us too."[129] Zhou replied that he had already instructed Wang Bingnan that "We will try to deal with the American side to make it reveal its bottom line first."[130]

The United States agreed to return to the negotiating table only reluctantly and with little expectation that anything would be resolved despite Dulles's public statement that there was "quite a lot to negotiate."[131] In his instructions for the first meeting, scheduled for 15 September, Dulles asked the chief U.S. negotiator, Jacob Beam, to emphasize the need to avoid a widening of the conflict and to press for an "informal cease-fire" followed by a discussion of ways to end provocation and ease tensions. Beam should also retain the right to raise previous issues (for example, prisoners and missing servicemen). He told Beam that Washington, however, was "under no illusions that Chinese Communists will use Warsaw talks for anything we would regard as constructive." Anticipating that the PRC would publish the record of the talks, Beam was told to ensure that his presentation emphasized an "open constructive" approach, refuted charges that the United States was the aggressor, and included a "carefully worded statement of support for position and dignity" of the ROC.[132]

The first meeting in Warsaw (the seventy-fourth meeting of the ambassadorial talks) took place at Mysliwieki Palace, provided by the Polish government, on 16 September 1958.[133] As the two countries were in the midst of the second Taiwan Strait crisis, "no genial mood and favorable atmosphere surrounded the

Talks." Each side had a separate waiting room, and they entered from opposite ends.[134] The situation in the Taiwan Strait was the main topic at ten meetings held between 16 September and 7 November, at intervals ranging from two days to almost two weeks. Despite Dulles's pessimism about their usefulness, as Steven Goldstein has suggested, the talks in Warsaw might actually have served as a port "in an ever-growing storm."[135] As Dulles told Beam in an "eyes only" letter on the eve of the first meeting, "Our basic objective is to bring about quickly a cessation of hostilities." Otherwise, Washington would have to resort to "drastic measures" in the Taiwan Strait.[136]

Beam took the initiative to speak first. He said that PRC actions were an unacceptable attempt to achieve "territorial changes . . . through use of military force," Beam asserted that the United States could not "stand idly by" given its defense treaty with Taiwan. Washington's position was that there should be an "immediate cease-fire in Taiwan Strait area," followed by discussions related to "terminating provocative activities and easing of tensions."[137]

Wang dismissed Beam's view by stressing the domestic nature of the conflict, the illegitimacy of the U.S.-ROC treaty, and American responsibility for the crisis. He presented an uncompromising draft of a five-point "agreed announcement" in which Beijing would reassert its claim to the offshore islands and Taiwan; the United States would agree to withdraw its armed forces from Taiwan; the PRC would agree to allow GMD troops to evacuate from Jinmen, Mazu, and other offshore islands without pursuit; the PRC would pledge to strive to liberate Taiwan and the Penghu Islands "by peaceful means and will, in a certain period of time, avoid using force" should such an evacuation take place; and both sides would agree on the need for freedom of navigation. Beam rejected the document as one that "involves [the] surrender [of ROC interests]."[138] The exchanges at the first meeting set a rigid pattern, and the two sides were again locked in an impasse. The subsequent discussions were hardly able to move beyond empty exchanges on the nature of the dispute (domestic or international), the nature of the ROC government (puppet regime or sovereign state), and which side presented the greatest danger to peace in the area (American occupation or PRC aggression).[139]

It is worth noting that immediately after the first meeting Dulles asked JCS's views with regard to "what alternative courses there might be to continuing the present support of the GRC in occupation of the off-shore islands." While stressing the importance of achieving a cease-fire in Taiwan Strait area, the JCS suggested that "certain concessions, subject to agreement by the GRC, might be made to achieve the U.S. objectives" if the United States was willing to depart substantively from its current China policy. It went on to discuss thirteen possible negotiating topics. While supporting the reduction of tension between the ROC and the PRC, the JCS argued that it was not possible for the United States either "to withdraw its Military Forces from the Taiwan Straits" or to withdraw its "Advisory Group Teams from the Forces on the Offshore Islands." It strongly opposed any decision that might lead to the suspension of U.S. support for Taiwan.[140] In light of the pressure from the military, it was not surprising that Washington would cling to a rigid position at the talks in Warsaw.

Beam presented the American counterproposal at the seventy-eighth meeting, on 30 September. It noted the support of the Soviet Union for the PRC position and the American treaty obligation to the ROC, and recognized that this was an "international dispute and threat of force which endangers international peace and security." The United States also proposed that the PRC "suspend hostilities," that it would be ready to pursue such remedies as mediation or judicial settlement, and that both sides refrain from "harassment or provocations."[141] While both parties at first had dealt with the offshore islands and Taiwan as a whole, each emphasized incompatible points of view. The American proposals were specific about the offshore islands and vague about Taiwan; the Chinese were specific about Taiwan but vague about the offshore islands.

Wang rejected the U.S. offer as a "deceitful proposal of yours which can never be realized,"[142] just as Beam had rejected the uncompromising PRC drafts at the start of the talks. Wang repeated the usual accusations and argued that the U.S. should withdraw its forces from the Taiwan area "as the only means of relieving tension." On the contrary, Beam insisted that cease-fire was essential to relaxation of tensions.[143] It is worth noting the subtle alteration of U.S. policy toward the offshore islands—on the same day this presentation was being made in private, Dulles spoke publicly of the possibility of a withdrawal from the offshore islands and a drawing down of Nationalist forces.[144] In response to journalists' questions, Dulles said that the United States had no obligation to defend the offshore islands, nor did it wish to assume such an obligation.[145]

Dulles's statement received much attention from Beijing leaders. At the Politburo Standing Committee meetings in early October, they concluded that the United States wanted to create "two Chinas." Zhou said that Dulles wanted China to renounce the use of force to liberate Taiwan; in exchange, the United States would most likely demand that Jiang abandon his aspiration to "recover the mainland" and that the GMD withdraw its troops from Jinmen and Mazu. Zhou's assessment led Mao to decide to put a halt to the bombardment of Jinmen and Mazu. He preferred to have Jiang keep GMD troops there, since that would make it more difficult for the United States to perpetuate the division of Taiwan and the mainland. Thus, on 6 October, PRC Defense Minister Peng Dehuai announced that, out of "humanitarian considerations," the bombardment of the offshore islands would be suspended for seven days, beginning immediately. Within this period, the GMD troops on the offshore islands could be resupplied as long as the United States did not escort the supply ships.[146] Beijing had announced a unilateral de facto cease-fire in the Taiwan Strait.

It seemed that the sense of crisis that had shaped the American approach at the beginning of the talks had now passed. In its instruction for the eightieth meeting, on 10 October 1958, the State Department notified Beam that the announcement had "changed [the] negotiating picture for [the] time being at least" and that he should work toward gaining an indefinite extension of the cease-fire and some sense of what U.S. actions that might provoke Beijing to resume hostilities. He was instructed to press for reconsideration of the U.S. proposal and to question Wang on whether the Warsaw talks had any meaning for the PRC, since despite its rejection at the talks, Beijing had announced a cease-fire.[147]

When the two sides met on 10 October, Wang refused to discuss a publicly announced cease-fire, declaring that Peng Dehuai's announcement had not been directed at the United States. Obviously, Wang feared that PRC action would be widely regarded as a response to the U.S. demand for a cease-fire. He claimed that Beam was not a representative of the "Chiang clique" and that Beam's attempt to initiate discussions on a cease-fire was an attempt to internationalize the issue. Wang reiterated that only an American withdrawal could pave the way for further negotiations.[148] Once again, any real resolution would have required a radical change on one side or the other. Washington was not prepared to accord greater prestige to the PRC or to weaken its ties with Taiwan. Similarly, Beijing was not ready to yield on the nature of the Taiwan issue or on the U.S. relationship with Taiwan.[149] It seemed that the date for solving the Taiwan question was still far away.

Christian A. Herter replaced the dying Dulles as secretary of state in April 1959, but the U.S. China policy changed little.[150] The ambassadorial talks continued with little progress on any substantial issue in 1959 and 1960. The two sides seemed to utilize the talks as a means of public diplomacy and an international public relations campaign.[151] Neither side would take the initiative to terminate the talks for fear of being held responsible for its collapse.[152] The departing Eisenhower administration seemed not the least interested in changing its "closed door" policy toward China. To the Chinese leaders, the direct aim of PRC's participation in the talks was no longer to seek improved Chinese-American relations but to maintain a channel of contact to facilitate their assessment of U.S. intentions.

The PRC's attitude hardened gradually. In his meeting with the British field marshal Sir Bernard Law Montgomery on 26 May 1960, Zhou Enlai said, "The prerequisite issues for improving Sino-American relations are: 1) The U.S. recognizes that Taiwan is part of China; 2) The U.S. withdraws its troops from Taiwan and the Taiwan Straits. If the United States recognizes these two principles, we, of course, are willing to talk with them."[153] Zhou reiterated the Chinese position in his talk with American journalist Edgar Snow on 30 August: "We should come to a principled agreement before solving concrete issues in

Sino-American negotiations."¹⁵⁴ On 13 September, China formally adopted a
"package" solution—that from now on China would not discuss "minor and
subsidiary issues" with the United States, only "fundamental issues," that is,
"the total withdrawal of U.S. troops from Taiwan and the Taiwan Strait area."¹⁵⁵
For the duration of the ambassadorial talks, the Chinese adhered to two principles: (1) the U.S. undertakes to withdraw immediately all its armed forces
from Taiwan and the Taiwan Strait area and dismantle all its military installations in Taiwan; (2) the U.S. government agrees to the signing of an agreement
on the Five Principles of Peaceful Coexistence between China and the United
States.¹⁵⁶

V

The Korean War had an immediate and lasting impact upon U.S.-China relations. China's Korean War experience gave the PRC leadership confidence in
the strength of the nation and status in world affairs. The Chinese leaders felt
it necessary and possible to expand PRC's international outreach, as China
was in the process of transforming from revolutionary diplomacy to normal
state-to-state diplomacy. China's participation as a great power in the 1954
Geneva Conference further encouraged PRC leaders to increase China's
international prestige. The Korean War armistice negotiations also confirmed
to American leaders the importance of talking to Beijing. When the repatriation of U.S. citizens became a thorny problem for the Eisenhower administration in the mid-1950s, Washington believed it was in its interest to start negotiating with the Chinese. Within this context, a face-to-face talk between
Chinese and American officials became a reality in Geneva in 1954, and they
maintained consul-level talks through mid-1955.

As U.S.-China tension rose high during the Taiwan Strait crisis of 1954–55,
both Washington and Beijing felt more urgency to retain the communication
mechanism, even at a higher level and on a more regular footing. PRC's shelling of Jinmen in 1954 was designed mainly to foil the U.S.-Taiwan security
treaty as Beijing worried about the division between mainland China and Taiwan. Although failing to achieve that end, Beijing's "tension diplomacy" made
America's European allies and some Asian allies, who were afraid of another
U.S.-China armed conflict in East Asia, nervous. Although committed to the
defense of Taiwan, Washington refused to risk a war with Beijing over the offshore islands. What the Eisenhower administration could realistically do was to
de-escalate the tension over the Taiwan Strait through negotiations. The U.S.
willingness to talk about the Taiwan issue would prove to be a diplomatic victory for Beijing, which had consistently and vigorously pressed Washington to
do so. The first Taiwan Strait crisis, in a way, launched the Sino-American ambassadorial talks, which lasted much of the second half of the 1950s.

The importance and utility of the ambassadorial talks were evident. The two sides negotiated on three formal written draft agreements: (1) the repatriation of civilians; (2) the renunciation of force; and (3) the exchange of newsmen. They concluded a formal agreement on repatriation in September 1955. Most of the seventy-six detained Americans in China at the beginning of the talks were released and left China. More importantly, the ambassadorial talks served as a "pressure reducer" during the two Taiwan Strait crises in the 1950s. It was evident that Beijing suspended military action in the Taiwan Strait area while the ambassadorial talks were in session.

Yet, the talks did not lead to a higher-level negotiation between Washington and Beijing, largely because of the lack of incentives for Washington. The Eisenhower administration's overall Cold War strategy was to "hold the line," not to fundamentally improve relations with a Communist state such as China. The U.S.'s interest in the talks was to work out the technical details for the release of American citizens and, if possible, to keep the Chinese under check through negotiations. As long as Beijing was at the negotiating table, Dulles reasoned, "it would not provoke conflict, thus contributing to a *de facto* cease-fire in the Taiwan Strait and providing stable conditions for a 'divided country' solution." Moreover, the talks were useful for deflecting domestic and international criticism of the Eisenhower administration's "closed door" policy. Although the talks could not produce substantial agreements over major issues, Dulles believed, they could be a useful public relations campaign for the Republican administration.[157] In addition, the Eisenhower administration did not want to annoy Taiwan and consequently upset the pro-ROC lobbyists. Believing that communism was only "a passing phase" on the Chinese mainland, Washington was only using the talks to subdue Beijing's militancy.

This was not what Beijing had expected. In mid-1950s, the Chinese leadership hoped to improve relations with the United States through serious negotiations. They then undertook a conciliatory position by showing willingness to unilaterally release some detained Americans and to discuss less controversial issues, such as the U.S. economic embargo against China and ban on cultural exchanges. Subsequently, Beijing expected to persuade Washington into serious discussions over significant issues, including recognizing PRC's legitimacy, resolving the Taiwan issue, and acknowledging China's rightful place in world affairs. From mid-1956, facing an uncompromising U.S. attitude on substantive issues, the Chinese leaders lost interest in improving relations through secret negotiations. Nonetheless, they still maintained this communication channel with the United States. Beijing's use of the suspension of the talks as an excuse to launch the second Taiwan Strait crisis in 1958 did bring the U.S. back to the negotiating table, but failed to change the U.S. negotiation position. The ambassadorial talks continued throughout the Eisenhower administration without much progress on the issues of Taiwan, the renunciation of force, the U.S. embargo of China, and cultural exchanges.

The ambassadorial talks, though, served as a useful platform of learning for the two antagonists. The talks offered the American negotiators an increased familiarity with PRC's negotiating style and a greater knowledge of Beijing's positions on various issues.[158] They were impressed by how good Beijing was at seeking moral high ground. For example, China showed itself skilled at using unilateral "goodwill" gestures to establish American "indebtedness." Beijing's release of eleven American pilots on the eve of negotiations, a gesture that cost China little and won U.S. gratitude, had become a hallmark of the bilateral relations. Also, American negotiators learned, the PRC was inclined to adhere to "principled" position: rather than initiating a negotiating exchange with exaggerated demands from which they would retreat in incremental compromises, the Chinese would press for acceptance of certain general principles.[159] Only after these had been codified and the negotiating counterpart's position tested against them over an extended period of time would the Chinese move to conclude an agreement. In 1954–55, U.S. acceptance of the "principle of equality and reciprocity" was a fundamental Chinese condition for the repatriation of Americans held in China. In 1955–57, Beijing vigorously pressed for a foreign ministers' meeting to discuss the Taiwan issue, trade, and cultural exchanges. The Americans refused to raise the level of talks before Beijing agreed to release all American prisoners. From 1958 on, Beijing insisted that the Americans unconditionally accept the principle of total withdrawal from the Taiwan area before Beijing would discuss or negotiate any specific agreements on lesser matters that Washington wished to discuss and settle.

Now it will be interesting to see how, with this value-added knowledge about how to negotiate with Communist China, the Democratic governments—the Kennedy and Johnson administrations—handled these issues at the ambassadorial talks in the 1960s.

CHAPTER FIVE

Negotiating at Cross-Purposes
The Ambassadorial Talks, 1961–68

T HE AMBASSADORIAL TALKS stalemated in the late 1950s when the two sides were bogged down on the major issue of contention—Taiwan. Yet, throughout most of the 1960s, Washington and Beijing carried on the talks, although less frequently: there were altogether thirty-two sessions from 1961 to 1968.

John F. Kennedy's taking office in Washington in 1961 seemed to unfold a new phase in Cold War international relations. While the Eisenhower administration succeeded in "holding the line," the two Democratic administrations— Kennedy and Johnson—expected to regain lost ground in the Cold War confrontation with the Communists. Adopting "Flexible Response," the "New Frontiersmen" demonstrated willingness to reconsider U.S. policy toward China. How much was China a threat to the U.S. interests in the 1960s? How much opportunity could the U.S. explore in the Sino-Soviet split in restructuring the Cold War international relations? What, then, did the Kennedy and Johnson administrations expect to achieve from the ambassadorial talks?

Beijing also faced different dynamics, domestic and international alike. Apart from border conflicts with India, China was confronted with two major threats, one from the north—the Soviet Union, a former ally—and another from U.S.-supported Chinese Nationalists across the Taiwan Strait. These external threats were compounded with a domestic disaster deriving from the Great Leap Forward (1958). How did Beijing perceive its external threats? What did Beijing expect to get from the ambassadorial talks? What role did these talks play in paving the way for more substantial and high-level talks in early 1970s?

I

Although America's China policy was not the top priority of the Kennedy administration—Cuba, Laos, and Berlin all ranked higher—the young Democratic president was anxious to make diplomatic if not strategic breakthroughs in overall Cold War confrontation. His less than three-year term in the White House, though, did not accord him a sufficient opportunity to institute fundamental changes. Administration officials did reconsider America's China policy. Such reconsideration was confined within the context of U.S.-Soviet confrontation, and more dealt with Washington's perception of threat from China and calculation of opportunities to reduce tensions between the two powers.

The Kennedy administration presented a different strategic outlook from its Republican predecessor's. Critical of the Eisenhower administration's overreliance on nuclear deterrence and heavy-handed techniques in responding to crises in Asia, the Middle East, and Europe, Kennedy and his advisers believed that "Flexible Response" would be a more rational alternative. Although Washington still believed that the Soviet threat was the predominant one, the Third World countries became a major battleground for the great power contention. The rise of nationalism as a result of Communist infiltration seemed to have posed an increasing threat to the United States and "Free World." It was within this area that China stood out as a large player, posing new threat to and new opportunities for the United States.

It is interesting to note that the Kennedy administration's threat perception of China, from the outset, focused on China's domestic crises. Administration officials noticed as a nationwide famine was unfolding in China. Early in February 1961, at the 475th NSC meeting, CIA director Allen A. Dulles reported to Kennedy "the serious agricultural situation in Communist China."[1] About two months later, a special national intelligence estimate (SNIE 13–61) explained that Communist China "is now facing the most serious economic difficulties it has confronted" since its founding. It further suggested, "Public disaffection probably would become a major problem for the regime" if malnutrition, disease, and starvation persisted.[2] Washington was concerned about the collapse and disintegration of the Communist regime in China and its grave consequence as famine refugees might rush to East and Southeast Asian countries. As a Defense Department report pointed out, "The threat of China has hung heavy over our heads in Asia."[3]

The Chinese leadership seemed to have become more reckless and aggressive since its growing dispute with the Soviet Union in late 1950s and early 1960s. China's hostility to the United States seemed to intensify in the wake of the failure of the Great Leap Forward. On 21–27 June 1960, a week-long "Opposing U.S. Imperialist Invasion, Resolutely Liberating Taiwan, and Safeguarding World Peace" campaign was staged in China. Anti-American demonstrations and mass rallies were held all over China.[4] China's bellicose rhetoric during the Cuban missile crisis in October 1962 demonstrated to the Kennedy administration that China presented a major challenge to U.S. interests.[5] The Sino-India border clashes in October and November 1962 sent Washington an ominous signal that Beijing had the ability to intimidate its neighbors. A policy analysis paper prepared by the Policy Planning Council on 30 November noted it was possible that Beijing leaders "will launch massive aggression across their borders."[6] After the war, Washington speeded up and augmented military aid to India.[7]

The Kennedy administration would also face a new crisis in the Taiwan Strait. Since the end of the Eisenhower administration, Jiang Jieshi had been pressing for the supplies and training he needed to mount large-scale cross-Strait operations. These demands continued into early 1962, when they became particularly intense (and public) due to the ROC's perception of the PRC's deteriorating internal and international situation. China's domestic economy was still recovering from the devastating Great Leap Forward. As the Sino-Soviet alliance was falling apart, Moscow was tilting toward India in the Sino-Indian border conflict. Jiang Jieshi believed it was the time to launch an invasion and recapture the mainland.[8] As the Chinese Communist military was building up in the Fujian area (the other side of the Taiwan Strait on the mainland), the Kennedy administration had to decide how to handle this crisis.[9]

Soon after taking office, the Kennedy administration was concerned about China's developing nuclear program. A PPS study in September 1961 noted that China would gain "psychological dividends" from its successful nuclear detonation. China could claim that "the Communist method of organizing a backward state's resource is demonstrably superior." To offset such an effect, the PPS study recommended that the U.S. should support a non-Communist Asian state, such as India, to detonate a nuclear device ahead of China.[10] Secretary of State Dean Rusk flatly turned down the proposal, noting "For us to assist some other country, even for important political and psychological reasons, would start us down a jungle path from which I see no exit."[11]

By the first half of 1963, Washington was even more obsessed with China's developing nuclear capacity. When briefed by McGeorge Bundy, the president's special assistant for national security affairs, and new CIA director John A. McCone about the Chinese nuclear programs early in January, Kennedy felt that "this was probably the most serious problem facing the world today. . . . [The United States] should prepare to take some form of action unless they [the Chinese] agreed to desist from further efforts in this field." Kennedy made it clear that he regarded such development as "intolerable to the United States and to the West."[12] In a more chilling public speech, he warned of "700 million people, a Stalinist internal regime, nuclear powers, and a great determination of war as a means of bringing about its ultimate success." The United States faced, he declared, "potentially a more dangerous foe than any we faced since the end of the Second World War."[13] The Kennedy and later Johnson administrations seriously considered using "preventive action against Chinese nuclear facilities."[14]

In spite of the perceived threats related to China, the Kennedy administration also identified diplomatic, political, and economic opportunities regarding China. At the outset, the Kennedy administration conducted a top-to-bottom review of Sino-Soviet relations within the context of the future of Communism and Washington's possible actions to exploit a potential Sino-Soviet split. A national intelligence estimate (NIE 1–61), dated 17 January 1961, explained that there was not much that the Soviet and Chinese Communist leaders could do to avoid an open breakup. Although it might be "calamitous," NIE 1–61 observed, it was unlikely that Moscow would go so far in trying to prevent it as to "surrender to the Chinese position, [because] both the USSR's determination to preserve its supremacy in the Communist movement and Soviet national interest in avoiding serious risk of general war would preclude such a course." By the same reasoning, the Chinese would not consider submitting to the Soviet stand, for "their pride, self-righteousness, and national aspirations are too heavily committed to permit it."[15] In May, the State Department confirmed that so long as "the security and the political-economic well-being of the Soviet state" remained the USSR's "primary concerns" and so long as China felt compelled to rely on Soviet economic and technological aid, the Soviet leaders had little incentive to mend the relations.[16]

In the first two years, administration officials also discussed the possibility of a "food-for-peace" arrangement, shipping grain to Communist China to help alleviate the food shortage in the hope to "calm China's alleged aggressiveness."[17] At a press conference on 25 January 1961, Kennedy stated that if there was both a desire and a need for food, "the United States would be glad to consider that need."[18] Some NSC and State officials even saw "an opportunity to break the deadlock" as "Chinese grain needs and American grain surpluses might be matched."[19] On 6 February 1962, Chester Bowles, then the president's special representative and adviser on African, Asian, and Latin American affairs, wrote to Kennedy that the Chinese food crisis offered the non-Communist world an opportunity "to gain some important leverage in its economic relations with the Peiping regime."[20]

Slowly but surely, the Kennedy administration started debating on a possible course of action in relation to changes in China policy. As a senator, John F. Kennedy had criticized the Republican White House's decision to defend the offshore islands, a stance that reflected the broader policy goal of disentangling the United States from the Chinese civil war. In a speech delivered in June

1960, Kennedy argued cautiously for improved communications with the mainland via the test ban talks in Geneva. After winning the election, Kennedy's secretary of state–designate Dean Rusk told the British ambassador to Washington
in December 1960 that he considered current American policy regarding the
PRC's UN membership "unrealistic" and that he would like to see the new administration get itself "off the hook" on it.[21] Adlai Stevenson, subsequently appointed as Kennedy's UN ambassador, had been even more vocal. In a *Foreign
Affairs* article published in January 1960, he called for an end to Beijing's exclusion from the United Nations, although he coupled this with the need to hold
a UN-supervised election in Korea and to achieve self-determination for Taiwan. In his view, China, "with a quarter of the world's population, would be
more accountable to world opinion than as an outcast."[22]

Mid-level officials at the National Security Council and the State Department saw opportunities for changes in China policy as well. NSC staffer Robert
W. Komer wrote to McGeorge Bundy in March 1961: "Let's face it; China problems may not wait for careful, leisurely review. . . . "[23] Edward Rice, a China
specialist and then a member of the Policy Planning Staff, prepared a long and
detailed paper in October 1961 outlining several possible policy initiatives toward Beijing.[24] This paper discussed the possible initiatives, which included the
matter of UN recognition; the opening of trade; authorized travel to China by,
for example, U.S. journalists, medical personnel, and scholars; the involvement
of China in arms negotiation; and Chinese Nationalist evacuation of the offshore islands, together with explicit assurances that the United States would not
support any attempt by the Taiwan authorities to use military means to reestablish their rule on the mainland. As Rosemary Foot has noted, this paper "largely
set the agenda for those searching throughout the 1960s for a means to improve
relations with the PRC."[25]

Moreover, the reorganization of the State Department at the beginning of
the Kennedy administration seemed to open new prospect for the China issue.
The appointment of W. Averell Harriman as assistant secretary of state for Far
Eastern affairs (from November 1961 to April 1963), signaled change as he was
replacing Walter P. McConaughy, the Dulles-era appointee and staunch opponent of the PRC. Harriman brought two new members to the bureau, Edward
Rice and Robert Barnett, who favored changes in China policy. These people,
joining with Chester B. Bowles, a key Kennedy adviser, first appointed as undersecretary of state (from January to December 1961), formed a critical group, willing to contemplate and propose new ways in dealing with Beijing. More importantly, the creation of the "Mainland China Affairs" desk, out of the "Republic
of China Affairs," suggested "opportunities for promoting a Beijing perspective
on events."[26]

These Kennedy officials were searching for a modified containment, which
was based on the argument that the Chinese Communist regime itself, despite

the vulnerabilities through which it would pass in the 1960s, was not "a passing phase" but was here to stay, at least for the medium term if not longer. The China policy speech by Assistant Secretary of State for Far Eastern Affairs Roger Hilsman (from April 1963 to March 1964) on 13 December 1963, three weeks after Kennedy's assassination, was viewed as "a landmark in the process of reducing tensions with China." He announced that the United States was "determined to keep the door open to the possibility of change (in Communist China) and not to slam it shut against any developments which might advance our national good, serve the free world, and benefit the people of China."[27] Hilsman tried to convey two new points: that the administration no longer believed the Chinese government to be a passing phenomenon, which was a reverse of the view held in the Dulles era, and that if Beijing gave up its preference for "foreign adventure," then it would find Washington to be flexible and willing to negotiate.[28] The GMD government in Taiwan was upset and disappointed by Hilsman's speech. Jiang Tingfu, the GMD ambassador to Washington, was asked to clarify with U.S. officials that Washington "has not adopted a new policy on China."[29]

While the Kennedy administration was reconsidering its China policy, the Communist leadership in Beijing was also at a crossroad in its policy toward Washington. Mao and his associates began to reassess the changing balance of power between the two camps in the early 1960s. The perception of threat in relation to the United States tended to be determined by both domestic pressure and international challenges. Whether China could survive and thrive in the new dynamics in domestic and international politics in next two or three years (1961–63) became a focal point for policy debate and subsequently a policy priority.

The Great Leap Forward ended in disaster. The direct consequence was the subsequent "three bitter years" of severe economic crisis (1959–61). It is submitted that at least 20 million people died of malnutrition and starvation.[30] Mao's self-reliant development model proved to be a total failure. China's serious economic crisis forced Mao and his associates to reorient PRC's development strategy. The Beijing regime was in severe domestic crisis.

The failure of the Great Leap Forward was also simultaneous with upheavals in its foreign relations. The divergences between China and the Soviet Union had steadily developed in the wake of the Twentieth Congress of the Communist Party of the Soviet Union in 1956. The Sino-Soviet summit in October 1959 was in fact a turning point marking the beginning of the collapse of the alliance. Immediately after the summit, Soviet leader Nikita Khrushchev openly criticized Chinese leaders and China's foreign policy. When the Soviet government decided to withdraw all its experts from China in the summer of 1960, the Sino-Soviet split became a reality. Mao was concerned about Soviet domination in China and annoyed at Khrushchev's "peaceful coexistence, peaceful

competition, and peaceful transition" policy toward the Western countries, especially the United States. Not willing to submit to the Soviet line on foreign
policy, Mao accused the Soviets of "revisionism." The Sino-Soviet dispute soon
spread from ideology to state-to-state relations. Soviet troops occupied Kelu-
chen Island on the Ergun River in Inner Mongolia near the Soviet border in
February 1960. In the summer of 1960, Soviet troops provoked a border incident
in the vicinity of the Potzuaikerh Pass, in China's Xinjiang Autonomous Region. In early 1962, the Soviet consulate in Ili instigated sixty thousand Chinese
residents to flee to the Soviet Union. From then on, there was no more peace
on the Sino-Soviet border.[31] After the Cuban missile crisis, the Soviet Union
made efforts to relax tension with the United States. Mao was vigilant about
Soviet-American collusion against China.

China's security situation was no better along its southern border. In the summer of 1959, India staged two armed conflicts with China, at Longju and the
Kongka pass, triggering a tense situation all along the Sino-Indian border. Before the second border conflict with India in 1962, Mao was very concerned and
tried to avoid military conflict. He instructed the Chinese army: "Never retreat,
but also avoid bloodshed."[32] China's relationship with its immediate neighbor
was at the lowest point after the second clashes.[33] With increasing U.S. military
involvement in Indochina, GMD's frequent small-scale raids along China's
coast, and Jiang Jieshi's active preparation to "mount a (large-scale) counterattack against the mainland," China now had to cope with external enemies
from both the south and the north.

China's deteriorating national security worried Beijing leaders. At a meeting
of the CCP Politburo Standing Committee, presided over by Mao Zedong,
held from 7 to 17 January 1960, it was decided that "strenuous and active efforts
should be made to open new prospects in China's foreign relations."[34] The pressure of the economic recession and the serious situation in foreign relations led
to calls within the PRC leadership for a comprehensive and systematic overhaul
of foreign policy. In the report delivered to an enlarged working conference of
the CCP Central Committee convened in January 1962, Liu Shaoqi, the president of the PRC, set a keynote for foreign policy. In his supplementary speech,
he stated at the very beginning: "Comrade Mao Zedong has pointed out that in
order to fulfill our international obligations, the essential thing for us is to do a
good job at home. . . . We should pay attention mainly to our domestic issues."[35] Liu advocated restraint and moderation in China's foreign policy.

II

Within all of those considerations in Washington and Beijing, the only one that
seemed to be accepted and persisted in was the continuation of the ambassadorial talks in Warsaw. U.S. officials attempted to pour more substance into the

Warsaw talks. At the outset of the Kennedy administration, a review of the ambassadorial talks during the Eisenhower administration, sent from Assistant Secretary of State for Far Eastern Affairs J. Graham Parsons (from June 1959 to March 1961) to Secretary of State Dean Rusk on 19 February 1961, prepared by John Holdridge, an officer in charge of Chinese affairs at the State Department, confirmed the utility and the justification of the talks. The report highlighted five major "political and psychological gains" for the U.S. from the talks with Communist China: (1) The talks showed to world public opinion that the U.S. was not "ignoring 650 million people," as the U.S. had been "dealing with the Chinese Communists on a regular basis." (2) As a result of the talks, the U.S. had been able "to an appreciable extent to place the onus for the tense relations" on the Chinese Communists. (3) The talks had apparently acted as a partial damper on Chinese Communist military actions against Taiwan, as Beijing resorted to force in the Taiwan Strait only during a period when the talks were not in session. (4) The continuation of the talks minimized the chance of third parties' attempting to set themselves up as middlemen between Beijing and Washington, which would complicate the relations. (5) The talks constituted a direct, private means of communications between the United States and Communist China, which made it possible to bring up a wide array of topics. The existence of such a contact, the report argued, provided the U.S. with "a convenient, rapid, and entirely confidential channel" to the PRC leaders.[36]

This document also suggested possible new subjects for the future talks, including disarmament and nuclear control and the Chinese reaction to a possible U.S. offer of food assistance and exchange of scholars, among others. Undersecretary Chester Bowles concurred and recommended that "the talks be continued." He believed that the talks "provide certain minor advantages to us at the present time and might be even more useful in the future."[37]

Beijing was interested in maintaining the communication channel as well. At the CCP Politburo Standing Committee meeting in January 1960, a basic guideline was laid down for the relations with the United States—"Keep on talking and don't break down; keep on talking but don't hurry." That is to say that China would continue its talks with the United States and would neither hurry to establish diplomatic relations nor terminate the talks. The Chinese leaders believed it was not the opportune moment to come to full diplomatic relations with the United States as Washington would not accept Beijing's condition to withdraw its troops from Taiwan, and Beijing would not accept Washington's solution of "two Chinas."[38] Such a guideline provided China's U.S. policy with a certain level of flexibility. To keep on talking with Washington might be a tactic that Mao would like to have while China was parting company with the Soviets. This became China's basic approach to the ambassadorial talks in the 1960s.

It was within this context that Chinese and American ambassadors held sixteen meetings during the Kennedy administration. The first was the 103rd meeting, on 7 March 1961, and the last, the 118th meeting, on 13 November 1963. Ambassador Wang Bingnan was the chief Chinese negotiator for the entire period, while Ambassador Jacob Beam represented the United States till the 107th meeting, on 28 November 1961. He was succeeded by Ambassador John Cabot, who took over from the 108th meeting, on 1 March 1962. Cabot was a career diplomat, having been in foreign services for thirty-six years by 1962. His selection as U.S. representative had much to do with his previous experience in China, serving as U.S. consul general in Shanghai in the 1940s.[39]

It was not surprising that the Kennedy administration, determined to contain "Communist expansion," did not plan to make big breakthroughs at the Warsaw talks—to discuss the withdrawal of U.S. troops from Taiwan. For the most part, there was little movement on the real issues that had deadlocked the negotiations: Taiwan, renunciation of force, detained U.S. prisoners in China, exchange of newsmen, and so on. However, the most obvious change of approach was the U.S. attempt to broaden the scope of the issues under discussion to include current problems—food supply to China, the Sino-Indian border clash, the Laotian crisis of 1961–62,[40] nuclear disarmament, and exchanges of journalists and scholars, among others.[41] For instance, during the course of the talks, the Kennedy administration debated the advisability of offering assistance in the form of food and medicine to mainland China.[42] In its instruction to Ambassador Jacob Beam for the 103rd meeting in March, the State Department asked Beam to tell his Chinese counterpart that "the United States will always do what it can to help on purely humanitarian grounds" if the Chinese side expressed "serious desire for food or need for food."[43] From the very beginning, the State Department had anticipated that the Chinese side might raise the issue. However, Ambassador Wang never touched on the issue at the first two meetings. When at the 105th meeting, on 29 June 1961 (the third session under the Kennedy administration), Ambassador Beam brought up the issue, and mentioned the U.S. proposal to grant permission on humanitarian grounds for individual Americans to send food parcels (purchased not in the U.S., but on the open market) to private individuals or groups in the PRC, Wang refused to discuss the sending of food parcels, even by private individuals, declaring that the PRC "was overcoming its difficulties by its own efforts," and thus "no 'relief' was required."[44] No further discussion over the issue was recorded at the ambassadorial talks, although U.S. officials continued to probe about such an opportunity.

There was not much progress on the issue of Taiwan—the withdrawal of U.S. troops—as Washington still regarded Taiwan as the legitimate government of China and a U.S. ally in the 1960s. Beijing was angry at Washington's initiation and UN adoption of the "important question resolution"[45] regarding PRC's membership at the UN in 1961, and about exchange visits between Vice President Lyndon Johnson (to Taiwan) and Chen Cheng, Taiwan's vice president (to the United States). At the 106th meeting, on 15 August 1961, Ambassador Wang blamed Washington for worsening "Sino-US relations with President's invitation [to] Chen Cheng's visit." He stated that exchange of newsmen was not possible "during the exchange of Vice Presidential visits between the US and GRC." He reiterated the usual Chinese position that Washington should withdraw from Taiwan. Wang warned that America's China policy "headed in the opposite direction."[46] Beam rejected Wang's accusation and insisted that "threat and use of force" against Taiwan by Beijing was the real issue. They exchanged the usual accusations, and the atmosphere was tense.

There seemed to be a small step forward from the U.S. side, but the result turned to be questionable. This happened on 31 August 1961 when Wang invited Beam to come to the Chinese Embassy for a talk the next day. The State Department replied positively to Beam's report, "No objection [to] your visit to Wang's Embassy." This was the first time that a U.S. ambassador went to talk at the Chinese embassy — obviously a breakthrough to Dulles's rule. However, when Beam arrived at the Chinese embassy, Wang read a prepared lengthy governmental statement, accusing the U.S. of creating tensions in Berlin, Laos, South Korea, and Okinawa, along with the Taiwan Strait area. He claimed that although President Kennedy had declared "his strategy of peace" during the presidential campaign, his actual policy moved the U.S. closer toward the "path of war." Beam was surprised and later noted, "His remarks about President surpassed bounds of common politeness."[47] Beijing had become increasingly disappointed with Kennedy's China policy and the lack of progress at the Warsaw talks. This ploy was intended as an early warning to the new Democratic administration. Washington was annoyed at Beijing's posture. When Foreign Minister Chen Yi proposed to upgrade Sino-American ambassadorial talks to the foreign ministers' level on 11 October 1961, Washington refused to concur.[48]

Ambassador John Cabot, however, did make clear during the Taiwan Strait crisis of 1962 Washington's willingness to deter Jiang's aggressive operation against the mainland. As the crisis atmosphere developed again in the Taiwan Strait due to Jiang's attempt to attack the mainland, the PRC was closely watching. At the end of May 1962, when Wang Bingnan was on vacation in China, Zhou Enlai called him in for a meeting to discuss the situation in the Taiwan Strait. The PRC leaders had concluded that Jiang Jieshi was eager to launch massive military attacks against the mainland, but that he would have difficulties in getting Washington's blessing. However, they remained uncertain about whether or not the United States would support a GMD military offensive. They decided that China should try to persuade the United States to use its influence to restrain Jiang. Zhou asked Wang to cut short his vacation and return immediately to Warsaw in order to seek an opportunity to feel out U.S. intentions.[49]

Upon his return to Warsaw, Wang made an appointment with Cabot on the pretext of having tea together. On 23 June, when Cabot arrived at the Chinese ambassador's residence, Wang told him that he would like to call to the attention of the U.S. government the tensions in the Taiwan Strait area. He claimed that Jiang Jieshi's preparations for attacking the mainland were made with U.S. support, encouragement, and cooperation and warned that the United States must bear full responsibility for Jiang's adventurous actions and their serious consequences.[50]

Cabot responded that he would relay Wang's concerns to Washington. He reassured Wang that under current circumstances, the United States would never support Jiang in launching military attacks against the mainland. He reported that Jiang was under obligation to Washington not to launch such a military attack without prior U.S. agreement. Cabot stated that the United States did not want a world war and would make every effort to prevent it from happening. He assured Wang that the United States would dissociate itself from any Taiwan attack. He even suggested that if Taiwan took military action against the mainland, the United States and China should continue to hold ambassadorial talks in order to restore peace. Cabot also warned Wang of the "serious danger US forces would be involved" in the event that the PRC attacked Taiwan.[51] The PRC leaders were satisfied with Wang's report on this meeting.[52]

This limited assurance was put to the test when an American-manufactured Chinese Nationalist–piloted U-2 aircraft was shot down over the mainland on 9 September 1962.[53] Upon Chinese request, the two ambassadors met on 20 September for a special, unnumbered session. Wang launched the "strongest protest" regarding the intrusion of the "American U-2" on an "espionage mission," and demanded that the "US stop such flagrant aggression." Wang said that this plane intrusion was not consistent with the U.S. pledge "not to attack China by armed force" on 23 June. It was an "important step by US to incite Chiang [Jiang] attack Mainland." Wang further claimed that if the present administration was "any different in China policy from previous" two administrations, it was that it was "more adventurous and irresponsible." Cabot responded that Taiwan purchased U-2 aircraft directly from the manufacturer, and the U.S. government was not responsible for its use. He argued that since Beijing wanted to overcome Taiwan "by any means including use of force," it was quite natural for the GMD to take precautions against the mainland. He again assured Wang of the U.S. pledge not to support Jiang in launching military attacks against the Chinese mainland.[54]

Beijing viewed the Kennedy administration as more threatening to its security, as it believed that Washington was behind Jiang's aggressive actions and the intrusion of the U-2 aircraft. During the Eisenhower era, Jiang never had a chance to seriously prepare an invasion of the mainland. Thus, Mao labeled the United States as China's major enemy after this incident. At the Tenth Plenum of the Eighth Party Congress on 24–27 September 1962, Zhou Enlai reported, "From the international relations' perspective, our struggle with American imperialists is the major issue. So Chairman Mao told us 'that the most important thing is to expose the U.S.-Jiang (Jieshi) clique [plot] of invading the mainland.'"[55] The perception of Washington as most "adventurous" with the deterioration of the Sino-Soviet dispute was meaningful. Beijing wanted to feel out Washington's real intention and to send the Kennedy administration an early warning and to exert pressure.[56] China, though, had no intention to terminate the talks. In his meeting with British Member of Parliament Malcolm MacDonald in late October 1962, Zhou Enlai stated that "Warsaw talks had been going on for seven years 'with no results,'" but China "was prepared to have them continue for another seven years."[57]

The talks in 1962 apparently played a role in defusing tension in the Taiwan Strait area. The Kennedy administration offered to continue the talks with the PRC despite possible conflict in the Taiwan Strait area. This was mainly because Washington came to accept the fact that there was no chance that the GMD could succeed in recovering the mainland. The Kennedy administration was now more in consensus that the Communist regime would stay in the mainland. Early in June 1962, in his memo to the president, Chester Bowles argued that "our ambiguous response to the GRC's request for assistance in operation against the Chinese mainland ('polite postponement' and limited cooperation) is highly dangerous." Bowles urged Kennedy to state explicitly that "under no circumstance will we support GRC operations against the mainland."[58] After further consultation, Kennedy wrote Jiang Jieshi in April 1963, "Given our present estimate of the situation, we cannot acquiesce in military action against the China mainland."[59] Washington was able to discourage Jiang from initiating any massive military operation against the mainland during the Kennedy administration. But small-scale raids occurred both before and after April 1963, and the United States seems to have acquiesced in them.[60]

Another issue also became a focus of the talks: control of nuclear weapons and disarmament. Nuclear disarmament was first brought to discussion at the 110th meeting, on 17 May 1962, when John Cabot presented a general statement on U.S. disarmament policy and its reasoning. Wang Bingnan countered by declaring that Beijing "favored general and complete disarmament," but the U.S. policy remained an obstacle. He claimed that "President Kennedy openly declared US ready strike first with nuclear weapons in preventive war."[61] When the First Test Ban Treaty was tentatively signed on 25 July 1963 (officially signed on 5 August),[62] the PRC government issued a statement condemning the treaty. But the condemnation did not go beyond a public call for total disarmament and a proposal for the creation of nuclear-free zones in Asia and the Pacific region, Central Europe, Africa, and Latin America, which could be realized by a U.S. withdrawal of atomic weapons from these areas.[63] On 2 August, Zhou Enlai sent a letter to heads of all nations of the world, relaying Chinese government proposals.[64]

Beijing renewed the discussion of the nuclear issue at the 116th meeting, on 7

August 1963. Wang Bingnan stated that the Test Ban Treaty increased the "hazard of nuclear war" through legalizing the "continued manufacture, transportation, underground testing and use of weapons by US while binding hands of peace-loving countries, denying them adequate means [to] protect [them]selves against nuclear threat." Wang further pointed out China's perception of nuclear threat from Washington's deployment in East Asia. He said that the United States should remove its nuclear threat to China, which came from all directions—from the fortifications in Guam, from the units in Korea and Taiwan, and from the U.S. Air Force, attack aircraft carriers, and submarines that operated in the Pacific Ocean. Wang presented Beijing's drafted agreed announcement, which declared that (1) the PRC and U.S. governments would jointly propose the establishment of a nuclear-free-zone in Asian Pacific regions, including China, the United States, the Soviet Union, and Japan, and (2) the U.S. government would "withdraw all its military bases, including nuclear bases, from the areas surrounding the People's Republic of China, and withdraw all its nuclear weapons and their means of delivery from those areas." Cabot countered by expressing regret at Beijing's rejection of the test ban treaty. He also explained U.S. policy "to promote general disarmament at some length."[65]

Beijing's ploy did not seem to work as Washington regarded the PRC's possession of nuclear weapons as "a menacing situation."[66] At the 117th meeting, on 11 September 1963, Cabot pointed out the "discrepancies in Chinese statements on disarmament." On the one hand, the PRC called for complete, absolute, and total disarmament, including the total prohibition of nuclear weapons. On the other hand, the Chinese official paper *Renmin Ribao* announced, "Universal and complete disarmament can be realized only after imperialism, capitalism and all systems of exploitation have been eliminated."[67] Following State Department instruction, Cabot declined to "answer Chou's letter [Zhou Enlai's letter on 2 August] or comment further on the agreed announcement" that Wang had proposed at last meeting. The State Department "believed the Chinese might be hoping for an outright U.S. rejection of their proposals [to be] used to justify their own nuclear tests."[68]

Wang expressed regret at Cabot's presentation and indicated that Washington was "not sincerely interested [in] preventing nuclear war." Cabot refuted Wang's accusation, indicating that the United States was interested in eliminating nuclear threat and had signed a limited test ban treaty as the first step forward, while Beijing's proposal was vague and not clear. As more than eighty-eight nations supported and signed the treaty, Cabot asked Wang why Beijing did not sign the limited test ban treaty, which was "important step in that direction." Each side was firm in its own position and waited for the other to give in. The State Department instructed that Cabot should "maintain an attitude of firmness without hostility" and "wait patiently until Wang's side is willing to cooperate in lessening tension."[69]

Washington was willing to adjust its China policy, but found it difficult to achieve the purpose. It tried to disentangle from the Chinese civil war and distance itself from Taiwan. However, it proved difficult, if not altogether impossible, for Washington to move closer to the PRC. In view of the Sino-Soviet rift, the State Department was considering whether a "more conciliatory tone" on the U.S. side in talks "might pay off." In his report to the State Department regarding the 117th meeting, Cabot stated that he saw "no signs whatever as yet it would," but he also suggested that the Department "should study situation in light [of] its overall knowledge to judge whether any change in atmospherics of the talks would be worthwhile experiment."[70] The Kennedy administration seemed to leave major changes in its China policy for Kennedy's expected second term.

III

Kennedy's assassination on 22 November 1963 had serious consequences at least in the domestic and international context within which the ambassadorial talks were conducted. Sworn into office, Lyndon B. Johnson promised to continue Kennedy's legacy and aspired to expand the Democratic administration's domestic and foreign policy agenda. However, the Johnson administration, which seemed to have placed its top priority on domestic reforms, known as the Great Society, was faced with a series of foreign policy crises. The biggest and unexpected challenge the Johnson White House encountered during its five-odd years in office was America's armed involvement in Vietnam. Suddenly, the PRC posed an outstanding threat and opportunity as far as U.S. military action in Vietnam was concerned.

American officials monitored the Chinese response during the Gulf of Tonkin Incident in August 1964. Initially, the CIA concluded that the incident would not trigger an immediate Chinese military response. A CIA memorandum reported on 6 August that the Chinese official newspaper *Renmin Ribao* declared that "aggression by the U.S. against the DRV means aggression against China." As the United States had "lit the flames of war" in Indochina, the PRC would "not sit idly by," and it asserted its "right" to help the North Vietnamese.[71] Allen Whiting, director of the State Department's Bureau of Intelligence and Research for the Far East, later noted that this phraseology reminded U.S. officials of Chinese warnings against U.S. troops advancing toward the Yalu in September 1950.[72]

Johnson administration officials worried that the two countries might repeat their Korean War tragedy in Vietnam. "Have we faced—and has the President faced—the full shape of the risk of Chinese intervention?" James Thomson Jr., a China specialist at the NSC, wondered on the eve of "Rolling Thunder" operations (the sustained bombing of North Vietnam in the spring of 1965). "Are we willing—and is the President willing—to face a ground war in Southeast Asia against the combined armies of North Vietnam and China?" Skeptical of "the systematic reprisal track," Thomson warned that it would be "folly for the sheer momentum of events (or of actions taken to bolster the morale of our friends in Saigon) to lead us into a land war with China in which our air and naval power would be relatively ineffective."[73] Undersecretary of State George Ball, a consistent skeptic on the efficacy of military escalation, likewise cautioned that pressures to "take out" air bases used by Chinese MIGs could set the United States "on a course that would escalate into all-out conflict with China."[74]

Concerned about Beijing's reaction, Washington did not send a large number of forces to Vietnam until the spring of 1965. By the summer of 1965, the CIA estimated that "as long as the Communists think they are winning in South Vietnam it is unlikely that Chinese Communists or Soviets will intervene with substantial military forces of their own, in combat." Moreover, the PRC would not send ground troops, as they had in Korea, even if it appeared that the United States and its South Vietnamese ally were winning in the South or if U.S. air strikes damaged the industrial and military sectors of North Vietnam. But the Chinese were likely to enter the war if the United States invaded North Vietnam or bombed their fighter bases in South China. They would certainly fight the United States if U.S. forces invaded North Vietnam and approached the Chinese border.[75] Six months later, U.S. military leaders and Secretary of Defense Robert McNamara concurred that China would intervene to prevent the destruction of the DRV authority, but probably not to prevent a DRV/Vietcong defeat in South Vietnam.[76]

China's successful explosion of its first nuclear device on 16 October 1964 posed a serious threat to Washington as well. At a National Security Council meeting on 16 October, which was scheduled to discuss the implication of Soviet leader Khrushchev's step-down and "the change of government in Moscow," attended by Johnson, Rusk, and other high-ranking officials, a preliminary report "about the explosion of a nuclear device in China arrived." Obviously surprised at the news, Washington believed that it had "pretty well prepared the world for expecting this event and not becoming alarmed by it."[77] A memorandum from Earle G. Wheeler, chairman of the JCS, to Secretary of Defense McNamara on 16 January 1965 further pointed out that although China's present nuclear capability had "not materially affected the existing balance of military power between the United States and Communist China," "the expansion of this capability will pose difficult problems in the future." The United States should stand ready to answer "requests by threatened countries for more definitive guarantees, including increased nuclear support."[78]

In 1966 and 1967, American officials were carefully watching China's Cultural Revolution with no clear idea as to what its implications were for U.S. policy.

NEGOTIATING AT CROSS-PURPOSES

Even Rusk was puzzled. On the one hand, he believed that China would become a great power that "would be expected to have close relations—political, economic, and cultural—with the United States." On the other hand, he was obsessed with the danger posed by "one billion Chinese armed with nuclear weapons."[79] A China study by some mid-level U.S. officials argued that as the Cultural Revolution was weakening China, it presented an opportunity for Washington to enhance its standing in East and Southeast Asia. It concluded that China's domestic troubles greatly "reduced the likelihood" that China would enter the war in Vietnam.[80] A CIA study noted a month later that the predominant theme of the Cultural Revolution had been "that the enemies are inside China." It concurred as the Cultural Revolution had so disrupted life in China that going to war was nearly impossible.[81]

There was more to China policy during the Johnson administration. Since Hilsman's speech in late 1963, administration officials had encountered no significant public or congressional opposition to the official changes of attitude in public statement regarding China policy.[82] The closeness of the 1965 vote at the UN to admit the PRC to the organization generated greater public and congressional interest in and debate about U.S. China policy. Public opinion surveys and polls also indicated that the mass public was ready for changes in policy toward the PRC. Various interest groups also supported an improved level of communication with Beijing.[83] The most important was the congressional support for changes. Many of the stalwarts of the China Lobby—men such as Walter Judd, Alexander Smith, and William F. Knowland—lost influence in Congress. In March 1965, a House subcommittee of the Foreign Affairs Committee issued a report on Sino-Soviet rift, which recommended "at an appropriate time, consideration to the initiation of limited but direct contact with Red China through cultural exchange activities with emphasis on scholars and journalists."[84] In March 1966, William Fulbright, as chair of the Senate Foreign Relations Committee, was instrumental in organizing televised Senate hearings on America's China policy. At the hearings, several Asian specialists urged trade in nonstrategic goods and movement toward eventual diplomatic and UN recognition, advocating U.S. China policy change from the Dulles/Eisenhower's "containment with isolation" toward "containment without isolation," a phrase first coined by the noted China scholar A. Doak Barnett.[85] More importantly, the Hearings promoted China's image as "troubled modernizer" rather than simply the "Red Menace."[86]

Top administration officials quickly endorsed this modified containment policy. Vice President Hubert Humphrey made remarks suggesting a new flexibility in policies toward Beijing in an appearance on NBC's *Meet the Press* at the time of the Senate Hearing.[87] On 12 July, in his radio address, President Johnson expressed the desire for eventual "reconciliation between nations that now call themselves enemies" and called publicly for the "free flow of ideas and people and goods" to China.[88] On 2 September 1966, the State Department broke its established rule and authorized U.S. chiefs of mission and principal officers "at their discretion, to permit responsible officers under their authority to establish informal social contacts with the Chinese Communists."[89]

At the height of the Vietnam War, U.S. allies, especially West Europe and Japan, also expected changes in China policy. Ambassador Edwin Reischauer, an eminent East Asian scholar, in his cable from Tokyo in August 1966 eloquently argued why America's China policy needed to be altered. From the perspective of his own posting, Reischauer described "Japanese unease at being linked to a China policy which they consider . . . basically unrealistic and not in Japan's long-range interests." In his judgment, it was "the most serious problem that now exists in U.S.-Japanese relations," and he added that "Japan is not the only country in which we pay a price for our present stand," that the United States paid "something of a price in practically every other of our major industrialized allies and in many other countries throughout the world." Such allies were similarly distressed by the U.S. pretense that the "twelve million people on Taiwan and not the seven hundred million in continental China, represent the great historical political entity known as China." Moreover, such a claim prevented Taiwan from recognizing reality, encouraged dangerous behavior among America's Asian allies, damaged regional solidarity in Southeast Asia, and stood in the way of building broad multilateral support for the U.S. role in that region. He proposed that the U.S. should support Beijing's representation at the United Nations, pledge not to interfere in its domestic affairs, and express willingness to live in peace with China. Reischauer argued that what was fundamentally required was a "redefinition of our attitude toward Beijing." Such a policy would not weaken the containment policy; on the contrary, it "would be more understandable to our own people as well as to outsiders.[90]

In mid-1968, as the turmoil of the Cultural Revolution was cooling down, the Johnson administration made a final gesture to Beijing by inviting Chinese correspondents to cover the forthcoming presidential campaign.[91] Undersecretary of State Nicholas Katzenbach made a major speech on China policy. He declared that the United States would be "happy to respond positively" to any future Chinese wish for better relations. Although he reiterated American interest in contacts and stressed strongly that there was no need for China to fear an American threat to China's security, he did not break any new ground. No major initiative could be expected in the last months of a troubled administration.[92]

While the Johnson administration was willing to adjust its China policy, Beijing seemed to have become more cautious and taken a more rigid stand toward Washington. In September 1962, Mao had turned down Wang Jiaxiang's suggestions for a more pragmatic and stable foreign policy, which included relaxing tension with the West, especially the United States.[93] Instead, Mao promoted a policy of "three struggles and one increase"—China should struggle against the imperialists, the revisionists, and the reactionaries of all countries, and give more assistance to anti-imperialist, revolutionary, and Marxist-Leninist political parties and factions.[94] The Sino-Soviet polemics and split hardened Beijing's rhetoric and attitude toward the United States. By the second half of the 1960s, Beijing became even more dogmatic and militant. With little hope to reconcile its fundamental and ever-widening differences with Moscow, Mao was aspiring more than ever before to lead an anti-imperialism and anti-hegemony campaign among the Third World nations. Mao's aspiration seemed to have been supported at home by China's success in exploding its first atomic bomb.

The dramatic escalation of U.S. military intervention in Vietnam caused great alarm and sense of threat to the Chinese leadership. The Chinese leaders believed that China's national security was under grave threat. The whole nation was close to the state of war. Mao noted that the danger of war was imminent. Immediately after the Gulf of Tonkin Incident in August 1964, Mao pointed out "[We must] base [our work] upon war. [We should] prepare to fight a general war on the assumption that it will break out any time soon and it will be on a grand scale and nuclear [*zaoda dada da hezhanzheng* in Chinese]." In June 1965, at a Politburo Standing Committee meeting, Mao instructed that in planning China's economic construction, the first priority was national defense, second agriculture, third industry—a reverse of China's third Five-Year Plan stipulated in 1964, which emphasized the importance of improving people's standard of living. China entered a twenty-year period of war preparedness.[95]

Top leaders anticipated that war with the United States would come anyway, and agreed that the entire nation had to be immediately mobilized to deal with a possible worst-case scenario. At the Foreign Ministry's Fourth Conference of Ambassadors and Envoys in January 1966, Zhou Enlai told Chinese diplomats that the United States was China's primary enemy in the international struggle as Washington attempted to dominate all over the world. Although the Sino-Soviet relationship was tense, the Soviet Union remained as the secondary enemy as it was only the accomplice of U.S. imperialism.[96]

China's successful nuclear explosion in October 1964 enhanced its national strength and international status, thus adding to its uncompromising position. Chinese leaders had come to understand the military and diplomatic importance of becoming nuclear since the mid-1950s. They now felt more confident of China's status and were satisfied with their nuclear success. In a cable to the Chinese scientists who contributed to the successful nuclear test, the State Council declared that "this successful nuclear test symbolized a new era in China's defense modernization. It was a great blow to U.S. nuclear monopoly and blackmail. It will greatly encourage all peace-loving countries and people of the world."[97] As China was now a nuclear power, more countries were calling for admitting Beijing to the United Nations. Many governments and individuals urged the U.S. to take initiatives to bring China into the international community.[98] Beijing scored more political, diplomatic, and psychological points from the success of its nuclear program.

IV

It was within these domestic and international contexts that the ambassadorial talks were carried on during the Johnson administration. During the five-plus years, there were only sixteen formal meetings: five in 1964, five in 1965, three in 1966, two in 1967, and one in 1968. The infrequency of the meetings made sustained discussions very difficult. The main issues discussed, aside from Taiwan and detained U.S. prisoners in China, were the Vietnam War, nuclear disarmament, China's UN membership, and scholarly and cultural exchanges. At a typical session during these meetings, the Chinese ambassador would denounce the United States for "occupying" Taiwan, for aggression in Vietnam, and for provocative hostility toward China, and would refuse to discuss other issues until these problems, especially the Taiwan issue, were resolved. The U.S. ambassador would defend the U.S. role in Southeast Asia and relations with Taiwan, would assure the Chinese side that Washington had no hostile intent and was willing to improve relations, would suggest a new initiative for cultural exchanges, and would demand the release of American prisoners remaining in China. The meeting would end with the only genuine negotiations of the session—on the question of the next date for the talks—with the U.S. ambassador pushing for an earlier date and the Chinese holding out for a latter meeting.[99]

Ambassador Wang Bingnan represented China for the first two meetings, No. 119 on 29 January and No. 120 on 8 April 1964. His successor Ambassador Wang Guoquan covered thirteen meetings, from No. 121 on 29 July 1964 to No. 133 on 14 June 1967. After Wang Guoquan was recalled to China to take part in the Cultural Revolution, Chinese chargé d'affaires ad interim to Poland Chen Dong served as Chinese chief negotiator at the 134th meeting, on 8 January 1968. For the U.S. side, Ambassador John Cabot was chief negotiator till the 127th meeting, on 15 September 1965. He was succeeded by Ambassador John Gronouski, who took over from the 128th meeting, on 15 December 1965.[100]

Nuclear disarmament became an important issue on the agenda and was a topic for almost all the talks afterward. After China's successful nuclear test in October 1964, Zhou Enlai used the occasion to repeat the call for a worldwide summit conference the Chinese had made when the partial test ban treaty was signed in summer 1963. He also stated that China would never be the first to use nuclear weapons. At the 123rd meeting, on 25 November 1964, immediately after China's nuclear explosion, the Chinese proposed a "no-first-use" agreement between the two sides.[101] This was an indication of how Beijing had been alarmed at a possible U.S. preemptive strike. Even rejected by Washington, Beijing could score favorable points in world peace movement. Washington, on the other hand, wanted first to prevent Beijing from becoming a nuclear power, or at least to prohibit it from further nuclear development.

Cabot agreed to transmit the draft announcement to Washington, but stated that the "question of verification and control" was a "vital consideration in any disarmament proposal." Cabot was contemptuous of the PRC draft, commenting it was "so patently unacceptable that I do not believe the Chinese themselves take it seriously."[102] At this time, Washington opposed the idea of nuclear disarmament because the U.S. seemed to count on nuclear weapons as the only means to counteract to China's tremendous manpower. Washington was not interested in a summit conference of all countries of the world for fear that such a meeting might degenerate into a propaganda forum. Thus, it insisted that only powers concerned should participate.[103] It was not possible to reach any agreement on this issue as the expectation gap was so wide.

The Chinese side seemed to have lost much interest in the talks after the 123rd meeting and proposed a longer interval: three months instead of usual two. Cabot noted, "Chinese clearly interested in talks only as propaganda forum" for the time being. He reported that there was "no value in lengthy and sterile polemics." He thus asked permission to "give somewhat shorter responses."[104] Ambassador Wang Guoquan, however, saw this change in Cabot's attitude differently. He and his assistants became very excited after learning that China had successfully exploded its first nuclear bomb. He noted that China's successful nuclear explosion "gives us new energy and powerful backing." He observed that China's nuclear acquisition and Khrushchev's fall out of power enhanced China's negotiation position. He personally felt much more confident as he was now the representative of a nuclear power in Asia. Thus, Wang believed that he surpassed his counterpart psychologically at the negotiating table since the 123rd meeting in Warsaw.[105]

The discussion over the nuclear issue led to no solution. At the 124th meeting, on 24 February 1965, Cabot informed Wang that Washington "could not accept PRC draft on nuclear disarmament, because it provided for no international control system." Washington also regarded a worldwide "summit conference as impractical."[106] The Chinese seemed not unhappy with Washington's rejection. Wang reiterated China's position on nuclear weapons, and declared "as long as the countries of the world have not reached agreement on the complete prohibition and destruction of nuclear weapons . . . China has a right to continue the testing and production of nuclear weapons."[107]

Beijing's concern over a possible U.S. preemptive strike on its nuclear facilities would linger on. After China's third nuclear test, on 9 May 1966, in a speech at a banquet for the visiting Albanian premier Mehmet Shehu the following day, Zhou claimed that the United States had turned down China's eighteen-month-old proposal for a Sino-American agreement on no-first-use of nuclear weapons.[108] Questioned at his press conference a week later, Dean Rusk stated that "disarmament measures should be carried out under strict and effective international control. . . . Mere declarations on such matters would not be adequate."[109] Washington felt it necessary to make a more positive response. At the 130th meeting, on 25 May, Ambassador Gronouski inquired whether the PRC government would consider an agreement to ban nuclear tests if it were linked to no-first-use agreement. Not prepared to discuss the connection of the two positions, Wang "made no mention of this statement nor did he refer again to subject of disarmament."[110] Beijing gave an indignant negative response through a *Renmin Ribao* article on 20 June. It declared that the U.S. proposal "was just another of its big frauds on the question of nuclear weapons. . . . [I]ts real intention is to fasten China to the tripartite partial nuclear test ban treaty."[111] It was clear that Beijing's position was firm. Beijing did not plan to yield an inch to Washington on the nuclear issue.

The Vietnam War was on the agenda for all sixteen meetings. In the aftermath of the Gulf of Tonkin Incident in the summer of 1964 and the subsequent U.S. retaliatory bombing of North Vietnam, James Thomson made a policy suggestion to McGeorge Bundy on 5 August. Thomson proposed that the United States call a special meeting in Warsaw to clarify the limited purposes of the bombing and to state that Washington's goal was neither to destroy North Vietnam nor to attack China. Only by using such a channel, Thomson argued, could "misinterpretation and miscalculation" be avoided. It was decided that, rather than call a special meeting about the bombing, Ambassador Cabot should communicate America's real purposes in Vietnam to the Chinese at the Warsaw talks.[112]

The Chinese wasted no time in accusing U.S. aggression and speaking out about China's support for the DRV after each major incident in Indochina. At the 122nd meeting, on 23 September 1964, after the second Gulf of Tonkin Incident, Wang Guoquan told his U.S. counterpart that the United States had fabricated the second attack in the Gulf of Tonkin "as a pretext to flagrantly launch an armed attack on the DRV." He warned the United States that it was "playing with fire" and promised Chinese support to the DRV. Wang repeated the Chinese statement that the "Chinese people will not sit idly by and we know how to deal with your aggression."[113] The atmosphere was so tense that it turned out to be one of the "most vitriolic" meetings, a "Panmunjom" type. Cabot described Wang as "loud, tendentious, impolite and arrogant, virtually spitting out his accusations, often with finger wagging."[114]

China also used the Warsaw talks to send Washington clear signals that Beijing would enter the Vietnam War when it deemed necessary. Shortly after Rolling Thunder began, Wang Guoquan derided the Americans at the 124th meeting, on 24 February 1965, by saying that "your defeat in South Vietnam is a

foregone conclusion." Wang maintained that the U.S. had destroyed the demarcation line and spread the war to North Vietnam. The signatories of the Geneva
Agreements had the right to action against U.S. aggression. Thus, China put on
record its views "designed to justify intervention in case of future needs."[115] At the
next meeting, on 21 April, he went further: "If you choose to fight on there," he
said, "the end of Nazi Germany and the Japanese militarists is a lesson for you to
learn." He rejected President Johnson's call for negotiations and a promise of
billions of dollars to redevelop the Mekong River valley. American calls for un-
conditional talks were, Wang said, a pretense to "legalize your aggressive actions." The proposed aid was nothing so much as a forlorn attempt to "buy over
the Vietnamese people with a few stinking dollars so as to save yourself from your
ultimate doom." He repeated Zhou Enlai's promise to "send [the] South Vietnamese people all their needs, including arms," and "[their] own men when
[the] South Vietnamese people wanted them." Cabot reported that Wang was
"rougher this time in both word and manner than at the last meeting."[116]

The efficacy of the Warsaw talks seemed to decrease in the wake of U.S. escalation of the war in Vietnam. The talks seemed to lose their function as the
reliable channel to convey sensitive messages between the two countries as the
discussions in Warsaw were not able to move forward. The Chinese leaders attempted to seek alternative avenues to convey to Washington their concerns
about America's expanded war in Vietnam through other diplomatic channels.
During his visit to Pakistan on 2 April 1965, Zhou Enlai asked the Pakistani
president, Mohammad Ayub Khan—who was scheduled to visit the U.S.
soon—to pass on Beijing's three-point policies to President Johnson: China will
not take initiative to provoke a war with the United States; the Chinese mean
what they say; China is prepared. Zhou also added his fourth point, "Once the
war breaks out, it will have no boundaries."[117] When the Pakistani president
postponed his visit to the United States,[118] Zhou repeated China's four-point
policy to "many foreign friends" over the next few months.[119]

Zhou reaffirmed his four-point statement in an interview with Ejaz Husain
of the Pakistani paper *Dawn* on 10 April 1966, pointing out that the four-point
statement was an indivisible whole. However, the four-point statement did not
appear in what was described as the full text of the interview in *Dawn* on 27
April. The Chinese official paper *Renmin Ribao* published this statement on 10
May 1966.[120] Ambassador Wang announced to the U.S. side China's four-point
policy at the 130th meeting, on 25 May 1966.[121] As the Warsaw talks were a mutual, confidential communication channel between the United States and
China, with the escalation of the war in Vietnam, the Warsaw channel seemed
to have degenerated into a forum for mutual accusations. The Chinese side
might think that Washington would not take seriously Beijing's statement via
the Warsaw channel. A message relayed to Washington through Mohammad
Ayub Khan, as the head of a major Asian nation known for its close tie to both

Beijing and Washington, certainly should carry more weight. The publication
of the statement by the official Chinese newspaper was designed to show to its
Communist allies and countries all over the world China's determination to
resist U.S. aggression and assist the Vietnamese people.

At the 131st meeting, on 7 September 1966, Washington attempted to lessen
China's sense of being threatened. Ambassador Gronouski assured the Chinese
that the United States did not want to maintain bases in Southeast Asia after the
war ended. The United States would even accept a neutral South Vietnam, if
that was what the South Vietnamese chose. Gronouski emphasized that if the
Chinese wanted "to see U.S. troops out of VN [Vietnam], they should use their
influence to prevail on DRV to halt infiltration and end conflict." Not convinced by U.S. reasoning, Ambassador Wang went over the usual accusation of
the Americans in Vietnam. He then suggested 11 January 1967 for the next meeting, refusing an earlier date and declaring that "he did not think more frequent
meetings were necessary" under current circumstances.[122] China was in the turmoil of the Cultural Revolution. It was indeed very difficult for Wang to conduct meaningful talks with the United States. However, the Chinese side might
still find "the existence of Warsaw channel useful both for façade of effort to
deal with [the] U.S. and for potential crisis communication but disinclined [to]
encourage frequent contact."[123]

At the same meeting, Wang expressed strong regret at U.S. violation of
confidentiality, alluding to past leaks from the U.S. side and especially the
speech by William Bundy (assistant secretary for Far Eastern affairs from March
1964 to May 1969) on 28 February, disclosing the U.S. offer on nonreciprocal
admission of Chinese journalists to the United States at the 128th meeting, on
15 December 1965.Wang told the U.S. side that Beijing would release his statement at the current meeting, which rejected all recent U.S. friendly overtures
and strongly condemned U.S. actions in Vietnam. He reiterated PRC support
for the DVR "in very strong terms." He claimed, "The USG will never be able
to obtain at the conference table what it has failed to obtain on the
battlefield."[124] The Chinese wanted to use this action to show to the world that
they were wholeheartedly supporting the Vietnamese people, rebutting the Soviet insinuations that Beijing talked belligerently about the Vietnam War but
was making behind-the-scene deals with the United States over Vietnam. The
Chinese leaders were under pressure from China's former ally the Soviet Union
and attempted to display China's revolutionary credentials to other socialist
countries: although Beijing was negotiating with Washington, it would never
"barter away principles" for its own national interest. Talking with the United
States was a tactic, the united-front strategy. It also designed to indicate to its
ally, North Vietnam, that China was supporting Vietnamese national liberation at any cost. China valued good faith and friendship, and would never be-
tray its friends.

The Johnson administration was cautious to avoid provoking PRC intervention. It also intended to create an "image of reason and responsibility" for the United States.[125] Washington made efforts to utilize the Warsaw talks in more subtle ways to reduce Beijing's apprehension regarding the U.S. war effort in Southeast Asia. In a memorandum to George Ball in December 1965, William Bundy noted that the United States should "balance" its intention of continued commitments to Vietnam and Taiwan with steps to "indicate to the Chinese that we still seek to avoid a major confrontation." He proposed that the United States would offer a broad menu of initiatives that would include the admission of PRC journalists, liberalized travel, and a joint examination of incidents involving American forces in the areas around China.[126]

With the Fulbright hearings in March 1966, the general atmosphere in the United States was more favorable to deal with China. The U.S. side would make a small friendly gesture at the Warsaw talks. At the 129th meeting, on 16 March 1966, Gronouski declared that "the United States government was willing to develop further relations with the People's Republic of China." Until then, Washington had never addressed China by its official name. Ambassador Wang regarded this as an important change in U.S. policy. He conveyed this to Beijing. "Unfortunately, this report did not receive sufficient attention and timely study" as China was on the eve of the Cultural Revolution, Wang recalled in his memoir.[127]

By the summer of 1966, the Johnson administration was considering new approaches to the question of Chinese representation at the UN[128] and restrictions on trade with China.[129] On 13 May, William Bundy drafted for President Johnson a letter to Zhou Enlai, proposing that talks be held at the foreign ministers' level.[130] The letter was considered for submission at that month's Warsaw meeting but was withheld at the last moment because George Ball, U. Alexis Johnson, and James Thomson at the State Department thought that in view of the situation in Vietnam, it might make the United States look weak. However, Gronouski was given the letter and told that its submission would be reconsidered "as soon as circumstances change."[131]

At the 132nd meeting, on 25 January 1967, Gronouski repeated his contention that the Chinese refused to believe any protestations of friendship from the United States. They saw any U.S. efforts to strengthen ties to other nations in Asia or East Asia as threats to China. "You continue to speak of the U.S. as threatening your country," Gronouski told Wang Guoquan. "Your leaders continue to talk of the U.S. as planning to attack or invade your territory." In actuality, the U.S. looked forward to Chinese help in arranging peace in Vietnam. "In our view," he continued, "peace in Vietnam does not mean the domination of any one country over Vietnam. It need not mean one country's victory and another's defeat."[132]

Even during the height of the Vietnam War, U.S. officials were exploring any opportunity to make small progress on China issue. The modification of the China travel ban was an interesting case in point. From 1961 to 1965, Rusk had categorically declined to approve a "China travel package."[133] A breakthrough came in late 1965. In "Proposed New Policy Initiatives for December 15 Warsaw Meeting," William Bundy proposed three new initiatives, including allowing "Chinese Communist journalists to visit the United States without an exchange agreement" and "Chinese doctors and scientists in the fields of public health and medicine to come to the United States" in the hope that Beijing would allow "similar American professional men to travel to China."[134]

At the 128th meeting, on 15 December 1965, Gronouski announced the U.S. proposal on exchanges of journalists, doctors, and scientists. Prior to this meeting, the principal type of cultural contact discussed at Warsaw was the exchange of journalists. Although Wang Guoquan responded by saying that "We have repeatedly made clear our position—no problems can be settled until major problem (Taiwan) settled,"[135] he regarded U.S. posture as a step forward toward negotiation. He saw this as a friendly gesture and "flexibility and concession" on the U.S.'s part.[136] The travel ban on U.S. journalists, doctors, and scientists was lifted, and the categories of those permitted to visit became steadily wider. During the subsequent meetings, these themes were reiterated and expanded upon to include exchanges of scientific data on herbal medicine and seeds and plants samples. The quickening pace and variety of U.S. cultural exchange initiatives were documented from the transcripts of the Warsaw talks.[137] For the American side, it was implementation of the new policy of "containment without isolation." Through this tactic, Washington was also able to put Beijing on the defensive, as Gronouski told Wang at the 130th meeting, on 25 May 1966, that "by not taking up our proposals for exchange [of] newsmen, doctors, educators," the Chinese side "was making it difficult to prevent" their own isolation.[138]

The Johnson administration's new moves led nowhere because China's Cultural Revolution intensified and brought about political turmoil in China starting in the summer of 1966. The times were unpropitious for major new American diplomatic initiatives toward China.[139] Yet, Washington "continued to send signals of openness and non-hostility,"[140] and Gronouski was instructed to do all he could to keep the talks going, as a "holding operation" in which the minimum U.S. objective was to "keep open some dialogue with the Chinese."[141] The State Department was even prepared to elevate the Warsaw talks to a higher-level (deputy undersecretary, undersecretary, or secretary) in case the Chinese moved to suspend or break the talks.[142] The Chinese did not go that far, but chose to meet less frequently, at an interval of five months instead of the previous three months. As China was in the Cultural Revolution, Beijing was attacking the Soviets for improving relations with Washington and was warning Hanoi against talking with the United States.[143] Rusk anticipated that Beijing might walk out of the talks to "be relieved of political embarrassment."[144]

Not anticipating changes in policy and attitude from the PRC in the current situation, the administration officials privately spoke of the Warsaw talks as serving an "educational" function.[145] Alfred Jenkins, a China specialist at the National Security Council, suggested in late 1968 that U.S. policy toward the PRC should be prepared for either a changed attitude by the current regime or a future, less radical leadership—a true "change of dynasty."[146] The record of the talks might also "provide both a general signal of openness to future leaders and a list of specific proposals that could form the basis for reconciliation."[147] Thus, the Johnson administration seemed careful not to propose anything in Warsaw that might limit the options of future PRC leaders if the current regime rejected it.[148]

This seemed to be the case in early January 1969, when the situation in China appeared to become stable. In the last two weeks of the Johnson administration, Walt Rostow, President Johnson's national security adviser (early 1966–January 1969), told Johnson that there were "faint signals" from China and suggested that it might be wise to respond with a small change in trade policy (to permit U.S. subsidiaries abroad to sell a limited range of nonstrategic goods to China). Although the change was "not substantial but psychological," Rostow argued it would open options for Johnson's successor. Johnson responded, "I don't want to rush these and do them in the last two weeks."[149]

The Chinese became even less enthusiastic about the talks as the Foreign Ministry was lost to the control of "Radicals" in the 1967.[150] Originally scheduled on 8 November 1967, the 134th meeting was postponed to 8 January 1968 at the request of the Chinese in late October. Between meetings, the two sides maintained a second secretary-level routine contact.[151] Luo Yisu, the second secretary at the Chinese Embassy in Poland, then Chinese contact person for the ambassadorial talks, phoned the U.S. Embassy that since Ambassador Wang Guoquan could not return to Warsaw for the meeting, the Chinese government proposed as a temporary measure that Chinese chargé d'affaires Chen Dong be chief negotiator at the meeting on 8 January. The U.S. side agreed to the arrangement, insisting this would be "a temporary solution, not a permanent change."[152]

At the 134th meeting, Gronouski indicated that he expected the next meeting would be at the ambassadorial level, and the two agreed to 29 May for the next meeting.[153] On 18 May, the Chinese Embassy handed the U.S. Embassy a letter, stating that since Ambassador Wang would not be able to return to Warsaw by 29 May, and "as there is nothing to discuss at present," the Chinese government suggested that 135th meeting be postponed until mid or late November. Although the State Department declared that "the U.S. side continued to feel the talks were of value," that it was prepared to meet again with Chen Dong on 29 May as an interim measure, and that there were "several pressing matters we would wish to take up on this occasion," the Chinese refused to meet earlier.[154] According to Luo Yisu, as North Vietnam was starting to negotiate with the United States in Paris, and China did not favor such negotiation, Beijing

believed it necessary to postpone its meeting with Washington to show its reservation regarding the Paris peace talks. By mid-November, it was the U.S. side
that demanded a change of date, as a new administration would soon take office
in Washington. The two agreed to hold the 135th meeting on 20 February 1969,
one month after Richard Nixon became president.[155]

V

The Kennedy administration's reconsideration of its China policy was shaped
largely by its threat perception. China's internal crisis in the wake of the Great
Leap Forward was believed to pose a serious threat to America's allies in East
and Southeast Asia. Beijing's determination to champion an independent
course in the Third World after its split with the Soviet Union was a growing
challenge to Kennedy's policy toward these countries. As America's war in Vietnam began to escalate, the Johnson administration was seriously concerned
about a possible Chinese intervention, and went the extra mile to decide what
Washington could realistically do to prevent Beijing from entering the war.
Closely watching Beijing's nuclear program, the two Democratic administrations were also eager to bring China to the international negotiations on nuclear disarmament.

Concerned about his narrow electoral victory, and annoyed at China's "anti-
Kennedy" propaganda, Kennedy was not ready to make fundamental changes
to America's China policy in his first term. Preoccupied with the war in Vietnam, the Johnson administration was hardly able to move forward in China policy. Worried about Beijing's strategic intention and threat to U.S. interests in
Asia, Washington was not prepared "to do much in terms of recognizing the
legitimacy of the Chinese government of the People's Republic of China."[156]
Their China policy was based on the assumption that Beijing must change first,
and then Washington could initiate fundamental changes. Washington still
maintained full diplomatic relations with the ROC government in Taiwan, and
was backing its membership in the United Nations. Nevertheless, with China's
growing strength and influence in the region and around the world, and given
the domestic and allies' pressure for change in its China's policy, the two Democratic administrations were compelled to take reconsideration of the China policy more seriously, and thus started to initiate "the concrete, practical level of
exchanges."[157]

One dramatic change in the 1960s was America's view of China's foreign policy. U.S. statements at the talks from 1962 to 1965 dwelt at length on Beijing's
aggressive expansionist designs in Vietnam and the rest of Asia. The theme
tended to fade away and was not mentioned after September 1966. By the end
of the Johnson administration, Washington was sending more positive signals
to Beijing for improving relations. Beijing's position, though, changed little if

at all, especially during the second part of the 1960s as China was caught in domestic chaos as a result of the Cultural Revolution. Annoyed at Washington's
interest only in "minor" issues, not the "major issue," and concerned about U.S.
escalation of war in Vietnam, Beijing was indignant and firm in its negotiating
posture. The asymmetric expectations, though, did not cause the breakdown or
suspension of the talks during the period of 1966–68, even when both were
faced with crises.

Both Washington and Beijing saw interest in and valued the importance of
maintaining this communication channel, as it helped to "clarify numerous
points of differences" between the two nations. For Washington, continuing
talks with Beijing would pacify its European allies and Japan and arouse suspicion in Moscow so as to deepen Sino-Soviet split. Thus, it would strengthen the
U.S. position in overall Cold War confrontation. It was also a useful mechanism
for crisis management and for dissemination of views to wide audience. The
talks, as Dean Rusk put it before the House Subcommittee on Foreign Affairs
in April 1966, "provide an opening through which, hopefully, light might one
day penetrate."[158] For Beijing, negotiation was an important venue of the united
front strategy. Although not expecting major changes in U.S. policy, Beijing
could use the Warsaw channel as a useful propaganda forum to voice its opinion on bilateral and international issues and to pour out its grievances against
U.S. imperialism. It served as a useful bargaining chip in managing relations
with its Communist allies, North Vietnam and North Korea. The Beijing-
Washington contacts may have served as a useful deterrence to GMD's attempt
to return to the mainland.

The Warsaw channel was an important facilitator for managing Sino-American
relations in the turbulent 1960s, since it offered a ready avenue for information
exchange and communication. In his assessment of the Johnson administration's China policy in late 1968, Alfred Jenkins argued that U.S. China policy
in those years "has accomplished" what could realistically be expected and had
laid the ground for improvement "when China is ready."[159] Reviewing the ambassadorial talks, Ambassador Wang Bingnan suggested in 1980s, "In a sense,
the ambassadorial talks constituted [a form of] mutual relations between the
United States and China under special historical circumstances. It provided a
useful channel for the two countries to air their views, propose solutions and
understand other's position and action during crises."[160]

As Steven Goldstein has suggested, the most important "unintended" outcome of the talks was "their role in stimulating American officials to rethink,
and in some cases to test, its policies regarding negotiations" with Beijing. To
provide information and instructions to U.S. negotiators in Warsaw, officials at
the State Department were compelled to devote considerable time to research
and intelligence estimates, trying to understand any subtle change of the PRC's
foreign policy. As the American record from 1961 to 1968 shows, preparations for

the talks were occasions for "fresh thinking" about policies toward Beijing.[161] It thus was an important part of the mutual learning process, which may have shortened the learning curve for policymakers in the immediate future. There is reason to assert that the thinking of these years left a rich set of policy options that could be drawn upon by future leaders, in both China and the United States.[162] The Warsaw talks seemed to have laid the foundation for Nixon's China policy.[163]

CHAPTER SIX

Entering a New Era
Toward Higher-level Talks,
January 1969–June 1971

T HE ELECTION OF Richard Nixon as president in 1968 marked a new era in U.S. Cold War strategy—the coming of "détente." Departing from the old bipolar system, the Nixon administration expected to reconfigure the great power structure by pushing for a five-part global order involving the United States, the Soviet Union, Europe, China, and Japan. Proclaiming the arrival of an "era of negotiation" upon entering office,[1] Nixon was able to achieve a "rapprochement" with the People's Republic of China in his first term. This was a great breakthrough to the twenty-odd years of the "mutual containment" between "Free World" and "Communist bloc."

The road to higher-level direct talks, however, was tortuous. It took almost two and half years in office before the Nixon White House was able to receive a secret message via the Pakistani channel in late May 1971 that the Chinese Premier Zhou Enlai invited Henry Kissinger, Nixon's national security adviser, to visit Beijing for high-level talks. What had Washington done that led to such an invitation from Beijing? What persuaded Beijing, still in the midst of the Cultural Revolution, to take a leap toward opening up with the United States, still cursed as the number-one imperialist in Chinese propaganda? More specifically, it is essential to examine how the two antagonists had communicated with each other since 1969, what moved the PRC and the U.S. to engage in secret diplomacy, and how and why Richard Nixon, a cold warrior, and Mao

Zedong, a staunch revolutionary, would decide to undertake such a historically significant course of action.

I

The Nixon administration's new China policy originated from its reconsideration of overall Cold War strategy. Recognizing the existence of a multi-polar world order, the Nixon administration "set out quite deliberately to eliminate ideology as the chief criterion by which to identify threats." As the Soviet Union "was approaching parity with the United States in long-range missile capability," the Nixon administration identified Moscow as more threatening.[2] With the deepening of the Sino-Soviet split in the 1960s, the Sino-Soviet alliance was no longer a threat to U.S. interests in Asia. As China was becoming a nuclear power in the 1960s and gained influence among the Third World countries, China's strategic asset increased. The Nixon administration came to appreciate China's importance in overall U.S. global strategy. As the United States was trapped in the Vietnam quagmire, with the federal budget in huge deficit, the Nixon administration was forced to make a strategic adjustment in its China policy.

The Nixon administration's China policy was an outgrowth of the efforts of the Johnson years. Nelson Rockefeller, Nixon's rival for the Republican nomination in the 1968 campaign, called for more "contact and communication" with China. Hubert Humphrey, the Democratic nominee, also proposed "the building of bridges to the people of Mainland China" and advocated a partial lifting of the American trade embargo against China.[3] A change in American policy toward China was clearly felt throughout the academic community. The day after Nixon's election on 6 November 1968, eight prominent China scholars, including law professor Jerome A. Cohen from Harvard University, political scientist A. Doak Barnett from Columbia University, and political scientist Lucian W. Pye from the Massachusetts Institute of Technology drafted a memorandum for the president-elect. The memorandum urged the Nixon administration to "move more positively toward the relaxation of tensions" between China and the United States and toward "the eventual achievement of reconciliation." The group, chaired by Professor Cohen, suggested, among other initiatives, sending an emissary to meet in secret with the Chinese to discuss prospects for a normal relationship between the two countries.[4]

While public opinion in the U.S. favored a fundamental change in China policy, by early 1969, China seemed to have a more urgent need to improve its relationship with Washington. The tension over Vietnam between China and the United States in 1968–69 seemed more intense than ever before. Beijing, in response to the escalation of the Vietnam War, dispatched large numbers of engineering and anti-aircraft artillery forces to North Vietnam while providing the Vietnamese Communists with other substantial military and economic support. Beijing and Washington thus were on the verge of fighting a direct war. Such security threats from China's southern borders were made worse with the sustained military standoff between the CCP and the GMD across the Taiwan Strait, as well as the hostile attitudes of Japan and South Korea toward the PRC. Consequently, Beijing perceived that, from Bohai Bay to the Gulf of Tonkin, all of China's coastal borders were under siege.[5] Since the Chinese-India border war of 1962, Beijing and New Delhi had viewed each other as a dangerous enemy; thus, the security situation along China's long western border with India was equally tense.

No less serious threat to China's security existed along the northern border, from the Soviet Union. Since 1965, both countries had continuously increased their military deployments along their shared borders. The situation along the border deteriorated further during the course of the Cultural Revolution as Beijing and Moscow now regarded the other "as 'traitor' to true communism." Each side had amassed several hundred thousand troops along the border areas by 1968–69. In early 1968, the Sino-Soviet conflict developed in the area of Qilixin Island, on the Chinese side of the main channel of the Ussuri River. This encounter was the prelude to large-scale armed conflict along the Sino-Soviet border.[6] Soviet invasion of Czechoslovakia in August 1968 heightened the Chinese leadership's apprehension.

When two bloody conflicts between Chinese and Soviet border garrison forces burst out on Zhenbao Island (called Damansky Island in Russian), located near the bank of the Ussuri River, in March 1969, China's security situation dramatically worsened. Soon border conflicts spread to other areas as tension increased along the entire length of the border. These incidents immediately brought China and the Soviet Union to the brink of a major military confrontation. According to Kissinger, the Soviet leaders even considered conducting a preemptive nuclear strike against their former Communist ally.[7] It is not surprising that Beijing leaders felt compelled to improve their nation's security by making major changes in China's foreign and security strategy.

After the CCP's Ninth National Congress in April 1969, the radical phase of the Cultural Revolution was over. Mao and Zhou were again in effective control of Chinese foreign policymaking. Chinese ambassadors, who had been recalled at the beginning of the Cultural Revolution, gradually returned to their posts.[8] Chinese diplomacy was returning to normalcy. The stabilization of Chinese politics was favorable to the improvement of Sino-American relations. Even before the Ninth Party Congress, Zhou Enlai had consciously selected articles regarding noticeable developments in international affairs, important commentaries, and possible policy alternatives from a large quantity of information for Mao's reference. This was a technique Zhou often employed when participating in important policymaking processes, so that he could, without much notice, influence Mao's decision-making.[9]

In mid-May, Zhou Enlai, following Mao's instruction, asked four marshals, Chen Yi, Ye Jianying, Xu Xiangqian, and Nie Rongzhen—to "pay attention to" international affairs. He urged them to meet "two to three times each month" to discuss "important issues" of international security and to provide the party Central Committee with their suggestions.[10] Zhou told the marshals not to be "restricted by any established frame of reference." They should try to help Mao "gain command of the new strategic developments" in the world. Zhou stressed that Mao had decided to assign them the task because they were marshals with much military experience and clear strategic vision. Hopefully, they would have a much better understanding of China's position in the changing world situation.[11]

Another major border clash, much larger than the two at Zhenbao Island in March, broke out between Chinese and Soviet garrisons in Xinjiang on 13 August.[12] Beijing immediately reacted to this incident, warning that Moscow probably was preparing for a major war against China. The situation deteriorated rapidly during the summer of 1969. On 27 August, the CCP Central Committee and Central Military Commission jointly issued an urgent order for establishing a new "National Leading Group for the People's Air Defense," with Zhou Enlai as the head, assigning to it the task of immediately organizing a large-scale evacuation of the population and main industries from the big cities.[13] On 28 August, the CCP Central Committee ordered the mobilization in the provinces and regions bordering the Soviet Union and the People's Republic of Mongolia.[14]

The marshal study group believed it unlikely that the Soviet Union would wage a large-scale war against China. They emphasized, however, the need for Beijing to be prepared for a worst-case scenario. Within this context, Chen Yi and Ye Jianying contended that in order for China to be ready for a major confrontation with the Soviet Union, "the card of the United States" should be played. In a written report, "Our Views about the Current Situation," completed on 17 September, they pointed out that although Moscow was intending to "wage war against China" and had actually deployed forces, the Soviet leadership was unable "to reach a final decision" because of political considerations. The marshals proposed that, in addition to waging "a tit-for-tat struggle against both the United States and the Soviet Union," China should use "negotiation as a means to struggle against them." Perhaps the Sino-American ambassadorial talks should be resumed "when the timing is proper."[15]

After submitting the report, Chen Yi proposed to Zhou Enlai that, while trying to resume the ambassadorial talks in Warsaw, China should "take the initiative in proposing to hold Sino-American talks at the ministerial level or even higher levels, so that basic and related problems in Sino-American relations can be solved." China should not set preconditions or demand that the United States accept Chinese positions. Merely holding a Sino-American summit would be a strategic move. American imperialism could benefit, but China would gain an even greater benefit. Chen Yi observed that this would be an "unconventional" initiative, but to the United States, it might be a welcome one.[16]

There has yet to be any evidence showing exactly how Mao responded to these reports, but he was concerned about the Soviet threat, and seemed to be interested in these "unconventional thoughts" on relations with the United States. The reports by the marshal study group thus helped reach consensus at the highest level within the Party. During the heyday of the Cultural Revolution, Mao himself had to take into consideration the possible opposition from the "ultra-leftists."[17] The study by the marshals' group provided the strategic analyses of the international situation for the Chinese leadership and gave concrete suggestions on improving Sino-American relations. As subsequent developments revealed, the marshals' reports to Mao and Zhou served as a basis for important decisions on opening up Sino-American relations. It was the prelude to Sino-American rapprochement.

It was the war scare, both strategically and psychologically, that created the necessary conditions for the CCP leadership to reconsider the PRC's long-standing policy of confrontation with the United States. The perception of an extremely grave threat from the Soviet Union pushed Mao Zedong to decide to break up existing conceptual restrictions in order to improve relations with the United States.[18] The key, then, was how to establish a communication channel.

At the outset of the new administration, it was by all accounts Nixon, not Kissinger, who seized the initiative on China.[19] In direct contrast to his reputation as a bitter anticommunist cold warrior, Nixon made reconciliation with China an early and high priority.[20] It was one of the subjects on his mind even during the transition period before he moved into the White House. Vernon Walters, who was then serving as the army attaché at the American embassy in Paris, called on Nixon at the Pierre Hotel in New York City. According to Walters's memoirs, Nixon told him that "among the various things he hoped to do in office was to open the door to the Chinese Communists. . . . He felt it was not good for the world to have the most populous nation on earth completely without contact with the most powerful nation on earth."[21] In his own memoirs, Nixon said that at the time he interviewed Kissinger for the job of national security adviser, he asked Kissinger to read his *Foreign Affairs* article and spoke to him of the need to reevaluate America's China policy.[22] At this time, Kissinger did not see any short-term possibility of a move toward China. According to Harry R. Haldeman, Nixon's chief of staff, when he told Kissinger on one early trip that Nixon "seriously intends to visit China before the end of the second term," Kissinger responded sardonically, "Fat chance."[23]

Nixon was fortunate as the American public was gradually becoming interested in "Red China" and the influence of the old China Lobby was declining.[24] Nixon hoped to use the opening to China to achieve several strategic interests.

As H. R. Haldeman observed, "He saw this as one of his contributions to his over-all objective of building a structure for peace—not just building peace, but building a structure that would maintain peace."[25] U.S. rapprochement with China would put the Soviets on the defensive, escalate the Soviet Union's military cost, and force it to be more cooperative with Washington. As Nixon had pledged that he would wind down the war in Vietnam, he saw the possibility of getting the Chinese to pressure the Vietnamese to accept some kind of a reasonable peace and thus to end the war if the opening to China could be achieved. As a foreign policy president, Nixon also anticipated that his China opening would "bring significant domestic political benefits" and thus contribute to his reelection campaign in 1972. He would be seen positively as a great "peacemaker and celebrated statesman." Also, access to the China market might help the American economy and strengthen the business community's support of the administration.[26]

With China's growing nuclear power, Washington and its Europeans allies felt a more urgent need to bring China back to international society and to engage China in disarmament talks. During his visit to Europe in February 1969, Nixon expressed to French president Charles de Gaulle his concern about growing Chinese nuclear power and the necessity to dealing with the Chinese. He stated, "In ten years, when China has made significant nuclear progress, we will have no choice. It is vital that we have more communications with them than we have today."[27] The French leader advised Nixon, "it would be better for the U.S. to recognize China before they were obliged to do it by the growth of China."[28]

Nixon, however, was uncertain how far he could go with his China policy. There existed no formal channel of communication between the two governments. The last meeting of the ambassadorial talks, which since had been indefinitely suspended, had been held in January 1968.[29] Beijing seemed to regard Nixon as no better than his predecessors. The Chinese government greeted Nixon's election with nothing but scorn. *Renmin Ribao* and *Hongqi* [Red Flag], the Chinese Communist Party mouthpieces, jointly published an editorial essay characterizing Nixon's inaugural address as nothing but "a confession in an impasse," which demonstrated that "the U.S. imperialists . . . are beset with profound crisis both at home and abroad."[30] Beijing Radio went so far as to report that during Nixon's swing through Europe, he was treated "like a rat running across the street."[31] The Chinese state-run radio also broadcast that Nixon was preparing to make a deal with the Soviet Union to divide the world into two spheres of influence. Even after the Zhenbao Incident, during the Ninth Party Congress, the CCP leadership, while emphasizing the danger of a major war with "social-imperialists" and "imperialists," was not yet moving to accommodate the United States. The harsh attacks on the United States continued. The main political report, delivered by Lin Biao, then Mao's second in command and designated successor, gave no indication that Beijing had changed its attitude toward the United States.[32]

Facing a hostile China, Nixon thought of collaborating with the Soviet Union in a Sino-Soviet war in the immediate aftermath of the Zhenbao Incident. In his April news conference, Nixon portrayed China as a global nuclear menace of equal concern to both the United States and the Soviet Union.[33] In a June memo to Nixon, Kissinger still advocated American neutrality, even cooperation, in the event of a Soviet attack on China. Thus, they hoped to get Soviet assistance in "winning a dignified exit from Vietnam and obtaining greater cooperation on the entire East-West agenda—arms control, Berlin, and the Middle East."[34] Moscow was not ready to strike a deal with the U.S. on China and unwilling to offer any concrete help on Vietnam.[35] As ending the war in Vietnam was his priority, Nixon was forced to drop the Soviet option and to probe the Chinese.

Several signs indicated that subtle changes were taking place in Washington's attitude toward China. On 26 June 1969, Nixon decided to relax economic controls and asked his Undersecretaries Committee to develop detailed plans for implementation.[36] The State Department announced on 21 July that it was relaxing restrictions on American citizens traveling to China. Tourists were permitted to bring back one hundred dollars worth of Chinese goods.[37] Five days later, Prince Norodom Sihanouk, Cambodia's chief of state, conveyed a letter to Zhou Enlai from U.S. Senate majority leader Mike Mansfield (Democrat-Montana). Mansfield was a former history professor and the Democrats' leading expert on Asia. In the letter, the veteran American politician expressed the desire to visit China to seek solutions to the "twenty-year confrontation" between the two countries.[38]

The worsening of the Sino-Soviet relationship alerted the Nixon administration. It would not be in U.S. interests if the Russians were to invade China and trigger a major regional war. During the first days of the administration, Kissinger, following the instruction of the president, had ordered the preparation of NSSM-14 (National Security Study Memoranda), an interagency study of the policy of the United States toward China and potential alternative policy direction.[39] Prepared primarily by the Department of State, the written response to NSSM-14 discussed three options—"Present Strategy, Intensified Deterrence and Isolation, or Reduction of PRC's Isolation and Points of US-CPR Conflict." The primary concern "tended to focus on how the United States could reduce tensions, and whether the PRC could be receptive to any initiative."[40] Newly declassified National Security Council institutional files reveal that at the meeting of NSC's Senior Review Group on 15 May 1969, Kissinger dissented from the view held by some Soviet experts that better relations with China would "ruin" ties with Moscow. From a balance-of-power perspective, he argued that "[h]istory suggested to him that it is better to align yourself with the weaker, not the stronger of the two antagonistic" powers.[41] He was taking a balance-of-power approach in forming U.S. policy. Thus, a better relationship with Beijing was necessary to strengthen the U.S. position with Moscow.

In the summer of 1969, Allen Whiting, former director of the State Department's Office of Research and Analysis for the Far East, and then a professor at the University of Michigan, counseled Nixon and Kissinger to assure the Chinese that the U.S. would not side with the Soviet Union in its attack against China's nuclear facilities. This would enable the United States to improve chances for Chinese concessions on the major issues blocking American-Chinese rapprochement. He argued that "the threat to China from the Soviet Union was so great that Taiwan—although China would never say as much—would be less important. Thus there would be some room for bargaining."[42] For Whiting, the new geopolitical situation gave the United States a singular opportunity to approach China.

On a round-the-world tour on July 1969, Nixon enunciated what was first called the Guam Doctrine and later the Nixon Doctrine, declaring that the United States should not be more concerned with the threat of internal subversion in a friendly country than was the country itself and that while the United States would supply military equipment to allies (especially in Asia) to deal with an internal threat, it would not contribute manpower. Although Nixon and Kissinger meant the doctrine as an assurance of continued American involvement in Asia, it was interpreted by many governments as a warning that the United States would be pulling out.[43] The adoption of this new policy by the Nixon administration must have been watched with interest by the PRC, possibly as another indication of U.S. intent to reduce hostility toward China.

Nixon wanted to use his Asian trip to send a signal to Beijing favoring improving relations. Recognizing Beijing's concerns about the Soviet threat, Nixon and Kissinger commented to Asian leaders that Washington would not take sides in the Sino-Soviet conflict and rejected any notion of a U.S.-Soviet "condominium" against the PRC.[44] Moreover, Nixon made his now famous initiatives to activate secret channels of communication with Beijing through Pakistan and Romania. Most significantly, in view of Pakistan's central role in facilitating early U.S.-PRC secret contacts, on 1 August Nixon asked Pakistani President Agha Muhammad Yahya Khan to inform Zhou Enlai of American interest in an accommodation with China.[45]

Other high-level officials were sending encouraging signals as well. In August, Secretary of State William Rogers made a public statement of American interest in a dialogue with China.[46] While traveling in Australia, Rogers said that the United States realized that "Mainland China will eventually play an important role" in Asia and that "Communist China obviously has long been too isolated from world affairs. This is one reason why we have been seeking to open up channels of communication." He then pointed to the recent American liberalization of trade and travel restrictions. Finally, he said that the United

States "look[s] forward to a time when we can enter into a useful dialogue and to a reduction of tensions. We would welcome a renewal of the talks with Communist China."[47]

By mid-August, Nixon was favoring Kissinger's balance-of-power approach in U.S. policies toward China and the Soviet Union. At the NSC meeting on 14 August, Nixon startled his Cabinet colleagues by announcing that the Soviet Union was more aggressive than China and that it was against U.S. interests to let China be "smashed" in a Sino-Soviet war. "It was a major event in American foreign policy when a President declared that we had a strategic interest in the survival of a major Communist country, long an enemy, and with which we had had no contact, " Kissinger recalls in his memoir.[48] This was the first NSC meeting of the Nixon administration to address China policy.[49]

The Nixon administration began now to send out messages publicly that it would not join the Soviets in threatening China's security and would not tolerate the defeat of China in a Sino-Soviet war. As Undersecretary of State Elliot Richardson, appearing before the American Political Science Association in New York on 5 September, pointed out:

> In the case of Communist China, long-run improvement in our relations is in our own national interest. . . . We could not fail to be deeply concerned with an escalation of this quarrel into a massive breach of international peace and security.[50]

In other words, the United States would not take sides in Sino-Soviet confrontation as the Soviets had hoped and the Chinese definitely feared. This was the most important public signal on U.S. China policy since Nixon took office.

II

The Soviet Union was unsatisfied with the U.S. stand in Sino-Soviet confrontation. In September 1969, the Soviet leaders attempted to hold a summit talk with their Chinese counterparts in order to relax tension, which had developed since March. After some complications,[51] the Soviet premier, Alexei Kosygin, was able to hold talk with his Chinese counterpart, Premier Zhou Enlai, at Beijing airport on 11 September. Beijing had several purposes in holding talks with Moscow. The Chinese leaders were interested in mitigating the tension with the Soviets after a number of bloody border clashes. They were looking to avoid a two-front war and retain certain security in face of the aggressive Soviet threat. Obviously, they wanted also to reduce the danger of Soviet-American collusion. More importantly, Zhou intended to utilize the occasion to provoke U.S. interest in expediting the Sino-American rapprochement process. For this purpose, Zhou tried hard to avoid "closeness" and "friendliness" with the Soviets, as Beijing was afraid of sending wrong information to Washington. The subsequent Sino-Soviet border negotiation at the vice foreign ministers' level gave the Americans another impetus.[52]

The Chinese strategy seemed to work well. Nixon was eager to catch up on U.S. China policy. During the fall of 1969 and the early winter of 1970, the Nixon administration made several attempts to establish direct talks with China. The White House had been in secret contact with the Chinese through the Pakistanis and Romanians during the summer.[53] To supplement the nascent Pakistani and Romanian channels, Nixon and Kissinger decided to reopen the long-frozen U.S.-China ambassadorial talks in Warsaw. In September 1969, they ordered Walter Stoessel, the American ambassador to Poland, to contact his Chinese counterpart for a new meeting. To Kissinger's irritation, it took Stoessel almost three months to find a chance to approach Chinese diplomats in Warsaw. Kissinger was exploring possible paths for an earlier meeting when U.S. intelligence learned of a secret directive issued by Zhou Enlai to Chinese embassies in November. This directive called for more diplomatic suppleness to protect China from the Soviet Union. Zhou declared that Beijing would follow "flexible tactics" by resuming talks with Washington. This might keep the Soviets off balance and exacerbate U.S.-Soviet tensions. Meanwhile, for domestic political consumption, Zhou stated that Beijing would not abandon "revolutionary principles."[54] Beijing would consistently state that it would remain firm on certain principles while dealing with the United States.

Stoessel acted in an unusual fashion when, on 3 December, he saw Chinese diplomats at a Yugoslavian fashion show at Warsaw's Palace of Culture and followed them outside the building after the show. The Chinese diplomats, caught off guard, quickly fled from the exhibition site. Stoessel ran after and was able to catch the Chinese interpreter, telling him that he had an important message for the Chinese embassy.[55]

Before this "encounter," China regarded Nixon's probing as only exploratory. This time Beijing's response was swift. The Chinese leaders seemed convinced that the U.S. gesture was serious. After receiving the Chinese embassy's report on the American ambassador's "unusual behavior," Zhou Enlai immediately reported to Mao Zedong, commenting that "the opportunity is coming; we now have a brick in our hands to knock at the door [of the Americans]."[56] Zhou acted at once to let the Americans know of Beijing's interest in reopening communication with Washington. As a goodwill gesture, on 4 December, with Mao's approval, Zhou ordered the release of two Americans who had been held in China since mid-February 1969, when their yacht had strayed into China's territorial water off Guangdong.[57]

In the making of China's American policy, Mao was the key figure with the final word. Mao laid particular emphasis on strategy, while Zhou focused on special planning details and operations. Zhou needed Mao's support in order to improve relations with the United States. The improvement in the Sino-U.S.

relationship would also consolidate Zhou's influence and power in domestic politics of the People's Republic.[58]

Stoessel's "encounter" with Chinese diplomats at the Yugoslavian fashion show was a turning point in the evolution of a new relationship between the two countries. It had at least three implications. First, it showed to the Chinese leadership U.S. good faith in improving relations with the PRC. Second, it happened at a time when the Chinese leaders were overestimating the war threat from the Soviet Union. They were looking for opportunities to ameliorate relations with the United States in order to offset the Soviet Union. Third, as a revolutionary regime, the PRC leaders were determined to restore China's rightful place in world affairs and would never show any sign of weakness in dealing with the United States. This "encounter" served as the right set of circumstances for the Chinese leaders to tell the Chinese public that "it is the Americans who need something from us, not the other way around." They would retell the story and repeat the theme time and again.[59]

In fact, the Chinese leaders had been carefully seeking opportunities to resume the ambassadorial talks as well. When the first group of ambassadors returned to their posts after the Ninth Party Congress, Lei Yang was appointed China's chargé d'affaires to Poland in June 1969. Although not an ambassador in rank, Lei was an intellectual and senior diplomat, having served as director-general of the Education Department of the Foreign Ministry for many years. Before Lei left for Poland, Zhou Enlai urged him to take close look at the development of Sino-American relations, especially the signs of change in U.S. policy, and to report back on anything significant. Zhou emphasized the importance of ensuring that "the Warsaw channel" would not break down. Following the Foreign Ministry's instruction, Lei carefully went through the records of the Sino-American ambassadorial talks and other written materials on U.S.-China relations before departing for Warsaw.[60]

The two sides quickly agreed to resume the ambassadorial talks on 20 January 1970. These meetings were to alternate between the Chinese and American embassies.[61] Beijing and Washington announced the meeting simultaneously. The U.S. spokesman in Washington, in announcing the event, was careful to refer to China for the first time as the "People's Republic of China,"[62] not "Red China" or "Communist China."

To prepare for the talks, the PRC Foreign Ministry drew up draft instructions for Lei Yang, along with a draft of his statement and submitted these drafts to Zhou Enlai for amendment. Zhou added the following instructions: "After your speech, if the U.S. reiterates that the U.S. and Taiwan have a relationship based on a treaty, you should reply in such terms as 'The U.S.-ROC (the Republic of China) Treaty' is not recognized by the Chinese people; if the U.S. side inquires about what the higher-level talks or other channels refer to, you should respond by saying that if the U.S. government is interested, it can make a proposal or work out a solution upon mutual agreement at the ambassadorial-level talks."[63] The Chinese leaders believed that since "at present, Nixon appears to be a bit more sober-minded than Brezhnev . . . the policy of engagement is necessary."[64]

Stoessel opened the talks on 20 January by declaring, "It is my Government's hope that today will make a new beginning in our relationship." He assured the Chinese that the U.S. had no objection to Beijing's peaceful diplomacy in Asia, and pledged that the Nixon administration's goal was "a reduced American military presence in Southeast Asia, which we recognize is near the southern borders of China."[65]

The Nixon administration was aware of the importance of the Taiwan issue to the PRC. Stoessel explained three new U.S. formulations on Taiwan. First, while America would honor its commitments to defend Taiwan, "the United States position in this regard is without prejudice to any future peaceful settlement between your Government and the Government in Taipei." Second, the U. S. would not support and in fact would oppose any offensive military action from Taiwan against the mainland. Third, Stoessel stated, "it is our hope" to reduce U.S. military facilities on Taiwan "as peace and stability in Asia grow." These three formulations were designed as a signal to show to the PRC the real intention of the U.S. to improve relations.[66] However, two questions remained to be clarified. First, it was not clear when Washington would withdraw troops from Taiwan and how many troops. Second, U.S. withdrawal would depend on the end of war in Vietnam. A link was also being drawn between the American presence on Taiwan and the Vietnam War. It was impossible for Beijing to force Hanoi to end the war on U.S. terms. Beijing was suspicious of Washington's real intention.

Stoessel made another offer. The Nixon administration, he said, would consider sending an emissary to Beijing or receiving a Chinese representative in Washington for "more thorough" talks. This change of attitude from the U.S. side was viewed as favorable for the new relationship as the Chinese had been seeking higher-level talks since 1955.[67]

Lei Yang, having already received detailed instructions from Beijing, repeated his government's "principled position" that Taiwan was the crucial issue preventing an improvement in the U.S.-PRC relationship. He accused the U.S. of occupying Taiwan and stated that "[t]he Chinese people will assuredly liberate Taiwan; . . . [they] will not allow any country to occupy Chinese territory and to interfere in its internal affairs." He then replied:

> We are willing to consider and discuss whatever ideas and suggestions the U.S. Government might put forward in accordance with the five principles of peaceful coexistence, therefore really helping to reduce tensions between China and the U.S. and fundamentally improve relations between China

and the U.S. These talks may either continue to be conducted at the ambassadorial level or may be conducted at a higher level or through other channels acceptable to both sides.[68]

Obviously, Lei's presentation was in accordance with the two principles that
Beijing had been adhering to in its relations with the United States since 1960:
the resolution of the Taiwan issue (meaning immediate withdrawal of U.S.
troops) and the signing of an agreement on the five principles of peaceful coexistence between the two countries. Without fulfilling these two conditions,
Beijing would not move ahead in its relations with Washington. Lei's new presentation left out the past demand for "immediate U.S. withdrawal." Therefore,
there were signs of changes in China's policy. The Nixon administration
seemed partly accommodating to both.

In his 18 February 1970 report to Congress on U.S. foreign policy, Nixon reiterated his desire for "improved practical relations" with Beijing. He described
the actions his administration had taken over the previous year as "specific steps
that did not require Chinese agreement but which underlined our willingness
to have a more normal and constructive relationship." He noted that the United
States had "avoided dramatic gestures which might invite dramatic rebuffs."[69]

Domestic politics played into China's foreign policymaking, especially policy toward the United States. In order to promote Sino-American rapprochement, Zhou had to spend much time and energy to patiently persuade, and to
get over obstacles and obstructions from, the ultra-leftists. As China was still in
the midst of the Cultural Revolution, it was inconceivable to even talk about
improving relations with the United States—the number-one imperialist
country. Even the Foreign Ministry, which was under Zhou's direct supervision, was not immune from leftist influence. The rank and file at the Foreign Ministry were understandably slow in responding to any change. They
were afraid of dealing with any organization with official U.S. background,
and tried to keep it a thousand miles away. Zhou was very worried and had to
report to Mao. After getting Mao's favorable support, Zhou immediately communicated Mao's instruction to his subordinates, ensuring them it was all
right to improve relations with the United States.[70]

The second formal meeting between Lei and Stoessel was held at the American embassy in Warsaw on 20 February. Top leaders in Beijing took it seriously.
On 12 February, Zhou Enlai chaired a CCP Politburo meeting to draft instructions for Lei Yang. The Politburo decided that Lei should inform the American
side that "if the U.S. government is willing to dispatch a minister-level official or
a special envoy representing the president to visit Beijing to explore further solutions to the fundamental questions in Sino-American relations, the Chinese
government will receive him." Mao approved the instructions on the same day.[71]

When Lei met with Stoessel on 20 February, he again highlighted the Taiwan issue, emphasizing that the Taiwan question was the "fundamental principle" in Sino-U.S. relations, and only when the Taiwan issue was solved could fundamental improvement in Sino-U.S. relations be achieved. Lei also informed the American ambassador that the Chinese government "will be willing to receive" a high-ranking American representative in Beijing.[72]

In responding to Lei's presentation, Stoessel agreed that the Taiwan question was "a major obstacle to better relations" between the U.S. and China. He stressed, however, that the two sides should move forward, not only on the Taiwan issue, but also other bilateral issues. He declared that the military presence in Taiwan was not designed to influence the political settlement of the Taiwan issue and that it was the Nixon administration's *"intention to reduce those military facilities which we now have on Taiwan as tensions in the area diminish."*[73] This was the language that later appeared almost word-for-word in the Shanghai communiqué.[74]

Stoessel's statement on the reduction of U.S. military facilities aimed for three objectives. It was an early commitment to China's demand for U.S. troop withdrawal from Taiwan, thus showing Beijing a tangible benefit for improving relations. It would contribute to altering the PRC's perceptions of the United States. It also attempted to give China an incentive to bring the Vietnam War to an end, and thus create the "peace and stability in Asia" that would allow the withdrawal to occur.[75]

The State Department was more cautious than the White House in "opening" China. Soviet specialists in the department feared it might worsen relations with Moscow. The playing of the "China card" should be cautious because it is difficult to explain it to allies, neutrals, the Russians, and the media.[76] After the 20 February meeting in Warsaw, the assistant secretary of state for East Asia and Pacific affairs, Marshall Green, argued "that a trip to Beijing, without prior progress on bilateral issues[77] discussed for fifteen years, implied a concession to the Chinese and risked misunderstanding by allies, not to speak of hostilities in Moscow."[78] In a memo to the White House on 5 March, Green claimed,

> The likelihood of success in achieving a genuine improvement in Sino-U.S. relations is small; the probability that the Chinese are interested in talks primarily for their impact on the Soviets is great; and the unsettling and potentially damaging impact on some of our friends and allies and their assessment of our China policy is substantial.[79]

Green warned that such a course would "weaken our ability to press the Chinese now to commit themselves further on their own intentions and negotiation position at higher-level meetings."[80] Thus, Green suggested that both sides have "one more exchange of formal messages" in order "to forestall the chance of early failure and to devise ways to ease reactions in East Asia" if the high-level talks became public.[81]

Kissinger and Nixon disagreed and, apparently unable to get responses quickly enough via the back channel, pushed hard for an immediate third meeting in Warsaw to further explore a higher-level meeting. The third meeting, however, was twice postponed,[82] and eventually it was scheduled to be held on 20 May. Earlier in the month, when Nixon ordered American troops in South Vietnam to conduct a large-scale cross-border operation aimed at destroying Vietnamese Communist bases inside Cambodia, the Chinese refused to talk in Warsaw.[83] At a Politburo meeting chaired by Zhou Enlai on 16 June, Chinese leaders decided that "given the current international situation," the ambassadorial talks "will further be postponed" and that only the Chinese liaison personnel would continue to maintain contacts with the Americans.[84]

The collapse of the Warsaw talks moved the venue of communications with the Chinese to the White House, which had been in secret contact with the Chinese through the Pakistanis since the previous summer. By late May, Nixon and Kissinger decided to pursue China policy on their own—covertly. Sino-American secret communications were also pursued through other channels: the American consulate in Hong Kong, the Pakistani and Romanian ambassadors in Washington, and the Norwegian ambassador in China. After the invasion of Cambodia, Nixon and Kissinger sent a secret message to the Chinese in June, through Vernon Walters, who was helping Kissinger in his secret talks with the North Vietnamese. The message informed the Chinese that the United States had no aggressive intentions in Indochina despite the Cambodian invasions. If the Chinese still were interested, they could talk with Henry Kissinger directly.[85] From this point on, U.S. communication with the PRC was under the direct control of Kissinger and General Alexander Haig, Kissinger's deputy at the NSC. It was the beginning of "secret diplomacy."

Beijing did not want to allow the progress toward opening relations with Washington to lose momentum completely. On 10 July, Beijing released Bishop James Walsh, an American citizen who had been imprisoned in China since 1958 on espionage charges.[86] This was Beijing's way of showing the U.S. that the PRC was still interested in improving relations. Nixon and Kissinger were satisfied with Beijing's gesture.

III

Beijing seemed ready to move ahead to higher-level talks with Washington as the United States withdrew from Cambodia and the weather cooled down in the fall of 1970.[87] This time, Mao and Nixon moved from behind the scenes to the front line, giving their personal pushes to Sino-American relations. On 1 October, leftist American journalist and writer Edgar Snow and his wife were invited to review the annual National Day celebration parade on the wall of the Forbidden City overlooking Tiananmen Square. They were escorted by Zhou

Enlai to meet Mao and stood by the chairman's side throughout the parade. Snow was the first American to be given such an honor. A picture of Snow and Mao together was printed on the front page of major Chinese newspapers on 25 December.[88] As a Chinese historian observes, "Mao was sending a message, which he intended not only for the Americans but also for people all over China." Mao was trying to use this public show as a first step to prepare the Chinese people psychologically for major changes in Sino-American relations.[89] The White House, however, failed to understand "the significance of this unprecedented gesture." It also turned down Allen Whiting's offer "to go to Switzerland" to debrief Snow.[90]

During a lengthy interview with Snow on 18 December,[91] Mao told Snow that Beijing was considering allowing Americans of all political persuasions—left, right, and center—to come to China. He particularly emphasized that he would like to welcome Nixon to Beijing because the U.S. president was the person with whom he could "discuss and solve the problems between China and the United States." Mao made it clear that he "would be happy to meet Nixon, either as president or as a tourist."[92] According to Nixon, Washington "learned of Mao's statement (on welcoming Nixon to Beijing) within days after he made it."[93] In actuality, the Nixon White House found out about the details of the Mao-Snow interview much later, possibly not until Snow's interview of Mao was published in *Life* magazine on 30 April 1971.[94] John H. Holdridge, a senior NSC staff member handling East Asia and Pacific Affairs, recalled, "Snow's article gave us great encouragement by suggesting that we were on the right track and that an improvement in U.S.-China relations was possible."[95]

The Nixon administration was also signaling, but not as subtly. In an October 1970 issue of *Time* magazine, Nixon declared that he viewed China as a world power. He observed, "Maybe that role won't be possible for five years, maybe not even ten years. But in 20 years it had better be, or the world is in mortal danger. If there is anything I want to do before I die, it is to go to China. If I don't, I want my children to."[96] This was a direct and very important statement. Zhou Enlai later recalled with emphasis how important it had been to the PRC leaders involved in initiating the normalization dialogue that Nixon was willing to deal with them on a personal level and treat China as an equal: "From the beginning he (Nixon) took the attitude that he was willing to come to Beijing to meet us."[97]

Late in October, Nixon gave another personal push. When a large number of chiefs of state and heads of government came to the U.S. to participate in the celebrations of the twenty-fifth anniversary of the founding of the United Nations, Nixon invited them to a state dinner at the White House in honor of the event. During the dinner, Nixon used Romanian president Nicolae Ceauşescu's presence to offer a toast, by praising the many common interests held by the people of the U.S. and Romania and the good relations that Romania had with the United States, the USSR, and China. He referred to "China" as the "People's Republic of China." This was the first time an American president had used China's official name.[98] Nixon considered it "a significant diplomatic signal."[99] In his private talk with Ceauşescu, Nixon was reported to have said "so far as he was concerned, Taiwan was not an international but an internal problem, to be resolved by the Chinese themselves in a peaceful way."[100] Nixon, meanwhile, had a private talk with the Pakistani president, Yahya Khan, during which he asked Yahya to pass a message to the Chinese leaders that his administration would like to send a high-level emissary to Beijing. He also promised that the United States would not enter into a "condominium" with the Soviet Union against China.[101] Nixon might have believed that he had adequately addressed China's deepest fears.

Shortly after, Yahya and his foreign secretary, Sultan Muhammad Khan, visited Beijing. During a private meeting with Zhou Enlai, Yahya passed on Nixon's message to Zhou, and brought a message back from Zhou to Washington. On 9 December, the Pakistani ambassador, Agha Hilaly, hand-carried to the White House the reply from the Chinese. In the letter Zhou declared that China "has always been willing and has always tried to negotiate by peaceful means. . . . In order to discuss the subject of the evacuation of Chinese territories called Taiwan, a special envoy of President Nixon will be most welcome in Peking." Zhou Enlai observed that many other messages had been received from the United States through various sources, "but this is the first time that the proposal has come from a Head [Nixon], through a Head [Yahya], to a Head [Mao]. The United States knows that Pakistan is a great friend of China and therefore we attach importance to the message."[102] Kissinger was excited. He claimed, "This was not an indirect subtle signal to be disavowed at the first tremors of difficulty. It was an authoritative personal message to Richard Nixon from Chou [Zhou] Enlai, who emphasized that he spoke not only for himself but also for Chairman Mao and Vice Chairman Lin Piao [Biao]."[103] A month later, the Romanian ambassador Bogdan passed to Kissinger another message from Beijing, saying Nixon himself would be welcome in China.[104]

While the communication from China seemed encouraging, it was only the beginning of making arrangements for high-level meetings. The Chinese paid much attention to agenda setting. These early and indirect contacts between the Nixon White House and Beijing involved delicate exchanges on setting up an agenda for direct talks between top leaders of the two sides. In these exploratory communications, the Chinese tried to focus the anticipated talks on the withdrawal of U.S. forces from Taiwan and establishment of U.S.-PRC diplomatic relations. The United States attempted to define a much broader, open-ended agenda that would include discussion of global and regional security issues. Employing the Pakistani channel, the Americans and Chinese haggled over the terms for high-level meetings. Zhou Enlai had stated that the sole purpose of the talks would be to discuss Taiwan, a limitation the Nixon administration could not accept. On Kissinger's memorandum of his conversation with Romanian ambassador Bogdan, Nixon added his instruction: "I believe we may appear too eager. Let's cool it. Wait for them to respond to our initiative."[105]

The Taiwan issue had been figuring prominently in U.S.-PRC relations since the outbreak of the Korean War. Edgar Snow reported that in his interview with Zhou Enlai on 13 December 1970, Zhou stated China's policy on Taiwan. He expounded to Snow China's two conditions for solving the Taiwan problem and establishing relations between China and the United States. First, the U.S. should recognize Taiwan as an inalienable part of the PRC and withdraw its own forces from the island and from the Taiwan Straits; second, despite their different political systems, China and the U.S. should establish relations on the basis of the five principles of peaceful coexistence. Zhou stated, "Formosa (Taiwan) is a domestic question concerning China, and only the Chinese people have the right to liberate the island. The armed aggression of the U.S. in that area is another question, an international one, and we are prepared to turn it into a topic of negotiation."[106]

The Nixon administration maintained that U.S. ties with Taiwan had been established over a long period of time, involving deep emotion as well as political considerations. Therefore, it could not be set aside easily. On the other hand, apart from Taiwan, there was no great conflict of national interests between the PRC and the United States.[107] Instructed by Nixon, Kissinger drafted a reply to Beijing that was handed to Hilaly on 16 December. The reply made it clear that the United States would be prepared for high-level talks in Beijing to discuss a broad range of issues concerning the two countries, including the issue of Taiwan. "The meeting in Peking would not be limited only to the Taiwan question," the note stressed, "but would encompass other steps designed to improve relations and reduce tensions." It went on to say, "With respect to the U.S. military presence on Taiwan, however, the policy of the United States Government is to reduce its military presence in the region of East Asia and the Pacific as tensions in the region diminish."[108] It was apparent that ending the war in Indochina and reducing "common hostility" in East Asia were conditions for U.S. withdrawal of forces from Taiwan.

Although bargaining hard, Washington did not hesitate to make further goodwill offers. On 25 February 1971, the Nixon administration issued its second Foreign Policy Report, which reiterated its desire to improve relations with China, and for the first time a written American official document referred to the People's Republic of China by its official name.[109] The administration further eased its restrictions on trade with China. On 15 March, the State Department revealed the president's decision to terminate all restrictions on the use of U.S. passports for travel to the People's Republic of China.[110]

To further prepare the Chinese people politically and psychologically for the forthcoming transformation of Sino-American relations, Mao Zedong decided to invite the American table tennis (Ping-Pong) team to visit China. China sent its Ping-Pong team to Japan in April 1971 to take part in an international tournament in Nagoya in which an American team also participated. Evidently with Zhou's encouragement, the members of the two teams encountered each other in a friendly fashion, and out of these meetings came out an "official" invitation for the U.S. team to visit China.[111]

In sending the Chinese team to Japan and inviting the U.S. team to visit China, Mao and Zhou came up against the dissenting views from the Foreign Ministry and the State Physical Culture and Sports Commission. When officials from the Foreign Ministry and State Physical Culture and Sports Commission recommended not sending the Chinese team to Japan, Zhou wrote to Mao on 13 March to solicit his support for sending the team. Mao concurred and instructed, "Act accordingly. Our team should go, and be prepared to be assassinated. Of course, it is better not to be killed. Not to be afraid of both hardships and death."[112] After receiving the request from U.S. Ping-Pong team to visit China, on 3 April, the Foreign Ministry suggested that it might not be advantageous for the Chinese side to invite the U.S. team. Zhou was unhappy with this recommendation, and again sent for Mao's decision. Mao overruled the Foreign Ministry and decided to invite the U.S. team.[113] It seemed that Mao took domestic politics into his policymaking calculations. Mao's decision to invite U.S. team was in the hope of improving relations with the United States. In his upcoming showdown with Lin Biao, Mao was afraid that Lin might turn to the Soviets for assistance.[114]

The Chinese leaders had ambivalent feelings toward dealing with the Westerners. On the one hand, they treasured Western science and technology. On the other hand, they sustained a remarkable degree of self-confidence that they could modernize their country while maintaining China's own cultural and historical traditions. It was no accident that when China sought to reengage the rest of the world during the Cultural Revolution, it did so by way of "Ping-Pong Diplomacy," a very symbolic gesture. It demonstrated a sport in which the Chinese had superior skills and would be seen in a positive light. Zhou Enlai artfully instructed the much better Chinese players to stress "friendship first, competition second."[115] Zhou confided to his top aides Huang Hua and Zhang Wenjin[116] after learning of Mao's approval of Beijing's invitation to the U.S. team on 7 April, "This [visit] has offered a very good opportunity to open the relations between China and the United States. In our handling of this matter, we must treat it as an important event, and understand that its significance is much larger in politics than in sports."[117] As Richard Solomon has noted, the Chinese leaders made "political use of a sport in which the Chinese were world champions—and thus were 'number one.'"[118]

The visit of the American Ping-Pong team to China was widely covered by

the Chinese media. Indeed, the matches between Chinese and American players received live television and radio coverage.[119] The highlight of the visit was
Zhou Enlai's meeting with the American and Chinese teams, together with
teams from four other countries at the Great Hall of the People on 14 April. The
Chinese premier announced, "Your visit has opened a new chapter in the history of the relations between Chinese and American peoples."[120] A few hours
after the meeting, Washington announced five new measures concerning China,
including the termination of the twenty-two-year-old trade embargo, permitting trade in commodities nearly equivalent to those traded with the Soviet
Union, ending U.S. currency controls relating to China, and expediting American visas for any Chinese seeking to visit the United States.[121] In a few short days,
Ping-Pong diplomacy had changed the political atmosphere between China and
the United States, making the improving relations between the two countries —
as Kissinger put it — "an international sensation" that "captured the world's
imagination."[122]

In the wake of the Ping-Pong diplomacy, Beijing and Washington moved to
make concrete plans for the high-level meetings that had been discussed since
early 1970. The Pakistani channel continued to play a crucial role in facilitating
communications between the two sides. On 27 April 1971, Washington received
a message through it. It was a hand-written two-page letter (as opposed to oral
or indirect statements) from Zhou Enlai in response to Nixon's message of 16
December. The message reads as follows:

> However, if the relations between China and the U.S.A. are to be restored
> fundamentally, the U.S. must withdraw all its Armed Forces from China's
> Taiwan and Taiwan Strait area. A solution to this crucial question can be
> found only through direct discussions between high-level responsible per-
> sons of the two countries. Therefore, the Chinese Government reaffirms its
> willingness to receive publicly in Peking a special envoy of the President of
> the U.S. (for instance, Mr. Kissinger) or the U.S. Secretary of State or even
> the President of the U.S. himself for direct meeting and discussions.[123]

Kissinger was excited when he read the message. Although the subject of the
proposed meeting was still Taiwan, the emphasis was on withdrawing U.S.
forces rather than abandoning its relationship with Taiwan altogether. The Chinese sought a high-level meeting to restore fundamentally the relations with the
United States. To that end, Beijing formally invited Nixon to visit China.

Although Nixon found that "in some important respects this message raised
as many problems as it solved," he and Kissinger immediately began to work
on formulating Washington's response. Because of domestic political considerations, Nixon thought it necessary for the contact with Beijing "to be kept
totally secret until the final arrangement for the presidential visit had been
agreed upon." In his oral reply to Zhou's message, Kissinger wanted Yahya to

convey to Zhou Enlai as Kissinger's personal view that "I feel that President Nixon is very anxious to handle these negotiations entirely by himself and not to let any politician come into the picture until a government-to-government channel is established."[124] In terms of who should be the person to go to China, Nixon finally decided that Kissinger was the choice.[125]

On 10 May, Kissinger handed Washington's formal response to Ambassador Hilaly to deliver to Beijing. In the reply, Nixon accepted Zhou's invitation to visit Beijing, but insisted on an open agenda. The message states,

> Because of the importance he attaches to normalizing relations between our two countries, President Nixon is prepared to accept the suggestion of Premier Chou En-lai that he visit Peking for direct conversations with the leaders of the People's Republic of China. At such a meeting each side would be free to raise the issue of principal concern to it. In order to prepare the visit by President Nixon and to establish reliable contact with the leaders of the Chinese People's Republic, President Nixon proposes a preliminary *secret* meeting between his Assistant for National Security Affairs, Dr. Kissinger, and Premier Chou En-lai or another appropriate high-level Chinese official. Dr. Kissinger would be prepared to attend such a meeting on Chinese soil preferably at some location within convenient flying distance from Pakistan to be suggested by the People's Republic of China. Dr. Kissinger would be authorized to discuss the circumstances which would make a visit by President Nixon most useful, the agenda of such a meeting, the time of such a visit and to begin a preliminary exchange of views on all subjects of mutual interest. . . . It is anticipated that the visit of President Nixon to Peking could be announced within a short time of the secret meeting between Dr. Kissinger and Premier Chou En-lai. Dr. Kissinger will be prepared to come from June 15 onward.[126]

Beijing received the message on 17 May,[127] but was not too happy with the Nixon administration's insistence that the entire visit should be kept secret. The Pakistanis explained to the Chinese officials Nixon's reasoning: if word of the visit leaked in advance, the Taiwan lobby in Washington might try to prevent the trip.[128] The American public was still skeptical about China. Nixon and Kissinger were obliged to secrecy, refusing until the last possible moment to inform American allies, the State Department, or even the secretary of state of the prospects for a presidential visit. Kissinger and Nixon later justified the resort to secrecy on the grounds of political necessity: their considerable achievements "could never have been carried out if subjected throughout to the full glare of publicity."[129]

After receiving the U.S. message, Zhou Enlai, following Mao's instruction, presided at a meeting attended by leading members of the Foreign Ministry to discuss how to respond to Nixon's messages on 25 May.[130] The next day, the Politburo met to formulate Beijing's specific strategies toward improving Sino-

American relations. Instructed by Mao, Zhou delivered a speech at the meeting, pointing out that the United States was at the height of its power at the end of World War II and thus could interfere with "anything anywhere in the world" afterward. U.S. power, however, had declined in recent years. America's intervention in Vietnam had lost the support of the American people, forcing Washington to withdraw its troops gradually from Vietnam. In the meantime, America's economic position as well as its political influence in the world had begun to decline. Under these circumstances, Zhou speculated, the American leaders had to consider whether to continue their "going-all-out" policy or to reduce America's international involvement. As a first step toward the latter choice, Washington needed to get out of Vietnam, and the Americans thus found it necessary to establish contact with China. These developments, Zhou stressed, had provided China with "an opportunity to improve Sino-American relations," which "will be beneficial to the struggle against imperialist expansion and hegemonism, beneficial to maintaining peace in Asia as well as in the world, and beneficial to maintaining our country's security and pursuing the unification of the motherland in a peaceful way."[131]

The Politburo meeting reached some consensus, which was summarized in "A Politburo Report on Sino-American Talks," drafted by Zhou Enlai after the meeting. The main points were the eight "basic principles," which became China's new guiding principles on relations with the United States:

1. All American armed forces and special military facilities should be withdrawn from Taiwan and the Taiwan Strait area within the fixed time. This is the key question in the restoration of relations between China and the United States. If no agreement can be reached on this principle in advance, it is possible that Nixon's visit would be deferred.

2. Taiwan is China's territory, and the liberation of Taiwan is China's internal affairs. No foreign intervention should be allowed. Vigilance toward the activities of Japanese militarism in Taiwan must be pursued.

3. We will try to liberate Taiwan through peaceful means, and the efforts concerning Taiwan affairs should be carried out conscientiously.

4. The activities aimed at creating "two Chinas" or "one China and one Taiwan" will be resolutely opposed. If the United States wishes to establish diplomatic relations with China, it must recognize the People's Republic of China as the sole legitimate government representing China.

5. If the abovementioned three terms [1, 2, and 3 above] are not realized fully, it is not suitable for China and the United States to establish diplomatic relations, but a liaison office can be established in each other's capital.

6. We will not initiate the question concerning [China's membership in] the United Nations. If the Americans touch upon this question, we will tell them clearly that we will not accept the arrangement of "two Chinas" or "one China and one Taiwan."

7. We will not initiate the question concerning Sino-American trade. If the Americans touch upon this question, we may discuss it with them only after the principle of American troops withdrawing from Taiwan has been accepted.

8. The Chinese government maintains that American armed forces should be withdrawn from the three countries of Indochina, Korea, Japan, and Southeast Asia to ensure peace in the Far East.[132]

These eight principles embodied three noticeable changes from China's previous position. First, while demanding that U.S. troops withdraw from Taiwan, China no longer insisted that the United States openly sever diplomatic relations with Taiwan as a precondition for exchanges between the Chinese and U.S. governments. Second, while continuing to claim that liberating Taiwan was a Chinese internal affair, China stressed only its interests in resolving the Taiwan issue through peaceful means. Third, China advanced the idea of establishing liaison offices in both capitals if the Taiwan problem would not be resolved in the immediate future.[133] These three changes reflected China's willingness to adopt a flexible and more constructive negotiating position.

These principles also demonstrated that Beijing leaders were not quite ready to make major concessions, especially on the Taiwan issue. Such an attitude—the Chinese not ready to make compromises—was foreseeable, given the profound differences that had existed between Beijing and Washington for over two decades. Besides, the Politburo report predicted that the Sino-American talks might fail. But the main point was that whatever the results, such talks would do no harm to China. If an agreement could be reached during Kissinger's visit, Nixon could come to China openly. If additional agreements could then be reached with Nixon, a formal announcement on normalization would most likely occur before the U.S. presidential election. China's guiding principle was to deal with the incumbent administration. However, if Kissinger's visit ended in failure, Nixon would not be likely to visit China. The Chinese leadership argued that China's positive attitude toward Sino-U.S. relations would help Nixon's rivals in the presidential election.[134]

To clear up suspicions within the party, the Politburo was fully aware that its endorsement of Kissinger's secret visit should not leave any impression that it had softened the party's combative spirit toward U.S. imperialism. The report thus specifically enumerated several possible outcomes of opening relations with the United States, arguing that a Sino-American rapprochement would not impair the American people's struggle against the "monopoly capitalist ruling class." It might cause a short-term "ripple" to the Indochina War and the Paris peace talks; but the progress in the Sino-U.S. discussions would eventually enhance Hanoi's position at the Paris talks. This would force Washington to withdraw troops from Indochina because Nixon had realized that the focus of Soviet-American rivalry was in Europe and the Middle East, rather than the Far East. In particular, the report argued that the opening of Sino-American communications represented the "victorious result of our struggles against imperialism, revisionism, and reactionary forces," as well as the "inevitable outcome of the internal and external crises facing the U.S. imperialists and the competition for world hegemony between the United States and the Soviet Union." If the opening succeeded, the "competition between the two superpowers" would be fiercer; if the opening failed, the "reactionary face" of U.S. imperialism would be further exposed, and "our people's consciousness" would be further enhanced.[135]

The Politburo analysis was evidently written from the leftist perspective and was full of revolutionary terms of the Cultural Revolution era. It indicated the difficulty that the Chinese leadership was facing in search of a formulation to justify the new relationship with the United States. It was relatively accurate in its assessment that U.S. strategic focus was in Europe rather than in the Far East, that Sino-U.S. talks reflected American domestic and international difficulties, and that ongoing U.S.-Soviet rivalry was inevitable. The Politburo report symbolized the formation of China's new U.S. policy, and thus provided a political foundation for China's rapprochement with the United States.

Mao approved Zhou's report on 29 May.[136] China set up the parameter of its upcoming negotiations with the U.S.: it would not raise preconditions to opening high-level meetings. The Chinese leaders would prepare to accept partial success in conducting high-level talks with the United States. However, Beijing leadership was aware of the strategic difficulties faced by the United States and saw opportunities to pressure the U.S. envoy to make concessions. The Politburo reasoned that Nixon needed a successful negotiation to support his reelection campaign. Thus Kissinger was under great pressure to reach an agreement. The same day, again via the Pakistani channel, Zhou sent Beijing's formal responses to Washington,[137] informing the Americans that

> Chairman Mao Tse Tung has indicated that he welcomes President Nixon's visit and looks forward to that occasion when he may have direct conversations with His Excellency the President, in which each side would be free to raise the principal issue of concern to it. It goes without saying that the first question to be settled is the crucial issue between China and the United States which is the question of the concrete way of the withdrawal of all the U.S. Armed Forces from Taiwan and Taiwan Straits area.
>
> Premier Chou En Lai welcomes Dr. Kissinger to China as the U.S. representative who will come in advance for a preliminary secret meeting with high level Chinese officials to prepare and make necessary arrangements for President Nixon's visit to Peking.
>
> Premier Chou En Lai suggests that it would be preferable for Dr. Kissinger to set a date between June 15 and 20th for his arrival in China, and that he may fly directly from Islamabad to a Chinese airport not open to the pub-

lic. As for the flight, he may take a Pakistan Boeing aircraft or a Chinese spe-cial plane can be sent to fly him to and from China, if needed.[138]

Kissinger felt relieved in particular at Zhou's acceptance of the U.S. proposal that each side should be free to raise the issue that most concerns it. This, of course, would guarantee a discussion of global issues—such as the war in Indo-china and the Soviet threat—in which the U.S. was mainly interested. Mean-while, Zhou had framed the Taiwan problem in a manner most susceptible to solution: the withdrawal of U.S. forces.[139] After learning of the message, Nixon noted, "This is the most important communication that has come to an Ameri-can president since the end of World War II."[140]

IV

When Nixon came to office in January 1969, the U.S. power position was on the wane. In Asia, the Vietnam quagmire evidentially showed that the American empire was on the retreat. Comparatively, Chinese leaders now felt more confident in dealing with the United States as they acquired nuclear weaponry, a much-aspired-to strategic asset, in 1964. They were more confident of resolv-ing the Taiwan issue without worrying too much that they would be coerced to make unwanted and unpopular concessions. On the other hand, Washington not only had an urgent need (to end the war in Vietnam) as a reason to engage China in a constructive dialogue, but also came to realize that to normalize re-lations with China would serve long-term U.S. interests (to contain the Soviet challenges).

To reduce the external threat and improve the security situation seemed to be a common goal Washington and Beijing expected to obtain with a high-level U.S.-China dialogue. As a foreign-policy president, Nixon was deter-mined to restore and enhance the U.S. position in world affairs. To get the U.S. out of Vietnam was Nixon's top priority. To that end, Nixon attached enormous importance to improving relations with China. For the Chinese leaders, the Soviet Union gradually but surely turned into China's number-one enemy in the late 1960s and early 1970s, while the U.S. was becoming less threatening. Thus, the mounting threat from China's northern neighbor, the USSR, became a blasting fuse in Mao's determination to reach a rapproche-ment with Washington. Both Washington and Beijing, indeed, hoped that the other side would help to enhance its own security.

Domestic political atmospheres in both countries were favorable to a better U.S.-China relationship. In the United States, the public was becoming more interested in "Red China," and the dissenting voice from the old China Lobby was weak. Although there was still a strong support of Jiang's regime in Taiwan, more and more congressional and public opinion leaders advocated "recognizing the People's Republic of China." Also, the American business community could no longer wait for any delay in lifting the trade and travel restrictions. China's domestic politics played out into the U.S.-China rapprochement process, as well. The political situation was being slowly improved as the radical phase of the Cultural Revolution came to an end after April 1969. Mao and Zhou, who were in favor of improving relations with the United States, were in control of China's foreign policymaking. However, the ultra-leftists, who were strong supporters of the Cultural Revolution, were not supportive of improving relations with the United States. They clung to Mao's revolutionary line in words, and were resistant to changes in Chinese foreign policy. In March 1971, they were not supportive of sending the Chinese Ping-Pong team to Japan. They proposed not to invite the U.S. Ping-Pong team to visit China in April. They also voiced their concerns in May at the Politburo meeting regarding Kissinger's secret visit to China. Mao had to overrule their policy suggestions and launch a propaganda campaign to prepare the whole nation theoretically and psychologically for a radical change in China's U.S. policy.

Both countries' allies did not seem to stand in the way of U.S.-China normalization. The U.S. allies in Western Europe and Japan had been supportive of an improved Sino-American relationship and were pleased at Nixon's vision and courage in integrating China into the international community. Meanwhile, as the United States was pulling out of Asia, the weight of its Asian allies (Taiwan, South Korea) in Washington's policymaking calculation was not as crucial as it used to be. Beijing's allies in Asia proved to be the same. Pakistan was more than enthusiastic in facilitating secret Chinese-American contacts. Although suspicious of Beijing's "softened" attitude toward Washington, Hanoi did not have much leverage; as long as China would not sell them out, the Vietnamese would retain their partnership with Beijing long after Nixon's trip to Beijing.

The decades-long talks between America and China had finally functioned toward obtaining substantive results. When Nixon took office, there was no direct high-level communication channel between Washington and Beijing. With complications, they were able to reopen the ambassadorial talks, which had been suspended for more than two years. Through the last two sessions of the ambassadorial talks, the Chinese side was assured that the Nixon administration was willing to send a high-level official to Beijing for direct talks with the Chinese leaders. This was an important breakthrough as the Chinese had been proposing and expecting higher-level talks from the outset of the ambassadorial talks in 1955. To seek a more effective and secure way to communicate with the Chinese leaders, even before the collapse of the Warsaw channel, the Nixon White House had been trying to establish back-channel communication with Beijing, one of which—the Pakistani channel—turned out to be instrumental in setting up the agenda for direct talks between Kissinger and Zhou Enlai.

Secret diplomacy seems to have facilitated the delicate exchanges between Washington and Beijing, and thus to have expedited the rapprochement process.

Both Beijing and Washington gained experience and drew lessons from the ambassadorial talks. The Chinese were informed earlier that the Nixon White House was willing to talk at a higher level. The top leaders, Mao and Nixon, were also ready to give their personal push (Mao's meeting with Edgar Snow in October 1970 and Nixon's interview with *Time* magazine the same month) in order to move the rapprochement process forward when it became stalemated. Mutual signaling facilitated the communication process. Zhou Enlai artfully made use of Ping-Pong diplomacy, which dramatically changed the political atmosphere between the two countries. Personal diplomacy seemed to work well and carry the day. In formulating its new U.S. policy in May 1971, the Chinese Politburo did not insist that Washington should openly sever diplomatic relations with Taiwan as a precondition for opening higher-level meetings. China's flexible and constructive negotiating position was instrumental in moving things forward. The Chinese leaders, especially Zhou, made every effort to make sure that the first high-level talk between Beijing and Washington would be a successful one. As the first high-level U.S. official to visit the PRC, was Kissinger able to match Zhou's savvy and insight?

CHAPTER SEVEN

Breaking the Ice
Kissinger and Haig in Beijing, July 1971–January 1972

W HEN PUBLICLY ANNOUNCED on 15 July 1971, Henry Kissinger's secret visit to Beijing stunned the world. Kissinger's second and open visit to
Beijing in October of the same year, and the visit of the advance team led by
Kissinger's deputy Alexander Haig in January 1972, finalized the diplomatic,
political, and even logistical preparations for President Nixon's trip to China
in February 1972. It seems that the two top American officials' visits verified
the old Chinese proverb *shui dao qu cheng* (when water flows, a channel is
formed). How Beijing and Washington could ultimately break the ice by insti-
tuting a summit meeting after twenty-plus years of hostility and confrontation
proved far more intricate.

For a better understanding, one needs to address several particular issues.
Other than discussions on detailed arrangements for Nixon's stay in China, issues embodying significant policy implications were vigorously tackled by both
the American visitors and their Chinese hosts. They included: What did Beijing
and Washington expect to achieve through the upcoming face-to-face talks at
the highest level? How did Kissinger and Zhou Enlai manage to overcome mutual suspicions and misperceptions in setting the agenda for the talks? What
concessions did each make in order to get the new relationship on the right
track from the outset? What, in the end, did they accomplish?

I

Early in 1971, Kissinger had asked John Holdridge, Winston Lord, his special assistant, and Richard (Dick) Smyser, his NSC Vietnam specialist, to begin preparing briefing books for his visit to Beijing, which he anticipated would be later in the year. Kissinger wanted Holdridge to create a detailed set of briefing papers in loose-leaf binders.[1] They included a scope paper describing what the Chinese objectives were, what the U.S. hoped Kissinger's visit would accomplish, and what his opening statement would be, and a series of position papers touching on every conceivable issue that might come up in his talks in Beijing. These issues comprised a summit, a communiqué, Taiwan, Indochina, great power relations, South Asia, Korea, and future contacts. This sort of briefing book was to prepare for any of Kissinger's significant meetings in Beijing.[2] As Kissinger explained in his memoirs, "I have always believed that the secret of negotiations is meticulous preparation. The negotiator should know not only the technical side of the subject but its nuances." He also found it essential to study the psychology and purpose of his opponents in order to reconcile them with his own.[3]

Holdridge and his team did just that. The briefing book anticipated that China was expecting to "make major political gains" from Kissinger's secret visit and Nixon's China trip. PRC's status would increase greatly, and it would secure its position as truly one of the "big five." Thus, the PRC would have a better chance to get into the UN. In agreeing to Kissinger's visit, the briefing book anticipated that the PRC had several objectives. They would include an agreement with the U.S. on reducing and eventually eliminating U.S. forces in Taiwan, U.S. acknowledgment of the PRC's importance in world affairs, a non-aggression treaty or agreement of "peaceful coexistence," and an affirmation of Nixon's visit to Beijing.[4]

The briefing book argued that in order to realize these objectives, the Chinese leaders would probably be ready to "pay a price." Kissinger expected that China would use its influence in Vietnam to force it toward a peaceful and acceptable settlement and to develop relations with the United States. Meanwhile, the United States could still maintain its diplomatic ties and mutual defense treaty with Taiwan. The U.S. and China would keep in direct contact so that mutual interests—arms control, expanded trade and travel, reduction of tensions in East Asia and Southeast Asia—could be discussed.[5]

The briefing book also laid out Kissinger's strategy in talking with the Chinese leaders. Kissinger noted that over the years of U.S.-China negotiations, the Chinese were tired of Americans saying "no, unless," while the Americans grew weary of China's hard-line approach. He would emphasize the common areas and play down the differences, leaving them unstated so long as the Chinese did not press him too hard.[6] His method in general terms would be to get the point across that the United States really expected the Chinese to pay a price for what they expected to achieve, particularly at the summit, and to help work out acceptable conditions for the new relationship.[7]

Kissinger went over all the major issues with Nixon and sent a copy of the 200-plus-page briefing book to Nixon for instruction in June. Nixon's handwritten notes show he gave specific instructions on issues of Taiwan, Indochina, the Soviet Union, Japan, and other matters. Nixon was reluctant to give up too much on Taiwan. He instructed Kissinger, "Don't be so forthcoming on Taiwan until necessary." During an important meeting on 1 July between Nixon, Kissinger, and Alexander Haig, deputy national security adviser, they discussed the briefing book extensively. Nixon instructed Kissinger not to show U.S. willingness to abandon its support for Taiwan "until it was necessary to do so." He emphasized that the issue of "one China vs. two Chinas" "should be mentioned only once in the conversation rather than threaded throughout it" as in the present briefing book.[8] He seemed to be not quite sure how to handle the Vietnam issue with the Chinese leaders. Nixon noted, "RN [Nixon] would try hard on Vietnam. . . . Gain on other trade. POW[s] in China." Nixon believed that Vietnam was a hard issue, but the United States could at least use the China opening to get the American prisoners in China released. He believed that one of the reasons why China was interested in contact with the United States was China's fear of the Soviet Union. He instructed Kissinger, therefore, to "play up over our possible move toward [the] Soviets." Nixon was also aware of China's problem with the Japanese and China's objection to the American presence in East Asia. He suggested that Kissinger "put in more fear re Japan."[9] He asked Kissinger to tell the Chinese that a total disengagement of the United States or a misapplication of forces in the area could result in a resurgent Japanese bellicosity, with considerable danger for all.[10]

Kissinger's negotiation counterparts in Beijing were also busy with preparation as well. Having set up the rules at the Politburo meeting in May, the Chinese leaders now made efforts to prepare the Party and the nation for a significant change of Chinese policy toward the United States. To this end, the PRC leaders convened a series of meetings, including the CCP Central Work Conference in Beijing from 4 to 18 June. Two hundred twenty-five "leading officials" from the Party, government, army, and different provinces attended the meeting. Zhou Enlai read out and explained the "Politburo's Report on the Sino-American Talks." Top officials from the Foreign Ministry and the CCP's International Liaison Department reported on the international situation and the international Communist movement. The participants also discussed the minutes of Mao's talks with Edgar Snow. Zhou made closing remarks on the significance of the upcoming new policy toward the United States.[11] Zhou stressed that it was Nixon and Kissinger who were coming to Beijing; thus "it is not we who need something from them, but they who need something from us."[12] This tone dominated

Beijing's effort to justify the Sino-American opening to the party rank and file in the years to come. The Chinese leadership was concerned about China's proper role in the world. They believed that as a great nation, China should occupy a central position in international affairs, not be a supplicant. On the strategic level, they would not allow any slights from the Americans.

On the tactical level, Zhou was particularly thoughtful and considerate. He would treat Kissinger and his team as state guests and accord them due respect. To achieve the desired result, Zhou demanded that the local governments coordinate their activities with the central government and do well in their reception work. "In receiving our foreign guests," Zhou stated, "we must be courteous. Neither haughty nor humble nor chauvinistic. We should also guard against ultra-leftist tendencies and the old sycophancy."[13] China's chief policymakers had thus confirmed and provided ideological underpinnings for its new policy toward the United States.

To prepare for Kissinger's arrival, Beijing established a special task force headed by Zhou Enlai and Marshal Ye Jianying, a senior Politburo member and vice chairman of the Central Military Commission, to handle all the technical and logistical matters.[14] According to Zhang Ying, the Chinese were very meticulous. Zhang, a middle-rank official in the Press Department of the Foreign Ministry, was assigned to read Kissinger's books and to write summaries and reports for the leaders' reference. Extensive surveys of American history, politics, society, and especially U.S. China policy since the founding of the PRC in 1949 had been prepared. By June, all the Chinese officials who were going to work with the visiting Americans moved into the state guesthouse. They were warned to keep Kissinger's visit secret even from their families. Zhou Enlai discussed almost every talking point with his senior associates and always sent the reports to Mao for his approval.[15] Zhou's handwritten notes on the document—"On Several Key Questions Pertinent to Sino-American Preliminary Talks," prepared by the Foreign Ministry—stating, "We will adhere to principles and make flexible adjustment if circumstances require. We will be ready for bargaining with the American side,"[16] set the tone.

Eventually, the date for Kissinger's visit was set for 9 to 11 July 1971. This was not the best time for China, as a high-level North Korean delegation was scheduled to be there. Having made the decision to accept a meeting, the Chinese acceded to U.S. wishes on the timing and went out of its way to assure the meeting's success.[17]

II

With the assistance of Pakistani President Yahya Khan, Kissinger, together with his small party of aides, including Winston Lord, John Holdridge, Richard Smyser, and two Secret Service agents, secretly flew from Islamabad to Beijing on 9

Marshal Ye Jianying greets Henry Kissinger at the Beijing Airport on 9 July 1971.
From left to right: Wang Hairong, Ji Chaozhu, Ye Jianying, Xiong Xianghui,
Huang Hua, Henry Kissinger, Zhang Wenjin, and Tang Wensheng.
National Archives (NPMP, 6825-03).

Zhou Enlai and Henry Kissinger shake hands at state guesthouse, Beijing,
on 9 July 1971. *National Archives (NPMP, 6825-02).*

July 1971. Zhou Enlai sent a team of four officials from the Foreign Ministry to Pakistan to escort the Americans to Beijing. They were Zhang Wenjin; Wang Hairong, Mao's niece on his mother's side, who was vice director-general, Protocol Department; Tang Wensheng, known as Nancy Tang, born in Brooklyn and speaking good American English, an interpreter for Zhou and Mao; and Tang Longbin, an official from the Protocol Department.[18] "We assured Yahya Khan that the gesture was welcome and appreciated," recalled Holdridge.[19]

During the forty-eight hours of his stay in Beijing, Kissinger spent a total of seventeen hours with Zhou and other high-ranking Chinese officials in six meetings. The Kissinger-Zhou talks focused on the Mao-Nixon summit, Taiwan, Indochina, relations with Japan and the Soviet Union, South Asia, further American-Chinese communication, and arms control. Kissinger also talked with Huang Hua and Zhang Wenjin for four hours on drafting a joint announcement.[20] Zhou and Kissinger quickly established respect for one another. While Zhou found Kissinger "very intelligent—indeed a Dr.," Kissinger found Zhou "one of the two or three most impressive men I have ever met."[21]

The two sides held the first formal talks on the afternoon of 9 July. Kissinger, Holdridge, Smyser, and Lord sat on one side of a conference table; Zhou Enlai, Ye Jianying, Huang Hua, Xiong Xianghui,[22] and Zhang Wenjin sat on the other side. Zhou opened the talks by saying that it was a Chinese custom always to let the guests speak first. Kissinger accepted the invitation and began with rather lengthy opening remarks. He praised China's long history and culture. At the end of his introduction, Kissinger said, "Many visitors have come to this beautiful, and to us, mysterious land." Zhou held up his hand and said, "You will find it not mysterious. When you have become familiar with it, it will not be as mysterious as before."[23]

In further response to Kissinger's remarks, Zhou told Kissinger, "The first question is that of equality, or in other words, the principle of reciprocity. All things must be done in a reciprocal manner."[24] Zhou emphasized the importance of being treated with "equality" and with full respect for China's sovereignty and national independence, the question which had bothered the Chinese nation for more than a century.

Zhou then turned to the Taiwan issue. He reminded Kissinger that Taiwan indeed was China's principal concern. He described Taiwan as the basic issue between the U.S. and the PRC, going back to the Korean War, when the U.S. declared—in contrast to its previous position—that Taiwan's status was "undetermined." He then went on to say that to establish diplomatic relations with the PRC, the U.S. must

— Recognize that Taiwan is an inalienable part of China, and a province of China.
— Recognize the PRC as the sole legitimate government of China.

— Withdraw all its armed forces and military installations from the area of
  Taiwan and the Taiwan Strait within a limited period.
— Consider that the US-ROC Mutual Defense Treaty is invalid.[25]

The briefing books did not anticipate the important issues that Zhou brought
up, namely the recognition of China's sovereignty over Taiwan and the PRC as
the sole legitimate government of China. Zhou's move on these issues was
surely a big surprise to Kissinger. He had to improvise his position.

Kissinger responded that Zhou was going beyond what the Chinese had said
to the Americans at the last two Warsaw talks in 1970 and in the secret channel
communications, in which the Chinese had requested the removal of U.S.
military presence only. Kissinger pointed out that the two sides had to distinguish between what could be done immediately and what had to be left to future development. He, therefore, would like to divide the Taiwan question into
two parts—first, U.S. forces in Taiwan, and second, the question of the normalization of relations between the U.S. and the PRC. As two-thirds of U.S. forces
in Taiwan were related to the Vietnam War, these forces could be withdrawn
after the end of the war in Vietnam, and the U.S. would continue to withdraw
more troops from Taiwan in concert with further improvements in Sino-
American relations. Kissinger emphasized that Washington firmly believed
that the Taiwan issue should be resolved in a peaceful manner. On the political
question of Taiwan, he made the important declaration, "We are not advocating a 'two Chinas' solution or a 'one China, one Taiwan' solution. The political
question could be settled within the earlier part of Nixon's second term."[26] He
also assured Zhou that the United States would not support a Taiwan independence movement.[27]

Kissinger made known to Zhou Enlai that the U.S. could not accept diplomatic recognition of the PRC as a condition to Nixon's visit to Beijing. Kissinger told Zhou that he believed the U.S. could settle the major part of the military question regarding Taiwan within Nixon's first term in office if the war in
Southeast Asia ended. The normalization of relations between the U.S. and the
PRC could be realized in Nixon's second term. After long discussion, Zhou
agreed that diplomatic recognition was not a precondition, but the visit should
set recognition as the ultimate direction of policy. He accepted Kissinger's position that some time was needed to establish diplomatic relations.[28] Thus, the
most important breakthrough was attained on the first day, as each leader was
trying to understand and accommodate the other's basic position.

Zhou made further efforts to secure new U.S. policy on Taiwan. He told Kissinger that if China was to be patient it needed three assurances: first, that the
U.S. would not support "two Chinas" or a "one China, one Taiwan" policy; second, that the U.S. would not support the indigenous Taiwan independence
movement; and third, that the U.S. would not permit Japanese troops to move

into Taiwan after U.S. withdrawal. Kissinger stressed that this would be the American policy but noted that some events on Taiwan might be beyond U.S. ability to control. Zhou interposed no objection.[29] Later, Kissinger assured Zhou that the Nixon administration would give no support to any Nationalist attempt to invade the mainland.[30] Although Beijing had repeatedly emphasized that unless progress could be made on the Taiwan issue, no other question would be discussed, Zhou showed flexibility. China would not set U.S. immediate withdrawal from and severance of diplomatic relations with Taiwan as preconditions for Nixon's visit and meeting with Mao.[31] Because each side had already revealed its basic position to the other through the back-channel communications, the face-to-face negotiation served the function of confirming those major points.

In explaining Washington's policy toward Indochina, Kissinger told Zhou Enlai in their first meeting on 9 July that the Nixon administration was committed to ending the Vietnam War through negotiation and thus was willing to establish a timetable to withdraw American troops from South Vietnam, if America's "honor" was protected. Kissinger emphasized, "If Hanoi is willing to accept a fixed date for our complete withdrawal, a cease-fire, a release of prisoners, and a guaranteed international status for South Vietnam . . . then we have a very good chance for a rapid peace."[32] From the outset, Kissinger tried to link the Indochina conflict to the relationship with Beijing. He stressed again to Zhou that two-thirds of U.S. forces in Taiwan were linked to the war and that their removal would depend on an end of the conflict, which in turn would accelerate improvement in Sino-American relations.

Zhou went back and forth between a formal theoretical defense of Hanoi's position and concrete questions that sought to discover areas of agreement. He stressed Beijing's support of Hanoi but denied that China had ever had advisers in Indochina.[33] He criticized American aggression but indicated China's interest in an "honorable exit" for the United States from Indochina. Zhou told Kissinger that China had only two objectives with regard to a Vietnam settlement: there must be a withdrawal of U.S. and Allied forces, and the peoples of the three Indochinese countries must be left to decide their own future. Zhou insisted that China would keep its hands off after a settlement.[34] In response to Kissinger's emphasis on protecting American honor in Indochina, Zhou pointed out that the Americans always liked to stress their prestige and honor. It would be the greatest honor and glory for the United States, Zhou commented, if it would completely withdraw its forces from Indochina. However, Zhou seemed satisfied with Kissinger's pledge and might have believed this was Washington's official position. Although he continued to insist that all the American troops must be withdrawn from Taiwan and the U.S.-ROC Mutual Defense Treaty must be abolished, Zhou stated that the differences between Beijing and Washington should not prevent the two sides from living in peace and equality.[35]

Before Kissinger arrived in Beijing, Nixon flew to Kansas City to address a large group of Midwestern news media executives on domestic policy. Nixon startled the assembled executives by using that venue to discuss the "broader context" and "the relationship between these [domestic] programs and the problems that America has in the world." Obviously excited at what he knew to be about to take place, Nixon wanted to place on record an outline of the reasons for approaching China. He praised the Chinese as "creative," "productive," and "one of the most capable peoples in the world." That was why it was "essential that this administration take the first steps toward ending the isolation of Mainland China from the world community." He foresaw a world of "five great economic superpowers" (the United States, Western Europe, Japan, the Soviet Union, and China) whose relationship would determine the structure of peace in our time. In order to prevent China from becoming "isolated" and out of touch with "world leaders," he said that "doors must be opened" and relations between Beijing and Washington normalized.[36] Zhou took Nixon's "Kansas City Address" very seriously and mentioned it to Kissinger in their first meeting, but rejected the appellation of "superpower," and reiterated that China would not play the game.[37]

Immediately after his first day's meeting with Kissinger, very late in the evening (11:20 P.M.), Zhou went to report to Mao Zedong. Mao was the behind-the-scenes strategist and final decision-maker. His reaction, however, was interesting. When Mao learned that Washington would withdraw some but not all American troops from Taiwan, he commented that it would take some time for a monkey to evolve into a human being, and that the Americans were now at the ape stage, "with a tail, though a much shorter one, on his back." Mao continued, "The United States should make a new start and . . . let the domino fall. The United States must withdraw from Vietnam. We are not in a hurry on the Taiwan issue because there is no fighting there," stated Mao. "But the Indochina issue is more important as there is a war in Vietnam and people are being killed there. We should not invite Nixon to come just for our own interests." Mao instructed Zhou not to focus on specific issues the next day but to "brag to" (*chui* in Chinese) Kissinger about the big "strategic picture," that "although all under Heaven is in great chaos, the situation is wonderful." In particular, Mao instructed, Zhou should tell the Americans that China was prepared "to be divided by the United States, the Soviet Union, and Japan, with them all coming together to invade China."[38] Mao wanted to find out Kissinger's response to this statement, as he was concerned with issues of strategic importance, especially the political structure of the world and China's national security. He wished to sound out America's real intentions through high-level contacts between the two countries so that China could develop its own international strategy.

Mao's attitude showed that he was going to accept partial improvement in Sino-American relations. He was willing to provide the Americans with the time needed to complete the change in its China policy. Since Beijing had always viewed the Taiwan issue as the single most important obstacle for restoring relations with the United States, Mao's attitude meant, as the historian Chen Jian has suggested, "the Taiwan issue would no longer block Zhou and Kissinger from reaching an agreement on the agenda for Nixon's visit."[39]

With Mao's instructions in mind, Zhou changed his negotiating approach the next day. Using ideologically aggressive language to draw a picture of "great chaos all under Heaven," Zhou presented Beijing's "principled stands" on a series of international issues, including Vietnam, India, Japan, Korea, and Taiwan, challenging Washington's policy toward them. He also brought up the issue of U.S. collusion with other countries to divide up China.[40] Kissinger assured Zhou that the U.S. would never collude with other countries in carving up China. China, therefore, did not have to worry about U.S. attack from the south, and could move its troops northward. He told Zhou that "there is no possibility, certainly in this administration, nor probably in any other, of any cooperation such as you have described between the U.S., the Soviet Union and Japan to divide up China."[41]

Zhou also raised the question of the alleged U.S. rearmament of Japan, which Chinese leaders regarded as a threat to China. Zhou maintained that the rapid development of Japanese economic power would inevitably carry rearmament in its wake. He said that Japan's economic expansion would lead to political expansionism. Kissinger declared that the U.S. was not encouraging, and indeed opposed to, any revival of Japanese expansionism. He agreed on the military implications of Japan's economic growth and indicated that the interests of the U.S. and the PRC coincided in trying to keep this growth under control. He pointed out that the USSR's powerful military buildup in the region lay behind Japan's rearmament—which could not threaten China—and that the U.S. nuclear umbrella and military relationship with Japan stabilized the region, turned the Japanese away from a revival of militarism, and deterred the Japanese from developing their own nuclear capability.[42]

The Korean question was also discussed. It originated from the fact that there was still no peace treaty despite China's effort in 1954 to extend the Geneva Accords to Korea. Zhou had proposed this, but the proposal was rejected by Britain and the U.S. in 1954. Zhou went on to say that there was conflict along the Demilitarized Zone; U.S. forces were still present; and ROK troops were in Vietnam. There was now a joint U.S.–South Korean army in which Thailand was also represented. Park Chong-Hee (then South Korean president) was as aggressive as Syngman Rhee (former South Korean president). Therefore, the Democratic People's Republic of Korea—and China—had a right to be concerned. Kissinger argued that there was no threat to anyone from the U.S. military presence, which, in actuality, helped to stabilize the military balance on the Korean peninsula. An increase in tensions on the peninsula was not in the interests of either China or the United States. Kissinger explained that what happened in Korea depended very much on the general relationships in the area. If the war in Indochina ended and U.S.-PRC relations developed, the ROK troops in Vietnam would return, and it was conceivable that before the end of President Nixon's second term, most of the U.S. troops in Korea would be withdrawn.[43] On Vietnam, each side simply reiterated its position, with Kissinger drawing attention to the U.S. withdrawal under "Vietnamization."[44]

As Chen Jian has suggested, Zhou's "fierce litany" (in Kissinger's words) was not designed to block the negotiations but to complete a particular "ritual procedure" that was needed for socialist China to reach a compromise with imperialist America.[45] In traditional Chinese belief, actors should perform in accordance with their ascribed roles. This means that the issue of identity is very important for China in international affairs. By attacking the U.S. on these international issues, Zhou intended to justify China's new relations with the United States.

The two sides did not agree easily on the wording of the announcement on Nixon's visit to China. Even before Kissinger's trip, the Chinese were anxious to get confirmation that Nixon was in principle willing to visit China, but they also tried to show that they had responded to Nixon's request. At first, Zhou took a hard position that the summit should be in the context of improving Sino-U.S. relations and that the best way to accomplish this was through the establishment of diplomatic relations. After considerable bargaining, Zhou eventually backed away from this position by reluctantly acknowledging that recognition was not an "absolute" precondition for a summit, but insisted that the direction should be set by it. Zhou proposed that the two sides discuss the date for Nixon's visit to China toward the end of the 10 July meeting. When Zhou suggested that President Nixon come to visit China in the summer of 1972, Kissinger indicated that a summer summit close to the election might be misunderstood. The two sides agreed to the spring of 1972.[46]

Zhou, who was scheduled to host a reception for a North Korean delegation visiting Beijing that evening, designated Huang Hua and Zhang Wenjin to work with Kissinger on the drafting of a joint announcement.[47] When Huang Hua, who was late to the meeting, finally arrived,[48] he proposed a draft indicating that Nixon had solicited the invitation to visit China for the purpose of discussing the Taiwan issue as a prelude to normalizing Sino-American relations. Kissinger made it clear that such a draft was absolutely unacceptable. He explained U.S. concerns about principles and domestic politics; it was not acceptable to appear as having solicited the invitation, and the summit should have a broader scope, not just normalization of U.S.-China relations. Huang Hua pointed out the shocking impact of the announcement on ordinary Chinese, who might not understand such a drastic change in policy.

When the meeting was resumed at 9:40 A.M. on 11 July, Huang presented a new draft, which Kissinger immediately found agreeable. It stated that "knowing of President Nixon's expressed desire to visit the People's Republic of China," Premier Zhou "has extended an invitation." The purpose of his visit was to seek "the normalization of relations" between the two countries and also "to exchange views on questions of concern to the two sides." Although the U.S. side preferred to include the phrase "peace in the world" to describe the purpose of the visit, Kissinger accepted the Chinese formulation since it met the principal U.S. concern of broadening the scope of the summit.[49] The draft joint announcement bridged U.S. and Chinese objectives, yet toned down the implication that the two sides would discuss matters of international security and peace. The United States and China simultaneously announced on 15 July that Kissinger had held talks with Zhou Enlai on 9–11 July and Nixon would visit Beijing in the spring of 1972.

According to John Holdridge, the concessions over the language of the announcement of the Nixon visit were all on the Chinese side, as they agreed to drop any reference to Taiwan.[50] In the process of communiqué drafting, the Chinese clearly made an effort to find a mutually acceptable compromise. Once China's principled stand was upheld, Zhou willingly accepted all the details for the summit that Kissinger had put forward.[51]

The United States and China confronted each other for twenty-two years before Kissinger's secret visit. China was still in the midst of the Cultural Revolution. A "war of liberation" against the U.S. was going on near China's southern border. Now China was dealing with the foremost capitalist country. It is understandable that the moral ambivalence of this encounter was revealed during the course of contacts.

Chinese officials greeted Kissinger and his party with considerable mistrust. They were afraid that the Americans might deceive them. The suspicions started from Nixon's and Kissinger's insistence upon total secrecy for the trip. The strongest indication of the lingering Chinese mistrust of America was that on the afternoon of 10 July, Zhou proposed that he and Kissinger tape-record a summary of their discussions.[52] Zhou apparently feared that the Nixon administration might back away in public from what Kissinger was telling him in private. He wanted Kissinger's promises on tape, above all his assurances concerning Taiwan. Zhou might also have hoped to use such a tape to protect himself in China's domestic politics. He might need the record to report to Mao and to defend his status in a future leadership struggle as the Chinese political culture attached importance to what was on record. Kissinger, however, thought differently. He might have been afraid of the leaking of these documents, as in the cases of the Pentagon Papers and the Anderson Papers.[53] These papers were causing great problems for the Nixon administration. Kissinger felt more comfortable with off-the-record talks, and was not in favor of the idea of tape-recording. After many exchanges of views, Zhou seemed to have more confidence in Kissinger. In the evening session, Zhou told Kissinger, "There is now no need for a tape-recording since we have fully exchanged our views today and will tomorrow."[54] Negotiation and face-to-face talks seemed to have dissipated suspicion and distrust.

III

To establish a workable channel of communication seemed to be the first pre-paratory step toward the Nixon-Mao summit. During his secret mission to Beijing in July, Kissinger secured Zhou Enlai's agreement that in the future the contact point between China and the United States would be Paris, with Chi-nese Ambassador Huang Zhen and the U.S. military attaché, General Vernon Walters, as point persons. As Kissinger had promised in Beijing that the U.S. would inform China in detail of any deal with Moscow that would affect Chi-nese interests, Nixon sent Zhou Enlai a message to confirm that promise on 16 July 1971. It was the first contact through this Paris channel. The message was delivered on 19 July by Walters to Huang Zhen.[55] It was drafted by Kissinger and his NSC staff, approved by Nixon, then hand-carried to Paris by a member of the Situation Room staff and delivered personally by General Walters.[56] The two sides soon began to use the secret Paris channel. Walters would visit Am-bassador Huang Zhen in his residence forty-five times before the U.S. and China decided to utilize Paris as the open point of contact, which occurred only after Nixon's trip to China in February 1972.[57] Kissinger also flew to Paris to talk secretly with Ambassador Huang three times in 1971.[58] The Paris channel "served chiefly as a transmittal belt for messages between the U.S. and the PRC."[59] Washington and Beijing intended "to use Paris as the primary channel for communications on major and longer-range policy issues and sensitive questions."[60]

In addition to the Paris channel, Washington and Beijing also set up a secret contact point in New York City. After the PRC's UN delegation arrived in New York in November 1971,[61] Kissinger and Huang Hua, then PRC permanent rep-resentative to the UN, held secret meetings at a CIA safe house in the Lower East Side of Manhattan and quickly developed a comfortable relationship. They exchanged views on a number of policy issues, including the India-Pakistan War. The two sides made it clear that these were "major questions of principle within the scope of the work of the United Nations and would not need to involve com-mitment."[62] Finding the meeting very useful, Kissinger and Huang Hua did, indeed, meet more than a dozen times in New York prior to the opening of li-aison offices in Beijing and Washington in mid-1973.

The first set of issues discussed through the Paris channel was how, during Kissinger's second visit to Beijing, to settle important details for Nixon's upcom-ing trip to China. The purpose of Kissinger's second visit was to make prepara-tions related to the political discussions and the technical arrangements for the president's visit. The two sides understood the importance of reviewing all major issues before the presidential visit.[63] During a secret Kissinger–Huang Zhen meeting in Paris on 26 July, Huang told Kissinger that the Chinese government "agreed" that Kissinger would visit Beijing in the later part of October, not in late September or early October as the U.S. had proposed. Making no objection, Kissinger suggested that Ambassador David Bruce, who had Nixon's full confidence and was conducting the Vietnamese peace negotiations in Paris, come with him. David Bruce, who was viewed as "one of the most respected diplomats of the post-World War II period," had been called out of retirement by Nixon to head the American delegation in Paris.[64] Huang Zhen, however, voiced objection to Bruce's coming to Beijing, possibly concerned about Moscow Radio's accusations that Beijing had made a deal on Indochina with the United States. Huang also pointed out that Beijing would prefer Kissinger to fly directly to Shanghai from Alaska. The Chinese did not like an American plane crossing a great portion of China's airspace.[65]

Kissinger seemed accommodating to China's requests. During his three secret meetings with Chinese Ambassador Huang Zhen in Paris in 1971, Kissinger briefed the Chinese on all U.S. moves with Moscow as well as the U.S. assessment of Soviet intentions. On 9 October, five days in advance, Washington informed the Chinese of the forthcoming announcement of the U.S.-Soviet summit in May 1972. The U.S. gave the Chinese a four-week advance warning of the contents of both the U.S.-USSR Agreement on Measures to Reduce the Risk of Accidental Outbreak of Nuclear War and the Berlin agreements. Both sides exchanged views on the deteriorating situation on the Indian subcontinent as well. Washington also turned down a Soviet proposal of a conference of five nuclear powers after learning of China's unwillingness to participate.[66] "The only way to protect the tender shoot of our China policy from being crushed by this combination of Soviet embrace and menace was to make sure Peking understood our actions," recalled Kissinger.[67] Later on, Kissinger went even further. He provided the Chinese with ultra-sensitive intelligence on Soviet military activities derived from top-secret National Security Agency intercepts of encoded communications and other sources. According to journalist Seymour Hersh's account, Kissinger showed Zhou high-resolution satellite photographs during his second trip to China.[68] In his memoirs, Kissinger admits that "I sometimes went so far as to let him [Zhou Enlai] see the internal studies that supported our conclusions."[69]

Eventually, a date for Kissinger's public visit was set for 20 October. The U.S. originally hoped that the Chinese government would make the announcement on 22 September, or 23 September, or 4 October, in that order of preference.[70] But the Chinese told Washington that they did not like the September dates as the UN would be discussing PRC's representation then. Neither would Beijing want to appear as accepting the U.S. dual-representation formula, advocating

Beijing's entry into the United Nations, but opposing the expulsion of Taipei.[71] After several rounds of negotiations, the U.S. agreed to release the public announcement of Kissinger's visit on 5 October.[72]

Kissinger came to Beijing with a larger party in his second trip to China. His delegation consisted of four categories of people according to the function they performed. Kissinger, Lord, and Holdridge focused on both the policy and some of the technical side of the president's trip. Dwight Chapin, deputy assistant to the president and head of the advance team, was fully responsible for technical issues. The advance team was also to seek out "photo opportunities" and lay out a preliminary schedule for President and Mrs. Nixon to follow. The security and communication technicians would familiarize themselves only with issues under their care. Finally, the State Department representative was Alfred Jenkins, who was the director of the Office of Mainland China and Mongolian Affairs, and an expert on the bilateral issues that had been discussed between the Chinese and Americans for two decades. Jenkins's appointment was arranged on Kissinger's order. The purpose was to give the State Department representative "a sense of participation without letting him in on key geographical discussions, especially the drafting of the communiqué."[73]

The October trip was much more comfortable for Kissinger and his staff as they were using the president's plane (Air Force One). They were testing the route planned for the Nixon trip, with stopovers in Hawaii and Guam. This route was planned to permit the presidential party to reach China without being too exhausted by time changes and jet lag. From Guam, the party flew directly to Shanghai and then to Beijing on 20 October 1971.[74]

Meanwhile, Beijing was preparing the Chinese people for an open and "comfortable" Kissinger visit. As Mao was in full control of Chinese politics, there was no Chinese language source indicating any senior leader, including Lin Biao, was openly challenging Mao's policy of rapprochement with the United States. But the Chinese leadership did have to nurture the ideological basis for rapprochement as the United States had been demonized by the Chinese Communist propaganda in the last twenty years. On 16 August 1971, *Renmin Ribao* published Mao's essay "On Policy." First formulated and published in 1940, the essay justified a policy of collaboration with Chinese Nationalists against the Japanese. The policy, designated for "an extremely complex struggle," called for a tactical united front with a less immediately dangerous adversary (the "secondary enemy") against a more dangerous "principal enemy."[75] A similar, slightly more explicit, explanation had also been given in a confidential internal CCP Central Committee document in mid-July, assuring the rank and file that Mao himself had invited Nixon and that the offer represented "another tactic in the struggle against imperialism."[76]

An unexpected political crisis in the CCP leadership in September 1971 made Kissinger's visit easier to sell to the Party. Lin Biao, who had been known as Mao's "closest comrade-in-arms" and "best and most loyal student," allegedly plotted a coup to assassinate Mao. Lin, together with his wife, his son, and a handful of supporters fled from Beijing but died in a plane crash in the People's Republic of Mongolia on 13 September.[77] Lin Biao's downfall enhanced the position of Zhou Enlai, who was a strong advocate of opening China's relations with other parts of the world in general and the United States in particular. As the Lin Biao Incident damaged the myth of Mao's "eternal correctness," Mao now was even eager to have a major breakthrough in China's foreign relation so as to cover up the domestic political crisis and salvage his declining reputation and authority.[78]

After the Lin Biao Incident, Zhou started to rectify China's domestic political atmosphere. He directed a nationwide policy education, toned-down anti-American propaganda, and restored the names of old stores and shops. All of these were permitted by Mao, as the chairman was eager to score diplomatic points.[79] Through Ambassador Huang Zhen in Paris, the Chinese side notified the U.S. that the Lin Biao Incident would not change China's attitude toward the U.S., and China would proceed with the preparation for Nixon's visit. The Nixon administration was very pleased at Beijing's stance.[80]

In Shanghai, Kissinger's party was greeted by the same four Chinese officials who had met him in Islamabad. Kissinger and his aides felt that although this visit was publicized, the Chinese officials remained restrained, and not as warm as expected. When escorted to the state guest house (*Diaoyutai* in Chinese) in Beijing, they were surprised to find that a special bulletin in English from the New China News Agency reprinted a *Renmin Ribao* editorial calling on the "peoples of the world" to overthrow the American "imperialists and their running dogs." Kissinger asked Holdridge to collect all the "offending" items and turn them over to one of the Chinese protocol officers, for he regarded this as a calculated effort to test their reaction to such a pointed slap.[81] In the car on the way to the Great Hall of the People the following day, Acting Foreign Minister Ji Pengfei explained to Kissinger that every country had its own means of communicating with its people. The Americans used newspaper and television; the Chinese used wall posters. In their later talks, Zhou Enlai mentioned obliquely to Kissinger that the United States should observe Beijing's actions, not its rhetoric, because, he explained, the anti-American propaganda was what the Chinese called "firing empty cannons of rhetoric" (*Fangkongpao* in Chinese).[82]

Kissinger stayed in Beijing from 20 to 26 October for what had been announced as a four-day visit.[83] He and Zhou Enlai held ten meetings, which lasted a total of twenty-three hours and forty minutes.[84] The Chinese side took the visit very seriously. On the day of Kissinger's arrival, the official Party newspaper listed the welcoming committee and on 21 October, *Renmin Ribao* carried two photographs of Zhou and Kissinger. This was the first time in twenty years that an American official had been pictured together with a Chinese leader.[85] In addition to exchanging opinions on a host of international issues and resolving specific items related to Nixon's visit (such as media coverage), the most difficult challenge facing the two leaders was to work out a draft summit communiqué to be issued at the conclusion of the presidential visit. After his first visit to Beijing, Kissinger had asked Holdridge to prepare the first draft of the joint communiqué. Not sure how to do it, Holdridge modeled his first attempt on some of the other joint communiqués that had been issued following visits by senior foreign leaders to Beijing for meetings with Mao. This U.S. draft was a standard diplomatic communiqué underlining agreement on the issues over which the two sides actually had sharp differences. On the Taiwan issue, it avoided mentioning U.S. withdrawal from Taiwan and asked the Chinese to use only peaceful means to solve the Taiwan issue.[86]

The negotiations over the communiqué draft turned out to be tortuous. When Kissinger first mentioned the issue of a communiqué with Zhou on 20 October, Zhou reported to Mao immediately. Mao told him that China should wait for Kissinger to present a draft. He added that if China had to present a draft, it should be a distinct, not a vague, one. On the evening of 22 October, when Kissinger handed the draft to Zhou Enlai, the Chinese premier did not respond right away, possibly because he needed some time to study it and get Mao's feedback.[87]

When the two met again on the morning of 24 October, Zhou told Kissinger that "our ideas regarding the joint Communiqué for the President's visit are different from yours." China and the U.S. differed in their attitudes toward issues concerning Taiwan, Vietnam, Indochina, Korea, Japan, and the subcontinent (India and Pakistan).[88] The Chinese premier pointed out that an acceptable communiqué must reflect the "fundamental differences" between Beijing and Washington, and should not present an "untruthful appearance."[89] Zhou argued that the two nations had fought against each other in Korea, disagreed on many world issues, and had gone through twenty-two years of mutual hostility and isolation, and the U.S. had "intervened in Taiwan." It would be very difficult for the Chinese people, the American people, and their mutual friends around the world to understand a communiqué that showed that China and the U.S. were getting together like two countries with "normal" diplomatic relations for a regular summit meeting. Zhou stressed that such a "friendly" communiqué was going to make China's allies nervous, and they might believe that China was selling them out. He also believed that the description of the world situation in the U.S. draft communiqué was "not sufficiently revolutionary" from his point of view. For these reasons, he said that the whole draft lacked credibility and candor, and, furthermore, it couldn't be defended by the Chinese ideologically in their own party circles, with their own people, or with their friends.[90] Therefore, Zhou suggested, they should issue a different kind of communiqué, in which each side should state its own position, although it would be unprecedented in the history of international diplomacy. Such a communiqué would certainly list those areas where they did have some agreement and some parallel interest.[91]

Behind Zhou's demand for dramatic change was Mao. As he was listening to Zhou's briefing on his meetings with Kissinger on the evening of 23 October, Mao told the premier, "I have said many times that all under Heaven is great chaos, so it is desirable to let each side speak out for itself." If the American side wanted to talk about "peace, security, and no pursuit of hegemony," the chairman continued, the Chinese side should emphasize "revolution, the liberation of the oppressed peoples and nations in the world, and no rights for big powers to bully and humiliate small countries." Mao acknowledged that stressing these goals was no more than "firing empty cannons," yet he stressed that "all of these points must be highlighted; and anything short of that would be improper."[92]

Mao's sensitivity, as well as his intervention, produced a would-be summit communiqué that would "truthfully" reflect China's overall position. This position revealed his determination not to allow Nixon's visit to tarnish his revolution's image at home and abroad. More important, though, Mao aimed to demonstrate to the Americans his moral superiority in handling important international issues. As Chen Jian has suggested, "What the Americans had proposed was a conventional agreement, one that would make Mao's unprecedented acceptance of Nixon's visit look like no more than an ordinary diplomatic venture." Mao wanted to emphasize the drama of the visit and thereby put the Chinese in an "equal" (as defined by Mao), thus a superior, position vis-à-vis the Americans.[93]

On the evening of 24 October, Kissinger was obviously surprised to receive the Chinese draft communiqué. But after he had finished reading this document full of "empty cannons" and had time to digest, Kissinger "began to see that the very novelty of the [Chinese] approach might resolve our perplexities."[94] Kissinger reasoned that "[a] statement of differences would reassure allies and friends that their interests had been defended; if we could develop some common positions, these would then stand out as the authentic convictions of principled leaders."[95] Kissinger and Lord spent a "frantic" night redrafting the Chinese draft with three goals in mind. First, they tried to tone down the fiery nature of the Chinese rhetoric, without overdoing it. Second, they set out to state firmly the U.S. position to balance the Chinese position. Third and perhaps most important, they had to work out the terms and language on Taiwan.[96] By the time of Kissinger's departure on the morning of 26 October, the two sides came to an understanding on all points except the Taiwan section.[97]

Taiwan, without doubt, was the most difficult issue. Kissinger explained to Zhou Enlai that he recognized China's need for some improvement in the U.S. position, but wanted Zhou to take into account U.S. problems. The Nixon administration, he told Zhou, could actually do more than it could say publicly.

The two basic contentious issues in the communiqué language were U.S. views on the resolution of the Taiwan issue and the U.S. military presence in Taiwan and the Taiwan Strait.[98]

Kissinger toned down the language somewhat on both issues and Zhou in turn showed some understanding. Kissinger had devised phraseology, which he admitted he borrowed from State Department language dating back to the ambassadorial talks in the 1950s, to the effect that "The United States side acknowledges that all Chinese on either side of the Taiwan Straits maintain there is but one China and that Taiwan is a province of China. The United States Government does not challenge that position."[99] Zhou accepted this statement, but found the following part of the U.S. position unacceptable:

> It emphasizes its view that the Chinese people should realize their objective by peaceful negotiation. It will support peaceful efforts to reach a resolution of the problem, and will not use its military presence in Taiwan Straits to produce additional obstacles to a peaceful solution. The United States accepts the ultimate objective of the withdrawal of its forces from the Taiwan Straits, and pending that will progressively reduce them as tensions diminish.[100]

Zhou emphasized that the crucial question of the normalization of relations between China and the United States was the Taiwan question. He told Kissinger, "on your formulation there are some superfluous words which complicate the situation." He appealed to Kissinger to indicate the U.S. position more clearly and to make changes along the following line:[101]

> *it hopes that the settlement of the Taiwan question consistent with this position will be achieved through peaceful negotiations and states that it will progressively reduce and finally withdraw all the U.S. troops and military installations from Taiwan.*[102]

Kissinger said it was hard for him to accept Zhou's wording on Taiwan. Zhou did not like to continue working on the wording through the Paris channel.[103] Without getting a mutually acceptable formulation, Kissinger assured Zhou that Alexander M. Haig would come in January with a new formulation.[104] The dates were set for President Nixon's visit: 21 to 28 February 1972.

One of the significant agreements in the draft communiqué was that neither side would seek hegemony in the Asia-Pacific region and both would oppose efforts by other countries to do so.[105] "American hegemony" had been a favorite epithet of the Chinese for the United States. With the United States removed from the list of offenders on this score, in the PRC leadership's view only the Soviet Union remained. The Kissinger trip laid the groundwork for Nixon to meet with Zhou to discuss the political issues, including the most sensitive issue of Taiwan.

One unpleasant distraction, however, was the coincident UN acceptance of the PRC as its member and rejection of a U.S. dual representation proposal.

While Kissinger was in Beijing, the United Nations General Assembly placed the Albanian resolution supporting PRC's membership on the agenda ahead of the U.S. resolutions for dual representation on 22 October. The UN General Assembly voted by an overwhelming majority to let Beijing have China's seat at the UN and expel Taiwan from it on 25 October. This development was immediately propagated throughout China as a "great victory" of Chinese foreign policy as well as an indication of the "significant enhancement" of PRC's international status and reputation.[106]

Critics of the Nixon administration asserted that the timing of the Kissinger visit in the early summer of 1971 had undercut the U.S. position on the dual representation issue and that the second Kissinger visit to Beijing, the announcement of which came just before the final vote in October, refuted the impression of sincerity on the part of the Nixon administration in pushing the dual representation issue.[107] When asked to explain about the coincidence of timing between his departure and the UN vote, Kissinger defended himself by stating that "it was a painful coincidence, but these events were totally unrelated and were planned at a time when we had every reason to believe that the vote would be well after my visit."[108] He explained that the decision to have a second visit was made during his secret trip to Beijing in July, and the general time frame for that visit was decided in the early part of September. During that time, the U.S. believed that the UN vote would be in the middle of November as in previous years. He assured journalists that he never discussed the UN issue with Zhou Enlai. Kissinger argued that he did not believe that his visit would affect the vote of any country that had voted against the U.S. or had abstained.[109] Nevertheless, Kissinger's visits to Beijing facilitated PRC's entry into the UN.

IV

As the summit was approaching, Kissinger and his staff were busy preparing briefing books for Nixon. John Holdridge, Dr. Richard Solomon, formerly of the University of Michigan and the Rand Corporation, and Foreign Service officer Jack Froebe, representing NSC, were responsible for preparing "books," which discussed sensitive matters in Sino-U.S. relations, particularly Vietnam and the Soviet Union. With Kissinger's permission, Alfred Jenkins and Marshall Green of the State Department were also brought into the planning to prepare their own briefing "book" on the working-level issues.[110]

As agreed, on 3 January 1972 an advance team headed by Alexander Haig arrived in Beijing. Its mission was to make technical arrangements for Nixon's visit. From 3 to 10 January, the group visited Beijing, Shanghai, and Hangzhou and surveyed each site that Nixon would visit, including residences, meeting rooms, and locations for various events.[111] The White House had decided to broadcast live the presidential visit. When the two sides discussed the means of televising directly from Beijing to Washington, Zhou Enlai turned down the U.S. offer to pay for the leasing of the ground satellite terminal and television production and transmission equipment, and insisted on the Chinese paying for the expenses.[112] Zhou was especially concerned that China was a sovereign and self-reliant state, and ought not to accept Western compensation. Haig did not insist. The Americans reluctantly accepted the Chinese condition that Nixon ride in Zhou Enlai's car when traveling with the premier and fly in a Chinese airplane on his visit to Hangzhou and Shanghai.[113] When Walters told the Chinese Ambassador Huang Zhen in Paris that no U.S. president had ever traveled in a foreign plane, Huang was pleased at this special concession from the U.S. side, which had great symbolic importance to the Chinese. "He looked as pleased as a Cheshire cat," Walters recalled.[114]

PRC Foreign Ministry developed a plan to receive Haig's team. Wang Hairong communicated further instructions from Mao on the proposed joint communiqué: (1) the original draft must be revised, as the situation in Indochina has changed; (2) the fact that the draft was too lengthy, according to Kissinger, would make Nixon feel embarrassed on the grounds that he did not want to fly 12,000 miles to China to be lectured; (3) since the U.S. wants to do business with us, let us just give them some *drizzle instead of heavy rain*.[115]

On 2 January, Zhou Enlai convened a meeting of the core group of the Foreign Ministry along with other related officials to discuss the revised Foreign Ministry–prepared draft. Zhou instructed that "the wording on Taiwan must not be changed. But they [Americans] can offer different opinions in the section about the international situation." On 3 January, the Foreign Ministry sent two alternative drafts to the decision makers, one with little change in China's statements on international situation, the other with major changes.[116]

Yielding to China's requests on minor issues, the advance team was to secure Beijing's commitment to "big issues," hopefully on the U.S.'s terms. Haig had two private meetings with Zhou Enlai on 3 and 7 January to discuss the India-Pakistan crisis, U.S.-Soviet relations, and Vietnam. He pointed out to Zhou that the events since October underscored the problem even more: Pakistan's defeat at the hand of India and the consequent Soviet action toward the encirclement of China made progress in U.S.-China relations even more imperative for Beijing. Since some leftist elements in the U.S. were joining the right wing to attack Nixon's China initiative—on the grounds that Nixon was alienating Tokyo and/or Moscow—Haig emphasized that both sides should show restraint in the Taiwan section of the communiqué and reinforce the positive sections, such as cultural and scientific exchanges and trade. These positive sections would give an immediate sense of accomplishment as a result of the visit. Zhou seemed persuaded.[117] Haig submitted to Zhou a new American counter-draft for the sensitive Taiwan passage in the proposed final communiqué—the major issue left over from Kissinger's October visit.[118] The Taiwan section now read,

The U.S. side declared: The United States acknowledges that all Chinese on either side of the Taiwan Straits maintain there is but one China and that Taiwan is a province of China. The United States Government does not challenge that position; it reaffirms its abiding interest that the settlement of the Taiwan question be achieved through peaceful negotiations; and it states that it will work to create the conditions which will permit the progressive reduction of the U.S. troops and military installations on Taiwan.[119]

Rather than rejecting this version abruptly, Zhou seemed accommodating. He said he would consult with the U.S. further, but probably needed to consult Mao first. However, Zhou continued, if the United States truly desired to improve Sino-U.S. relations, it should adopt a positive attitude toward settling the Taiwan issue. "If [we have to] yield to certain forces opposed to the normalization of Sino-U.S. relations and backing down from the former position, that will bring no benefit to China and the United States," Zhou declared.[120]

Haig inadvertently offended the Chinese when he delivered an assessment from Nixon and Kissinger about the recently concluded India-Pakistan crisis. During the crisis, Haig told Zhou, the Soviets tried hard to encircle the PRC by inviting Kissinger "to visit Moscow personally on several occasions as a guest of Mr. Brezhnev" and offering "to reach agreements with the U.S. in areas of accidental war and military provocative act." The United States rejected the Soviet offer on two grounds. The first was that the U.S. "could not tolerate use of force to dismantle" Pakistan. Second was that maintaining China's viability was in the fundamental interests of the United States.[121] When Zhou reported the meeting to Mao, the chairman commented: "Why should our viability become America's concern? . . . If China's independence and viability should be protected by the Americans, it is very dangerous [for us]."[122] Mao said that China would adhere to the position of self-reliance.

Finally, Zhou asked Mao whether additional changes should be made in the non-Taiwan sections of the draft communiqué insofar as they seemed acceptable to the United States. Mao answered,

> OK, just forget it. However, if any changes are made, just change "the people desire progress" into "the people desire revolution." They [Americans] are just too afraid of revolution. The more scared they are, the more we want to mention it. In fact, this communiqué fails to cover the basic issue. The basic issue is this: No matter whether it is the United States or China, neither of us could fight simultaneously on two fronts. It is OK to say that you will fight on two, three, four, and five fronts; in fact, no country can do it. Of course, it will not do any good if you write it into the communiqué.[123]

Mao thus sounded out his understandings of Sino-American rapprochement— a mutual need for strategic concentration of their forces to deal with their respective adversaries.

On 7 January, Zhou formally told Haig that he was "greatly surprised" by the American leaders' concern for protecting "China's independence and viability." It was Beijing's firm belief, Zhou asserted, that "no country should ever rely on external forces to maintain its independence and viability," otherwise the dependent country "can only become a protectorate or a colony."[124] As the PRC leaders were determined to maintain China's independence and self-esteem, it was no small wonder that they took the viability issue so seriously.

Zhou also refused to discuss the Vietnam peace process. He defended Hanoi's position in the war. Responding to Haig's charge that the Democratic Republic of Vietnam had "insulted" the United States by its recent attack on American forces, Zhou said that North Vietnam was a victim of the latest U.S. bombing and that China had no choice but to support the DRV. If the United States really wanted to end the war and have its forces completely withdrawn from Vietnam, Zhou went on, it had no reason to reject the reasonable demands of the DRV.[125] However, Zhou seemed to be annoyed by Soviet–North Vietnamese cooperation and indicated that Chinese aid to North Vietnam was the minimum requirement to prevent a deterioration of relations between Beijing and Hanoi.[126] There were indications that China was prepared to face the negative outcome of a worsening of Sino–North Vietnamese relations and closer Moscow-Hanoi ties as a result of the Sino-American rapprochement. In November 1971, when North Vietnamese premier Pham Van Dong visited Beijing, he had one meeting with Mao and three formal talks with Zhou Enlai. In his conversation with Mao on 22 November, Pham Van Dong asked the Chinese government to cancel the planned Nixon trip to China. Mao rejected Pham's request.[127] When Haig told Zhou Enlai on 4 January 1972 that the continuation of the war in Southeast Asia could only provide the Soviet Union an opportunity to increase its influence in Hanoi and to implement its plan to encircle the PRC, Zhou replied that Soviet intervention in Indochina was an "inevitable reaction" to the improvement of Sino-American relations and that China was prepared to "bear the consequences of the Sino-American accommodation."[128]

The Nixon administration, however, did not let slip the possibility of using Beijing to resolve the Vietnam conflict. On the eve of the presidential trip, Nixon and Kissinger tried one more time. On 6 February, through the secret Paris channel, they had proposed that Beijing would arrange a meeting between Kissinger and Le Duc Tho, the North Vietnamese negotiator, on Chinese soil during the Nixon visit. If the meeting took place, the White House promised, the situation in Indochina could be discussed "with generosity and justice."[129] From Nixon's perspective, such a meeting would have been a diplomatic coup, one that would have enabled him to show that he was trying to end the Vietnam War and, in the process, to demonstrate to the American public the concrete benefits that could flow from the opening of China. The White House, however, had not thought about the possible negative impact this demand would have on China's image as a revolutionary state and thus, its ideological leverage with North Vietnam. Within five days, China responded via the Paris channel that it supported North Vietnam and would not be drawn into Hanoi's negotiation with the United States.[130] It is interesting to note that the Chinese and Americans were cordial to each other through the secret Paris channel even when they disagreed. As Walters recorded, after delivering the message, which stated that the Chinese would not help to arrange a meeting between Kissinger and Le Duc Tho, "All of them were obviously a little embarrassed by the harshness of the tone of the note they had handed me."[131]

In private, but never in public, Nixon came to recognize that his opening up to China would not bring about what had been one of its original objectives: that is, China's direct help for a negotiated peace settlement in Vietnam. On 15 February, two days before he departed for China, Nixon wrote down what he planned to tell Zhou Enlai about Vietnam:

> V. Nam:
> 1. We are ending our involvement—
> 2. We had hoped you would help—but now it doesn't matter
> 3. We must end it honorably—+ will.[132]

There can be little doubt that Nixon was disappointed but not totally dismayed at the not-so-helpful Chinese. He seems to have developed more bargaining power early in 1972.

Before Nixon's trip to China, U.S.-Soviet relations had improved as the Kissinger-Gromyko back-channel arms-control talks had culminated in the 20 May 1971 agreement. Early in 1972, the arms-control talks took an important step forward when Moscow agreed to limits on heavy missiles.[133] It was further agreed that following the Beijing summit, Nixon would visit Moscow and presumably announce significant progress in arms control. In contrast, Beijing and Moscow had yet to move beyond media polemics. Thus Washington's negotiating position was bolstered. Early in February, the Nixon administration issued its third annual foreign policy report. It included a long review of the development of U.S. policy toward China. The purpose was to help prepare the American people for the rapprochement with China and to reassure them and others of the continuing U.S. commitment to Taiwan. The report reaffirmed that "our policy is not aimed against Moscow." It stated that the United States would not "use our opening to Peking to exploit Sino-Soviet tensions . . . because it would be self-defeating and dangerous. . . . We will try to have better relations with both countries."[134]

V

Although the Sino-American rapprochement might have been driven by common interests and threats, the actual process toward it, starting from Kissinger's meetings in Beijing with Premier Zhou Enlai, played a significant role. No one could have done a better job than Kissinger in persuading the Chinese to set a new relationship on a strategic or geopolitical basis. His success in achieving that removed any possible serious hurdle that Nixon might have felt compelled to overcome.

Between Kissinger and Zhou Enlai, a framework that would guide future U.S.-USSR-PRC relations was established. Explaining U.S. concerns about Soviet foreign policy, Kissinger looked directly into Zhou's eyes and promised that the Nixon White House would inform Chinese leaders of any U.S.-Soviet arrangement that might affect Chinese interests, something that Washington would do with only its close allies. Kissinger's secret visit to Beijing rendered immediate dividends for the Nixon administration in dealing with Moscow. It seemed that the Kremlin was so impressed with a possible U.S.-China rapprochement that it began to reorient its confrontation with the U.S. The Soviet ambassador to Washington, Anatoly Dobrynin, suddenly was ready to set a date for a Nixon-Brezhnev summit, and Russian negotiators came to an agreement over Western access to Berlin, quieting another crisis point between the two superpowers.[135] Kissinger's triangular diplomacy seemed to have worked. Obviously, the Soviets were concerned about U.S.-China rapprochement as it would reverse the strategic balance in world affairs.[136]

Kissinger did not score high in obtaining Chinese help to bring an end to the Vietnam War. He tried to link China's interest in resolving the Taiwan issue with America's interest in ending the Vietnam War. Although Zhou tacitly suggested his sympathy for and interest in U.S. efforts to avoid a humiliating defeat in Indochina, he made it clear that Beijing would not pressure Hanoi to alter its negotiation position. He, in particular, resisted Kissinger's request that the Chinese influence Hanoi to change its policy on the issue of prisoners of war.[137] There is good reason to assert that Zhou was instructed to do so by Mao, who was probably concerned about his own revolutionary credentials among other national liberation movements around the world. But Kissinger's presence in Beijing might have aroused suspicions in the minds of the Vietnamese leaders. Two days after Kissinger's trip, Zhou made a secret visit to Hanoi in order to assure the North Vietnamese of China's continued support. Obviously worried about U.S.-China rapprochement, the Vietnamese leaders issued an editorial in their party newspaper making pointed allusion to it.[138]

Without having to accept Kissinger's request on Vietnam, however, the Chinese leaders secured much needed, although not completely satisfactory, U.S. assurances regarding Taiwan. The PRC had been trying hard both to prevent Nationalists from attacking the mainland and to ensure that Taiwan would not become independent. The U.S. position was vital to China's cause in this regard. Without U.S. support of the Nationalists, politically and militarily, there would have not been any serious challenge to the Communist regime on the mainland from the Taiwan Strait. Kissinger perfectly understood the Chinese concerns and did assure Zhou that the U.S. would soon disengage itself from Taiwan. More specifically, he said, the Nixon administration would not seek "two Chinas" or a "one China, one Taiwan" policy, would not support Nationalist action against the mainland, and would not support the Taiwan independence movement.[139] Without Kissinger's assurances on Taiwan, it would have been impossible for the Chinese to invite Nixon to China. These commitments were at best "a nod to reality."[140]

Kissinger made these assurances not just on his own, although they were not in line with the official U.S. position announced by the State Department less than three months earlier, that sovereignty over Taiwan was "an unsettled question subject to future international resolution."[141] In effect, the State Department had been exploring possible new approaches to the Taiwan issue since a year and half before. Preparing directives for Stoessel's talks with the Chinese at Warsaw in early 1970, Marshall Green pointed out that the U.S. eventually had "to decide whether we can agree to" the PRC position (Taiwan is part of "one China") "without seriously adversely affecting our relations with and the international position of the ROC."[142] Along these lines, Kissinger's NSC staff, together with the State officials, gradually came up with these general principles on Taiwan and had them confirmed by Nixon.[143] They were not, in short, Kissinger's personal improvisations.

Kissinger, on the other hand, skillfully resisted Zhou Enlai's further demands on Taiwan. During the talks, Zhou presented China's three conditions for normalization. These involved the acknowledgment of the PRC as the sole legitimate government of China and Taiwan as a province of China; the withdrawal of American forces from Taiwan by a fixed deadline; and the abrogation of the 1954 U.S.-ROC Mutual Defense Treaty. Kissinger agreed to the first demand by indicating that the acknowledgment of the PRC as the sole legitimate government could be achieved only in Nixon's second term. He declared that troop reductions could begin once the war in Vietnam ended, and circumvented the third by noting that it was a historical issue and would be solved by history.[144] This is a typical example of the Chinese cultural propensity for reaching agreement on broad and philosophical principles, which Kissinger seems to have understood. In retrospect, there was no fundamental change in the U.S. stance regarding the status of Taiwan. While Zhou had argued that diplomatic normalization depended on U.S. recognition that Taiwan was a province of China, Kissinger successfully avoided a direct response on that point.

During those secret and open talks, the Chinese leaders softened their stance on Taiwan as well. Although the Chinese still regarded Taiwan as the basic issue between the U.S. and the PRC, the Chinese leaders now showed willingness to settle it in due course, and did not insist on its being a precondition for a summit. Neither did China insist on immediate U.S. withdrawal and severance of relations with Taiwan. This was an unusual Chinese compromise. As H. R. Haldeman records in his diary on 13 July 1971 after Kissinger's return from his China trip, "Henry hung very tight on our points apparently. At least the way he tells it, and came out extremely well, in that we got the visit and the announcement set up pretty much the way we want it. It is pretty clear that the Chinese want it just as badly as we do and that makes it easier to negotiate."[145] Indeed, on Taiwan, both Kissinger and Zhou seemed firm but flexible. Therefore, it was a successful example of international negotiation in which the two negotiators tried to accommodate each other's needs in order to reach a solution. Without the so-called "Taiwan concession," the Sino-American rapprochement would not have occurred during the Nixon administration.

At the personal level, both Kissinger and Zhou Enlai deserved credit for the success of the talks. The two men were masters of negotiation. Drawing lessons from the decades-long U.S.-China ambassadorial talks, Kissinger knew that the old approach had not worked and would not work. Therefore, "something more upbeat is required." The thrust of his effort, Kissinger reasoned, was "to establish the right climate."[146] Coming to Beijing after twenty-two years of no high-level direct contact, he was adopting an integrative negotiating approach by trying to split the difference for a win-win agreement in which both sides achieved enough of their goals to feel successful. When holding his first formal talks with Zhou Enlai on 9 July 1971, Kissinger praised China's long history and civilization, and assured Zhou that the U.S. accepted China as a great power with a legitimate role to play in international, and particularly Asian, affairs and that the U.S. bore no hostility toward the Chinese government and people.[147] This was not the usual Western empirical approach to negotiation, which had insisted on specificity in both the conduct and the outcome of negotiations. By adopting the Chinese approach—showing respect and admiration to your hosts—Kissinger succeeded in engaging them. For his part, Zhou Enlai did almost the same thing. Appearing considerate and understanding of the difficulties the Nixon administration was faced in opening up to China, he showed his talent in penetrating issues and caring about the details. Speaking up for the PRC leadership without alienating the Americans, he knew exactly what principles to adhere to and when and how, and, more importantly, he balanced persistence and flexibility very well. Reading between the lines of the available Kissinger-Zhou meeting minutes, one may detect that the two were actually enjoying talking to each other, even though often for long hours.

The visits by Kissinger and Haig set the stage for Nixon to perform. How would Nixon play his part in dealing with the Chinese leaders, Mao and Zhou? How would Mao, a revolutionary and autocratic leader of a large socialist state, treat Nixon, a vehement anticommunist cold warrior?

CHAPTER EIGHT

Summit Talks
Nixon's China Trip,
February 1972

A FTER NEARLY FOUR YEARS of contemplation and secret diplomacy, Richard Nixon was finally en route to China. Toasting his Chinese hosts at the banquet on his last night in China on 27 February 1972, Nixon said, "We have been here a week. This is the week that changed the world."[1] Although that sounds a bit self-congratulatory, Nixon's one week in China no doubt represented a profound turning point in U.S.-China relations. It seemed that the summit diplomacy worked to its best potential. How, then, did Nixon talk with Chinese leaders Mao Zedong and Zhou Enlai? What were the major issues? How were they approached by both sides? Did the leaders make any compromise; if so, why? Was there any secret deal between the two? How did the top leaders overcome the long-sustained mutual suspicions and misperceptions? How did these talks shape the subsequent steps toward U.S.-China rapprochement directly or indirectly? What impact, if any, did the visit have on the overall Cold War international relations?

I

The American public seemed supportive of Nixon's China trip. No American president had ever visited China. Only a handful of Americans had ventured onto the mainland during the previous two decades. The *New York Times* exaggeratedly claimed that more Americans had been to the moon than to China.[2]

Messages flooded into the White House wishing Nixon well. Nixon confided to H. R. Haldeman and Kissinger that the Americans were hopelessly naïve, willing to pay almost any price for peace. Nixon also knew that public naïveté would help him sell the opening up of China.[3] On 17 February, one day before his departure for the China trip, Nixon assured congressional leaders that there were no preconditions requested or granted by either side in the agreement to hold meetings. Instead, he stressed, there would be tough hard bargaining with the Chinese leaders in Beijing. To him, twenty-two years of hostility and no high-level contact would not be swept away in one week of discussion.[4]

On 18 February, Nixon was on his journey across the Pacific to China. He was contemplating his coming meetings with the PRC leaders, with whom America had been engaging in confrontation and hostilities for more than two decades. To prepare for the trip, Nixon had read extensive background materials on China, listened to specialists' advice on how to deal with his Chinese counterparts, and even practiced eating with chopsticks.[5] Nixon wrote down his thoughts. His handwritten notes offer insight into the nature of what Nixon sought and how he viewed the new relationship with Communist China. He used very vivid and direct expressions to define what the American and Chinese governments were trying to obtain from one another. He jotted down notes in his yellow pad:

> What they want:
> 1. Build up their world credentials.
> 2. Taiwan.
> 3. Get U.S. out of Asia.
>
> What we want:
> 1. Indochina (?)[6]
> 2. Communists—to restrain Chicom [Chinese Communist] expansion in Asia.
> 3. In Future—Reduce threat of a confrontation by Chinese Super Power.
>
> What we both want:
> 1. Reduce danger of confrontation and conflict.
> 2. A more stable Asia.
> 3. A restraint on USSR.[7]

Since Kissinger's secret visit to China, the Nixon administration had been trying to link Taiwan and Vietnam in their talks with the Chinese leaders. In the talking points, Kissinger recommended that Nixon tell the Chinese leaders that the U.S. would be ready to end the war in Vietnam. However, as a global power, the U.S. couldn't simply do what Hanoi had insisted on, that is, not only withdraw unconditionally from Vietnam but also replace those with whom the U.S. had worked. The U.S. position was not to maintain any particular government in Saigon; its purpose was to let the political forces in South Vietnam develop freely. It was not possible for the U.S. to help North Vietnam remove the Saigon government. The United States would welcome Beijing's constructive attitude toward the American proposal for ending the war, but it was not a precondition for other understandings between the two countries. Washington would not ask Beijing to stop giving aid to Hanoi.[8] According to Winston Lord, Nixon already knew that Zhou Enlai was "a formidable interlocutor" and that he himself "had to be up to that." Nixon wanted to use the trip to gain Chinese confidence, to project firmness, to induce them to cooperate, and to point out the advantages of cooperation.[9]

In addition to these issues, Nixon was anxious to meet with Mao. He was contemplating how to play his best in the upcoming summit diplomacy. Kissinger and his staff had attempted to give Nixon some insights into the nature of Mao Zedong, the revolutionary leader and founding father of the PRC. No American official had met Mao since Marshall's failed mission in 1946. In his memorandum to Nixon on 5 February, Kissinger explained to Nixon that the summit was unprecedented. Nixon's personal experiences, philosophy, world outlook, and personality were fundamentally different from those of the Chinese leaders.[10] Based on his two previous visits, Kissinger told Nixon that "Mao was the boss, although he left day-to-day administration and tactics to his Prime Minister." Kissinger tried to compare Mao's and Zhou's different styles as well. "Chou will talk on philosophic and historic planes, but his main thrust will be on the concrete substantive issues. . . . Mao is the philosopher, the poet, the grand strategist, the inspirer, the romantic."[11] Kissinger told Nixon that Mao's stature as "one of the 20th century's outstanding political figures" derived from "a combination of personal assertiveness, charismatic self-confidence, and a creative native intelligence." Mao knew where he wanted China to go.[12]

A few days before the China trip, Kissinger reminded Nixon that the Chinese were very different from the Russians. The Russians "are physical" and "wanted to dominate" while the Chinese "really believe that virtue is power." To indicate the importance of the rapprochement with the PRC, Kissinger argued that the United States should "lean toward the Chinese against the Russians" in the next fifteen years. To be more explicit, Kissinger told the president, "We have to play this balance of power game totally unemotionally. Right now, we need the Chinese to correct the Russians, and to discipline the Russians."[13]

During their Hawaii stopover, Kissinger sent Nixon another memo on 19 February, assuring him of the possibility of tangible results for the China trip, but also reminding him of the difficulty and potential possible adverse outcome. He told Nixon, "The crucial factor, however, will be the Chinese judgment of our seriousness and reliability: this litmus test will determine their future policy." Kissinger warned that the Chinese leaders might change course if they couldn't trust Nixon. They might resort to people's diplomacy by "inviting in opposition politicians, dealing with unfriendly private groups and hostile journalists and lambasting us in the United Nations."[14] Kissinger advised Nixon to make clear to the Chinese leaders that he could "be counted up to move ahead surely and steadily." On the other hand, Nixon should make the Chinese fully aware of U.S. international and domestic imperatives. The Communists "will only respect strength and resoluteness,"[15] Kissinger reminded the president. Taking Kissinger's advice, Nixon wrote down notes for his talk with Mao:

> Treat him (as Emperor)
> 1. Don't quarrel [*sic*].
> 2. Don't praise him (too much).
> 3. Praise the people—art, ancient.
> 4. Praise poems.
> 5. Love of country.[16]

Kissinger had even offered Nixon a way to find common cause with Mao. Kissinger told Nixon on 15 February that "Mao carries a deep personal distrust of intellectuals."[17] "RN and Mao, men of the people," Nixon wrote to himself; both he and Mao had had "problems with intellectuals."[18] Nixon couldn't rival Mao as a popular figure in his own country. Nevertheless, he still felt nervous and was worried that he might be subjected to the humiliation previously encountered by Western barbarians who had journeyed to the court of the Chinese emperor in an earlier age.[19] Nixon wrote down how Mao would evaluate him when they met. He wrote:

> 1. What is he like inside?
> Strong
> Decisive
> Spartan
> Earnest
> 2. "Is he strong so that I must respect him or weak so that I can attack him?"
> 3. Does he have determination & shrewdness?
> 4. Is American Culture strong or weak?[20]

However, it was not Mao but the fundamental strategy of his China trip that was most prominent in Nixon's thinking. Kissinger had also advised Nixon that it was Mao's and Zhou's pragmatism that had led them to deal with one "barbarian" nation in order to control another, but the relationship would not develop unless the Chinese believed they could depend on Washington. Because the United States would be making important commitments on withdrawal of forces from Taiwan and normalization of relations, Kissinger explained to Nixon that "our basic task is to get across to them that we *can* make certain moves they want in the future because it is in our own self-interest, and that we *will* make such a move because we are reliable."[21] While preparing what he would say to Mao Zedong and Zhou Enlai, as James Mann observes, "Nixon came up with an idea that would have special resonance in China two decades later, after the end of the Cold War."[22] This was what Nixon told Zhou in their first meeting on 22 February 1972, "in terms of the safety of these nations which are not superpowers in the world, they will be much safer if there are two superpowers, rather than just one."[23]

II

With respect to the reception of Nixon's party, the Chinese government was very concerned and careful on general principles and details. On numerous occasions, Zhou stressed, "We are a sovereign nation. Nothing should be allowed to impinge upon our sovereignty." He especially instructed on 2 December 1971 that the reception of Nixon "must reflect the principles, styles, and strict disciplines of the proletarian class."[24] On 8 February, at a meeting attended by senior officials from Beijing, Shanghai, and Zhejiang, the locations where Nixon would visit, Zhou issued guidelines for receiving Nixon: "Neither cold nor warm; neither humble nor haughty; receiving him with politeness; and not imposing our opinions on him."[25]

At 11:30 A.M. on 21 February 1972, Nixon's party arrived in Beijing. Nixon would not let the presentation of the arrival go unplanned. Nixon and Haldeman had decided that the president should be alone when the television cameras filmed his first encounter with Zhou Enlai. When the time came, a burly aide blocked the aisle of *The Spirit of '76* (Nixon changed *Air Force One* to the new name shortly before this trip). Nixon and his wife stepped down the steps alone. When he reached the bottom step, he made a point of extending his hand as he walked toward Zhou. This became a famous photograph. Here, Nixon intentionally made use of this important handshake with Zhou to correct the wrong that Dulles had inflicted on the Chinese in the mid-1950s.[26] Zhou was also conscious of the importance of the handshake, and he had to act properly. He was standing there, smiling, but not in great hurry and eagerness.[27] "When our hands met, one era ended and another began," Nixon recorded in his memoirs.[28] On their way to the state guesthouse, Zhou told Nixon, "Your handshake came over the vastest ocean in the world—twenty-five years of no communication."[29]

The Americans felt the welcoming ceremony was formal and correct, but chilly.[30] There were about one hundred Chinese officials and social celebrities at the airport to meet the Americans, including Guo More, vice chairman of the National People's Congress; Li Xiannian, senior vice premier; Marshal Ye Jianying; Wu De, mayor of Beijing; and Ji Pengfei, foreign minister. Two flags, one Chinese and one American, flew over the reception area, and the band played both national anthems. Nixon inspected a military honor guard, with contingents from each of the three People's Liberation Armies. There were no other spectators. The absence of spectators was mainly due to political reasons, as there had been no formal diplomatic relations between the two countries for so many years. The Chinese leaders decided to give a low-key welcome to the American president.[31]

The uneasiness of the Americans soon dissipated. Shortly after Nixon settled down at the state guesthouse, Zhou Enlai informed him that Mao was ready to meet him. When the U.S. party departed for China from Andrews Air Force Base, they did not have an agreed time for the Nixon-Mao meeting. By not confirming the schedule for the president, Nixon aides believed, the Chinese wanted to keep the Americans off balance.[32] This was a typical practice of the Chinese emperor, indicating that the emperor (Mao) was the head of the Central Kingdom and that the U.S. was coming to pay "tribute." Nixon recalled that as soon as he entered Mao's study, his worries and anxieties vanished "when he reached out his hand, and I reached out mine, and he held it for about one minute."[33] This one-minute handshake symbolized the end of hostilities between China and the United States that had begun more than twenty-five years earlier with the failure of General Marshall's attempted mediation and the renewed outbreak of China's civil war.

The meeting between the Chinese chairman and the U.S. president lasted a little over an hour and seems not to have had a central theme.[34] Actually, it could be seen to have laid down definitive guidelines for the new Sino-American relationship. Mao refused to get into details on any specific issues, declaring that he would only "discuss philosophical questions."[35] The transcript of the conversation shows that Mao wanted to set the direction for the coming Sino-American talks. He hoped to explore these issues from philosophical, long-term, principled, macro, and strategic perspectives.[36] It appears that Mao was eager to demonstrate his broad vision, showing the Americans that not only was he in total control of matters concerning China, but also he occupied a privileged position to comprehend and deal with *anything* of significance in world affairs. In a sense, what was most meaningful for the chairman was not the specific issues he would discuss with the U.S. president but the simple fact that "Nixon and Kissinger came to *his* study and listened to *his* teachings."[37] Mao probably was revealing some of his truest feelings when he said that he had "only changed a few places in the vicinity of Beijing."[38] Yet, at the bottom of his heart, he also must have believed that he had indeed changed the world. Otherwise, the "head of international imperialism" would not have come to visit his country in the first place.[39]

On the question of trade, Mao conveyed his decision in the form of an explanation of Chinese slowness in responding to the Nixon administration's easing of controls during the previous two years. China, he said, had been "bureaucratic" in insisting that the solution of major issues precede the resolution of smaller issues like trade and reciprocal visits of private individuals. "Later on, I saw you were right, and we played table tennis." In this disarming, understated way Mao gave his green light to progress on those matters at the summit. Other

Mao Zedong and Richard Nixon shake hands at Zhongnanhai, Beijing, on 21 February 1972. *National Archives (NPMP, 8528-01).*

One of the private sessions between the U.S. and Chinese negotiators during Nixon's China trip in February 1972. *National Archives (NPMP, C8546-13A).*

views were thrown out seemingly offhandedly, to avoid loss of face if Nixon's visit failed. Taiwan was placed on a subsidiary level as a relatively minor internal Chinese dispute. In a discussion of Chinese security concerns, Mao made his point by omission: the threat of American or Chinese aggression, he opined, was "relatively small. . . . You want to withdraw some of your troops back on your soil; ours do not go abroad." By a process of elimination, it was the threat from the Soviet Union that was to be feared. At the same time he had in a few words ("ours do not go abroad") touched on a whole list of American preoccupation. He eliminated the U.S. nightmare of Chinese interventions in the Vietnam War. He was also disclaiming any Chinese wish to challenge vital American interests in Japan and South Korea. But what about the ideological struggle? Mao disposed of the ringing anti-American slogans that had marked his rule with equal facility. Laughing uproariously, he dismissed them as the "sound [of] a lot of big cannons." In sixty-five minutes, Mao succeeded in providing a set of signposts for his American guests and the Chinese bureaucracy.[40]

Mao had been suffering from heart problems and a lung infection, which he had refused to allow his doctors to treat until 1 February. Mao, for whom Nixon's visit would confirm China's "equal" position in the world of nations, was eager to meet with the U.S. president. As a result, Mao agreed to undergo physical therapy so he could walk and be in a condition to receive visitors.[41] For this eventful day, Mao put on a new suit and a new pair of shoes. His hair was freshly cut and his face cleanly shaved. He kept asking his aides for details of the exact arrival time and subsequent schedule. Awaiting the arrival of his guest, he was gripped by greater anxiety.[42]

Nixon reminded Mao, "What brings us together is a recognition of a new situation in the world and a recognition on our part that what is important is not a nation's internal political philosophy. What is important is its policy toward the rest of the world and toward us."[43] Nixon and Kissinger may have gotten what they wanted out of it — the opportunity to leave China's "fanatic" but pragmatic leaders with an impression of "our seriousness and reliability." Nixon, perhaps taking Kissinger's advice, made statements that he hoped to encourage Mao and Zhou to view him as reliable, even though they had no reason to trust him: "You will find I never say something I cannot do. And I will always do more than I can say."[44] Indeed, not long after Nixon had left Beijing, he ordered the withdrawal of nuclear-capable F-4 Phantom bomber units from Taiwan to validate his pledge to withdraw U.S. military force from the island.[45]

Whatever the restraint of the initial reception, the fact that Mao met Nixon within the first couple of hours of his arrival was truly significant. The following day, the Chinese official paper *Renmin Ribao* carried the photograph of Chairman Mao's meeting with President Nixon. It sent a clear signal to the world and to the Chinese people that Mao personally was behind this visit and also showed the historic importance of the event. Mao even told Nixon at the closing of the meeting, "It is all right to talk well and also all right if there are no agreements, because what use is there if we stand in deadlock? Why is it that we must be able to reach results?"[46] Mao officially put his seal of approval on the improvement of relations between China and the U.S. and, in effect, gave his blessing to progress on bilateral issues, even before major issues such as Taiwan were clearly decided. The common Soviet threat and Chinese strategic concerns had compelled the chairman to sidestep the Taiwan issue.[47] For Nixon, the summit with Mao instantly put the whole China trip on a higher plain. It was the highlight of the week. No matter what was achieved on the diplomatic front, Nixon had gotten the image he wanted—the first meeting ever with Mao Zedong by an American president, embarked on a quest for peace.

At the state dinner for the entire American party that evening, Zhou Enlai proclaimed that despite ideological differences, normal state-to-state relations could be established on the basis of the five principles of coexistence. However, no element of controversy such as Vietnam and Taiwan was mentioned.[48] Nixon's reply was more emotional. He stressed that the two sides had common interests, which transcended the ideological gulf. He even quoted from a poem by Mao that "a journey of ten thousand *li* begins with but a single step" and that one should "seize the day, seize the hour," implying that he was looking forward to the continued growth of Sino-U.S. ties and a better future.[49]

While Nixon was in China, there were three levels of talks between American and the Chinese leaders. The first level was the Nixon-Zhou talks. They held four talks in Beijing and one in Shanghai. President and Mrs. Nixon spent the mornings sightseeing, and after lunch Nixon talked with Zhou Enlai and his advisers in a conference room at the Great Hall of the People. In the evenings, the Nixons attended entertainment functions, after which the president was briefed on the day's progress or on the latest important revisions to the draft of the joint communiqué.[50]

The second-level negotiation was between William Rogers and Ji Pengfei. Secretary of State Rogers and Marshall Green met with Foreign Minister Ji Pengfei and Special Assistant to the Premier Xiong Xianghui in Rogers's *Diaoyutai* state guesthouse conference room to negotiate bilateral problems. These included the repatriation of American citizens remaining in China (there were still a few in early 1972), and the question of Chinese assets frozen by the U.S. from the time China entered the Korean War and American property confiscated by the Chinese following the Nationalist defeat in 1949. Rogers's party included people who were well qualified to address these questions: Marshall Green, Al Jenkins, and Charles (Chas.) Freeman. Freeman was a Foreign Service officer fluent in Chinese, acting as an interpreter for the president and the secretary.[51] When Rogers underscored the importance of establishing permanent organizations, trade and travel offices to promote the relations, Ji indicated it was very difficult to discuss other U.S.-China problems before the Taiwan issue was resolved.[52]

The third-level negotiation was the Kissinger-Qiao talks. Kissinger held ongoing meetings with Vice Foreign Minister Qiao Guanhua to work out details of the communiqué wordings. Anything they would work out would be cleared when necessary with Nixon, and separately with Zhou Enlai and the CCP Politburo; the separate versions and responses had again to be reconciled with the opposite side.[53] It was at this level that "We had really tough negotiations on Taiwan, day after day, right down to the wire," recalled Winston Lord.[54]

III

Nixon and Zhou Enlai discussed foreign policy considerations and international issues from their own perspectives, focusing particularly on matters of concern to both sides, such as mutual problems in relations with Taiwan, Vietnam, the Soviet Union, India, and Japan.[55] Following Kissinger's recommendation, Nixon tried to acquaint Zhou with his thoughts and to know why he believed certain things to be important.[56] He repeatedly stressed to Zhou that it was not philosophy, not friendship, but national security that brought the two countries together.[57] With the complete declassification of Nixon's conversations with Zhou and Nixon's handwritten notes he made before and during his China trip, we now have a much better understanding of how Nixon and Zhou negotiated.[58]

Taiwan was, of course, the first issue on the agenda. Nixon was engrossed in the possibility of getting China's help in obtaining a peace settlement in Vietnam and was ready to make concessions on Taiwan. He was also aware that he could not take immediate action. As Nixon's handwritten notes indicate:

> *Taiwan = Vietnam = trade off*
> 1. Your people expect action on Taiwan.
> 2. Our people expect action on Vietnam.
>   Neither can act immediately—But both are inevitable—Let us not embarrass each other.[59]

Referring to Taiwan and Vietnam as "irritants,"[60] Nixon tried to explain to Zhou how the United States and China might collaborate in dealing with the other large powers in Asia: the Soviet Union, India, and Japan. It would be easier for Washington and Beijing to work together if they could smooth over Taiwan and Vietnam. But Nixon stressed, "We can't handle [Taiwan and Vietnam] in [a] way that destroys or weakens our position of leadership."[61]

Zhou's refusal to link Vietnam with Taiwan made the latter a touchier subject. The Taiwan issue needed to be addressed not just in the private talks between Nixon and Zhou, but also in the formal communiqué. On 2 February, almost three weeks before the trip, Secretary of State Rogers presented to Nixon an analysis on U.S. policy toward Taiwan. Abandoning its long-held position that Taiwan's status was "unsettled," the State Department paper sug-

gested Nixon should do nothing to close the door to the idea that Taiwan
might eventually be reunited with the rest of China. It urged the president to
"take note" of the Beijing position that there was only one China. The president should "encourage the establishment of some direct contacts between
the PRC and Taiwan," and "emphasize the economic aspect of Taiwan's separate existence over the political and military." It also speculated that Beijing's
position on Taiwan might soften as the Republic of China ceased to be a cred-
ible rival and thus Sino-U.S. antagonism would subside. The State Department paper predicted that "the time may come when either Taiwan's existence as a separate entity will be recognized as a *fait accompli* by the PRC, or
the island undergoes some form of peaceful integration with the PRC."[62] It
was obvious that Rogers's report underestimated the importance of the Taiwan issue to the PRC and the symbolic as well as substantial importance to the
Chinese leaders.

Kissinger, on the other hand, did not want Nixon to go that far on Taiwan.
The talking points prepared by Kissinger and his staff advised Nixon "to set the
tone of the meeting," by taking "the initiative in confirming personally certain
assurances which I gave them last year with respect to the status of Taiwan, our
willingness to normalize relations with the PRC, and the role of Japan."[63] Nixon
went further on the Taiwan question in his private talks than in the public communiqué. As the notes for his opening presentation to Zhou Enlai indicate:

> *Taiwan:*
>   I reiterate what our policy is
>   1. Status is determined—one China, Taiwan is part of China—
>   2. Won't support Taiwan independence
>   3. *Try* to restrain Japan—
>   4. Support peaceful resolution
>   5. Will seek normalization—[64]

These were the five assurances that Nixon made to Zhou at their first private meeting on the afternoon of 22 February. Nixon stressed to Zhou that China could
count on these statements no matter what the U.S. might say about other subjects.
These were such important issues that Nixon elaborated on each to Zhou:

> Principle one. There is one China, and Taiwan is a part of China. There
> will be no more statements made—if I can control our bureaucracy—to the
> effect that the status of Taiwan is undetermined.
>   Second, we have not and will not support any Taiwan independence
> movement.
>   Third, we will, to the extent we are able, use our influence to discourage
> Japan from moving into Taiwan as our presence becomes less, and also dis-
> courage Japan from supporting a Taiwan independence movement. I will
> only say here I cannot say what Japan will do, but so long as the U.S. has
> influence with Japan—we have in this respect the same interests as the

Prime Minister's government — we do not want Japan moving in on Taiwan and will discourage Japan from doing so.

The fourth point is that we will support any peaceful resolution of the Taiwan issue that can be worked out. And related to the point, we will not support any military attempts by the Government on Taiwan to resort to a military return to the Mainland.

Finally, we seek the normalization of relations with the People's Republic. We know that the issue of Taiwan is a barrier to complete normalization, but within the framework I have previously described we seek normalization and we will work toward that goal and will try to achieve it.[65]

Nixon tried to convince Zhou that, due to domestic constraints, he could not "abandon his old friends" on Taiwan right now. He told Zhou there was certain force in the U.S. who "believes that no concessions at all should be made regarding Taiwan."[66] He restated his intention to normalize relations with the PRC during his second term in office.[67] In a later conversation between Nixon and Zhou on 24 February, Nixon assured Zhou again that the United States would not support Taiwanese independence, but he was also careful to note that his administration could not use force to prevent it if it happened.[68]

Zhou, however, did not seem altogether convinced. He responded, "the Taiwan question is the crucial question between our two countries, and here I cannot but add that it was the result of a mistake by former President Truman."[69] Zhou told Nixon that the PRC would strive for peaceful liberation of Taiwan, but the Nationalists might not want a peaceful resolution. "What will we do if they don't want it?" asked Zhou. Zhou reminded Nixon, "it would be good if the liberation of Taiwan could be realized in your next term of office. . . . Of course, that's our internal affair."[70] Zhou also promised even after Taiwan was returned to China, the PRC would not build a nuclear base in Taiwan and not use Taiwan against Japan.[71]

Nixon emphasized, "my goal is normalization with the People's Republic. I realize that solving the Taiwan problem is indispensable to achieving that goal." The direction for normalization of relations is settled.[72] Therefore, the problem now "is not in what we are going to do, the problem is what we are going to say about it."[73] Nixon attempted further to persuade Zhou by saying,

I must be able to go back to Washington and say that no secret deals have been made between the Prime Minister and myself on Taiwan. So what I must do is to have what we would call "running room" which the communiqué language I hope will provide, which will not make Taiwan a big issue in the next two or three months and next two, three, or four years. So I can do the things to move us toward achieving our goal.[74]

Zhou replied that he understood that there should be some "running room," and no time limit. Having succeeded in persuading Zhou to accept his interpretation, Nixon tried to clarify his points. He declared, "I cannot, for the reasons just mentioned, now make a secret deal and shake hands and say that within the second term it will be done. If I did that, I would be at the mercy of the press if they asked the question."[75]

Nixon was careful not to arouse excessive expectations from the Chinese side. He was aware of his difficulty in realizing normalization with the PRC. Nixon had been preoccupied with finding the right "language which will meet the Prime Minister's need" and also would not give opponents ammunition to attack him after his return. Otherwise, "it will make it very difficult to deliver on the policy which I have already determined I shall follow."[76] For this reason, Nixon had written the following in his notes:

> *Can we deliver?*
> 1. Reduce troops—yes
> 2. But if it appears we sold out Taiwan Left egged on by Soviet & Right will make it an issue—
> 3. Must say we keep our commitments; no secret deals—but I know our interests require normalization and it will occur.[77]

The "no secret deals" wording would later become the basis for Nixon's and Kissinger's public commitments and press briefings about the trip.

Vietnam was another tough issue. Zhou had singled out Indochina as the most "urgent" issue in the relations. During their first meeting on 22 February, Zhou stressed to Nixon that Indochina was the crucial question for the relaxation of tensions in the Far East. He tried hard to persuade Nixon to agree to a "total withdrawal." "The war is going on there and people are dying every day,"[78] Zhou continued. Although the question of Taiwan was very important for U.S.-China relations, China was willing to wait on Taiwan. But China had the obligation to give the Indo-Chinese people assistance if the war continued, although this did not mean that China would intervene in their internal affairs.[79] Zhou stressed again that China insisted on total U.S. withdrawal from Indochina without "leaving a tail" of advisers or technicians behind. China concentrated on the military questions, saying that only the Indo-Chinese people should take care of their own political problems.[80] Therefore, China would like to see Indochina removed as a distortion in U.S.-China relations and as an issue for Soviet exploitation. Nixon told Zhou that he agreed with Zhou and had offered to withdraw all Americans and to have a ceasefire throughout Indochina if he could get all U.S. prisoners back. He agreed that the political decision should be made by the Indo-Chinese people without outside interference. But the U.S. could not consent to remove the South Vietnamese government as requested by North Vietnam.[81]

During the meeting on 22 February, Zhou appealed to Nixon to withdraw U.S. armed forces from Vietnam, and he found brilliant ways of deflecting their eagerness for Chinese help in bringing about a settlement. As James Mann has suggested, Zhou "played to Nixon's sense of grandeur by saying that French President Charles DeGaulle, whom Nixon revered, had been right to withdraw from Algeria."[82] Zhou also appealed to Nixon's anxiety over the Soviet Union by suggesting that the U.S. "should take bold action on Vietnam, or otherwise the Soviet Union benefits [from a protracted war]."[83] Obviously, Zhou was using his power of persuasion. He told Nixon, "if the U.S. Government would take a very bold move in Indochina you would gain very good feelings on the part of the Indochinese people."[84]

Nixon replied that he respected Zhou's views and had offered to withdraw all Americans and to have a cease-fire covering all Indochina if he could get all U.S. prisoners back. He agreed that political decisions should be made by the Indo-Chinese people without outside interference. But the U.S. could not consent to removing the South Vietnamese government as requested by North Vietnam. Nixon argued, as the U.S. was a world power, it could not "get out and at the same time join those who have been our enemies to overthrow those who have been our allies." This would do great harm to U.S. prestige and honor, he stressed.[85] He insisted on bringing about an honorable end to the war.

Zhou handled the Vietnam issue, furthermore, "by touching Nixon's rawest nerve, his fear and loathing of his Democratic opponents."[86] The Democrats had "put us on [the] spot," Zhou told Nixon, and "have come to China to settle Vietnam." Zhou assured Nixon, "Of course, [that is] impossible."[87] Zhou might want to remind Nixon that China still could deal with the Democrats. It was also an implicit warning to Nixon not to make the same mistake as the Democrats by assuming that China would help the United States in reaching a settlement on Vietnam.

Nixon's handwritten notes show that Zhou assured Nixon that Chinese policies toward Vietnam were "different from [those regarding] Korea." This statement further eased American fears that China might send its troops to fight in Vietnam as it had in Korea. President Truman had compelled Chinese intervention in Korea by sending the Seventh Fleet to Taiwan Strait and pressing toward the Yalu River. Zhou told Nixon on 22 February that America had been more careful about China in the Vietnam War than it had been in Korea.[88]

China still needed to maintain its revolutionary credentials in the Communist world. Thus, Zhou's consistent private line had been that he wished the U.S. well in the peace negotiations, but that a settlement was entirely up to Hanoi and Washington.[89] On 24 February, Nixon reaffirmed that he understood China's problem on the Vietnam issue and that the U.S. would settle Vietnam in its own way. He hoped, however, that China would not encourage the North Vietnamese to refuse to negotiate with the United States.[90] This was all that Nixon could get from Zhou on Vietnam. The impression that Nixon and Kissinger drew from the talks was that China gave highest priority to advancing its relationship with

Washington. In the words of Kissinger, "We indeed understood each other; the war in Vietnam would not affect the improvement of our relations."[91]

The Soviet Union was one of the principal subjects. At the beginning of his first meeting with Zhou Enlai on 22 February 1972, Nixon promised that Kissinger would give a briefing to the Chinese officials about what Nixon termed "sensitive info" and that Kissinger would also brief them after the U.S. talks with the Soviet Union.[92] Newly declassified records confirm that the next day, in a three-hour meeting with Vice Foreign Minister Qiao Guanhua, with Marshal Ye Jianying in attendance, Kissinger told the Chinese about Soviet military deployments against mainland China and about the state of negotiations between Washington and Moscow.[93]

Nixon's handwritten notes for his meeting with Zhou show that he made a series of points and assurances about the Soviets:

> *Russia:*
> 1. Maintain balance of power—
> 2. Restrain their expansion (if our interests are involved)
> 3. Try to reduce tension between us
> 4. Not make them irritated at you—
> 5. Make no deals with them we don't offer to you—
> 6. Will inform you on all deals[94]

The talking points for Nixon-Kissinger's briefing to the Chinese on the "sensitive" information regarding the Soviet Union indicate that America had two basic objectives in discussing the Soviet issue with the Chinese leaders. First, America planned to utilize Chinese worries about the Soviet Union to gain Chinese assistance on other issues. Kissinger had earlier suggested that Nixon should make clear the Soviet encirclement of China and tell the Chinese that the U.S. would try to help divert Soviet pressure on the PRC. Kissinger advised Nixon to avoid mentioning that the PRC needed U.S. protection. The PRC could express contempt for Russia, but would never admit fear. As realists, in Kissinger's judgment, the Chinese would appreciate the counterweight the U.S. could provide in Asia and in other areas. Second, Nixon should assure the Chinese leaders that the U.S. would not choose sides in the Sino-Soviet dispute. The U.S. would not collude with Moscow against China, and at the same time, China would have no veto on U.S. dealings with Moscow. There can be no doubt that Nixon and Kissinger believed that the successful U.S.-China summit in Beijing would have a favorable impact on the United States' position vis-à-vis the Soviet Union.[95]

Through their presentation, Nixon and Kissinger attempted both to prepare China for the possibility of Soviet-American agreements on arms control and to ease any lingering Chinese fear that the United States and the Soviet Union would collude against China. They were addressing China's fears of a Soviet invasion by declaring that the United States would, at least within limits, seek to stop Soviet expansion. In the meantime, they were giving China an incentive to go along with improvements in Soviet-American relations: the United States would offer China whatever it gave to the Soviets.[96]

In response, Zhou stated China's four-point policy toward the Soviet Union. First, China would not provoke Russia; second, should the Soviets invade Chinese territory, China would fight back; third, the Chinese meant what they said; fourth, if the Soviets launched air attacks against China, the Chinese would fight back. Nixon assured Zhou that it was not in U.S. interests to see the Soviet Union and China at war, as war between major powers could never be contained.[97]

Nixon and Zhou Enlai discussed other power relations, including those with India and Japan. Nixon had, in effect, outlined how American and Chinese leaders should deal with the countries on China's periphery in his talking-point preparation. On India, Nixon's notes show that his presentation was rather brief:

> India:
> 1. Will go in tandem
> 2. We should balance Russia —[98]

As indicated in the talking points, the United States regarded South Asia as the one region in which the PRC and the U.S. had some similar interests.[99] The United States would coordinate its policies with China toward the subcontinent and had indeed done so during the India-Pakistan War in the previous year. In his talks with Zhou, Nixon made it known that the U.S. would continue to support Pakistan. The Soviets were assisting India with military equipment; therefore, Nixon was going to provide Pakistan with "substantial amounts of economic assistance" to enable Pakistan to acquire arms from other sources. In addition, Nixon informed Zhou that the U.S. would soon recognize Bangladesh, as requested by Pakistan's president, Zulfikar Ali Bhutto. This measure would counter Indian and Soviet influence, but in the meantime, the U.S. would also try to improve relations with India so as not to leave the field to Moscow.[100]

Japan turned out to be a more sensitive subject. The talking points Kissinger and his aides had prepared for Nixon admitted that both China and the United States had difficulties with Japan. The suggested approach for Nixon was that the "thought you will want to plant in the minds of the Chinese is that a Japan without the U.S. in the picture could be much more dangerous to them than a Japan preserving the basic aspects of the present U.S. relationship."[101] Indeed, in the week before his arrival in Beijing, Nixon had carefully prepared what he would say to the Chinese about Japan, which had so brutally invaded and occupied China less than four decades earlier, but now was an American ally. Nixon and Kissinger were meticulous with every word. "Don't say, 'We oppose rearmament of Japan,'" Kissinger, for example, inculcated in Nixon in one of their prep sessions, but rather "We oppose [a] nuclear Japan."[102]

Nixon's principal objective was to preserve America's bases and troops and its nuclear protection for Japan. The troop deployments in Japan were to be one of the cornerstones of America's continued presence and military power in Asia as the United States slowly withdrew its forces from Vietnam and gave Asian allies more responsibility for their own defense. Nixon and Kissinger were also worried about the return of Okinawa to Japan. The Japanese government had insisted upon the removal of nuclear weapons from Okinawa, although Nixon had obtained assurances that the United States could reintroduce them in an emergency. The PRC had been vehemently opposed to the American presence in Japan for more than two decades. Nixon and Kissinger, therefore, were seeking Chinese acceptance of, and accommodation to, the American military alliance with Japan. In answering Zhou's criticism of the U.S.-Japan security treaty, Nixon asked the Chinese premier to ponder the alternative—a Japan completely uncoupled from its American anchor. "Do we tell the 2nd most prosperous nation to go it alone—or do we provide a shield?" Nixon asked Zhou. Was not a "U.S. Japan policy with a U.S. veto" less dangerous than a "Japan only policy"? Nixon tried to encourage Zhou to take a more positive view of the U.S.-Japan security relationship, which he deemed to be for a "peaceful, independent, and neutral Japan."[103]

Nixon, as his handwritten notes show, aimed to explore the Chinese worry about the implications of Japan's growing economic power. Zhou Enlai had already told Kissinger that "Japan's feathers have grown on its wings and it is about to take off." He had asked Kissinger, "Can the U.S. control the 'wild horse' of Japan?"[104] China was especially worried that the United States, while withdrawing its own troops from Taiwan, might encourage the Japanese to station its forces on the island. A feasible solution was to work out an understanding with China that the United States would protect Japan but would restrain both its military development and its political influence in Asia. Nixon wrote this note in Hawaii as he was en route to China:

> Best to provide nuclear shield—
> 1. To keep Japan from building its own.
> 2. To have influence for U.S.
> We oppose Japan "stretching out its hands" to Korea, Taiwan, Indochina.[105]

These themes were the basis of Nixon's message to Zhou about Japan in their first talk. Nixon's notes for the meetings state that "our friendship with Japan is *in your* interests—not *against*" [Nixon's emphasis]. Nixon also raised the specter of "a very great danger" concerning Japan, a danger that he described as "Korea, Taiwan." That was an allusion to the prospect that Japan, if not controlled by the United States, could regain its once-dominant influence in these parts of Northeast Asia,[106] certainly a dire prospect for China. Newly declassified files show that Nixon made a general commitment on 23 February

that the United States would "restrain the Japanese from going from economic expansion to military expansion."[107] He reiterated his pledge that Washington would use its "influence" to "discourage" Japanese intervention in
South Korea.[108]

IV

Taiwan not only was a touchy issue in the private talks, but also had to be addressed in the formal communiqué. The climax of Nixon's "journey for peace"
was to be a joint U.S.-China communiqué that served to herald a new era of
relations. One of the main challenges was to find a mutually acceptable expression of America's stand toward the linkage between Washington's agreement to
withdrawal of U.S. troops from Taiwan and Beijing's commitment to a peaceful
settlement of the Taiwan issue.

The Americans agreed that Taiwan was not an "international dispute" between the Americans and the Chinese but an "internal matter" for the Chinese
to settle.[109] Chinese officials sought to nail down an American commitment to
withdrawing all U.S. troops from Taiwan, preferably within a fixed time period.
Nixon and Kissinger wanted a conditional withdrawal upon an end of the war
in Vietnam, a linkage that would give China an incentive to help end the
conflict in Indochina. The Americans also hoped for language about a "peaceful settlement" in Taiwan, in a way that would prevent China from trying to
take the island by force, and more importantly, would pacify the Taiwan sym-
pathizers or lobbyists in the United States.[110]

China wanted the United States to say it merely hoped for, but did not insist
upon, a peaceful resolution to the Taiwan issue. The U.S. stated, "It reaffirmed
its abiding interests" in the peaceful settlement of the Taiwan question. The
problem of U.S. troops in Taiwan had been the most important item addressed
at the 26 May 1971 Politburo meeting, which emphasized that "All U.S. armed
forces and military installation should be withdrawn from Taiwan and the Taiwan Strait area in a given period."[111] Having already failed to set up a time limit
for U.S. troop withdrawal from Taiwan, Chinese negotiators were reluctant to
make any more compromises. They even raised the possibility of excluding
from the communiqué a discussion of cooperation in exchanges and trade, and
even foregoing a communiqué if the two sides could not reach agreement on
the wording of the Taiwan section.[112]

On the morning of 24 February, Qiao Guanhua suggested a formulation.
"The U.S. side . . . hopes that the Taiwan question will be settled by the Chinese themselves through peaceful negotiations. It will progressively reduce
and firmly withdraw all the U.S. troops and military installations from Taiwan."[113] But Kissinger told Qiao he still could not accept this wording on
Taiwan as he and Nixon would be attacked by conservatives on the grounds

that they sold out Taiwan."[14] This might have simply been Kissinger's tactic. The two sides did not easily back down from their positions.

Gradually, the negotiators were able to make some progress. On the afternoon of 24 February, Kissinger suggested the idea of separating the two problems—the final objective of total withdrawal and U.S. willingness to withdraw troops progressively in the interval, which up to then had been in the same sentence. Kissinger's proposal was to tie the final withdrawal to the premise of peaceful settlement, and to link the progressive reduction of forces to the gradual diminution of "tension in the area."[15] Qiao Guanhua made a counterproposal. He preferred to speak of the "prospect" of a peaceful settlement, rather than "premise," claiming that it had a more active and more bilateral connotation; "premise" sounded like a unilateral imposition by Washington. Although not yet ready to accept linking U.S. withdrawal to its other requirement, and the diminution of "tension in the area,"[16] Qiao's proposal certainly closed the gap between the two.

After a few rounds of bargaining, the two sides came very close to a mutually acceptable draft communiqué. Now the United States would regard the withdrawal of all American forces from Taiwan as its "ultimate objective." It would "progressively reduce" these forces "as the tension in the area diminishes." Such a characterization fell short of what China wanted, as the United States made no specific public concessions on when or whether it would break diplomatic relations with the Republic of China and abolish the U.S.-ROC Mutual Defense Treaty. In addition, the two agreed to replace the sentence "Taiwan is a province of China" with "Taiwan is part of China" in the English version, which showed Chinese concession to the United States.[17] Moreover, the U.S. "hopes" for a peaceful settlement was replaced by the "U.S. reaffirms its interests in a peaceful settlement of the Taiwan question by the Chinese themselves."[18] This, indeed, was less than what the Americans wanted, since China did not itself commit to a peaceful settlement. The Chinese also specified the areas of exchanges "in such fields as science, technology, culture, sports and journalism" and introduced the question of trade, which was not mentioned in the October draft at all.[19] It is clear that both compromised but did it on a quid pro quo basis.

The Chinese leaders were willing to make some concessions because, in the larger context, they thought they had scored points on the Taiwan issue. They had upheld principles, namely, the Americans had reiterated their adherence to a "one China" policy. They might also have believed that this was what Nixon and Kissinger could realistically do for the moment. Nixon also gave Zhou the impression that he was very sincere and wanted to get things done. Nixon wrote, "In the official plenary sessions with Chou [Zhou], therefore, I spoke very frankly about the practical political problems a strongly worded communiqué on Taiwan would cause me." One of Nixon's arguments to the Chinese was that if he lost the election as a result of the American concessions on Taiwan, "my successor might not be able to continue developing the relationship between Washington and Peking."[120] Nixon again assured Zhou that he could do more privately than he could say publicly. This argument seemed to carry the day. In any event, the Chinese leaders seemed to have bought it. The Chinese and American leaders were moving toward a new relationship that would help China to counteract the threat from the Soviet Union. As Kissinger later suggested, the U.S. and China agreed on "a carefully crafted formulation that accepted the principle of one China but left the resolution to the future."[121]

The White House negotiators needed the endorsement of the State Department before the communiqué could be announced. However, State Department officials were reluctant to approve the communiqué. After Secretary of State Rogers had actually signed off on the communiqué, State Department officials discovered a potentially serious flaw in the document. In the U.S. statement, they pointed out, Washington reaffirmed its treaty commitments to all its treaty allies in Asia—Japan, South Korea, the Philippines, and Thailand—with the exception of Taiwan, despite the continued validity of the U.S.-ROC Mutual Defense Treaty. The omission of Taiwan, Marshall Green noted, was strikingly similar to Secretary of State Dean Acheson's famous exclusion of the Korean peninsula from the U.S. defense perimeter just prior to the North Korean invasion of South Korea in 1950.[122] It was unlikely that the exclusion of Taiwan would mislead the PRC officials, as it could be easily compensated for by subsequent unilateral U.S. statements. Green, though, pointed out that the similarity to Acheson's mistake would undoubtedly attract the wrath of the right wing of the Republican Party, and Nixon could not afford to provide his domestic adversaries with additional bullets.[123]

At the last moment, State Department representatives were able to bring the issue to Nixon's attention.[124] Nixon concurred and asked Kissinger to talk to the Chinese for further changes. Kissinger tried to reopen negotiations with Qiao Guanhua later the night of 26 February. Qiao refused to redo the draft on the grounds that the two sides had gone this far and China had made many concessions in response to American wishes. "The Chinese Politburo had approved the final draft the previous night on the basis of U.S. assurance that the President had accepted it." Qiao asked, "How could we reopen this discussion less than 24 hours before the formal announcement of the communiqué?"[125] Zhou Enlai, however, seemed more considerate of Nixon's dilemma after knowing the situation. He handled the matter quite skillfully. Zhou explained to Qiao that creating a psychological basis for the new relationship with the United States was more important than these valid objections. Zhou reported to Mao, who instructed him, "All could be reconsidered except the part concerning Taiwan. Any attempt to change the Taiwan section would preclude issuing a communiqué."[126] Thus, Kissinger and Qiao Guanhua reopened the talks. The problem was resolved by eliminating the references to the other treaty commitments, so that Taiwan would not be singled out.[127]

But the State Department officials had found yet another problem. Many Taiwanese, they pointed out, did not agree with the Nationalist government's position that Taiwan was part of China. Therefore, they argued, the language in the communiqué should say merely that "Chinese on either side of the Taiwan Strait" rather than "*all* Chinese" agree on the status of Taiwan. Chinese negotiators refused to budge on this point.[128]

The actual release of the joint statement, which was followed by a news conference, took place in Shanghai on the afternoon of 27 February 1972. As the two nations had no formal diplomatic relationship, the joint communiqué acquired the appellation "the Shanghai Communiqué."[129] The willingness of both sides to make concessions on Taiwan and their mutual agreement that both powers had a more menacing adversary in common provided the underpinnings for the "Shanghai Communiqué." Thus, while China affirmed its support for wars of national liberation and social revolution, and the United States affirmed its commitment to peace, both euphemistically conveyed their opposition to "hegemony"—Soviet influence—in Asia and the Pacific. Not only did this confirm the anti-Soviet underpinnings of the Beijing-Washington rapprochement (in word, not in action or in reality; it was rhetoric), but it represented a rebuff to Moscow's earlier proposals for a U.S.-Soviet partnership in the event that Beijing turned hostile to both.[130]

The Shanghai Communiqué became the basic instrument upon which an entirely new relationship was built. Its four "principles of international relations" stated that

1. Progress toward normalization of relations between China and the United States is in the interests of all countries;
2. Both wish to reduce the danger of international military conflict;
3. Neither should seek hegemony in the Asia-Pacific region and each is opposed to efforts by any other country or group of countries to establish hegemony; and
4. Neither is prepared to negotiate on behalf of any third party or to enter into agreements or understandings with the other directed at other states.[131]

The Shanghai Communiqué did not specify any timetable concerning "progress toward the normalization of relations," nor did it mention the terms under which full normalization would take place. It embodied a modus vivendi for Chinese-American relations that fell short of full normalization, but recognized that the two countries had common interests and that there was a need to communicate as well as to work to gradually overcome the remaining difficulties. It served as the basic charter for the Sino-American relationship until the two countries finally normalized relations in 1979.

V

Nixon's splendid summit meetings with the Chinese top leaders, in effect, replicated Kissinger's earlier visits to Beijing. Determined to move ahead but firm on principal issues, the leaders of the two sides proved worthy negotiation opponents. Friendly in gesturing but candid in negotiating, they covered a wide array of issues, philosophical and practical alike, and all came out feeling fulfilled. Although optimistic about the prospect of final U.S.-China normalization, both sides agreed to play slow and safe.

At the core of the U.S.-China summit diplomacy was the common concern over the Soviet threat. Nixon and Kissinger aspired to utilize China to balance the Soviet threat, as did Mao and Zhou. Without forming an anti-Soviet alliance, the American and Chinese leaders reached a tacit agreement on "opposing international [Soviet] hegemony." With such an understanding, Nixon believed that the Chinese leaders would not make excessive demands regarding Taiwan[132] and might be willing to help the U.S. to resolve the Vietnam conflict. On the opposite side, Mao and Zhou seemed keenly aware of exactly what China would want regarding Taiwan and could offer in Vietnam. On both issues, scores were mixed.

Nixon and Kissinger did repeatedly make efforts to link U.S. troop withdrawal from Taiwan with Chinese direct help to end the war in Vietnam. Zhou, however, rejected the linkage, was firm on "total U.S. withdrawal from Indochina," and reiterated China's support for Vietnam. When China declined to arrange a meeting between Kissinger and Le Duc Tho on Chinese soil, Nixon was not at all disappointed. To get China's direct help to a settlement in Vietnam might be Nixon's operational strategy, but certainly not his first priority. As he later recalled, "I said that I fully understood the limitations of our talks and that I had no illusions about being able to settle the Indochina war in Peking."[133] Yet, Nixon's successful trip to China indirectly put pressure on North Vietnam. China did encourage the North Vietnamese to reach a settlement with the U.S. in the coming year.[134]

Coming to China, Nixon and Kissinger knew that they had to state clearly to Zhou the U.S. position regarding Taiwan. The end result was Nixon's five private assurances. These were the substantial concessions the Nixon administration had to make to the Chinese. In response, the Chinese leaders backed down from their long-held position when they stopped asking the U.S. to sever relations with Taiwan immediately and pressing to set a time limit for troop withdrawal. Although the Taiwan issue remained unresolved, Zhou assured Nixon that "we are not rushing to make use of the opponents of your present visit and attempt to solve all the questions and place you in an embarrassing position."[135] Indeed, Nixon and Kissinger in effect needed more time to prepare both at home and abroad for U.S.-PRC normalization and were in no position to promise when they could withdraw U.S. troops from Taiwan and switch recognition from the ROC to the PRC. They succeeded in persuading Mao and Zhou to accept their concerns. Chinese pragmatism also seemed to have prevailed over the ideological stiffness.

Nixon's China trip did accomplish its preset strategic as well as political goals. Nixon broke a twenty-two-year taboo in dealing with the People's Republic of China. Without any apology, he engaged Mao in a discussion that ended the isolation of the PRC from the West and America's isolation from China. Nixon had confided in Zhou that when he was serving in the Eisenhower administration, his views had been no different from those of John Dulles. "But the world had changed since then," he said, "and the relationship between the People's Republic and the United States must change too."[136] No doubt Nixon's opening to China served American national interests and helped the Republican president to win reelection.

Nixon's trip, as complex as its motivations were, had cut through one of the great knots of international politics of the twentieth century, and many recognized that it would stand as an example of farsighted and pragmatic diplomacy — Nixon's diplomacy. It made triangular diplomacy a reality and tipped the balance of power to the U.S. advantage by opening "seemingly endless opportunities for achieving other goals, most specifically an end to the Vietnam War and an advantageous set of agreements with the Soviet Union."[137] As Nixon had projected, the trip helped to guarantee that any future friction between the United States and the People's Republic of China would be decided not on a battlefield but at a negotiating table, hence diminishing any misunderstanding that might lead to war.[138]

Nixon was not the only winner. The historic Nixon-Mao handshake stood as a great diplomatic victory for Beijing. A CCP Central Committee document hailed the summit for its success in "utilizing [others'] contradictions, dividing up enemies, and enhancing ourselves," and credited this to Mao's "brilliant decision" to invite the U.S. president.[139] The Chinese leaders could now focus their attention on the Soviet threat and avoid the possibility of fighting a two-front war. In addition, China gained U.S. and world recognition of its legitimacy, the validity of its national interests, and its status as a major regional power with a role to play in shaping current and future international policies. Moreover, China gained access to and enlisted the badly needed economic and technological resources of the United States in the buildup of Chinese industry and defense capability.

It is also interesting to note that the seemingly better understanding between the two sides as a result of their previous talks contributed to the U.S.-China summit success. Almost two decades of de facto diplomatic talks between the two antagonists had proved useful in paving the way for the high-level negotiations. Nixon and Kissinger knew how they should get prepared in order to convince the Chinese. Both agreed, as noted in Kissinger's 5 February 1972 memo to Nixon, that "frankness was one of the dominant elements in our talks with Chou [Zhou]," because "the rather unconventional approach of genuine (as opposed to feigned) frankness" had served Kissinger well in his conversations with Zhou.[140] It turned out that even the more "philosophical" Mao liked the "rightist" Nixon.

Both sides seemed to be operating in a different mindset at the negotiating table. Nonetheless, there had been hardly any bargaining in the context of threats of arms race and armed conflict after Kissinger's secret visit, as both believed that mutual cooperation would serve each other well. The issue was the degree of U.S.-China cooperation. Instead of facing the risk of escalated adversarial relations, China and the United States weighed the benefits of cooperation and the costs of reduced cooperation should negotiation fail. As Kissinger commented after his long negotiation with Qiao Guanhua on the communiqué, "We have made this communiqué on the basis that both sides should benefit and not that it was a victory for one, and the other was the loser."[141] They were striving to create a win-win situation in lieu of a "zero-sum game," in which "gains" for one side invariably meant "losses" for the other.

From the human standpoint, the summit success could be attributed to the style, educational backgrounds, and personalities of the negotiators. Nixon and Kissinger, not Secretary of State Rogers,[142] were intellectually capable of grand strategic thinking and able to engage in meaningful dialogue with their Chinese counterparts. Nixon seems to have formed a personal relationship with Zhou and even Mao. Years later, when Nixon resigned from his presidency as the result of the Watergate scandal, the Chinese leadership invited the disgraced president to pay a return visit as a state guest, and he did so in February 1976.

CHAPTER NINE

Conclusion

WITH THE U.S. RETAINING diplomatic relations with the ROC government in Taiwan after Nixon's China trip in 1972, Washington and Beijing agreed to establish diplomatic representation in the other's capital with a "liaison office" in 1973. The new relationship, however, did not grow as smoothly as expected, partly because of the resignation of Nixon after the Watergate scandal and the failing health of Mao and Zhou and partly because of President Gerald Ford's reluctance to relinquish U.S. military presence in Taiwan. It would take a few more years and many more talks until President Jimmy Carter announced in December 1978 that the United States would extend full diplomatic relations to the PRC and withdraw its diplomatic recognition from Taiwan in January 1979.

The story of the Chinese-American talks from 1949 to 1972, without doubt, reveals the intricacy of Cold War international history. Security interests, ideological differences, and historical enmity explained in part the confrontational relationship between Beijing and Washington. Behind the veil of intense hostility and confrontation, however, the chance for eventual conciliation existed. A careful scrutiny of the Chinese-American Cold War diplomatic contacts indicates that the two distinctly different and widely separated nations and peoples who were locked in intense conflicts ended up as the victims, in some measure, of their own strategic, political, and cultural baggage.

I

This study, first of all, demonstrates that the two-decade-long mutual hostility between the U.S. and China, no matter how bitter it had been, did not preclude continuous contact and talks between the two, sometimes productive, other times in vain. The dynamics of the overall Cold War not only defined the Chinese-American confrontation, but also shaped the Beijing-Washington communication and negotiation.

Without the Cold War, the Chinese Communists might not have been inevitably hostile toward the United States. The CCP foreign policy approach developed a great deal of pragmatism after Mao assumed leadership in 1935. The CCP leadership worked hard to win U.S. support during and immediately after World War II. Even during the latter period of the Chinese civil war, although indignant at U.S. assistance to the Nationalists, the CCP leaders were carefully looking for opportunities to avoid confrontations with the Americans. They supplemented talks of "persuasion and accommodation with carefully considered, coordinated political propaganda" designed to "demonstrate the steel of resolve" behind their rather flexible policies toward the U.S. and other Western governments.[1]

In total control of CCP's policy toward the U.S., Mao seemed to have adopted an opportunist attitude toward Washington but would not give in on his revolutionary principles. As early as in July 1947, the CCP headquarters had publicly proclaimed the principles of equality and mutual benefit as the basis for dealing with other countries, capitalist and socialist alike. In November 1948, the CCP Central Committee again announced its wish "to establish equal and friendly relations with all foreign countries, including the United States," but on the condition of full respect for China's territorial sovereignty.[2]

In early 1949, however, Mao was convinced that the Truman administration would not meet his basic preconditions. "The imperialists," he explained to his colleagues, "who have always been hostile to the Chinese people, will definitely not be in a hurry to treat us as equals. As long as the imperialist countries do not change their hostile attitude, we shall not grant them legal status in China." If Washington would handle diplomatic ties on a "wait-and-see" basis, then so would the CCP.[3] To this end, Mao quietly probed Washington's intentions. Progress on the diplomatic front would be well worth the effort if it would help isolate the Nationalists, neutralize the perceived threat of U.S.-sponsored intervention, and facilitate access to the much needed Western technology and foreign trade.

When Ambassador John Stuart did not evacuate with the GMD government after Nanjing fell to Communists, Mao saw an opportunity to ascertain American intentions and perhaps even to influence U.S. policy toward China. He authorized Huang Hua to hold private and secret talks with Stuart. With these exchanges underway came Mao's public statement on 15 June 1949 showing guarded interest in establishing diplomatic relations with Western countries.[4]

By the summer of 1949, however, Mao reached the conclusion that diplomatic relationship with the U.S. on terms acceptable to the CCP was impossible. He was determined to overturn the old rules, which allowed the Western powers to define their positions in China. This stance set him directly at odds with the U.S., which claimed to have diplomatic privileges while simultaneously refusing to recognize the official standing of CCP authorities, even in areas under their de facto control. Even then, Mao still believed economic relations with the United States were possible. While in Moscow, Mao urged his colleagues in Beijing to pursue the possibility of trading with the United States and other capitalist countries in 1950.[5]

Dismayed at Communist takeover in China and heavily preoccupied with the unfolding Cold War in Europe, U.S. China policy was at no point a top priority and remained unsettled. Truman's dispatching of General Marshall to China in December 1945 to mediate the CCP-GMD conflict, and Marshall's insistence on including the CCP in a coalition government—precisely the kind of settlement the Americans were opposing in Europe at the time—suggested that Washington was prepared to deal with Mao and his followers. By mid-1949, however, boxed in by domestic politics and rating China lightly in U.S. overall Cold War strategy, Truman decided not to consider Mao's terms. When Stuart asked for Washington's authorization to negotiate with the CCP leaders in Beiping, Truman denied the request.

To neutralize a Communist China, Dean Acheson and his State Department wanted to "drive a wedge" into the Sino-Soviet partnership. Searching for an "Asian Tito," the State Department regarded Mao Zedong as a plausible candidate. Acheson felt that the United States might be compelled to recognize Communist China during the first months of 1950, as most of its allies would do so by that time.[6] Even after Beijing and Moscow formed an alliance in February 1950, Acheson and many State Department China experts still regarded a CCP independent from Moscow as an option. Only the domestic political hurdles prevented the State Department from pursuing a more positive policy such as recognition.

The outbreak of the Korean War in 1950 disrupted any positive development of Chinese-American relations, but not the "wedge" approach. As late as in May 1951, well after the Chinese had intervened in Korea, Truman's NSC still listed as the first objective of American policy in Asia the goal of "detach[ing] China as an effective ally of the USSR" by "stimulat[ing] differences between the Peiping and Moscow regimes" and by "creat[ing] cleavages within the Peiping regime itself by every possible means."[7] Given China's hostility, Washington easily leaned toward a "hard-line" through toughening the China embargo, firming support of the Nationalist government in Taiwan, and further isolating the PRC.

Although feeling compelled to intervene in Korea, the CCP leaders expected the war to have political and diplomatic effects. Viewing war as a means of making an opponent more susceptible to persuasion, they placed a greater emphasis on war, or the threat of war, as an instrument for converting their opponents to the Chinese viewpoint than on its inherent nature as an instrument of conquest. Thus war and formal negotiation were but two complementary tactics available to Chinese leaders for managing China's external relations. Mao had several sleepless nights before making the difficult decision to send Chinese "volunteers" to fight in Korea. When the war stalemated in the spring of 1951, the Chinese were ready to come to the negotiating table. The Chinese and the Americans, however, differed fundamentally on setting up the negotiating agenda. The United States was interested only in a cease-fire, while the Chinese wanted to include difficult political issues. Although bargaining hard, the two adversaries were able to reach an armistice agreement after more than two years of negotiation.

By 1955, the PRC leadership was more confident of its domestic control and readier to pursue a less adversarial foreign policy. Interested in creating a peaceful environment conducive to China's domestic economic development, the PRC leaders adopted a more flexible foreign policy, including an initiative to develop relations with the United States. The beginning of the ambassadorial talks was to serve as a viable channel for extending and continuing contact with the United States. Although agreeing to the talks, the Eisenhower administration, which pledged to hold the containment line, had no intention to push for diplomatic breakthrough in U.S.-China relations. Lasting through the end of 1950s, the ambassadorial talks were not able to achieve substantial breakthrough.

The Kennedy administration could have made a significant progress in reducing U.S.-China hostilities, and the ongoing ambassadorial channel would have served that purpose well. Taking up a more practical Cold War policy, the Kennedy administration's China policy showed some positive signs. It planned to ship wheat to China to help famine victims if Beijing made a firm request. It sought an exchange of journalists and expressed interest in cultural exchanges. Assistant Secretary of State Roger Hilsman's speech on China in December 1963 expressed a moderate attitude and new thinking on China.[8] It turned out that Beijing was interested only in resolving more fundamental issues, of which an outstanding one was Taiwan. Much as the Eisenhower administration, Kennedy's White House felt handicapped by the pro-ROC establishment at home and the Soviet challenge abroad. China's desire for and pursuit of nuclear weapons further dissuaded Kennedy from improving Chinese-American relations through diplomacy and negotiations.

In redefining the China policy, Kennedy's successor encountered the same Cold War difficulties. There existed signs of changes in U.S. China policy during the Johnson years. At the end of 1965, the State Department unveiled its first major modification of the China travel ban since 1957. The first half of 1966 seems to have been a turning point, when two congressional hearings were held on the subject of whether it would be in the best interest of the U.S. to continue isolating China. In March, Vice President Hubert Humphrey publicly embraced the new policy formation—containment without isolation. On July

1966, Johnson himself spoke of mainland China as no president had done in seventeen years. Urging to build a relationship of "co-operation, not hostility," he defined the central objective of U.S. China policy as "reconciliation."[9] State Department officials seriously considered upgrading the talks with the Chinese in the later years of the Johnson administration. The time, however, was not ripe for a major change in U.S. China policy, especially when the U.S. found itself sunk in the Vietnam quagmire.

These twenty-plus years of constant confrontation and continuous communication between Washington and Beijing saw both adopting a Cold War approach to one another. A drastic change came along in the early 1970s when Nixon and Mao came to realize that a greatly improved U.S.-China relationship would drastically change the Cold War reality. Both expected such a relationship to significantly better their overall strategic positioning vis-à-vis the Soviet Union. Had it not been for the Cold War confrontation, Washington and Beijing would not have engaged in hostilities and talks for twenty-plus years. Had it not been for the dynamic changes of the Cold War in the late 1960s, U.S.-China rapprochement would have not been realized in just three years.

II

Along with the Cold War context, this study has illustrated, domestic politics proved to be a crucial factor in determining the scope and nature of negotiations and communications between the U.S. and the PRC, and rendering it a difficult but lasting process. Nonetheless, such a process proved to be useful for discovering both sides' intentions, settling minor disputes, and paving the way for real and substantial high-level talks.

Domestic politics is part of the "internal setting" of the foreign policy decision-making process.[10] In a democratic society, domestic constraints on foreign policy include the forces of public opinion, Congress, the media, and powerful interest groups. During the period under study, PRC foreign policy decision-making was the sphere of the small group of party elite. There was little influence on foreign policy decision-making from interest groups, the wide society—the so-called public opinion. However, even in an authoritarian state such as China under Mao, domestic factors restrained foreign policy conducts. There seem to have existed three domestic determinants of Chinese foreign policy: "the primacy of politics, the weight of the past, and ideology."[11] When combined, they tend to explain most of the direction, timing, and specifics of Beijing's policies toward Washington.

When the People's Republic of China was founded in 1949, Mao, as head of state and the chairman of the Chinese Communist Party, retained in his own hand the power of setting foreign policy orientation and guidelines for the new regime. He consigned Zhou Enlai to the role of a manager to overlook day-today operation of foreign affairs. The role of the five-man CCP Secretariat, and later the Standing Committee of the Politburo, was to accord legitimacy to a major policy decision made by Mao. The Politburo meetings were to help him weigh the pros and cons of a major foreign policy decision. These meetings also served the function of overcoming opposition and reservation, building consensus once Mao had made the final decision.[12] In the early days of the Republic, Mao had allowed inner-Party debates on foreign policy decision-making,[13] but these inner-Party contentions over foreign policy issues virtually disappeared after the Korean War. Up to the Cultural Revolution in 1966, "Mao alone received Foreign Ministry options papers from Zhou Enlai for decision, with information copies to Liu Shaoqi, Deng Xiaoping, and Peng Zhen."[14] This structure was temporarily interrupted during the early period of the Cultural Revolution, especially from May to August 1967, when the "rebel faction" was in actual control. Mao and Zhou, however, were able to resume total control of foreign policy decision-making after August 1967.

During the period of U.S.-China rapprochement, although encountering no open opposition to his U.S. policy, Mao, nonetheless, had to take care to nurture the Party and the nation for a dramatic transformation in China's foreign policy. Mao's public meeting with Edgar Snow on China's National Day in October 1970 at the top of Tiananmen was designed to create a positive image of the Americans. In sending China's Ping-Pong team to Japan and inviting the U.S. team to China in the spring of 1971, Mao had to overrule the decisions made by the Foreign Ministry. Mao's main purpose in Ping-Pong diplomacy was to further prepare the Chinese people politically and psychologically for the forthcoming U.S.-China rapprochement.

For the U.S., domestic politics proved to be a powerful force affecting the U.S.-China talks. Although Eisenhower was convinced of the need for a channel of direct contact with the Chinese Communists in order to settle unresolved disputes such as getting detained U.S. citizens back, and approved the opening of bilateral talks at the ambassadorial level in Geneva, Dulles's "closed door" strategy to the China problem blocked the negotiation from moving to an ideal direction.[15] However, the talks were useful for deflecting domestic and international criticism of the Eisenhower administration's China policy. Annoyed at Washington's obstinate posture, Beijing became impatient and thus adopted a hard-line approach after 1958. It insisted that no subsidiary issues could be discussed or negotiated until the United States agreed in principle to withdraw from Taiwan.

Kennedy was concerned about his narrow electoral victory, and was apprehensive, even obsessed, about China's nuclear program and also contemplated military action against the PRC's nuclear facilities. Some of his advisers saw a need for reaching a modus vivendi with Beijing, but Kennedy's own anti-communist feelings and fears of congressional reaction prevented him from taking any major initiative during his brief term in office. There was no substantial movement on the issues that had been discussed at the Warsaw talks.

Lyndon Johnson viewed China generally through the prism of Vietnam, but nonetheless shared the view that opening lines of contact with Beijing might be beneficial—and thus he personally approved some private visits to the PRC. Some of Johnson's advisers—notably W. Averell Harriman, George Ball, Marshall Green, Allen Whiting, and others in the State Department—similarly sought an opening to China, but the escalation of the Vietnam War and the outbreak of China's Cultural Revolution made that move impossible.[16] Early in 1963, Green wrote a "toe in the water" speech, suggesting change in the China policy. He and others in the State Department had been working to "craft the best actions to take when the right time came."[17] Although there were talks of changes at the high level, no substantial proposal had ever been put on the table for discussion at the ambassadorial talks in Warsaw.

Although seemingly limited, the fifteen years of ambassadorial talks played its role for settling minor disputes and paving the way for real and substantial high-level talks. By 1967, thirty-six Americans imprisoned in China had been released, and only four remained by the closing of the Warsaw talks in February 1970.[18] The ambassadorial talks also served useful crisis management functions during the three Taiwan Strait crises in 1954–55, 1958, and 1962.

The objective conditions for the 1971–72 Sino-U.S. détente were in place a decade earlier (since the early 1960s); it took a crisis to break through preconditions and expectations, and to start the process.[19] Only then could policy innovation occur. Decade-long reflections and preparations were crucial for the eventual reconciliation. They laid the groundwork for Nixon and Kissinger to do what Kennedy and Johnson could not.

III

Aside from the Cold War context and domestic restraints, individual negotiators mattered. Their educational background, professional experiences, and communication and negotiation style and abilities did play a role in shaping how the talks were conducted and, more importantly, what attitude negotiators would adopt toward their counterparts.

During this twenty-two-year period, on the Chinese side, there had been some continuity in the personnel managing relations with the United States. The primary individual was Mao Zedong. He was aided by Zhou Enlai and a number of Western-educated foreign policy specialists, such as Qiao Guanhua, Huang Hua, Wang Bingnan, and Zhang Wenjin, whose diplomatic involvement with the United States dated back to the Yan'an period in the late 1930s and the Marshall mission in 1945–46. From the beginning, the making of the CCP's foreign policy was highly centralized and personalized. Mao and Zhou not only were the ultimate decision-makers, but also supervised the implementation of China's foreign policy. The Chinese-American negotiation experiences showed that Mao made all the important policy decisions, Zhou managed the day-to-day operations and the implementation of policy decisions, and the front-line Chinese negotiators were messengers in most situations.

The Western encroachment inflicted on China in the nineteenth century served as "the intellectual crucible for the founding fathers" of the PRC as well as their associates.[20] The starting point for CCP's foreign policy, especially its policy toward the United States, was its leadership's visceral reaction to foreign danger and yearning for a restoration of China's greatness. At the new Political Consultative Conference on 22 September 1949, Mao informed the delegates that "[t]he Chinese People have always been a great, courageous and industrious nation; it is only in modern times that they have fallen behind. And that was due entirely to oppression and exploitation by foreign imperialism and domestic reactionary governments."[21]

Mao viewed domestic and international development as intrinsically linked. He looked at policy issues from a strategic viewpoint. Zhou, on the other hand, was responsible for making detailed analyses of complex issues. He placed priority on ensuring policy continuity, and never attempted to deviate from Mao's overall policy framework. Zhou had the best Western education among the top CCP leaders and was the most familiar with international affairs. He understood better than Mao the rather severe limitations imposed by China's strategic weakness on its ability to work its will in its relations with other countries.

Early in 1950, when discussing China's relations with the United States, Zhou stated that the U.S. was trying to feel out CCP intentions. He believed that the PRC should not entirely cut off ties with the Americans; neither should it be anxious to enter into diplomatic relations with Washington. If China sought immediate U.S. recognition, Zhou felt, the CCP would be cast in a passive position. In addition, Zhou believed that the CCP must make it clear to the United States that China would not tolerate any humiliation and that no country could interfere in China's internal affairs.[22] Zhou was determined to end old China's diplomacy of humiliation. He stressed that the key to maintaining independence was not to subject oneself to the influence of other countries and become their tool.

After the Korean War, Zhou believed that "the main international contradiction today is that between war and peace," and that "a new war can be both postponed and prevented."[23] To Zhou, "war and peace" was a common concern of the peoples and governments of the world. The support of world peace was both the point of convergence of the vast majority of countries and the point of departure for China's foreign policy. Zhou proposed the Five Principles of Peaceful Coexistence, revised the tactics of the united front, and made a huge effort in opening up a new frontier for China's foreign relations. The beginning of

Sino-U.S. ambassadorial talks in 1955 was a sign of relaxation in Sino-American relations.

Mao had originally advocated and supported this approach. But after almost three years of negotiations without substantial achievements, Mao became impatient. It seemed that China's moderate foreign policy did not produce instant and obvious results. From late 1957, Mao again decided to fight against the Western countries. The revolutionary foreign policy corresponded to the Great Leap Forward of 1958–60 and indeed escalated into virtually all-out frenzy during the early stage of the Cultural Revolution (1966–68). China's practical foreign policy would reemerge only in the early 1970s.

Under Mao and Zhou, the Chinese front-line negotiators played some, although limited, roles while negotiating with the United States. According to one study, the Communist diplomats did not reveal "the slightest difference between their own position and that of their government."[24] It was true that Chinese negotiators were all Communist Party members experienced in the art of persuasion. Although the Chinese negotiators were culturally Chinese and armed with Marxist-Leninist ideology, their understandings of and approaches to Sino-American relations and actual behaviors in negotiations varied. The role of individual Chinese negotiators was confined largely to understanding directives accurately, interpreting the intentions of top leaders, and forming their own positions during negotiations. The role of each of these representatives in the grand strategy of the central leadership varied between messenger and real negotiator.

A messenger's role was limited to delivering prepared statements, setting forth established government positions, and receiving opposing communications. Negotiators should be able to make decisions, offer counterproposals, conclude agreements, or terminate discussions at their own discretion.[25] When Huang Hua met with Ambassador Stuart, he was actually a messenger since Mao instructed him to "spend more time listening than talking" in his meeting with Stuart. The five PLA officers, Deng Hua, Xie Fang, Bian Zhangwu, Ding Guoyu, and Chai Chengwen, held positions on the four-man Chinese/North Korean negotiation team. Deng, Bian, and Ding were more ceremonial heads, while Xie and Chai did the actual talking for the Chinese side. Xie was very eloquent and at ease with bargaining, and Chai was also well qualified first as a senior liaison officer, then as a negotiator.

The Chinese representatives assigned for the ambassadorial talks also assumed different roles. Wang Bingnan's assignment was more that of a negotiator, as the Chinese leadership was serious about building a working relationship with the United States in the mid-1950s. Alexis Johnson regarded Wang as a professional diplomat. Early in the negotiation, Johnson noted that "he [Wang] is acting much more in tradition of old time Chinese bargainer than communist diplomat."[26] Wang Guoquan succeeded Wang Bingnan as China's chief negotiator at the height of the Vietnam War in July 1964, when the talks were seen as a potential "pressure reducer" for tension in Sino-American relations. A former provincial party chief and one-term ambassador to East Germany (1957–64), Wang Guoquan was neither an "American hand" nor Zhou's closest aide in foreign affairs. His appointment indicated Beijing's lowered expectations on the ambassadorial talks. The Warsaw channel now served less as a negotiation avenue, but more of a listening post or mailbox. Succeeding Wang Guoquan in 1969, Lei Yang acted as a messenger as well as a negotiator.

During the rapprochement talks, Zhou Enlai negotiated directly with Kissinger, although largely on Mao's behalf. Qiao Guanhua conducted negotiations with Kissinger over the final version of the "Shanghai Communiqué" during Nixon's visit to China. Qiao's negotiating style resembled Zhou's more than did that of any of Zhou's other close associates. According to Kissinger, "this impressive man was a lesser copy of Chou's charm, erudition and intelligence."[27] Behind each negotiator was Zhou Enlai, who provided each with a degree of autonomy commensurate to the situation, his ability, experience, and closeness to Mao and Zhou.

In contrast to the longer tenure of Chinese diplomats, the U.S. negotiators came and went more or less in tandem with each administration. The twenty-two years of talks cut across five U.S. administrations from Truman to Nixon. According to U.S. liberal democratic traditions, it was possible for an individual diplomat to maintain his/her own views on foreign affairs. Fred Ikle has suggested, "He may even act as a mediator between his government and that of the opponent instead of as an advocate of his own side."[28] In 1949, Ambassador Stuart made policy suggestions to the State Department and advocated his staying in Nanjing and his meeting with CCP leaders in Beiping for the purpose of establishing contact with Chinese Communists. In spite of his eagerness to assume the role of a real negotiator, Truman and Acheson were hesitant to confer upon Stuart that role. Ambassador Alexis Johnson was a seasoned diplomat. He worked hard to put forward effective proposals, even "pressured" Secretary Dulles to compromise on several occasions. However, Dulles's "closed door" approach to the China issue nullified Johnson's efforts. Johnson's successors, Ambassadors Jacob Beam, John Cabot, and John Gronouski, did not take substantial personal initiatives to advance the course of negotiations. Dean Rusk, skeptical of the Chinese Communists, was not in the least interested in bringing about a modification of U.S. policy toward China. As a senior aide to President Johnson summarized in December 1965, "The President [Johnson] will never take the steps on China policy that you and I might want him to take unless he is urged to do so by his Secretary of State. And this Secretary of State will never urge him to do so."[29]

Nixon came to office at the right moment in history in terms of Beijing's changing security environment and evolving worldview, America's difficulty

in Vietnam, the American public's changing view toward China, and the bureaucracy's stage of development. He saw and seized the opportunity at hand.
Kissinger, a faithful believer in geopolitics, was crucial in planning, foment-
ing, and implementing Nixon's China policy initiatives. The changing approaches toward China during the Nixon administration were crucial for the
breakthrough. It was important that Nixon was willing to deal with the Chinese leaders on a personal level. This was in sharp contrast to Dulles's attitude
toward Zhou Enlai at Geneva. In one of the early Sino-American exchanges,
carried out indirectly via the secret Pakistani channel, Zhou expressed concern that Nixon's reference to his desire to establish "secret talks" between the
two countries meant only that he wanted to establish a "hot line" communication channel such as the one between Washington and Moscow. He was
very pleased to learn that Nixon planned to send a personal envoy secretly to
China to prepare the way for his own visit. Zhou later mentioned to Kissinger
his appreciation of Nixon's sincerity.

One study points out that to establish friendly and cordial interpersonal relations in negotiations "may strengthen the tendency to observe rules of accommodation and may make a large set of these rules feasible."[30] This seems to be
the case during the U.S.-China rapprochement negotiations. In cultivating the
new relationship, Kissinger and Nixon were both impressed by Zhou's diplomatic skills. To Kissinger, Zhou Enlai appeared "urbane, infinitely patient, extraordinarily intelligent, [and] subtle." He moved through their discussions
"with an easy grace that penetrated to the essence of our new relationship as if
there were no sensible alternative."[31] Kissinger wrote that the talks between
Zhou and him "were longer and deeper than with any other leader I met during
my public service, except possibly Anwar Sadat."[32] He also observed that "Chou
never bargained to score petty points."[33] When he returned to Washington from
his secret China visit, Kissinger gave a background briefing to reporters, and
stated, "On the human level, we were treated extraordinarily well. The mood
of the session was very businesslike, very precise; no rhetoric on either side."[34]
While in China, Nixon was enthralled by Zhou's manner. "My other most vivid
memory of the trip is the unique personality of Chou Enlai. . . . But many
hours of formal talks and social conversation with Chou made me appreciate
his brilliance and dynamism," Nixon recalled in his memoirs.[35] After returning
from his China trip, Nixon also praised Zhou as "a totally delightful man with
great inner strength. . . . Zhou adds to Chinese subtlety the far-ranging experience of a world diplomat."[36]

Both Nixon and Kissinger also undertook extra efforts to build a cordial personal relationship with Mao and Zhou. Before his secret trip to China, Kissinger's staff made extensive background preparation. In his first meeting with
Zhou, Kissinger was ready to praise Chinese culture and arts. To prepare for
his China trip, Nixon read extensive background materials on China, listened

to specialists' advice on how to deal with the Chinese leaders, planned to cite Mao's poems, and even practiced eating with chopsticks. Both of them showed obvious willingness to shake Zhou's hands. Aiming to dispel twenty-two years of historical wrongs, hostility, and confrontation, they believed personal amity contributed to U.S.-China rapprochement.

IV

Yet another finding of this study is that ethnocentrism, or ignorance of culture-bound factors such as belief, value, and historical consciousness, is an important element in fostering misunderstanding, misperception, or misjudgment, all of which seem to have protracted the U.S.-China antagonism, as well as the bilateral talks.

The historian Akira Iriye defines *culture* as "the sharing and transmission of memory, ideology, emotions, life-styles, scholarly and artistic works, and other symbols."[37] Although the term *culture* has many definitions, in this study, *culture* refers to "the shared values and beliefs of a group of people."[38]

As John King Fairbank has observed, "Contact between cultures begets conflict, and the invasion of another culture area has usually heightened the invaders' consciousness of their own cultural values, their own sacred principles worth fighting for."[39] Since the end of World War II, U.S. leaders have believed that America's ultimate foreign-policy objective is to ensure its national security—its independence and its way of life. They saw Communism in China as an "aberration" and harmful to American interests in Asia. After the outbreak of the Korean War, American leaders viewed China as a growing threat to U.S. national security interests. As historian Shu Guang Zhang has observed, "It did not matter, for example, whether the threat of a Chinese Communist regime was 'real' or not. What mattered was that the perception and fear of the threat was real."[40]

It was clear that Americans and Chinese were operating on fundamentally different value systems. The Chinese leaders, like policy makers everywhere, brought to their encounters with the complexities of foreign affairs mental preconditions such as sets of presuppositions, values, expectation, preferences, and operating assumptions, as well as, according to Steven Levine, a formal system of ideas and an informal ideology. The ideology of Marxism-Leninism provided a prism through which the PRC leaders viewed the world, and they believed that it explained reality and served as the formal system of ideas. An additional cluster of ideas, values, assumptions, and prejudices, "which often operated at an unconscious level—also shaped the external outlook and influenced the foreign policy choices of Chinese elites," were grouped as informal ideology.[41]

Given these factors, the PRC leaders viewed the U.S. policy of containment against China as gravely detrimental to the core values of their political system and regime. With a strong nationalistic sentiment, they attached tremendous importance to political independence. The PRC leaders "clung to an illusory belief" that China would eventually defeat U.S. containment. They were "pre-occupied with the romantic vision that weakness and inferiority were not necessarily detrimental to China but could be transformed into a source of strength."[42] In the meantime, the PRC leadership emphasized the value of formal, face-to-face negotiation as another tactical "form of struggle" against the United States.

The most enduring cultural influence on PRC's negotiating behavior came from the Chinese historical experience. "Military power and economic performance may ebb and flow," Akira Iriye has aptly pointed out, "but historical consciousness will linger."[43] To the PRC leaders, negotiation was not an end in itself, to be treated in isolation, but simply one episode in an ongoing relationship, implying that short-term wisdom may be long-term folly. Chinese negotiating behavior can be seen as reflecting a similar attention to the long-term dimension of relationship rather than just short-term issues. Without the confidence born of a long acquaintance, a Chinese negotiator would never make concessions to his opponent if he could not trust his discretion and integrity. The Chinese leaders would not make any compromise on the Taiwan issue before they were convinced that the United States no longer "conspired" to seek their downfall and was willing to move toward a live-and-let-live arrangement with Beijing.

In the negotiation realm, different verbal and nonverbal expression, ways of organizing information, and relationships to time and space are major elements reflecting cultural traits.[44] In the Anglo-Saxon tradition, great emphasis has been laid upon creating conditions for an equitable contest. The most distinctive American negotiating approach is the "manipulative," or "can-do" style. This derives from the belief that "man can freely manipulate his environment for his own purposes." This view implies "a behavioral sequence whereby a person sets his objective, develops a plan designed to reach that plan." Little attention, however, is paid to the need to cultivate personal ties or to special circumstances. Choices are "either-or" and are made on the basis of instrumental or ends-means criteria alone.[45] In short, results rather than relationships are paramount. While emphasizing the distinction central to the manipulative style (and alien to the adaptive approach), I. William Zartman and Maureen R. Berman stress "that the problem, not the opponent, is the 'enemy' to be overcome." To them, it is the problem that "prevents good and beneficial relations and sours the other party's perception of things (including yourself), so the other party needs help to solve the problem, often against his own will and perception."[46]

Traditional Western negotiating norms, such as reciprocal concessions, revision of starting positions, and give-and-take, were consistently reflected in U.S. use of trades, exchanges, and mutual concessions as inducements to force the PRC to U.S. terms. During this twenty-two-year period of Sino-American hostility, the Americans also resorted to some "abnormal" approaches while negotiating with the Chinese. Dulles's "closed door" strategy was a case in point. The United States was stalling to a certain degree at the talks in Geneva and Warsaw.

Nevertheless, cultural factors are not usually decisive by themselves but are amplified by other circumstances. During the ambassadorial talks from 1958 to 1970, Beijing insisted on prior U.S. agreement to withdraw from Taiwan before talking about other issues, and rejected Washington's proposal to enlarge the scope for discussion, such as the visit of journalists and cultural exchanges. Looking back from the vantage point of 1971, Mao seemed to have alluded to this past error when he told Nixon that the United States was right to propose tackling small issues before big ones. The earlier atmosphere of distrust had exacerbated the gap between the two parties. As Raymond Cohen observes, "By 1971 a convergence of supreme national interests—primed by subtle diplomacy—diminished the impact of cross-cultural discordance."[47]

This study shows that the American perception of the PRC's negotiating style underwent significant changes with time. In the 1950s, the adversarial negotiations between Washington and Beijing were characteristic of mistrust, suspicion, manipulation, and the utter lack of good faith. Personal acrimony was common during the Korean armistice talks in the early 1950s. Even in the much more relaxed mid-1950s, the two sides still posed as adversarial negotiators. Ambassador Johnson noted that the PRC leaders were "proud, stubborn, unpredictable, sometimes harsh opponents. They ignored written commitments when it suited them, as they did with the Agreed Announcement on prisoners."[48] Although Johnson's observation was biased, it actually reflected U.S. perception of the PRC's negotiation styles in the 1950s. Kenneth Young also describes the Chinese negotiating styles as "adversary negotiations" at the ambassadorial talks.[49]

In the early 1970s, the U.S.-China negotiations became more and more cordial. After Kissinger's secret visit to Beijing, the U.S. no longer viewed the PRC as a hostile or at best incomprehensible nation. Henry Kissinger observed that the top leaders of the PRC were still tough, shrewd bargainers, but very patient. He saw Beijing's style of diplomacy as more positive than the Soviets'. He highlighted three points: (1) PRC leaders "use friendship as a halter in advance of negotiation." (2) Having been culturally preeminent, the Chinese can "use self-criticism as a tool." (3) The Chinese diplomats "proved meticulously reliable"; as Zhou often stressed, "Our word counts."[50]

It is said that Asians attach greater importance to pre-negotiation informal social functions. The Chinese tend to use the preliminary stages—broad discussion of issues, sightseeing trips, and banquet talks—as part of a purposeful process of establishing personal relationships. In Chinese culture, good interpersonal relationships are central to "getting things done." The Chinese officials were highly skilled in drawing the American negotiators into personal relationships in order to work with them.

A number of studies have discussed China's emphasis on negotiating from a "principled position."[51] This study, however, finds that Beijing's insistence on principle was not altogether invariable. In 1949, the CCP insisted on the U.S. severing relations with the Chinese Nationalists as a precondition for contact. During the ambassadorial talks, the PRC adhered to U.S. withdrawal from Taiwan as its "principled" position. By the time of the U.S-China rapprochement talks, however, Beijing made an important compromise on this principle by suspending its insistence on immediate U.S. withdrawal from Taiwan as a precondition for the new relationship.

The Chinese have also shown themselves skilled at using unilateral "good will" gestures to establish American "indebtedness." For example, Beijing released a group of eleven U.S. pilots on the day before the opening of the civilian repatriation talks in 1955. The release of political prisoners on the eve of negotiation, a gesture that cost China little and won U.S. gratitude, had become a hallmark of bilateral relations. From 1969 to 1972, the Chinese implemented a whole series of unsolicited concessions. These included the release of prisoners, the famous invitation to the U.S. Ping-Pong team, and the gift of pandas.[52] All these goodwill signals were shrewdly directed at public opinion, and did not need to be reciprocated (and hence evaded possible snubs). They put China in the best possible light, and ensured that the United States was put under a moral obligation for favors already received.

Fairbank contended in the early 1960s that "[t]he U.S. policy failure in the 'Chinese culture area' has resulted from a conflict between modern Western and traditional Confucian concepts of government."[53] While the cultural determinant was important, negotiators could not ignore power reality and economic interests. This study confirms that the two adversaries locked in an ideological, political, and military Cold War were compelled to conduct long, lasting, and often fruitless talks for political and international security interests, and yet, cultural factors played an important role in hindering communications and negotiations between China and the United States from 1949 to 1972.

CHRONOLOGY

1944

June	U.S. Vice President Henry Wallace led a mission to China.
22 July	Dixie Mission arrived in Yan'an.
18 Aug.	CCP Central Committee issued "Instructions on Diplomatic Affairs," regarded as its first formal diplomatic document.
	President Roosevelt appointed General Patrick Hurley as his personal representative to China.
21 Oct.	Hurley was appointed U.S. ambassador to China.
24 Oct.	General Stilwell was recalled from China.

1945

2 April	Hurley announced that U.S. support to China would go only to the Nationalist government.
23 April–11 June	The CCP convened its Seventh Party Congress.
14–23 Aug.	Jiang Jieshi three times invited Mao Zedong to Chongqing (Chungking) for negotiations.
28 Aug.	Mao arrived in Chongqing, entering talks with Jiang Jieshi and Hurley over the long-standing Communist-Nationalist struggle for control of China.
10 Oct.	The CCP and GMD issued summary of Mao-Jiang conversations.
27 Nov.	Hurley resigned as ambassador to China, protesting U.S. decision to end military aid to Jiang Jieshi, and charging that pro-Communist State Department officials had undermined U.S. efforts to resolve the Communist-Nationalist conflict.
	General George Marshall was appointed President Truman's special representative to China.
20 Dec.	Marshall arrived in China, trying to get the Communists and Nationalists to agree to a cease-fire and enter into a coalition government.

1946

10 Jan.	The CCP and GMD reached truce agreement.
14 Jan.	The Executive Headquarters at Beiping began its official functions.
30 June	CCP-GMD truce expired; an overall civil war began.

11 July	U.S. Senate confirmed Stuart's appointment as U.S. ambassador to China.
2 Nov.	Sino-American Treaty of Friendship, Commerce, and Navigation was signed in Nanjing.

1947

6 Jan.	Marshall returned to U.S. to become secretary of state after more than a year of failed mediation efforts in China.
29 Jan.	The United States announced end to its mediation efforts in China, and immediate withdrawal of U.S. troops.
1 Feb.	The CCP announced that it would no longer recognize any treaty or agreement reached between the GMD government and foreign countries.
9 July	The United States announced General Albert Wedemeyer's mission to China.

1948

3 April	Truman approved China Aid Act of 1948.
1 Nov.	The PLA occupied Shenyang.
10 Nov.	CCP Central Committee ordered that the diplomats from Western countries should be treated as ordinary foreign residents.
17 Nov.	Mao instructed Gao Gang to inform the Soviets that the CCP would adopt an identical position with the Soviet Union in making its foreign policy.
20 Nov.	U.S. consul-general in Shenyang Angus Ward and his staff were put under house detention.

1949

1 Jan.	In his New Year message, Mao called for "carrying the revolution through to the end."
6–10 Jan.	CCP Politburo convened an enlarged meeting to discuss New China's domestic and foreign policies.
19 Jan.	CCP Central Committee issued comprehensive instructions on diplomatic affairs, making it clear that the CCP would "make a fresh start" in China's foreign policy.
21 Jan.	Jiang Jieshi announced his retirement; Li Zongren became acting president.
31 Jan.	The PLA occupied Beiping.
31 Jan.–7 Feb.	Soviet Politburo member Mikoyan secretly visited Xibaipo to meet Mao and other CCP leaders.
5 Feb.	The main body of the Nationalist government moved from Nanjing to Guangzhou (Canton).
5–13 March	CCP Central Committee convened its second plenary session of the Seventh Party Congress, which decided that the CCP would not hurriedly pursue diplomatic relations with Western imperialist countries.
21 April	The PLA crossed the Yangzi River and occupied Nanjing.

May–June	Stuart held a series of meetings with Huang Hua in Nanjing.
27 May	The PLA seized Shanghai.
2 June	The PLA seized Qingdao.
15 June	With the Communists in control of several major cities, Mao Zedong stated that he was willing to discuss establishing diplomatic relations with any foreign government, on "the basis of the principles of equality, mutual benefits, and mutual respect for territorial integrity and sovereignty," and on the condition they would sever relations with the Nationalists.
22 June	The CCP announced that former American diplomats in Shenyang had been involved in espionage activities.
26 June–14 Aug.	Liu Shaoqi secretly visited the Soviet Union.
30 June	Mao announced that New China would adopt a "lean-to-one-side" approach in international affairs.
5 Aug.	U.S. State Department issued the *China White Paper*.
21–30 Sept.	The Chinese People's New Political Consultative Conference was convened in Beiping.
1 Oct.	The People's Republic of China was established, with Mao Zedong as chief of the state and CCP chairman.
24 Oct.	Ward and four other U.S. consulate staff were arrested by the Shenyang Public Security Bureau.
8–10 Dec.	Jiang Jieshi and Nationalist officials fled mainland China for the nearby island of Taiwan, where they installed the exiled government of the Republic of China.
11 Dec.	Ward and his American staff, after one year's detention, were deported from China.
16 Dec.–17 Feb. 1950	Mao visited the Soviet Union.

1950

5 Jan.	President Truman stated that the United States would stay out of the Chinese civil war and would "not provide military aid or advice to Chinese forces" in Taiwan.
6 Jan.	Beijing Municipal Military Control Commission announced the requisition of former American military barracks (then U.S. Consulate General office building) in Beijing.
10–31 Jan.	After the United States announced that it would block a Soviet proposal to give China's UN seat to the PRC, the Soviet delegate staged a walkout.
12 Jan.	In his National Press Club speech, Secretary of State Acheson excluded Taiwan and South Korea from U.S. Western Pacific defense perimeter.
15 Jan.	State Department recalled all American diplomats remaining in mainland China.
30 Jan.	For the first time Stalin endorsed Kim Il-sung's plan to attack South Korea.
14 Feb.	Zhou Enlai and Vyshinskii signed the Treaty of Friendship, Alliance, and Mutual Assistance between the PRC and the Soviet Union.
13–16 May	Kim Il-sung secretly visited Beijing and met Mao Zedong.

25 June	North Korea launched an early morning surprise invasion of South Korea.
27 June	President Truman ordered U.S. air and naval forces to defend South Korea, and sent the U.S. Seventh Fleet to the Taiwan Strait to protect Taiwan against attack.
28 June	Zhou Enlai denounced Truman's decision to send the U.S. Seventh Fleet into the Taiwan Strait as "armed aggression against the territory of China," adding that "the fact that Taiwan is part of China will remain unchanged forever."
7 July	General MacArthur was appointed commander for UN forces in Korea.
15 Sept.	U.S. Tenth Corps landed at Inchon.
30 Sept.	South Korean troops crossed the 38th parallel. Zhou Enlai warned that China would not stand idly by if "the imperialists wantonly invade the territory of North Korea."
1 Oct.	Kim Il-sung asked for Chinese assistance. Stalin urged Mao to send Chinese troops to Korea.
3 Oct.	Zhou Enlai warned that if U.S. forces moved across the 38th parallel, China would enter the war.
4–5 Oct.	CCP Politburo confirmed the decision to send Chinese troops to Korea.
7 Oct.	U.S. troops crossed the 38th parallel into North Korea.
19 Oct.	"Chinese People's Volunteers" crossed the Yalu River.
25 Oct.	CPV launched the first campaign against UN forces in Korea.
24–28 Nov.	PRC's special representative, Wu Xiuquan, attended the UN Security Council meeting to present the PRC's charges against the United States for its activities in Korea.
25 Nov.	CPV began second offensive campaign in Korea.
6 Dec.	Chinese/North Korean forces recaptured Pyongyang.
8 Dec.	U.S. Commerce Department announced a total trade embargo on China. It would remain in place for 21 years.
13 Dec.	Mao ordered CPV to cross the 38th parallel.
31 Dec.	CPV began third offensive campaign in Korea.

1951

1 Feb.	At the urging of the United States, the UN General Assembly adopted a resolution branding China an aggressor in the Korea conflict. The UN adopted the "moratorium" procedure on PRC's representation. The General Assembly agreed annually not to make any changes in China's representation and not to debate the issue.
11 April	General Douglas MacArthur was dismissed by President Truman from all commands in East Asia after repeatedly ignoring White House orders not to publicly demand that the war be expanded against Communist China.
18 May	Assistant Secretary of State for Far Eastern Affairs Dean Rusk set the tone for U.S. China policy for the next two decades when he stated, "The regime in Peiping . . . is not the government of China. . . . We recognize the national government of the Repub-

	lic of China, [which will] . . . continue to receive important aid and assistance from the United States."
10 July	The Korean Armistice talks began between UN Command and Chinese/North Korean representatives at Kaesong.
8 Sept.	The U.S., the UK, and 47 other nations signed peace treaty with Japan in San Francisco. The USSR and PRC were not parties to the San Francisco treaty.
25 Oct.	The Korean Armistice talks resumed in Panmunjom.
27 Nov.	The UNC and Chinese/North Korean negotiators agreed "that the actual line of contact between both sides be made the military demarcation line, and that both sides withdraw two kilometers from this line so as to establish the demarcation zone."

1952

10 July	The Korean Armistice talks entered a second year.
8 Oct.	The new UN chief negotiator, William K. Harrison, suspended the armistice talks indefinitely.

1953

2 Feb.	In his State of Union address, President Dwight D. Eisenhower announced that he was "issuing instructions that the Seventh Fleet no longer be employed to shield Communist China" from possible attack by Nationalist forces, adding that "we certainly have no obligation to protect a nation fighting us in Korea."
10 April	The exchange of Korean War POWs occurred in Panmunjom.
25 April	The Korean War Armistice talks resumed in Panmunjom.
27 July	The Korean War Armistice was signed in Panmunjom.
2 Sept.	Secretary of State John Dulles warned that if China renewed the Korean conflict or sent Communist forces into Indochina, the U.S. might declare war against the mainland.

1954

26 April–21 July	The Geneva Conference on Korean and Indochina issues was convened.
5–21 June	The U.S. and PRC representatives, U. Alexis Johnson and Wang Bingnan, held four talks in Geneva.
29 June–15 July 1955	The U.S. and PRC held 11 consul-level talks in Geneva.
3 Sept.	The PLA began shelling the small Nationalist-held offshore island of Jinmen (Quemoy) in the Taiwan Strait, inaugurating the beginning of the Taiwan Strait crisis of 1954–55.
8 Sept.	The U.S. joined seven other countries in signing a regional defense treaty, establishing the Southeast Asia Treaty Organization (SEATO).
2 Dec.	The United States entered into a mutual defense treaty with the Republic of China, pledging American support for Taiwan against any attack from mainland China. In response, the ROC made clear that it would not attack mainland China without first consulting the United States.

1955

6–13 Feb.	After Nationalist troops withdrew from Dachen Island with the assistance of the U.S. Seventh Fleet, the PLA took over the Island.
8 March	In a nationally televised address, Dulles warned China not to underestimate U.S. determination to meet aggression in East Asia, adding that the U.S. could employ a "new and powerful weapon of precision."
23 April	Zhou Enlai stated that China did not want war with the United States and was willing to negotiate with the U.S. government.
1 Aug.	Sino-American ambassadorial-level talks between U. Alexis Johnson and Wang Bingnan started in Geneva.
10 Sept.	At the 14th session of the Sino-American ambassadorial talks, the two sides reached an agreement concerning the return of civilians to their respective countries.

1956

12 May	Zhou Enlai proposed meeting with Dulles to discuss Taiwan and other problems.
12 June	Dulles rejected Zhou's offer of discussions because of short notice and because 13 captured Americans were still imprisoned in China.
7 Aug.	One day after the Chinese government offered visas to 15 U.S. newsmen who had requested them, the State Department announced that Americans would be allowed to travel to the mainland only when all U.S. prisoners were released.

1957

28 June	In a major address on China policy to Lions International, San Francisco, Dulles uncompromisingly reaffirmed the U.S. position and stated his belief that Communism was, in China as elsewhere, "a passing and not a perpetual phase."
22 Aug.	State Department authorized 24 news agencies to send correspondents to China for a seven-month trial period, but would not issue reciprocal visas to Chinese newsmen.
25 Aug.	*Renmin Ribao* denounced State Department's plan as "completely unacceptable to the Chinese people."
October	In a *Foreign Affairs* article, Senator John F. Kennedy called for a new foreign policy toward China, calling current U.S. policy "exaggeratedly military" and "probably too rigid."
15 Oct.	The Soviet Union signed secret agreement with the PRC, agreeing to provide a training model of an atomic bomb and related equipment. But the Soviet Union deliberately left it open as to exactly what equipment would be delivered and when and how.
12 Dec.	The Sino-American ambassadorial talks were suspended after the 73rd meeting on the day.

1958

13 June	China's first atomic reactor, built with Soviet help, began operating.
22 July	China announced the start of a campaign to "liberate" Taiwan and began building up forces opposite the island.
23 Aug.	Chinese forces began intensive shelling of the Nationalist-held offshore island Jinmen, inaugurating the beginning of the Taiwan Strait crisis of 1958.
4 Sept.	The PRC government declared that the extent of its territorial waters was 12 nautical miles. The same day, Dulles issued a statement that the U.S. "would not hesitate" to use armed force "in insuring the defense of" Taiwan.
6 Sept.	Zhou Enlai proposed resumption of Sino-U.S. ambassadorial talks to discuss the Taiwan Strait crisis. The U.S. agreed to talks the same day.
7 Sept.	China lodged first "serious warning" against U.S. intrusion to its territorial water. Over the years, China kept an account of these warnings. By mid-1971, the Chinese government had lodged 476 serious warnings against U.S. intrusions to its territorial waters and sky.
16 Sept.	Chinese and U.S. ambassadors Wang Bingnan and Jacob Beam reopened talks in Warsaw during the Taiwan Strait crisis of 1958.
6 Oct.	PRC defense minister Peng Dehuai announced the suspension of the bombardment of the offshore islands. It was regarded as the de facto cease-fire in the Taiwan Strait.

1959

20 June	Soviet leader Khrushchev informed the Chinese leader that the Soviet government had decided to postpone the delivery of a training model of atomic bomb and atomic technology to China.
7 Dec.	Rockefeller Report on future U.S. foreign policy called for improved relations with the Chinese people, while acknowledging China's hostile stance toward the U.S.

1960

23 May	The "Liberal Project," a group of House members, scholars, and scientists, released a study advocating opening direct communications with Beijing and withdrawing U.S. opposition to PRC's UN membership.
18 June	In a visit to Taiwan, President Eisenhower told a rally, "The United States does not recognize the claim of the warlike and tyrannical Communist regime in Beijing to speak for all the Chinese people. In the United Nations we support the Republic of China, a founding member, as the only rightful representative of China in that organization."
16 July	Moscow recalled thousands of Soviet advisers from China and canceled economic and military aid to the PRC.
13 Sept.	China formally adopted a "package" solution at the ambassado-

rial talks—that from now on China would not discuss "minor and subsidiary issues" with the United States, only "fundamental issues," that is, "the total withdrawal of U.S. troops from Taiwan and the Taiwan Strait area."

1961

7 March   The 103rd session of Sino-American ambassadorial talks, the first in the Kennedy administration, was held between China's Ambassador Wang Bingnan and the United States' Ambassador Jacob Beam in Warsaw.

August   President Kennedy secretly promised Jiang Jieshi that the U.S. would veto any UN decision to seat the Beijing government, and agreed to cooperate with Jiang's forces in covert operations against the mainland.

1 Dec.   Debates in the 16th UN General Assembly on whether to admit the PRC, the first time since 1950 that the question of China's admission made it to the General Assembly. The UN adopted U.S.-engineered and New Zealand–sponsored "important question resolution."

1962

20 June   The Third Taiwan Strait Crisis began.

26 June   Ambassador John Cabot received instructions to secretly assure the Chinese that the U.S. would not support "any Nationalist attempt to invade the mainland." Publicly, Kennedy told newsmen the next day that the U.S. would "take the action necessary" to defend Taiwan and the offshore islands from Communist attack.

16–28 Oct.   The Cuban Missile Crisis.

1963

April   Kennedy wrote Jiang Jieshi, "Given our present estimate of the situation, we cannot acquiesce in military action against the China mainland."

July   Kennedy sent W. Averell Harriman to Moscow to explore the opportunity of joint U.S.-Soviet preemptive strike against China's nuclear installations.

1 Aug.   In a news conference, Kennedy stated that China, with its population of 700 million, its nuclear potential, and "a government determined on war as a means of bringing about its ultimate success," might pose "a more dangerous situation than any we have faced since the end of the Second World War."

5 Aug.   The United States, the Soviet Union, and Britain signed a treaty prohibiting nuclear testing in the atmosphere, underwater, or in outer space.

22 Nov.   John F. Kennedy was assassinated in Dallas, Texas.

13 Dec.   Assistant Secretary of State Roger Hilsman's China policy speech implied that the U.S. was ready to coexist with Communist China while maintaining its commitments to the Nationalists on Taiwan.

1964

3 May	In response to questions from Western reporters, Chinese foreign minister Chen Yi stated that the initiative for better Sino-American relations would have to come from the United States, and that China could only wait for U.S. recognition and the withdrawal of U.S. forces from Taiwan.
7 Aug.	Following reports of North Vietnamese attacks on U.S. destroyers in the Gulf of Tonkin, Congress overwhelmingly passed the Gulf of Tonkin Resolution, approving President Johnson's request for authority to bomb North Vietnam and widen U.S. involvement in the Vietnam War.
13 Sept.	Johnson, Rusk, and Bundy met to decide whether to make a preemptive strike against China's nuclear installations.
16 Oct.	China successfully exploded its first atomic bomb.

1965

2 March	The United States and South Vietnam joined in heaviest air strikes against North Vietnam. Six days later, the first U.S. combat troops arrived in South Vietnam.
15 March	Richard Nixon declared that the Vietnam conflict was a de facto war between the U.S. and China: "A United States defeat in Vietnam means a [Chinese] Communist victory."
25 March	An article in *Renmin Ribao* announced that China would "join the people of the whole world in sending all necessary material aid, including arms and other war materials" to South Vietnam, adding that China was ready to send "our own men whenever the South Vietnamese people want them, to fight together with the South Vietnamese people to annihilate the United States aggressors."
2 April	During his visit to Pakistan, Zhou Enlai asked Pakistan's President Mohammad Ayub Khan—who was scheduled to visit the U.S. soon—to pass on Beijing's three-point policies to President Johnson.
28 July	Johnson announced an increase in troops to Vietnam from the current 75,000 to 125,000.

1966

January	At the Foreign Ministry's Fourth Conference of Ambassadors and Envoys, Zhou Enlai told Chinese diplomats that the United States was China's primary enemy in international struggle as Washington attempted to dominate all over the world.
8–30 March	The Senate Foreign Relations Committee began hearings on the need for a new policy toward mainland China.
16 March	At the 129th Sino-American ambassadorial meeting in Warsaw, Ambassador John Gronouski reassured Wang Guoquan that despite its buildup in Vietnam, the United States had no plans to invade China.
10 April	In an interview with Mr. Ejaz Husain of the Pakistani paper

Dawn, Zhou Enlai stated that "China will not take the initiatives to provoke war with the United States," but cautioned that China would support any government that "meets with aggressions by the imperialists."

16 May — The beginning of China's Cultural Revolution.

16 June — Senate Majority Leader Mike Mansfield (D-Montana) called for an "initiative for a direct contact between the Beijing government and our own government on the problem of peace in Vietnam and Southeast Asia."

12 July — In a nationally televised address, President Johnson called for Sino-American reconciliation and stated that the U.S. would try to reduce tensions between the two countries.

20 July — Senator Edward Kennedy (D-Massachusetts) told the Senate that both Communist and Nationalist China should be seated in the UN. At a news conference the next day, President Johnson said that while the administration would "do everything we can to increase our exchanges" with China, the U.S. would not adopt a "two-China" policy.

27 Oct. — China announced that it had successfully conducted a guided missile nuclear weapons test the day before.

29 Nov. — The UN General Assembly rejected a resolution to seat the PRC and expel the Nationalists in Taiwan.

1967

17 June — The PRC exploded its first hydrogen bomb.

12 Oct. — Dean Rusk defended U.S. actions in Vietnam as a means of blocking Chinese expansion in Southeast Asia.

Oct. — Presidential hopeful Richard Nixon published his article "Asia after Vietnam" in *Foreign Affairs*.

1968

1 May — Governor Nelson Rockefeller of New York called for more "contact and communication" with China in his campaign for the Republican presidential nomination.

2 May — U.S. Information Agency invited Chinese journalists to cover the 1968 presidential campaign.

13 May — DRV and U.S. negotiators started talks in Paris.

12 July — Vice President Hubert Humphrey called for an end to trade restrictions with China and a shift of U.S. policy away from "confrontation and containment" to one of "reconciliation and engagement."

8 Aug. — In his acceptance speech for the Republican presidential nomination, Richard Nixon said that he would "extend the hand of friendship to all peoples," specifically, to the people of China and Russia.

20 Aug. — The USSR invaded Czechoslovakia. Three days later, Zhou Enlai condemned the invasion as "the most barefaced and most typical specimen of fascist power politics played by the Soviet revisionist clique of renegades and scabs."

11–16 Nov.	In what becomes known as the "Brezhnev Doctrine," Leonid Brezhnev defended the invasion of Czechoslovakia by claiming that the USSR had the right and duty to intervene in other Communist states to "protect" them from anticommunist influences.
25 Nov.	The PRC and the U.S. agreed that the 135th ambassadorial talks be held on 20 February 1969, one month after Nixon took office.

1969

20 Jan.	In his inaugural address, President Nixon hinted at future changes in U.S. foreign policy: "After a period of confrontation, we are entering an era of negotiation."
23 Jan.	*Renmin Ribao* carried an editorial denouncing Nixon as "an agent of the American monopoly groups which have now chosen him as their front man."
27 Jan.	In his first presidential news conference, President Nixon stated, "Until some changes occur on their side . . . I see no immediate prospect of any change in our policy" toward China.
1 Feb.	In a secret memo to his new national security adviser, Henry Kissinger, Nixon stated, "I think we should give every encouragement to the attitude that this Administration is 'exploring possibilities of rapprochement with Chinese.'"
18 Feb.	China abruptly canceled Warsaw talks with the U.S., scheduled to be reopened in two days.
2 and 15 March	Two bloody border conflicts between Chinese and Soviet garrison forces at Zhenbao Island. There were more than 400 skirmishes along the Sino-Soviet border in 1969.
1–24 April	The CCP convened its Ninth Party Congress, symbolizing the end of the radical phase of the Cultural Revolution.
21 April	Secretary of State William Rogers announced a new U.S. "two-Chinas" policy that accepted the existence of a Communist China on the mainland and a Nationalist China on Taiwan as "facts of life."
24 May	At Nixon's request, Rogers asked Pakistani chief of state Yahya Khan to feel out the Chinese on expanded talks with the U.S.
7 June	Four-marshal study group, including Chen Yi, Ye Jianying, Xu Xiangqian, and Nie Rongzhen, met for the first time.
21 July	State Department announced a slight easing of travel and trade restrictions on China.
25 July	During his round-the-world tour, Nixon announced the Guam Doctrine (later called Nixon Doctrine), which was interpreted by many governments as a warning that the United States would be pulling out.
1 Aug.	President Nixon asked Pakistani chief of state Yahya Khan to secretly explore the possibilities for expanded talks between the U.S. and China. The next day, Nixon made a similar request of Romanian leader Nicolae Ceaușescu.
28 Aug.	As Sino-Soviet border fighting continued, State Department acknowledged reports that the Soviet Union was considering a preemptive strike against China's nuclear installations.

	The CCP Central Committee ordered the mobilization in the provinces and regions bordering the Soviet Union and the People's Republic of Mongolia
Sept.	Nixon and Kissinger ordered U.S. ambassador to Poland Walter Stoessel to contact his Chinese counterpart and ask to resume the Warsaw talks.
11 Sept.	The Soviet premier, Alexei Kosygin, held talks with his Chinese counterpart, Premier Zhou Enlai, at Beijing airport to ease tension between the two sides.
20 Oct.	The beginning of Sino-Soviet border negotiation at the vice foreign ministers' level.
7 Nov.	The U.S. ended its 19-year patrol of the Taiwan Strait.
3 Dec.	Stoessel told Chinese diplomats in Warsaw that Nixon would like to open direct talks with the Chinese.
19 Dec.	Ending a ban in place since 1950, the U.S. announced that subsidiaries and affiliates of U.S. firms abroad would be allowed to buy and sell nonstrategic goods with China.

1970

8 Jan.	State Department announced that Warsaw talks between the U.S. and the PRC would resume on 20 January. The U.S. spokesman in Washington, in announcing the event, was careful to refer to China for the first time as the "People's Republic of China," not "Red China" or "Communist China."
20 Jan.	U.S. Ambassador Stoessel and Chinese chargé d'affaires Lei Yang met for the 135th session of the Sino-American ambassadorial talks.
18 Feb.	In an address to Congress, Nixon stated that the U.S. had made unilateral overtures to China "which underlined our willingness to have a more normal and constructive relationship," adding that "we have avoided dramatic gestures which might invite dramatic rebuffs."
20 Feb.	U.S. Ambassador Stoessel and Chinese chargé d'affaires Lei Yang met for the 136th session of the Sino-American ambassadorial talks.
21 Feb.	Kissinger began secret talks with North Vietnamese negotiator Le Duc Tho.
15 March	U.S. State Department further eased restriction on travel to China.
18 March	With U.S. support, pro-American General Lon Nol overthrew the government of Prince Norodom Sihanouk.
1 May	U.S. troops invaded Cambodia.
18 May	China canceled the next day's ambassadorial meeting in Warsaw to protest U.S. invasion of Cambodia.
20 May	Mao issued a statement written in tough anti-American language, calling for "the people of the world to unite and defeat the U.S. aggressors and all their running dogs."
20 June	China suspended the Warsaw talks.
30 June	U.S. invasion of Cambodia ended.

1 Oct.   American leftist writer Edgar Snow and his wife were invited to review the annual National Day celebration parade with Mao Zedong on the wall of the Forbidden City overlooking Tiananmen Square in Beijing.

5 Oct.   In a *Time* magazine interview, Nixon stated, "If there is anything I want to do before I die, it is to go to China."

25 Oct.   White House press secretary Ron Ziegler publicly hinted at the continued shift toward a U.S. "two-China" policy when he announced, "The U.S. opposes the admission of the Beijing regime into the UN at the expense of the expulsion of the Republic of China."
                  At the White House State dinner, in his conversation with Romanian president Nicolae Ceauşescu, Nixon referred to "China" as the "People's Republic of China." This was the first time an American President had used China's official name. Nixon also asked Pakistani president Yahya Khan to pass on a secret proposal to China: the U.S. wants to conduct high-level talks in Beijing, and promises it won't enter into any anti-China alliance with USSR.

10 Nov.   Yahya Khan passed on Nixon's proposal to Zhou Enlai.

18 Dec.   Mao Zedong told Edgar Snow that he would like to welcome Nixon to Beijing because the U.S. president was the person with whom he could "discuss and solve the problems between China and the United States." Mao made it clear that he "would be happy to meet Nixon, either as president or as a tourist."

9 Dec.   After weeks of silence, Nixon and Kissinger received Zhou Enlai's reply: In order to discuss the vacation of Chinese territories called Taiwan, a special envoy of President Nixon will be most welcome in Beijing. Nixon White House replied that they could send an envoy, but that talks could not be confined only to Taiwan.

1971

25 Feb.   In his second annual Foreign Policy Report, Nixon stated, "The United States is prepared to see the People's Republic of China play a constructive role in the family of nations." It is the first time an American official document referred to the People's Republic of China by its official name.

15 March   State Department ended restrictions on U.S. travel to China.

10 April   Nine American table tennis players, four officials, and two spouses arrived in China, ushering in an era of "Ping-Pong diplomacy."

11–17 April   The American Ping-Pong team's visit to China received extensive U.S. media coverage.

27 April   Nixon and Kissinger received Zhou Enlai's message, through the Pakistani channel, that China was willing to receive Nixon's envoy.

30 April   *Life* magazine published Edgar Snow's interview with Mao Zedong on 18 December 1970.

17 May   Beijing received Nixon's formal response via Pakistani channel. In the reply, Nixon accepted Zhou's invitation to visit Beijing, but insisted on an open agenda.

29 May	Zhou Enlai sent a message to Washington, through the Pakistani channel, indicating that Mao Zedong welcomed Nixon to visit China.
10 June	The White House announced the end of its 21-year embargo on trade with China.
6 July	Nixon's Kansas City remarks: In his address to a large group of Midwestern news media executives, Nixon wanted to place on record an outline of the reasons for approaching China. He foresaw a world of "five great economic superpowers" (the United States, Western Europe, Japan, the Soviet Union, and China) whose relationship would determine the structure of peace in our time. He claimed that "doors must be opened" and relations between Beijing and Washington normalized.
9–11 July	Henry Kissinger held extensive talks with Zhou Enlai during his secret visit to Beijing.
15 July	In a nationally televised surprise announcement, Nixon announced that he would visit China in early 1972.
28 July	The U.S. government announced the suspension of intelligence-gathering missions over China.
2 Aug.	Secretary of State Rogers announced that the U.S. would end its 20-year policy of opposition to Communist China's admission to the UN, but would not vote to expel the Nationalists.
5 Aug.	In a *New York Times* interview, Zhou Enlai stressed that "the question of Vietnam and Indochina should be solved, and not the question of Taiwan or other questions," but stated that China would refuse to enter the UN so long as Nationalist China remained seated.
13 Sept.	Marshal Lin Biao, Mao's designated successor, died in an airplane crash while fleeing to Moscow.
16 Sept.	In an unscheduled news conference, Nixon said that the U.S. would support the PRC's seating in the UN Security Council because it "reflects the realities of the situation," but added that "we will vote against the expulsion of the Republic of China."
20–25 Oct.	Kissinger's second visit to China to prepare for Nixon's upcoming visit.
25 Oct.	The UN General Assembly voted to admit the PRC and expel Nationalist China. U.S. supported "duel representation" resolution that the PRC should hold the Security Council seat, but that both Chinas should be in the General Assembly; it failed to pass.
11 Nov.–22 Dec.	PRC delegation attended the 26th UN General Assembly.
3 Dec.	India, supported by Soviet aid, invaded Pakistan. Both the U.S. and China sided with Pakistan.

1972

3–10 Jan.	Deputy National Security Adviser Alexander Haig led an advance party to China to make technical arrangements for Nixon's visit.
17 Feb.	After a farewell ceremony on the White House lawn, President and Mrs. Nixon departed for Hawaii, en route to China.

21–27 Feb.	Nixon's historic trip to China.
27 Feb.	The United States and China issued the Shanghai Communiqué.
1 May	The United States and China opened liaison offices in Beijing and Washington, D.C., respectively, operating as de facto embassies.

1979

| 1 Jan. | The United States extended full diplomatic relations to the PRC and withdrew its diplomatic recognition from the ROC in Taiwan. |

NOTES

Abbreviations Used in Notes

CCA	Chinese Central Archives, Beijing
CWIHPB	*Cold War International History Project Bulletin*
DZJJG	Han, *Dangdai Zhongguo Jundui de Junshi Gongzuo*
FRUS	Foreign Relations of the United States
HAK	Henry A. Kissinger
JYMZW	Mao, *Jianguo Yilai Mao Zedong Wengao*
LBJPL	Lyndon Baines Johnson Presidential Library
MZN93	Pang, *Mao Zedong Nianpu, 1893–1949*
MZW	Mao, *Mao Zedong Wenji*
MZWW	Mao, *Mao Zedong Waijiao Wenxuan*
MZX	Mao, *Mao Zedong Xuanji*
MZZ49	Pang, *Mao Zedong Zhuan, 1949–1976*
NA	National Archives II (College Park, Maryland)
NPMP	Nixon Presidential Materials Project
NSCF	National Security Council Files
RG	Record Group
WHSF	White House Special Files
ZEJW	Zhou, *Zhou Enlai Junshi Wenxuan*
ZEN98	Jin, *Zhou Enlai Nianpu, 1898–1949*
ZEN49	Li, *Zhou Enlai Nianpu, 1949–1976*
ZEWHD	Pei, *Zhou Enlai Waijiao Huodong Dashiji, 1949–1975*
ZEWW	Zhou, *Zhou Enlai Waijiao Wenxuan*
ZEZ	Jin, *Zhou Enlai Zhuan, 1949–1976*
ZHJH	Wang Bingnan, *Zhongmei Huitan Jiunian Huigu*
ZRGW49	Pei, *Zhonghua Renmin Gongheguo Waijiaoshi, 1949–1956*
ZRGW57	Wang, *Zhonghua Renmin Gongheguo Waijiaoshi, 1957–1969*
ZRGW70	Wang, *Zhonghua Renmin Gongheguo Waijiaoshi, 1970–1978*
ZZWX	Zhonggong Zhongyang Wenjian Xuanji

1. Introduction

1. See, for example, Zhang Shu Guang, *Economic Cold War*; idem, *Deterrence and Strategic Culture*; Chen Jian, *Mao's China and the Cold War*; Christensen, *Useful Adversaries*; Sheng, *Battling Western Imperialism*; Zhai, *Dragon, the Lion, and the Eagle*.

2. Jiang Jieshi was the leader of Chinese Nationalist government from 1927 to 1949. He fled to Taiwan after the Communist takeover of the Chinese mainland, and was president of ROC in Taiwan from 1950 to 1975.

3. E.g., Zhang Shu Guang, *Economic Cold War*; idem, *Deterrence and Strategic Culture*; Chen Jian, *Mao's China and the Cold War*; Christensen, *Useful Adversaries*; Zhai, *Dragon, the Lion, and the Eagle*; Gordon H. Chang, *Friends and Enemies*; Gaddis, "Dividing Adversaries," 147–94; and Mayers, *Cracking the Monolith*.

4. Joy, *How Communists Negotiate*; Goodman, *Negotiating While Fighting*.

5. Dean, "What It's Like to Negotiate with the Chinese," 44–45; U. Alexis Johnson, *Right Hand of Power*; Beam, *Multiple Exposure*.

6. See Nixon, *Memoirs of Richard Nixon*; Kissinger, *White House Years*; Holdridge, *Crossing the Divide*; Walters, *Silent Missions*, 523–50.

7. See Vatcher, *Panmunjom*; Foot, *Substitute for Victory*; Bailey, *Korean Armistice*.

8. Young, *Negotiating with the Chinese Communists*; Goldstein, "Dialogue of the Deaf?"

9. See Solomon, "China: Friendship and Obligation in Chinese Negotiating Style," 1–16; idem, *Chinese Negotiating Behavior*.

10. Wilhelm, *Chinese at the Negotiating Table*.

11. Raymond Cohen, *Negotiating across Cultures*, 25.

12. Ibid, 26.

13. Ibid.

14. Zhang Shu Guang, *Meiguo Duihua Zhanlue Kaolei Yu Juece*, ix.

15. Kennan (Mr. X), "The Sources of Soviet Conduct," 566–82.

16. Kennan, *American Diplomacy*, 101.

17. Lippmann, *Cold War*, 51 and 60.

18. This author disagrees with Fredrik Logevall's argument that "it can be said that the United States had no meaningful diplomacy with Communist adversaries through long stretches of the Cold War." See Logevall, "Bernath Lecture: A Critique of Containment," 473. It is not true of U.S. relations with the PRC, to say nothing of those with the Soviet Union.

19. Ikenberry, *American Foreign Policy*, 124.

20. Gaddis, *Strategies of Containment*, especially conclusion; Buhite, *Soviet-American Relations in Asia*, conclusion; Zhang Shu Guang, *Deterrence and Strategic Culture*, conclusion; idem, *Meiguo Duihua Zhanlue Kaolei Yu Juece*, viii and conclusion.

21. See Walt, *Origins of Alliances*, 19–21, 172–74; Jervis and Snyder, *Dominoes and Bandwagons*.

22. "Comparative advantage," an international economy term, is adapted here to compare countries' comprehensive national power. See Kenen et al., *International Economy*, 19–82; Deardorff, "The General Validity of the Law of Comparative Advantage," 941–57.

23. Ikenberry, *American Foreign Policy*, 285–89.

24. Although I relied heavily on *FRUS*, I also made extensive use of the National Archives (Records of the Department of State, Nixon Presidential Materials Project). I found that archival records regarding ambassadorial talks, Paris secret talks, and U.S.-China rapprochement negotiations are very revealing.

25. Dangdai Zhongguo Series, *Kangmei Yuanchao Zhanzheng*; Xue, *Dangdai Zhongguo Waijiao*.

26. ZEWHD; ZRGW49; ZRGW57; ZRGW70.

27. ZEN49; ZEZ; MZZ49.

28. E.g., Jia, *Wei Shixian de Hejie*; Su, *Meiguo Duihua Zhengce Yu Taiwan Wenti*; Tao, *Zhong Mei Guanxi Shi*; Zhang Baijia and Niu, *Lengzhan Yu Zhongguo*.

29. Xu Jingli, *Jiemi Zhongguo Waijiao Dang'an.*
30. Gao, *Wannian Zhou Enlai.*

2. Establishing Contact

1. "The United States Policy toward the People's Republic of China, 1949–1969, Part I," box 8, Executive Secretariat Historical Office Research Project, 1969–1974, RG 59.

2. Warren I. Cohen, "Acheson, His Advisers, and China," 13–14.

3. Mayers, *Cracking the Monolith*, 19–21.

4. NSC 6, "The Position of the U.S. Regarding Short-term Assistance to China," 26 March 1948, *FRUS*, 1948, 8: 44–45.

5. The above two paragraphs are based on NSC 6, ibid., 46–50.

6. Cited from Mayers, *Cracking the Monolith*, 24.

7. Tsou, *America's Failure in China*, 2: 475.

8. For a good discussion of this point, see Stueck, *Road to Confrontation*, 56–57.

9. Kennan to Marshall, "The Situation in China and U.S. Policy," 3 November 1947, "China 1947–1948," box 13, Records of the PPS, RG 59.

10. Gaddis, "The American 'Wedge' Strategy," 159.

11. PPS/39, "To Review and Define United States Policy toward China," 7 September 1948, *FRUS*, 1948, 8:148; Memorandum by Charlton Ogburn Jr., 2 November 1949, *FRUS*, 1949, 9: 160–61.

12. PPS/39, *FRUS*, 1948, 8: 147, 155.

13. Ibid., 147–55.

14. "United States Policy toward the PRC, 1949–1969," p. 9, box 8, RG 59.

15. The China Lobby, an influential pro-Nationalist coalition of publishers, businessmen, military generals, and Republican congressmen, came into to existence in the early 1940s. They, including freshman senator Richard Nixon, attacked the Truman administration for being "soft" on Chinese Communism, and blamed the Nationalists' defeat on a handful of allegedly treasonous State Department China specialists. It was the antecedent of the Committee of One Million. By the later 1960s, the China Lobby lost much of its strength. See Koen, *China Lobby in American Politics*, 29–30.

16. The previous two paragraphs draw heavily on Mayers, *Cracking the Monolith*, 30–31.

17. The CCP Central Committee to the CCP Northeast Bureau, 1 November 1948, cited in ZEN98, 814.

18. ZZWX 17: 35–39.

19. ZEN98, 796. The unpublished part of the telegram, the part concerning "squeezing out" Western diplomats in Shenyang, can be found in Chinese Central Archives, Beijing. Cited from Chen Jian, "The Myth of America's 'Lost Chance,'" 78.

20. Gao Gang, a member of the CCP Politburo who had risen in the CCP leadership in the 1940s, was then CCP's top official in the Northeast. After Stalin's death, however, he was purged, and then he committed suicide. For a discussion of Gao's case, see Teiwes, *Politics at Mao's Court*; see also Salisbury, *New Emperors*, 90.

21. Mao Zedong to Gao Gang, 17 November 1948, CCA, cited in Chen Jian, "The Myth of America's 'Lost Chance,'" 78.

22. Mao Zedong to Gao Gang, November 18, 1948, CCA, cited ibid., 78.

23. For a detailed account of the Ward case see Chen Jian, "The Ward Case," 149–70; Yang Kuisong, "The Ward Case," 104–18.

24. Chen Jian, "The Ward Case," 153–54; Yang Kuisong, "The Ward Case," 107.

25. For a plausible discussion of the Soviet attitude toward the Northeast in the early stage of China's civil war, see Yang Kuisong, "The Soviet Factor and the CCP's Policy toward the United States in the 1940s," 24–28.

26. Goncharov, "Stalin's Dialogues with Mao Zedong," 65–66. Goncharov points out that it was Kovalev who proposed to the CCP that it isolate the American diplomats and confiscate their radio transmitter. The Soviets passed this message to Gao Gang, who reported the Soviets' strong advice that the CCP treat the American diplomats in Shenyang the same way the GMD had treated the Soviet commercial representatives in the Northeast in 1946—that is, to cut off their external channels of communication. According to Gao, the Soviets believed that the Americans would be compelled to leave. Yang Kuisong's study shows that it was Malining, the Soviet consul general in Harbin, who called Gao Gang and urged him to confiscate all radio transmitters of U.S., U.K., and French consulates general in Shenyang. See Yang Kuisong, "The Ward Case," 107.

27. Chen Jian, "The Ward Case," 154–55; Yang Kuisong, "The Ward Case," 111.

28. Beijing (Peking) was called "Beiping" by the Chinese Nationalists from 1928 to 1949. In late September 1949, the Communist named Beijing, the capital of the Ming and Qing dynasties, as the new seat of government for the PRC. "Beijing" is used in this book for events after 1 October 1949.

29. Li Rui, "Random Notes on the Takeover of Shenyang," 58–59. Li was then Chen Yun's political secretary.

30. Telegram: Northeast Bureau to the Central Committee, 24 November 1948, cited from Yang Kuisong, "The Ward Case," 110. In carrying out the policy of "squeezing out" the Westerners, the Northeast Bureau tried to treat the British and French diplomats differently. The main target of struggle was the Americans as the U.S. was supporting the Chinese Nationalists in the civil war. Ibid., 108.

31. Mao Zedong, "The Present Situation and the Task of the Party in 1949," *MZW* 5: 231. On 6 January, when talking about the issue, Mao stressed, "We are not eager to seek the recognition of imperialist countries as we are anti-imperialism. We may discuss the issue of recognition when we want to do business in the future. Neither are we in a hurry to recognize them. We have to protect foreign nationals in China. We are in a hurry to establish diplomatic relations with the Soviet Union and democratic countries." Ibid., 235–36 n. 6. The report was delivered by Mao to the Politburo on 6 January 1949. It was then adopted by the Politburo and issued as a formal document on 8 January.

32. The British Embassy to the Department of State, 10 January 1949, *FRUS*, 1949, 9: 821.

33. NSC 34/1 "United States Policy toward China," Draft Report by the National Security Council, 11 January 1949, *FRUS*, 1949, 9: 474–75; also see Martin: *Divided Counsel*, 4–7.

34. Mao Zedong, "Comments on the abstract of conversation with Lei Wenhe," 4 December 1948, CCA, cited in Yang Kuisong, "The Ward Case," 110. Also see Niu Jun, "The Origins of the Sino-Soviet Alliance," 68.

35. *MZN*93: 3: 410–11.

36. Mao Zedong, "Carry the revolution through to the end," 30 December 1948, *MZX* 4: 1374.

37. Yang Kuisong, "The Ward Case," 110.

38. The detention, trial, and imprisonment of American consul general Angus Ward and his staff from November 1948 to December 1949.

39. Xue, *Dangdai Zhongguo Waijiao*, 4; Mao Zedong's conclusion at the Second Plenary Session of the Seventh Central Committee, 13 March 1949, minutes, CCA, cited in Chen Jian, "The Myth of America's 'Lost Chance' in China"; Mao Zedong,

"Report on the Second Plenary Session of the Seventh Central Committee of the CCP," *MZX* 4: 1435–36.

40. Mao's telegram to the Party Center, 3 January 1950, *JYMZW*, 1: 213.

41. He, "The Evolution of the Chinese Communist Party's Policy toward the United States," 43.

42. NSC 34/1, "United States Policy toward China," Draft Report by the National Security Council, 11 January 1949, *FRUS*, 1949, 9: 474–75.

43. Tucker, *Patterns in the Dust*, 2.

44. Memorandum by Marshall S. Carter, 7 February 1949; Acheson Memorandum of Conversation with Truman, 7 February 1949; and Memorandum by Sidney W. Souers for National Security Council, 8 February 1949, *FRUS*, 1949, 9: 485–7.

45. Memorandum of Acheson-Bevin Conversation, 4 April 1949, *FRUS*, 1949, 7: 1138–41.

46. The last three paragraphs are based on NSC-41, "Draft Report by the National Security Council on United States Policy Regarding Trade with China," 28 February 1949, *FRUS*, 1949, 9: 826–34.

47. Cabot to the Director of the Office of Far Eastern Affairs (Butterworth), 30 December 1948, *FRUS*, 1948, 7: 707–18; Memorandum by Chief of Division of Commercial Affairs for Paul H. Nitze, 7 January 1949, *FRUS*, 1949, 8: 16–19.

48. "United States Policy toward the PRC, 1949–1969," pp. 19, 13, box 8, RG 59.

49. Zhang Shu Guang, *Deterrence and Strategic Culture*, 24.

50. Telegram, Zhou to the General Front Command Commission, 25 April 1949, in *ZEN98*, 824.

51. See Chen Xiaolu, "China's Policy toward the United States," 186.

52. Yang Kuisong, "The Ward Case," 112; Niu Jun, "The Origins of the Sino-Soviet Alliance," 64–65.

53. "Stalin Cable to Kovalev re Trade with Capitalist Countries," 15 March 1949, cited in Goncharov, Lewis, and Xue, *Uncertain Partners*, 230–31.

54. Goncharov, "Stalin's Dialogues with Mao Zedong," 63; also Goncharov, Lewis, and Xue, *Uncertain Partners*, 231.

55. "Philip Fugh's Letter to Zhou Enlai, Deng Yingchao and Dong Biwu," 8 December 1948, cited in Xu Jingli, *Jiemi Zhongguo Waijiao Dang'an*, 1.

56. "Mills Memorandum," 1949; Saul Mills, *Mission to China*, 1949; "Summary of Mills' Talk with Zhou Enlai," 18 May 1949, cited in Yang Kuisong, "The Ward Case," 113.

57. Memorandum, "Mr. Chen Ming-shu's Report on American Ambassador's Secret Visit to Shanghai," 26 March 1949, cited in Yang Kuisong, "The Ward Case," 113. Stuart's diary (25 March 1949) indicates that he had a three-hour meeting with Chen Ming-shu, and Lo Haisha on 25 March. See Stuart, *John Leighton Stuart's Diary*, 30.

58. Mao Zedong to the CCP's General Front-line Committee, 28 April 1949, *Dangde Wenxian* no. 4 (1989): 43.

59. Mao Zedong, "Statement by the Spokesman of the General Headquarters of the Chinese People's Liberation Army," 20 April 1949, *MZX*, 4: 1464.

60. Zhonggong Zhongyang Dangxiao Jiaoyanshi, ed. *Zhonggong Dangshi Cankao Ziliao*, 60.

61. *Mao Zedong Yijiusanliunian Tong Sinuo de Tanhua*, 110.

62. *FRUS*, 1942, 1: 98–103, 197–99, 206; *FRUS*, 1943: 10: 192, 197, 201–3, 214–16.

63. For accounts of the Dixie Mission to Yan'an, see Barrett, *Dixie Mission*; Also Carter, *Mission to Yenan*.

64. Zhang Shu Guang and Chen, *Chinese Communist Foreign Policy*, 13–17.

65. *ZHJH*, 37.

66. Mao's conversation with John Service recorded by Service, 27 August 1944, is in Esherick, *Lost Chance in China*, 307.

67. *Hu Qiaomu Huiyi Mao Zedong*, 336, 341–42; Esherick, *Lost Chance in China*, 295–307.

68. George Elsey, "The President and U.S. Aid to China," p. 42, box 165, Map Room Files, Franklin Delano Roosevelt Library, Hyde Park, New York.

69. *Hu Qiaomu Huiyi Mao Zedong*, 342.

70. For a general discussion of Hurley's mission, see Westad, *Cold War and Revolution*, chapter 1; for a critical Chinese account, see Niu Jun, *Cong Heerli dao Maxieer*; for the text of the five-point agreement, see Van Slyke, *China White Paper*, 74–75.

71. *Hu Qiaomu Huiyi Mao Zedong*, 354.

72. Ibid., 359

73. *FRUS*, 1944, 7: 203.

74. For an account of the *Amerasia* incident, see Service, *Amerasia Papers*.

75. *Hu Qiaomu Huiyi Mao Zedong*, 361–62.

76. For discussion of the origin of the Marshall Mission, see Westad, *Cold War and Revolution*, chapter 6; for a recently published collection of essays on different aspects of the Marshall Mission, see Bland, *George C. Marshall's Mediation Mission to China*.

77. Statement by President Truman on United States Policy toward China, 15 December 1945, in Van Slyke, *China White Paper*, 607–609.

78. *Hu Qiaomu Huiyi Mao Zedong*, 426, 428–29. To achieve a peaceful solution to the CCP-GMD conflict would have required both parties to cooperate and share power in a way neither would have accepted. The GMD demanded that the CCP submit its military forces to the "unified leadership" of the GMD government. The CCP insisted that the "democratization" of Jiang's regime should come before the nationalization of China's armed forces.

79. Marshall to President and Secretary of State, 1 February 1946, *FURS* 1946, 9: 151–52.

80. Goncharov, Lewis, and Xue, *Uncertain Partners*, 49.

81. *MZX* 4: 361–75, 401–403.

82. "United States Policy toward the PRC, 1949–1969," p. 12, box 8, RG 59.

83. Li Zongren succeeded Jiang Jieshi as acting president on 21 January 1949.

84. Shaw, *American Missionary in China*, 243.

85. Ibid., 247.

86. The Secretary of State to Stuart, 26 January 1949, *FRUS*, 1949, 8: 667–68.

87. "United States Policy toward the PRC, 1949–1969," pp. 49–50, box 8, RG 59.

88. Stuart to the Secretary of State, 10 March 1949, *FRUS*, 1949, 8: 173–77.

89. The Secretary of State to Stuart, 6 April 1949, *FRUS*, 1949, 8: 230–31.

90. The Secretary of State to Stuart, 22 April 1949, *FRUS*, 1949, 8: 682–83.

91. Huang, "My Contacts with John Leighton Stuart,"24.

92. Ibid.

93. Chen Guangxiang, "Why Didn't the PLA Liberate Shanghai Immediately?" 21; Also Chen Jian, *China's Road to the Korean War*, 52.

94. Goncharov, "Stalin's Dialogue with Mao," 50; and Goncharov, Lewis, and Xue, *Uncertain Partners*, 43.

95. "Mao Zedong to the CCP Nanjing Municipal Committee," 10 May 1949, *MZN*93, 3: 499–500; Huang, "My Contacts with John Leighton Stuart," 26–27.

96. "Mao Zedong to the CCP Nanjing Municipal Committee," 10 May 1949.

97. Huang, "My Contacts with John Leighton Stuart," 26.

98. "Mao Zedong to the CCP Nanjing Municipal Committee," 10 May 1949.

99. Stuart to the Secretary of State, 14 May 1949, *FRUS*, 1949, 8: 745–46.

100. Xu Jingli, *Jiemi Zhongguo Waijiao Dang'an*, 26.

101. Chen Xiaolu, "China's Policy toward the United States," 186. Wusong Kou is the water gateway of the city of Shanghai.

102. The CCP's General Front-line Committee to Su Yu and Zhang Zhen, 21 May 1949, telegram, CCA; Chen Xiaolu, "China's Policy toward the United States," 186; Chen Jian, *China's Road to the Korean War*, 53.

103. Stuart to the Secretary of State, 8 June 1949. *FRUS, 1949*, 8: 752–53; Huang, "My Contacts with John Leighton Stuart," 28–29.

104. Huang, "My Contacts with John Leighton Stuart," 29–30. Webb's cable to Stuart could not be found in *FRUS*; thus it might be Fugh's pretext.

105. Sprouse Memoranda of Conversations, 6 January 1949, and 10 February 1949, *FRUS, 1949*, 9: 5–6, 823–26.

106. Yu Huamin. "The Secret Contact between the U.S. and Chinese Communists," 30; Huang, "My Contacts with John Leighton Stuart," 30.

107. Yu Huamin, "The Secret Contact between the U.S. and Chinese Communists," 30.

108. Mao Zedong, "The Chinese people are willing to cooperate with people all over the world," 15 June 1949, Mao's remarks at the preparatory session of the New Political Consultative Conference, in MZWW, 91.

109. Stuart to the Secretary of State, 30 June 1949, *FRUS, 1949*, 8: 766–67; Stuart's diary (26 and 28 June 1949), see *John Leighton Stuart's Diary*, 42–43.

110. Stuart to the Secretary of State, 30 June 1949, *FRUS, 1949*, 8: 766–67;

111. See Tsou, *America's Failure in China*, 2: 530–34.

112. Davies to Kennan, 30 June 1949, *FRUS, 1949*, 8: 768–69.

113. Huang Hua dismissed the idea that a Stuart visit to Beiping might have opened the way to improved relations. He argued that Mao and Zhou were not interested in anything more than forestalling a major American intervention to save Guomindang. See Warren I. Cohen, "Conversations with Chinese Friends," 283–89.

114. The Secretary of State to Stuart, 20 July 1949, *FRUS, 1949*, 8: 769, 780–81, 794. Also see Tucker, *Patterns in the Dust*, 174.

115. The Secretary of State to Stuart, 1 July 1949, *FRUS, 1949*, 8: 769.

116. Huang, "My Contacts with John Leighton Stuart," 31.

117. Stuart's diary (26 June 1949), in *John Leighton Stuart's Diary*, 42.

118. Mao Zedong, "Address to the Preparatory Meeting of the New Political Consultative Conference," MZX, 4: 1470.

119. Stueck, *Road to Confrontation*, 124–25; Nakajima Mineo, "Foreign Relations: From the Korean War to the Bandung Line," 263.

120. MZX, 4: 1470; see also Zhou Enlai, "Report on Problems Concerning the Peace Talks," *Zhou Enlai Xuanji*, 1: 322–23.

121. The CCP charge was not totally groundless. The Chinese sources show that the U.S. consular officers were involved in espionage activities. See Xu Jingli, *Jiemi Zhongguo Waijiao Dang'an*, 213–17, 220–25. Even the U.S. sources indicate that U.S. consular officers at Mukden "worked closely with an American naval intelligence unit stationed in the area, and the radio of the Consulate General transmitted messages on behalf of the Nationalist forces." See "United States Policy toward the PRC, 1949–1969," p. 21, box 8, RG 59.

122. *Renmin Ribao*, 19 June 1949; Clubb to Acheson, 19 June 1949, *FRUS, 1949*, 8: 965.

123. Mao Zedong to the CCP Northeast Bureau, 22 June 1949, telegram, CCA, cited in Chen Jian, *China's Road to the Korean War*, 55.

124. Mao Zedong's Instruction to Hu Qiaomu, 24 June 1949, *Mao Zedong Shuxin Xuanji*, 327–28.

125. *Dongbei Ribao*, 20 June 1949; the Consul General at Beiping (Clubb) to the Secretary of State (Acheson), 19 June 1949, *FRUS*, 1949, 8: 965.

126. Stuart to the Secretary of State, *FRUS*, 1949, 8: 968–69.

127. ZRGW49, 3.

128. For a detailed discussion of Liu's visit to the Soviet Union from late June to August 1948, see Zhu, "Liu Shaoqi's Secret Visit to the Soviet Union in 1949," 74–80; and Jin, *Liu Shaoqi Zhuan*, 646. Liu's delegation arrived at Moscow on 26 June 1949.

129. According to one Chinese source, General Chen Ming-shu was invited to Beiping to attend the preparatory session of the New China Political Consultative Conference by the CCP in June 1949. In his meeting with Mao, Mao stated that the CCP placed great hopes on Stuart. He hoped that the United States would cut off its assistance to Jiang's reactionary government. If the United States would "act and formulate [its China] policies in the manner of President Roosevelt, General Stilwell and Mr. [Henry] Wallace," then [Communist] China would be friendly to the United States. See Yu Huamin, "The Secret Contact between the U.S. and Chinese Communists," 31–32. This could be confirmed by U.S. sources. See Memorandum by General Chen Ming-shu, Chairman of the Shanghai Board of the Kuomintang Revolutionary Committee (*KmtRC*)–Supplementary Memo to Conversation with Mr. L. Stuart, *FRUS*, 1949, 8: 773–79. Also see *John Leighton Stuart's Diary*, 9 July 1949, 44.

130. "United States Policy toward the PRC, 1949–1969," p. 70, box 8, RG59.

131. Mao Zedong, "Cast Away Illusions, Prepare for Struggle," "Farewell, John Leighton Stuart," "Why It Is Necessary to Discuss the White Paper," "'Friendship' or 'Aggression'?" "The Bankruptcy of the Idealist Conception of History," *MZX* 4: 1486–520.

132. He, "The Most Respected Enemy," 148.

133. O. Edmund Clubb was American consul general in Beiping before the Communists took over the city.

134. *Zhonghua Renmin Gongheguo Duiwai Guanxi Wenjianji*, 4–5; see also Clubb to Acheson, 2 October 1949, *FRUS*, 1949, 9: 93–94.

135. Mao Zedong to Liu Shaoqi and Zhou Enlai, 19 December 1949, *JYMZW*, 1: 193; Xue, *Dangdai Zhongguo Waijiao*, 7–9.

136. Memorandum by Freeman (Acting Deputy Director of the Office of Chinese Affairs), 3 October 1949, *FRUS*, 1949, 9: 96–97.

137. *New York Times* (3 October 1949): 1.

138. Zhou Enlai, "New China's Diplomacy," in *ZEWW*, 1–2.

139. Ward, Ralph Rehberg, and three non-American members of the consulate general were arrested.

140. According to Ward, Ji was fired by the consulate in late September and was found hidden in the consulate compound by Ward on 11 October. Ward tried to escort him out of the area. When Ji lay down on stairway and refused to move, Ward endeavored to take "him by hand intending to turn him as trespasser to armed sentry at street entrance." This prompted a scuffle with Ji's brother, who was also in the compound. Ji was then sent to hospital, although Ward believed "[At] no time did I or any member my staff strike, kick or injure Chi [Ji] in any way." Ward to Acheson, 11 September 1949, *FRUS*, 1949, 8: 1049. The Chinese sources contend that Ward and his staff did beat, kick, and injure Ji. See Xu Jingli, *Jiemi Zhongguo Waijiao Dang'an*, 218–20.

141. *Dongbei Ribao*, 25 October 1949; for related Chinese reports on the case, see *Dongbei Ribao*, 28 October and 2 November 1949.

142. Memorandum by the Under Secretary of State (Webb), 14 November 1949, *FRUS*, 1949, 8: 1008; Memorandum by the Acting Secretary of State, 31 October 1949, *FRUS*, 1949, 9: 1355. Also see Chen Jian, *China's Road to the Korean War*, 61.

143. "Angus Ward Released by Communists — Secretary Acheson Sends Personal Letter to Thirty Nations," *Department of State Bulletin* v. 21, no. 543 (28 November 1949): 799–800.

144. *Dongbei Ribao*, 27 November 1949; *Xinhua Yuebao* 1, no. 3 (1949): 620–23; Ward to Acheson, 11 December 1949, *FRUS, 1949*, 8: 1049–50.

145. Stuart's diary (18 and 19 July), *John Leighton Stuart's Diary*, 45.

146. "United States Policy toward the PRC, 1949–1969," pp. 123–25, box 8, RG 59.

147. "United States Policy toward Formosa — Statement by President Truman," *Department of State Bulletin* v. 22, no. 550 (16 January 1950): 79; "China Telegram" (4 January 1950), Foster Papers, box 26, cited in Kuznitz, *Public Opinion and Foreign Policy*, 41 n. 64.

148. Yang Kuisong, "The Ward Case," 118.

149. Memorandum by the Acting Secretary of State to the President, 10 January 1950. *FRUS, 1950*, 6: 270–72. U.S. Consul General Clubb and his staff were forced to remove American property and evacuate the three-story barracks office building by midnight on 13 January.

150. *Renmin Ribao*, 19 January 1950; Xue, *Dangdai Zhongguo Waijiao*, 18–19.

151. "United States Policy toward the PRC, 1949–1969," pp. 127–28, box 8, RG 59; "Communists Take U.S. Property in China," *Department of State Bulletin* v. 22, no. 551 (23 January 1950): 119.

152. Mao Zedong to Liu Shaoqi, 13 and 17 January 1950, JYMZW, 235, 241.

153. *Renmin Ribao*, 19 January 1950.

154. "United States Policy toward the PRC, 1949–1969," box 8, RG 59.

155. *Zhonghua Renmin Gongheguo Duiwai Guanxi Wenjianji*, 75–78. The English version is from Rhode and Whitlock, *Treaties of the People's Republic of China*, 15 b.

156. Zhou Enlai, "International Situation and Diplomatic Tasks after the Signing of the Sino-Soviet Treaty," 20 March 1950, ZEWW, 11–17.

157. Mao Zedong's "Address to the Sixth Session of the Central People's Government Council," 11 April 1950, JYMZW, 1: 291.

158. "United States Policy toward the PRC, 1949–1969," pp. 79–80, box 8, RG 59.

159. Mao Zedong's conclusion at the Second Plenary Session of the Seventh Central Committee, 13 March 1949, CCA, cited in Chen Jian, "The Myth of America's 'Lost Chance' in China," 81.

160. Yang Kuisong, "The Ward Case," 114.

161. For the "Lost Chance" debate, see Warren I. Cohen, "Symposium: Rethinking the Lost Chance in China," 71–115.

162. The author agrees with Nancy B. Tucker, William W. Stueck, John Gaddis, and Gordon Chang that there existed a chance for developing a working relationship between the PRC and the United States in late 1949 and early 1950. See Tucker, *Patterns in the Dust*; Stueck, *Road to Confrontation*; Gaddis, "The Strategic Perspective," 61–118; Chang, *Friends and Enemies*, 7–75.

3. Negotiating While Fighting

1. Acheson, *Present at the Creation*, 652.

2. Resolution Adopted by the United Nations Security Council, 25 June 1950, *FRUS, 1950*, 7: 155–56.

3. Resolution Adopted by the United Nations Security Council, 27 June 1950, ibid., 7: 211.

4. "United States Policy toward the PRC, 1949–1969," p. 129, box 8, RG 59.

5. Kaufman, *The Korean War*, 30.

6. Zhou Enlai, speech at the CCP Central Military Commission's Enlarged Meeting, 26 August 1950. In this speech, Zhou Enlai clearly pointed out that from Beijing's perspective, the settlement of the Korean issue should be related to Taiwan and China's seat at the UN. For a full transcript of the speech, see *ZEJW* 4: 42–49; For an English translation of part of the speech, see Zhang and Chen, *Chinese Communist Foreign Policy and the Cold War in Asia*, 158–59; Chen Jian, *Mao's China and the Cold War*, 89.

7. Chai and Zhao, *Kangmei Yuanchao Jishi*, 47.

8. The UN forces under the command of General Douglas MacArthur succeeded in landing in Inchon on 15 September 1950, catching the North Korean forces off guard.

9. For a comprehensive discussion, see Chen Jian, *China's Road to the Korean War*, chapters 6–7.

10. *Peng Dehuai Zishu*, 259.

11. For the text of the proposal, see *FRUS, 1951*, 7: 64; for the background of the proposal, see Stueck, *Korean War*, 152–54; For a Chinese description of the proposal, see Chai and Zhao, *Kangmei Yuanchao Jishi*, 75.

12. Acheson, *Present at the Creation*, 513.

13. Ciphered Telegram, Roshchin to USSR Foreign Ministry, 13 January 1951 in *CWIHPB*, nos. 6–7 (Winter 1995–96), 34, 54.

14. *ZEWHDJ*, 25; Also, "Editorial Note, Chou Enlai to the Acting Secretary-General of the UN," 17 January 1951, *FRUS, 1951*, 7: 90–91; Foot, *Substitute for Victory*, 30.

15. *FRUS, 1951*: 7: 91–92, January 17; 7: 117, January 22; 7: 130, January 25. The text of Zhou's reply is in RG 59, Records of the Director of the Office of North East Asian Affairs, U. Alexis Johnson, box 4, 22 January 1951, NA.

16. Acheson, *Present at the Creation*, 536.

17. Memorandum Containing the Sections Dealing with Korea from NSC 48/5, 17 May 1951, *FRUS, 1951*, 7: 439.

18. Ibid., 439–42.

19. Acheson, *Present at the Creation*, 531.

20. Vatcher, *Panmunjom*, 18.

21. Telegram, Mao to Peng, 4 December 1950, cited in Chinese Academy of Military Sciences, *Zhongguo Renmin Zhiyuanjun Kangmei Yuanchao Zhanshi*, 76–77.

22. Rees, *Korea: The Limited War*, 225–56.

23. Pillar, *Negotiating Peace*, 46.

24. *Nie Rongzhen Huiyilu*, 2: 742.

25. Ibid.

26. Chai and Zhao, *Banmendian Tanpan*, 125; Qi, *Chaoxian Zhanzheng Juece Neimu*, 177.

27. Stueck, *Rethinking the Korean War*, 139. In reality, Kim Il-sung had lost much of his commanding power over North Korean troops after December 1950, when the Chinese and North Korean forces signed an agreement to establish a joint Chinese/North Korean headquarters. The contract put the commanding power of all Communist forces in Korea into the hands of Chinese commanders. For the agreement, see *ZEJW* 4: 122–24; see also telegram, Peng Dehuai to Mao Zedong, 7 December 1950, in which Peng reported that Kim Il-sung had agreed "not to intervene in military command affairs [in Korea] in the future." See Wang Yan, *Peng Dehuai Nianpu*. Peng Dehuai was reported to have told Kim that he, not Kim, was in charge of the war. Peng is alleged to have told Kim that the Korean War was a fight between himself and General MacArthur, and Kim had no part in it. See Suh, *Kim Il Sung*, 137. In a recent article, Chinese historian Shen

Zhihua explores the tensions in Sino-Korean relations at the highest levels during the Korean War. Shen contends that the Chinese and North Koreans at least quarreled over the following four issues: (1) the North Korean government did not notify the Chinese leadership when it launched an attack on South Korea on 25 June 1950—Kim Il-sung preferred to depend on Soviet aid and avoid having China's intervention in the war; (2) after the Chinese entered the war, the two sides had difficulty creating a United Sino-North Korean Command; (3) once the CPV pushed the front line toward the 38th parallel, the two sides differed in the timing of advancing south of the 38th Parallel; (4) the two sides also conflicted over how best to manage the railroad system in order to guarantee army's supply line. See Shen Zhihua, "Sino-North Korean Conflict," 9–24.

28. Memorandum of Conversation, by Frank P. Corrigan and Thomas J. Cory of the United States Mission at the United Nations, 3 May 1951, *FRUS, 1951*, 7: 401–10; Memorandum by John P. Davies, Jr. of the Policy Planning Staff to the Director of the Policy Planning Staff (Nitze), 8 May 1951, *FRUS, 1951*, 7: 421–22.

29. Cited from Stueck, *Korean War*, 205.

30. Acheson, *Present at the Creation*, 532–33; Memorandum by George F. Kennan Concerning Events from May 18 to May 25, 1951, *FRUS, 1951*, 7: 460–62, 483–86, and 507–511.

31. Editorial Note, Malik's radio address on Korean cease-fire, 23 June 1951, *FRUS, 1951*, 7: 547. Also Kaufman, *Korean War*, 191; Stueck, *Korean War*, 208. The next day, Stalin wrote to Mao, "[Y]ou must always know from Malik's speech that our promise about raising the question of an armistice has already been fulfilled by us. It is possible that the matter of an armistice will move forward." See ciphered telegram, Filippov [Stalin] to Mao Zedong, 2 June 1951, *CWIHPB*, nos. 6–7 (Winter 1995–96): 62.

32. Stairs, *Diplomacy of Constraint*, 171–82; Porter, *Britain and the Rise of Communist China*, 116–20; Stueck, *Korean War*, 210–15.

33. *FRUS, 1951*, 7: 547; Stueck, *Korean War*, 209.

34. Memorandum of Conversation, by John R. Heidemann of the Bureau of Far Eastern Affairs, *FRUS, 1951*, 7: 595.

35. U. Alexis Johnson, *Right Hand of Power*, 121.

36. Acheson to the Embassy in the Soviet Union, 25 June 1951, *FRUS, 1951*, 7: 553–54; Kirk to the Secretary of State, 26, 27 June 1951, ibid., 7: 555, 560–61; Stueck, *Korean War*, 209; Foot, *Substitute for Victory*, 37.

37. The Joint Chiefs of Staff to the Commander in Chief, Far East (Ridgway), 28 June 1951, *FRUS, 1951*, 7: 577–78; "Memorandum of Conversation, by John R. Heidemann of the Bureau of Far Eastern Affairs," 29 June 1951, ibid., 7: 593–95; Acheson, *Present at the Creation*, 533–34.

38. This message was drafted by Admiral Davis, JCS, and U. Alexis Johnson, who was then director of the Office of Northeast Asian Affairs, and approved by Secretary of State Dean Acheson and Secretary of Defense George Marshall. For details, see Johnson, *Right Hand of Power*, 122.

39. Memorandum of Conversation, by the Director of the Office of Northeast Asian Affairs (Johnson) 28 June 195, *FRUS, 1951*, 7: 566–71, 577–78, 583–87.

40. Memorandum of Conversation, by John R. Heidemann of the Bureau of Far Eastern Affairs, 29 June 1951, *FRUS, 1951*, 7: 593–95.

41. U.S. Consulate General, Hong Kong, *Survey of the China Mainland Press* (SCMP), 26–27 June and 1–3 July 1951, cited in Stueck, *Korean War*, 216.

42. Stueck, *Korean War*, 216. It is interesting to note that the North Korean reply to the call for cease-fire talks was signed by both Peng Dehuai and Kim Il-sung, stating that "we are authorized" to begin negotiation. The wording was completely proper for Peng

as commander of the Chinese volunteers, but Kim was the head of state and needed no authorization from anyone to negotiate. The Chinese takeover of the Korean War was so comprehensive that the United States dealt primarily with the Chinese and not with Kim Il-sung directly. See Suh, *Kim Il Sung*, 138.

43. Ciphered Telegram, Filippov [Stalin] to Mao Zedong, 30 June 1951, *CWIHPB*, nos. 6–7 (Winter 1995–96), 64.

44. Editorial, 25 June 1951, *Renmin Ribao*; the CCP Central Committee Instruction: "On Issues Related to Korean Armistice Negotiation," 3 July 1951, cited in Qi, *Chaoxian Zhanzheng Juece Neimu*, 188.

45. Ibid.

46. Simmons, *Strained Alliance*, 199.

47. It's interesting to note that Mao stated it was possible to omit the question of PRC representation at the United Nations as a condition "since China can refer to the fact that the UN has in fact become an instrument of aggression, and therefore China does not at the present time attach a special significance to the question of entrance into the UN." On Taiwan, Mao believed that "the question should be raised in order to bargain with them," but "if America firmly insists that the question of Taiwan be resolved separately, then we will make a corresponding concession." See Ciphered Telegram, Mao Zedong to Gao Gang and Kim Il Sung, 13 June 1951, *CWIHPB*, nos. 6–7 (Winter 1995–96), 61.

48. Johnson, *Right Hand of Power*, 162.

49. The Joint Chiefs of Staff to Ridgway, 30 June 1951, *FRUS, 1951*, 7: 598–600.

50. The above three paragraphs are based on "The Joint Chiefs of Staff to Ridgway," ibid.

51. General MacArthur had established JSPOG on 20 August 1949 and staffed the group with Army, Navy, and Air Force representatives. The group had responsibility for high-level planning in the theater and served as the principal planning agency for the UN Command during the Korean War.

52. Hermes, *Truce Tent and Fighting Front*, 16–17.

53. Foot, *Substitute for Victory*, 11 12.

54. Chai, "Material on . . . the Korean War Armistice Negotiations," 22.

55. Ciphered Telegram, Mao Zedong to Filippov [Stalin]; Filippov [Stalin] to Mao Zedong, 30 June 1951, *CWIHPB*, nos. 6–7 (Winter 1995–96), 64–65.

56. Ciphered Telegram, Filippov [Stalin] to Razuvaev with message for Kim Il Sung, 1 July 1951, ibid., 65.

57. Mao to Peng and Kim Il-sung, 25 June 1951, in Qi, *Chaoxian Zhanzheng Juece Neimu*, 187.

58. Mao to Peng Dehuai and Kim Il-sung, 2 July 1951, *JYMZW*, 2: 379–80.

59. MZZ49, 1: 160; Chai, *Banmendian Tanpan*, 129–30.

60. Qu, ". . . An Interview with General Chai Chengwen," 47.

61. Kang, *Waijiao Douzhi Renwu*, 95.

62. Joy, *How Communists Negotiate*, 12–13.

63. "Mao Zedong to Kim Il-sung, Li Kenong and Peng Dehuai," original manuscript, 4 July 1951, cited in MZZ49, 1: 161; Stueck, *Korean War*, 224;

64. Kang, *Waijiao Douzhi Renwu*, 113.

65. Wu Xiuquan was director-general, Department of Soviet and East European Affairs, Foreign Ministry, in November 1950. He was promoted to be vice foreign minister after returning from his mission to the UN. See Wu Xiuquan, *Zai Waijiaobu Banian de Jingli*.

66. Li Lianqing, *Waijiao Yingcai Qiao Guanhua*, 54–60.

67. Joy, *How Communists Negotiate*, 13–14. Also see Chai and Zhao, *Banmendian Tanpan*, 131.

68. Stueck, *Korean War*, 210.

69. Ciphered Telegram, Mao Zedong to Filippov [Stalin] conveying 2 July 1951 telegram from Mao to Peng Dehuai, Gao Gang, and Kim Il-sung, 3 July 1951, *CWIHPB*, nos. 6–7 (Winter 1995–96), 67.

70. Ciphered Telegram, Mao Zedong to Filippov [Stalin], 3 July; 13, 27 August 1951, *CWIHPB*, nos. 6–7 (Winter 1995–96), 66–68.

71. Ciphered Telegram, CC Politburo decision with approved message, Filippov [Stalin] to Mao Zedong, 19 November, 1951, ibid., 72.

72. Qu, ". . . An Interview with General Chai Chengwen," 39–40.

73. A territory under UNC military control, where the UNC set up base camp in Munsan-ni, about ten miles south on the road to Seoul and 21 miles away from Kaesong by road.

74. Chai and Zhao, *Banmendian Tanpan*, 133.

75. Qu, ". . . An Interview with General Chai Chengwen," 10.

76. Wilhelm, *Chinese at the Negotiating Table*, 74.

77. Chai and Zhao, *Banmendian Tanpan*, 136–37.

78. Hermes, *Truce Tent and Fighting Front*, 23–24.

79. Ibid., 24.

80. Chai, "Material on . . . the Korean War Armistice Negotiations," 23.

81. Mao to Li Kenong, 11 July 1951, *JYMZW*, 2: 392.

82. Ibid., 422; Telegram from Mao Zedong to Li Kenong, Kim Il-sung and Peng Dehuai, 17 July 1951, cited in *MZZ49*, 1: 166.

83. Mao to Li Kenong, 11 July 1951, *JYMZW*, 2: 415.

84. Hermes, *Truce Tent and Fighting Front*, 29.

85. Ridgway to the Joint Chiefs of Staff, *FRUS*, 1951, 7: 726.

86. Chai, "The Decision-making Path Taken by Mao," 12; *MZZ49*, 1: 167.

87. Ridgway to the Joint Chiefs of Staff, 25 July 1951, *FRUS*, 1951, 7: 727–28; *MZZ49*, 1: 167.

88. Ridgway to the Joint Chiefs of Staff, 26 July 1951, *FRUS*, 1951, 7: 735; *MZZ49*, 1: 167–68.

89. *FRUS*, 1951, 7: 740.

90. Chai and Zhao, *Banmendian Tanpan*, 176–77.

91. Telegram, Mao to Peng, 26 July 1951, *JYMZW*, 2: 426.

92. Joy, *How Communists Negotiate*, 173–74; Hermes, *Truce Tent and Fighting Front*, 118–19, 408.

93. Acheson, *Present at the Creation*, 537.

94. Ridgway to the Joint Chiefs of Staff, 27 July 1951, *FRUS*, 1951, 7: 742; Joy, *How Communists Negotiate*, 24.

95. Ridgway to the Joint Chiefs of Staff, 28 July 1951, *FRUS*, 1951, 7: 748–52.

96. Zhou Enlai, "The Korean Armistice Talks and the Question of Signing a Peace Treaty with Japan," 3 September 1951, *ZEJW* 4: 235; Du, *Zai Zhiyuanjun Zongbu*, 375–76.

97. Vatcher, *Panmunjom*, 53–54.

98. Hermes, *Truce Tent and Fighting Front*, 39.

99. Foot, *Substitute for Victory*, 48.

100. Kaesong was formerly controlled by ROK special forces, and Rhee might have provoked these incidents to disrupt the talks.

101. Ciphered Telegram, Mao Zedong to Filippov [Stalin], 27 August 1951, *CWIHPB*, nos. 6–7 (Winter 1995–96), 68.

102. Ciphered Telegram, VKP (b) CC Politburo decision with approved message from Filippov [Stalin] to Mao Zedong, 28 August 1951, ibid., 69.

103. Stueck, *Rethinking the Korean War*, 151.

104. Downs, *Over the Line*, 46.

105. Chai, "The Decision-making Path Taken by Mao," 13.

106. Stueck, *Rethinking the Korean War*, 154.

107. Chuck Downs contends that the Communists may have hoped to detract from the San Francisco discussions of the U.S.-Japan peace treaty by portraying the United States as responsible for the breakdown in negotiations. See Downs, *Over the Line*, 55.

108. Ciphered telegram from Mao Zedong to Filippov [Stalin], 27 August 1951, cited in Kathryn Weathersby, "Stalin, Mao, and the End of the Korean War," 101.

109. Ridgway to the Joint Chiefs of Staff, 6 September 1951, *FRUS*, 1951, 7: 884–86.

110. Goodman, *Negotiating while Fighting*, 63–64.

111. Chai and Zhao, *Banmendian Tanpan*, 181.

112. Vatcher, *Panmunjom*, 82.

113. The Joint Chiefs of Staff to Ridgway, 13 November 1951, *FRUS*, 1951, 7: 1128–30.

114. Ridgway to the Joint Chiefs of Staff, 13 November 1951, ibid.

115. Ciphered Telegram, Mao Zedong to Filippov [Stalin], 14 November 1951, *CWIHPB*, nos. 6–7 (Winter 1995–96): 70–71; *ZEJW* 4: 249–51.

116. Ciphered Telegram, VKP (b) CC Politburo decision with approved message, Filippov [Stalin] to Mao Zedong, 19 November 1951, *CWIHPB*, nos. 6–7 (Winter 1995–96): 72.

117. Kathryn Weathersby suggests four reasons why Stalin believed that a stalemated war in Korea benefited the Soviet Union: (1) it tied down American forces, and made it more difficult for the United States to engage in military action in Europe; (2) it drained U.S. economic resources, and caused political difficulties for the Truman administration; (3) it provided the Soviet Union with a superb opportunity to gather intelligence on U.S. military technology and organization; (4) it created great hostility between the Chinese and the Americans, and thus tied the PRC more firmly to Moscow. See Weathersby, "Stalin, Mao, and the End of the Korean War," 102.

118. Chai, "The Decision-making Path Taken by Mao," 15.

119. Chai and Zhao, *Banmendian Tanpan*, 188–91.

120. Ridgway to the Joint Chiefs of Staff, 21 November 1951, *FRUS*, 1951, 7: 1159–61.

121. Ridgway to the Joint Chiefs of Staff, 27 November 1951, ibid., 1186–88.

122. Ridgway to the Joint Chiefs of Staff, 4 December 1951, ibid., 1229–30, 1234.

123. Telegram, Mao to Li Kenong, 28 December 1951, *JYMZW*, 2: 642–43.

124. Chai and Zhao, *Banmendian Tanpan*, 121; Vatcher, *Panmunjom*, 86.

125. Telegrams, Mao to Peng Dehuai, 18 and 24 November 1950, *JYMZW*, 1: 672 and 685. Mao even authorized the CPV commanders to decide when and how many POWs should be released without asking his permission in advance.

126. Hermes, *Truce Tent and Fighting Front*, 141–42; Chai and Zhao, *Banmendian Tanpan*, 187.

127. Hermes, *Truce Tent and Fighting Front*, 142–43.

128. Following the end of World War II in 1945, tens of thousands of German and Japanese soldiers taken prisoner by the Soviet Union were kept captive in order to help in the country's massive reconstruction effort. In order to prevent this from happening again, Article 118 of the Geneva Convention of 1949 provided for the quick and compulsory return of all POWs at the end of a war; it did not provide for POWs who did not want to be repatriated. Although the United States did not sign the Convention until 1951, it announced very early in the Korean War that it would abide by its provisions, as did North and South Korea. For more details, see Whalen, *Drawing the Line*, 331.

129. Foot, *Substitute for Victory*, 88–89.

130. Qu, ". . . An Interview with General Chai Chengwen," 43.

131. Bernstein, "The Struggle over the Korean Armistice," 279.

132. Hermes, *Truce Tent and Fighting Front*, 150–51.

133. Joy, *How Communists Negotiate*, 149–54.

134. Hermes, *Truce Tent and Fighting Front*, 171–72; Bernstein, "The Struggle over the Korean Armistice," 284.

135. Charles Stelle to Nitze, "The POW Issue in the Armistice Negotiations," January 24, 1952, PPS Files, cited in Bernstein, "The Struggle over the Korean Armistice," 285.

136. Qu, ". . . An Interview with General Chai Chengwen," 42.

137. Xu Yan, *Diyici Jiaoliang*, 313–14.

138. U. Alexis Johnson, *Right Hand of Power*, 139.

139. Xu Yan, *Diyici Jiaoliang*, 285.

140. Ciphered Telegram, Mao to Filippov [Stalin], 18 July 1952, *CWIHPB*, nos. 6–7 (Winter 1995/96), 78.

141. Telegrams, Mao to Li Kenong, 14 July 1952, cited in Xu Yan, *Diyici Jiaoliang*, 285; MZZ49, 1: 173.

142. Weathersby, "New Russian Documents on the Korean War," 34.

143. *FRUS*, 1952–1954, 15: 554–57. Harrison replaced Joy on 22 May 1952.

144. Chai, "The Decision-making Path Taken by Mao," 18.

145. Bernstein, "The Struggle over the Korean Armistice," 303, 307; U. Alexis Johnson, *Right Hand of Power*, 152.

146. President Eisenhower and Secretary of State John F. Dulles believed that the Eisenhower administration's threats of use of nuclear weapons in Korea compelled the Chinese to end the war. See Eisenhower, *White House Years*, 1: 180–81. Chinese sources suggest that Beijing's leaders had in fact discounted a nuclear attack. See Zhang Shu Guang, *Deterrence and Strategic Culture*, 133.

147. MZZ49, 1: 179.

148. Chai, "The Decision-making Path Taken by Mao," 19–20.

149. Clark, *From the Danube to the Yalu*, 240–41.

150. Ciphered Telegram, Resolution, USSR Council of Ministers with draft letters from Soviet Government to Mao Zedong and Kim Il-sung and directive to Soviet delegation at United Nations, 19 March 1953, *CWIHPB*, nos. 6–7 (Winter 1995–96), 80; MZZ49, 1: 180.

151. Ibid. Many researchers of the Korean War have noted that a dramatic change in the Chinese/North Korean position came after Stalin's death in March 1953, although they disagree on the origins of such a change. On the one hand, Kathryn Weathersby contends that Stalin's death played an important, if not decisive, role in the softening of the Communist attitude toward the POW issue, and the tough Chinese approach over the POW issue reflected Stalin's unwillingness to end the Korean War. See Weathersby, "Stalin, Mao, and the End of the Korean War," 108–110. On the other hand, Chen Jian argues that it is implausible to completely attribute the changing Chinese attitude over the POW issue to Stalin's death. Chen indicates that new Chinese sources demonstrate that a more conciliatory approach on Beijing's part had its own logic, which can be understood only in a broader and more complex framework. Beijing's unyielding stand on the POW issue should be regarded more as a response to America's use of the issue to put Beijing on the defensive than as an unwilling gesture made under Stalin's pressure. China's changing attitude toward the POW issue in late March 1953 appears "more an outgrowth of Beijing's existing policies based on Chinese leaders' assessment of the changing situation than a reflection of altering Soviet directives." See Chen Jian, *Mao's China and the Cold War*, 112–13. Chinese historian She Zhihua has noted that the Soviet sources show that Mao reported and asked Stalin's advice on every issue regarding the Korean armistice negotiation. However, after Stalin's death, Mao seldom sought advice from the Soviet new

leadership. While respecting the general policy line of the Soviets—a voluntary concession—Mao maintained complete independence on implementing concrete negotiations
and ending the war—continuing his strategy of negotiating while fighting. On the contrary, the Soviet leadership had to comply with Mao's view in this regard. See Shen Zhihua, "Ending the Korean War," 182–215. On armistice and ending the war in Korea, Shen
has argued that it was the Soviet new leadership who deferred to Mao's decision.

152. Refer to the exchanges of sick and wounded POWs between Communists and
UNC in April 1953.

153. Chai, "The Decision-making Path Taken by Mao," 20.

154. Pillar, *Negotiating Peace*, 83.

155. Clark, *From the Danube to the Yalu*, 243.

156. Editorial Note: Chou Enlai's radio address, 30 March 1953, *FRUS*, 1952–54, 15:
824; Hermes, *Truce Tent and Fighting Front*, 411–14; MZZ49, 1: 182–83.

157. Chai, "The Decision-making Path Taken by Mao," 20.

158. *FRUS*, 1952–54, 7 May 1953, 15: 979–81; MZZ49, 1: 183–84.

159. *FRUS*, 1952–54, 7 May 1953, 15: 982; Hermes, *Truce Tent and Fighting Front*, 425–26.

160. Stueck, *Rethinking the Korean War*, 174–5; Foot, *Substitute for Victory*, 175–76.
There is a discrepancy between Chinese and English sources regarding June 8's agreement. According to Chinese scholars, "non-repatriate POWs should be released from custody and be turned over to Neutral Nations Repatriation Commission within 60 days of
an armistice. Then the home countries of these non-repatriate prisoners will have 90 days
for meeting and explaining. After that, those non-repatriates will be turned to a political
commission to decide within 30 days." See Chai and Zhao, *Banmendian Tanpan*, 265–66;
Xu Yan, *Diyici Jiaoliang*, 299.

161. The South Korean president, Syngman Rhee, was unhappy with the development of the situation, so he released 25,000 anti-Communist North Korean prisoners
held by South Korean forces on 18 June. The Chinese/North Korean forces launched a
week-long offensive campaign on 13 July in order to punish the South Koreans. See
Foot, *Substitute for Victory*, 183–87.

162. Johnson, *Right Hand of Power*, 169.

163. Xu Yan, *Diyici Jiaoliang*, 285, 313.

164. Foot, *Substitute for Victory*, x–xi, 158.

165. Peng Dehuai's speech at the Twenty-fourth Session of the Central People's Government of China, *Peng Dehuai Junshi Wenxuan*, 445.

166. In deciding to enter negotiations, Mao listed restoration of the status quo antebellum and creation of a neutral zone along the 38th parallel as China's conditions for
an armistice. Cited from ciphered telegram, Mao Zedong to Gao Gang and Kim Il-
sung, 13 June 1951, in CWIHPB, nos. 6–7 (Winter 1995/96): 61.

167. Acheson, *Present at the Creation*, 529–38, 651–57.

168. Many junior diplomats, interpreters and staff members, such as Ji Chaozhu, Bi
Jilong, Guo Jiadian, and others, serving either at Panmunjom during the negotiations
or at the post-armistice talks, later attained important positions in PRC's foreign services. For them, Panmunjom became a useful diplomatic training institution. Many of
them were also China's American experts from the 1950s up to 1990s.

4. Creating a Special Channel

1. Mao Zedong, "Unite and consolidate with any peace-loving country," 7 July 1954,
MZW, 6: 333.

2. Niu Jun, "The Evolution of New China's Diplomacy," 38.

3. These five principles are mutual respect for each other's sovereignty and territorial integrity, mutual nonaggression, mutual noninterference in each other's internal affairs, equality and mutual benefit, and peaceful coexistence.

4. Xie Li, "An Analysis on Zhou Enlai's Diplomatic Strategy," 243–44.

5. ZEWW, 62.

6. ZEN49, 1: 356.

7. Xu Jingli, *Jiemi Zhongguo Waijiao Dang'an*, 251.

8. Johnson, *Right Hand of Power*, 235.

9. ZHJH, 23–24.

10. Liu Shaoqi was then China's No. 2 leader, Mao Zedong's designated successor.

11. ZEN49, 1: 375.

12. *FRUS, 1952–54*, 14: 462–67, 476–79. In the second meeting between Wang and Johnson on 10 June 1954, Wang stated the Chinese position: The Chinese people are friendly to the American people and all are free to leave China, unless they have (a) engaged in espionage or, (b) taken part in Jiang Jieshi's civil war, or (c) violated Chinese territorial air or waters. In these cases China had the right and duty to prosecute according to the laws of a sovereign state. To prove they are free to leave, he noted that 1,485 Americans had left China since 1949: "582 in 1950, 727 in 1951, 143 in 1953, 33 in 1953 [1954]." *FRUS, 1952–54*, 14: 464–66. The United States focused on the approximately 155 Americans who were in prison or denied exit permits between 1949 and 1955. Johnson, *Right Hand of Power*, 232. In 1954, the PRC focused on the 5,400 students in the United States, probably because of the need in China for their talents; because they are likely to be the most vulnerable both to appeal to patriotism and to family ties; and they are the easiest to identify. *FRUS, 1952–54*, 14: 441. In the wake of the Korean War, the Truman administration issued orders to bar 175 of the Chinese from leaving the United States because of their U.S. education in such technical fields as weapons design, nuclear energy, and rocketry, and the remainder were free to leave at any time. Johnson, *Right Hand of Power*, 235–43.

13. *FRUS, 1952–54*, 14: 462–67.

14. Ibid., 464–72, 478.

15. According to State Department minutes, "Johnson stated Wang raised issues beyond scope of these discussions which he not prepared discuss . . . [and] indicated his belief that further discussions between himself and Wang no longer necessary. . . . [Johnson] suggested staff officers might be designated by each side for purpose passing on information." Ibid., 478.

16. Memorandum of Conversation, Department of State, Washington, 6 July 1955, *FRUS, 1955–57*, 2: 632. From 29 July 1954 to 15 July 1955, the U.S. and the PRC held 11 consul-level talks in Geneva. See Li Changjiu and Shi, *Zhongmei Guanxi Erbainian*, 186.

17. ZHJH, 25. Johnson recalls, "I deliberately chose a sitting room in the UN Building with several sofas but no table, hoping to make the atmosphere as easy and informal as I could contrive, and when Wang Ping-nan and his aides arrived I made a point of shaking hands and made some light conversation before moving to business." See Johnson, *Right Hand of Power*, 234–35.

18. ZRGW49, 336–38.

19. Mao Zedong, "The relationship between mainland China and Taiwan is different from that between the two Germanys, the two Koreas, and the two Vietnams," 2 October 1959, in MZWW, 381.

20. The memoirs of General Ye Fei, commander of the Fuzhou Military Command, responsible for the bombardment of Jinmen, reveal that orders Beijing sent on 25 August 1954 instructed Ye Fei to shell Jinmen, not as preliminary to an assault on the island but

as a special and limited response to what was perceived as an increase in U.S. and Nationalist military provocations in the area and the rumored negotiation of a mutual defense treaty between Washington and Taipei. It was Ye Fei personally, not the central authorities, who recommended 3 September for the shelling for the simple reason that General Ye believed that the Nationalists planned to supply the island by ship on that day. PRC shelling of Jinmen after 3 September 1954 and in early 1955 was, in fact, infrequent and light. See *Ye Fei Huiyilu*, 643. Other Chinese military commanders supported Ye Fei's contention. General Zhang Aiping, commander of the Zhejiang forces, and Lei Yingfu, military secretary to Zhou Enlai and an aide to Mao Zedong, both independently confirm that the only military plan developed at the time was one to take the Dachen, an offshore island group far to the north of Jinmen and Mazu held by the Nationalists; the plan included neither Jinmen nor Mazu. See Gordon J. Chang and He Di interviews with Zhang Aiping, Ye Fei, and Lei Yingfu in Chang and He, "The Absence of War," 1507.

21. During the propaganda campaign, the CCP Central Committee issued instructions to its cadres at different levels. CCP Central Committee Propaganda Department and the Political Department of the Central Military Commission, "Instruction on Military Report Regarding the Taiwan Issue," 24 July 1954; and "Instruction on Propaganda Principle Regarding the Liberation of Taiwan," 25 September 1954. In Zhongyang Dang'anguan, comp., *Zhonggong Zhongyang Wenjian Huibian: 1954*, 1711–19 and 2722–24.

22. Gordon J. Chang and He, "The Absence of War," 1514.

23. ZEWW, 134.

24. *FRUS, 1955–57*, 2: 506–9; 519–20. What was clear, above all, was that Dulles wanted only "direct" negotiations. He was "fed up with all the intermediaries," a judgment with which President Eisenhower concurred. Ibid., 531–34, 605, 630–31.

25. ZEN49, 1: 474–75.

26. Memorandum of a Conversation, Department of State, Washington, 24 March 1955, *FRUS, 1955–57*, 2: 392.

27. Zhou Enlai's three points can be found in ZRGW49, 344–45.

28. "Report of Premier Zhou Enlai on the Afro-Asian Conference at the fifteenth enlarged conference of the standing committee of the NPC," in *Zhongmei Guanxi Ziliao Huibian*, 2: 2264.

29. ZEZ, 1: 478.

30. ZRGW49, 345.

31. The following discussion draws on Gordon H. Chang, *Friends and Enemies*, especially chapter 3. Also see Gaddis, "The American 'Wedge' Strategy," 157–83.

32. *FRUS, 1955–57*, 2: 563–64, 659. In his memoirs, Johnson also noted that Dulles was concerned about what might happen at a forthcoming summit in Geneva. See Johnson, *Right Hand of Power*, 237.

33. See "Guanyu Zhongmei Shuangfang Dashiji Daibiao Zai Rineiwa Huitan de Fang'an" [Scheme Regarding Sino-American Ambassadorial Talks in Geneva], no. 111–00009–02 (1), PRC *Waijiao Dang'an*; ZRGW49, 346.

34. This wording comes from the message sent through the Indian government. See Telegram from the Secretary of State to the Embassy in Italy, 7 July 1955, in *FRUS, 1955–57*, 2: 637–38. The message sent through the British government was similar, except that it used terminology referring to future agenda issues (certain other practical matters then at issue) that found its way into the formal announcement of the talks. See Telegram from the Secretary of State to the Embassy in the United Kingdom, 11 July 1955, in *FRUS, 1955–57*, 2: 643.

35. Editorial note, ibid., 678. In August 1955, the United States focused on 41 civilians and 35 military personnel detained in China. See Johnson, *Right Hand of Power*, 233. In

March 1956, the Chinese accounted for the 99 Americans in China at the end of July 1955; of 59 ordinary residents, 13 had asked to leave and 46 remained free to leave whenever they wish; of 40 criminals, 27 had finished their term and left and 13 remained in prison. Over the next 15 years the number in prison was gradually reduced. The PRC expanded its interests in Chinese aliens in the United States to all 117,000, probably because it provided a vehicle for seeking de facto recognition by the United States in lieu of the ROC, as well as influence within this community. A total of 767 students returned to mainland China using U.S. government financial aid from April 1949 to 30 June 1955.

36. Johnson, *Right Hand of Power*, 238.

37. Secretary of State to Johnson, 29 July 1955, *FRUS, 1955–57*, 2: 685.

38. *Department of State Bulletin*, v. 33, no. 841 (8 August 1955): 220–21.

39. Editorial Note, *FRUS, 1955–57*, 2: 679–80; and *Department of State Bulletin*, v. 33, no. 841 (8 August 1955): 220–21. Also see Johnson, *Right Hand of Power*, 238–40.

40. Tucker, *China Confidential*, 98.

41. Secretary of State to Johnson, 29 July 1955, *FRUS, 1955–57*, 2: 685.

42. Goldstein, "Dialogue of the Deaf?" 205. As Dulles noted in his announcement, there were signs of a lull in the Strait. To use his words, a "pistol" to the head of the U.S. had been "laid down" by the PRC, and he was determined to see that it stayed that way. *Department of State Bulletin*, v. 33, no. 842 (15 August 1955): 261. Robert Accinelli makes the same point about Dulles's view of the talks in Accinelli, *Crisis and Commitment*, chapter 2.

43. Johnson, *Right Hand of Power*, 239.

44. ZHJH, 32.

45. Ibid., 40–41.

46. Ibid., 32.

47. See "Guanyu Zhongmei Dashiji Daibiao Zai Rineiwa Huitan de Zhishi" [Instructions on Sino-American Ambassadorial-level Talks in Geneva], Top Secret, 30 July 1955, no. 111–00009–01 (1), PRC *Waijiao Dang'an*.

48. ZEN49, 1: 492–93; Editorial Note, *FRUS, 1955–1957*, 2: 688; also see *People's China*, no. 16 (August 16, 1955): 3–8.

49. ZEWHD, 122.

50. ZHJH, 48–49. These 11 pilots were freed and left China on 31 July 1955.

51. Ibid., and "A Résumé of the Warsaw Talks, 1955–1970," box 2187, Pol Chicom U.S. 1970–73, RG 59, p. 2.

52. ZHJH, 47.

53. Goldstein, "Dialogue of the Deaf?" 205.

54. Wang Bingnan insisted that "American nationals [would be] treated like all other aliens in China and accorded protection as long as they respect Chinese law. If they breach Chinese law [they would be] treated as the law provides." Johnson to Secretary of State, 2 August 1955; and Johnson to Secretary of State, 18 August 1955, in *FRUS, 1955–57*, 3: *Supplement*. See also *FRUS, 1955–57*, 3: 40.

55. Johnson to Secretary of State, 2 August 1955, *FRUS, 1955–57*, 3: *Supplement*.

56. "A Résumé of the Warsaw Talks," box 2187, RG 59, p.6.

57. This was no surprise, of course. From the moment the talks were announced, the Republic of China's ambassador was protesting American interference in a domestic affair as an apparent weakness in confronting the mainland. At the start of the talks, the State Department had sought to assure the ROC regarding the nature of the talks by sending a copy of Johnson's instructions to its Foreign Ministry. However, the copy omitted two key sections that would have increased suspicions on Taiwan: the permission for Johnson to meet socially with the Chinese and the suggestion that the United States

might relax rules on travel to the mainland in exchange for a repatriation agreement. Dulles was not above misleading allies to avoid conflict. See "Memorandum of a Conversation, Department of State, Washington, August 9, 1955," in *FRUS, 1955–57*, 3: 22.

58. The Secretary of State to Johnson, at Geneva, 14 August 1955, *FRUS, 1955–57*, 3: 38.

59. Johnson to Secretary of State, 12 August 1955, *FRUS, 1955–57*, 3: *Supplement*.

60. The Secretary of State to Johnson, at Geneva, 14 August 1955, *FRUS, 1955–57*, 3: 38.

61. Johnson to the Secretary of State, 18 August 1955; Secretary of State to Johnson, 19 August 1955; and McConaughy to Johnson, 19 August 1955, ibid., 45–47, 50.

62. Johnson to Secretary of State, 20 August 1955, ibid., 52.

63. Johnson to Dulles, 24 August 1955, ibid.; Dulles to Johnson, 2 September 1955, ibid.

64. "A Résumé of the Warsaw Talks," box 2187, RG 59, pp. 20–22.

65. Agreed Announcement of the Ambassadors of the United States of America and the People's Republic of China, 10 September 1955, *FRUS, 1955–57*, 3: 85–86.

66. "A Résumé of the Warsaw Talks," box 2187, RG 59, p. 19.

67. *New York Times*, 13 September 1955.

68. *Department of State Bulletin*, v. 33, no. 848 (26 September 1955): 492.

69. Dulles to Johnson, 2 September 1955, and McConaughy to Johnson, 2 September 1955, *FRUS, 1955–57*, 3: *Supplement*.

70. Goldstein, "Dialogue of the Deaf?" 209.

71. McConaughy to Johnson, 9 and 12 September 1955, *FRUS, 1955–57*, 3: *Supplement*.

72. "A Résumé of the Warsaw Talks," box 2187, RG 59, p. 23.

73. *ZHJH*, 56.

74. Ibid., 57.

75. Ibid.

76. Hoover to Johnson, 27 September 1955, *FRUS, 1955–57*, 3: *Supplement*.

77. Johnson to Secretary of State, 5 October 1955, *FRUS, 1955–57*, 3: *Supplement*.

78. Johnson to Secretary of State, 28 September 1955, *FRUS, 1955–57*, 3: *Supplement*; *ZHJH*, 58–59.

79. Johnson to Secretary of State, 5 October 1955, *FRUS, 1955–57*, 3: *Supplement*; *ZHJH*, 58–59.

80. Johnson to Secretary of State, 5 October 1955, *FRUS, 1955–57*, 3: *Supplement*.

81. "A Résumé of the Warsaw Talks," box 2187, RG 59.

82. In the meetings, Johnson made several arguments to clarify or elaborate on these assumptions: that at the moment, China was a divided country (like Germany and Korea); that the ROC was recognized internationally as a sovereign state; that, therefore, the Mutual Defense Treaty of 1954 was a valid international treaty, which justified an American presence in the area, and that for this reason, the United States would not surrender (nor did it expect the PRC to surrender) the right to "individual or collective self-defense." Examples of these arguments can be found in the following reports of meetings with the Chinese: Johnson to Secretary of State, 22 December 1955; Johnson to Secretary of State, 4 February 1956; Johnson to Secretary of State, 19 April 1956; and Johnson to Secretary of State, 17 May 1956, *FRUS, 1955–57*, 3: *Supplement*.

83. Johnson interpreted Beijing's mention of a presidential representative as suggesting that Beijing saw the State Department as hostile. Johnson to McConaughy, 28 March 1956, *FRUS, 1955–57*, 3: *Supplement*. Such a proposal is interesting in light of Henry Kissinger's later trip.

84. Goldstein, "Dialogue of the Deaf?" 213.

85. See, for example, Johnson to State Department, 19 January 1956, *FRUS, 1955–57*, 3: *Supplement*.

86. Johnson to State Department, 2 December 1955, *FRUS, 1955–57*, 3: *Supplement*.

87. Still, as late as 18 April 1956, Johnson continued to argue for a reconsideration of the intransigent position on the question of self-defense. Johnson to Secretary of State, 2 December 1955; Secretary of State to Johnson, 6 December 1955; Secretary of State to Johnson, 7 December 1955; Secretary of State to Johnson, 12 December 1955; Johnson to McConaughy, 18 April 1956, *FRUS, 1955–57*, 3: *Supplement*.

88. Kenneth Young describes this in his *Negotiating with the Chinese Communists*, chapters 3 and 4. Indeed, most of Young's analysis draws from public statements.

89. "A Résumé of the Warsaw Talks," box 2187, RG 59, p. 46.

90. Li Changjiu and Shi, *Zhongmei Guanxi Erbainian*, 191.

91. *People's China*, no. 4, 16 February 1956.

92. *New York Times*, 5 March 1956 and 7 March 7 1956; and *Department of State Bulletin*, v. 34, no. 873 (19 March 1956): 451.

93. *People's China*, no. 7, 1 April 1956, p. 19.

94. ZHJH, 66–67; *Renmin Ribao*, 29 June 1956.

95. ZEN49, 1: 588.

96. "A Résumé of the Warsaw Talks," box 2187, RG 59, p. 23.

97. ZHJH, 62–63.

98. Memorandum from the Deputy Under Secretary of State for Political Affairs (Murphy) to the Deputy Assistant Secretary of State for Far Eastern Affairs (Sebald), 6 August 1956, *FRUS, 1955–57*, 3: 416–17; and Dulles to Johnson, 8 August 1956, *FRUS, 1955–57*, 3: *Supplement*.

99. Significantly, Wang Bingnan argued that at this stage, a foreign ministers' meeting would be "absolutely indispensable to solve question of relaxation and elimination of tension in the Taiwan area." Johnson to Secretary of State, 26 July 1956, and Johnson to Secretary of State, 9 August 1956, *FRUS, 1955–57*, 3: *Supplement*.

100. Secretary of State to Johnson, at Geneva, October 12, 1955, *FRUS, 1955–57*, 3: 125–26. See especially 126 n. 2.

101. Dulles to Johnson, 19 July 1956; Johnson to Secretary of State, 26 July 1956, and Johnson to the Secretary of State, 9 August 1956, *FRUS, 1955–57*, 3: *Supplement*.

102. "A Résumé of Warsaw Talks," box 2187, RG 59, pp. 88–89.

103. *FRUS, 1955–1957*, 3: 639 and 641 n. 2; also Department of State to Johnson, 12 December 1957, *FRUS, 1955–1957*, 3: *Supplement*.

104. Dulles to Johnson, 4 December 1957, *FRUS, 1955–57*, 3: *Supplement*.

105. Tucker, *China Confidential*, 99. Edwin Martin was first secretary at the U.S. embassy in London from 1956 to 1958. In his memoirs, Wang Bingnan mistakenly regarded Edwin Martin as "counselor." See ZHJH, 65.

106. Johnson to Secretary of State, 19 December 1957, *FRUS, 1955–57*, 3: *Supplement*.

107. Mao Zedong, "Some policy issues in Chinese diplomacy," in MZWW, 288.

108. Quoted in Chen Yi, "Zai Waijiaobu Dangzu Wuxuhui Shang de Fayan" [Speech at a general meeting of the Party committee of the Foreign Ministry], 17 June 1953, cited in Jiang Changbin and Ross, *Cong Duizhi Zouxiang Huanhe*, 181, 193 n. 30.

109. Guoji Zhanlue Xuehui, comp. *Huanqiu Tongci Liangre*, 266–67.

110. Transcript of Mao Zedong's Talk on International Situation, 16 June 1958, cited in MZZ49, 1: 851.

111. Hunt and Niu, *Toward a History of Chinese Communist Foreign Relations*, 92.

112. *Renmin Ribao*, 1 July 1958, cited in MZZ49, 1: 851.

113. Letter from the Director of the Office of Chinese Affairs (Clough) to John B. Dexter at the Consulate General in Geneva, June 27, 1958, *FRUS, 1958–60*, 19: 27–28.

114. MZZ49, 1: 851.

115. Roberson to Beam, 25 July 1958, *FRUS, 1958–60*, 19: *Supplement*.

116. Young, *Negotiating with the Chinese Communists*, 140.

117. *New York Times*, 12 August 1958. In a major address on China policy on 28 June 1957, Dulles uncompromisingly reaffirmed the U.S. position and stated his belief that communism was, in China as elsewhere, "a passing and not a perpetual phase." See "Dulles's Speech on China Policy to Lions International, San Francisco, June 28, 1957" in MacFarquhar, *Sino-American Relations*, 134–42. The statement here was even harsher. See also "Our Policies toward Communism in China," 28 June 1957, in *FRUS*, 1955–57, 3: 566.

118. *MZZ49*, 1: 858.

119. *DZJJG* 1: 387.

120. Revolution broke out in Iraq on 14 July 1958. The following day, U.S. marines landed in Beirut, Lebanon, to interfere in the Iraqi Revolution. See *MZZ49*, 1: 852.

121. Wu Lengxi, *Yi Maozhuxi*, 74–75.

122. *DZJJG* 1:394; *MZZ49*, 1: 860.

123. *Ye Fei Huiyilu*, 655; *MZZ49*, 1: 860–61.

124. *ZHJH*, 70–71.

125. Wu Lengxi, *Yi Maozhuxi*, 79.

126. Li Changjiu and Shi, *Zhongmei Guanxi Erbainian*, 195; *MZZ49*, 1: 867.

127. Liao, "Historical Review of Mao Zedong's Decision to Bombard Jinmen," 33; *MZZ49*, 1: 866.

128. *ZHJH*, 73.

129. "Mao's letter to Zhou Enlai and Huang Kecheng," original manuscript, 13 September 1958, cited in *MZZ49*, 1: 872.

130. "Zhou Enlai to Mao Zedong, 13 September 1958," cited in *ZEZ*, 1: 470.

131. Beam, *Multiple Exposure*, 122.

132. Dulles to Beam, 11 September 1958, *FRUS*, 1958–60, 19: *Supplement*.

133. There is a discrepancy regarding the date. Polish time was 16 September 1958, while Washington time was 15 September 1958.

134. Young, *Negotiating with the Chinese Communists*, 161.

135. Goldstein, "Dialogue of the Deaf?" 222. Kenneth Young suggested that the ten sessions held during September-November 1958 "justified the twelve years of the talks" and that the meetings in Warsaw "played a useful part in controlling and calming the crisis." See Young, *Negotiating with the Chinese Communists*, 14, and chapter 7.

136. Dulles to Beam, 14 September 1958, *FRUS*, 1958–60, 19: 187.

137. The transcript of the meeting can be found in Telegram from the Embassy in Poland to the Department of State, September 15, 1958, *FRUS*, 1958–60, 19: 191–95.

138. Ibid., 190–91 and 194.

139. Beam to the Department of State, 18 September 1958, *FRUS*, 1958–60, 19: 209–16.

140. "Memorandum for the Joint Chiefs of Staff "-Appendix to Enclosure "A: Negotiations with the Chinese Communists," 17 September 1958, Records of the U.S. Joint Chiefs of Staff, Geographic File 1958, box 6, RG 218.

141. The Department of State to the Embassy in Poland, 28 September 1958, *FRUS*, 1958–60, 19: 293–96.

142. Telegram from the Embassy in Poland to the Department of State, 30 September 1958, *FRUS*, 1958–1960, 19: 306.

143. "A Résumé of the Warsaw Talks," box 2187, RG 59, p. 106.

144. Editorial Note, *FRUS*, 1958–1960, 19: 301.

145. *ZEZ*, 1: 472.

146. Ibid., 472–73, 475.

147. Dulles to Beam, 3 October 1958, *FRUS*, 1958–60, 19: 354–56.

148. Beam to the Department of State, 10 October 1958, and Beam to Secretary of State, 13 October 1958, *FRUS, 1958–60*, 19: *Supplement.* It should be noted that in talks with the Australians and the British, the Eisenhower administration denigrated the value of the talks. *FRUS, 1958–60*, 19: 394, 408–411.

149. Goldstein, "The Dialogue of the Deaf?" 225.

150. Rosemary Foot notes that the year 1959 brought forth a number of indications for greater flexibility in China policy, but the domestic signals still were not strong enough. See Foot, *Practice of Power*, 93–96.

151. As a State Department instruction to Ambassador Beam stated on 3 October 1958, "We are desirous of keeping Warsaw talks going, at least through this period, as their existence may provide some sort of cover or excuse for Chicoms not raising level of their offensive operations." It noted that the talks and other U.S. activities "would enable us to get increased support at U.N." See Telegram from the Department of State to the Embassy in Poland, in *FRUS, 1958–60*, 19: 323.

152. Mao Zedong brought up this point in his talks with Czechoslovakia governmental delegation in March 1957. See *MZWW*, 287.

153. *ZEWHD*, 281.

154. Ibid., 286–87.

155. *Peking Review*, 14 September 1960.

156. *ZHJH*, 91. Also "A Résumé of Warsaw Talks." The Chinese would make adjustment to these two policies during U.S.-China rapprochement talks in early 1970s.

157. This part is drawn from Steven Goldstein. See Goldstein, "Dialogue of the Deaf?" 234–35.

158. See, for example, Young, *Negotiating with the Chinese Communists*, 302–303.

159. Kenneth Young, Alfred Wilhelm, Richard Solomon, and Raymond Cohen all argued on China's "principled" position.

5. Negotiating at Cross-Purposes

1. Record of actions taken at the 475th NSC meeting, 1 February 1961, *FRUS, 1961–1963*, 8: 20.

2. SNIE 13–61, "The Economic Situation in Communist China," 4 April 1961, ibid., 22: 40–41.

3. Lansdale to Secretary of Defense McNamara, 3 April 1961, ibid., 22: 38–39.

4. Li Changjiu and Shi, *Zhongmei Guanxi Erbainian*, 200.

5. See Foot, "Redefinitions," 281.

6. Paper Prepared in the Policy Planning Council: US Policy toward Communist China, 30 November 1962, *FRUS, 1961–1963*, 22: 325–32.

7. Roger Hilsman to Dean Rusk (Suggested United States Responses to likely Chinese Communist Initiatives), 31 July 1963, box 3858, POL 1, ChiCom, RG 59.

8. *ZHJH*, 86.

9. Memorandum from Acting Secretary of State Ball to President Kennedy, 21 June 1962, *FRUS, 1961–63*, 22: 258–59.

10. "Anticipatory Action Pending Chinese Communist Demonstration of a Nuclear Capability," 13 September 1961, Records of the PPS, PPS 1957–61, box 129, RG 59.

11. "Memorandum For S/S–Mr. Battle," 7 October 1961, ibid.

12. Kennedy's comments at a meeting with Bundy and McCone, 11 January 1963, enclosed in editorial note, *FRUS, 1961–1963*, 22: 339.

13. Kennedy's "Stalinist" remarks are quoted from "Kennedy's Assessment of the

Chinese Threat at His Press Conference, August 1, 1963" in MacFarquhar, *Sino-American Relations*, 200.

14. For the most recent study, based on newly declassified U.S. sources on this topic, see Burr and Richelson, "Whether to 'Strangle the Baby in the Cradle,'" 54–99.

15. NIE 1–61, "Estimate of the World Situation," 17 January 1961, *FRUS, 1961–1963*, 5: 17–19.

16. PMK-D/2, background paper, "President's Meeting with Khrushchev, Vienna, June 3–4, 1961," prepared in the Department of State, 25 May 1961, ibid., 5:153–57.

17. Thomson, "On the Making of U.S. China Policy," 227.

18. *Public Papers of the Presidents, John F. Kennedy, 1961*, 15.

19. Thomson, "On the Making of U.S. China Policy," 227.

20. Bowles to Kennedy (U.S. Initiative Regarding the China Mainland Food Crisis), 6 February 1962, Records of the PPS, box 214, RG 59; parts of the memo also are enclosed in editorial note, *FRUS, 1961–63*, 22: 185.

21. See Foot, "Redefinitions," 264.

22. Stevenson, "Putting First Things First: A Democratic View," 203.

23. Komer to Bundy (Quick Thoughts on China), 1 March 1961, *FRUS, 1961–63*, 22: 19–20.

24. Draft Paper Prepared in the Policy Planning Council (U.S. Policy toward China), 26 October 1961, *FRUS, 1961–63*, 22: 162–67.

25. Foot, "Redefinitions," 267.

26. Ibid., 266–67.

27. Thomson, "On the Making of U.S. China Policy," 230. Hilsman said, "We don't love the Chinese Communists. We think that they would be happier, and the world would be happier, if they had a more relaxed view of other people's rights to select their own government. But we think these people are going to be around and we're going to dealing with them." Also Hilsman, *To Move a Nation*, 350–57.

28. "Assistant Secretary of State for Far Eastern Affairs Roger Hilsman's Speech on China Policy to the Commonwealth Club, San Francisco, December 13, 1963" in Mac-Farquhar, *Sino-American Relations*, 201–205. Hilsman's China policy speech was noticed in Beijing, but was denounced by the Chinese as an attempt to promote "peaceful evolution" in China, and to pursue old policies in a new way. See Li Changjiu and Shi, *Zhongmei Guanxi Erbainian*, 203.

29. Memorandum of Conversation (Mr. Hilsman's Speech to the Commonwealth Club, San Francisco, 13 December 1963), 17 January 1964, box 3862, Central Foreign Policy File, 1963, RG 59.

30. See Spence, *Search for Modern China*, 583; Short, *Mao: A Life*, 505. Edwin E. Moise claims that "the total number of deaths seems to have been at least 16 million more than it would have been in three years of normal food supply." See Moise, *Modern China*, 142.

31. See ZRGW57, 229–30, 235–37, 245–47, 254.

32. MZZ49, 2: 1225.

33. ZRGW57, 75–80.

34. Wu Lengxi, *Shinian Lunzhan*, 1:248.

35. For Mao's discussion about foreign policy, see ibid., 1: 243. For Liu's speech, see *Jianguo Yilai Zhongyao Wenxian Xuanbian*, 15: 61.

36. Parson to Rusk, 19 February 1961, *FRUS, 1961–63*, 22: 9–11.

37. Ibid.

38. Wu Lengxi, *Shinian Lunzhan*, 1: 247. The term "two Chinas" is from the original Chinese text. The Kennedy administration in some contexts was willing to admit that

the Communist government on the mainland was a government, but in other contexts (notably its rejection of proposals for a two-China policy at the United Nations) it was not willing to do even that.

39. See "A Résumé of Warsaw Talks," box 2187, RG 59; ZHJH, 85.

40. The Laotian crisis of 1961–1962: In early 1961, a civil war between a right-wing general, Phoumi Nosavan, the neutralist force headed by Prince Souvanna Phouma, and the left-wing Pathet Lao broke out in Laos. The civil war triggered an international confrontation between major powers. On 16 May, 14 nations gathered at Geneva to discuss a solution to the Laotian crisis. Beijing sent a large delegation to the conference, headed by Vice-Premier and Foreign Minister Chen Yi. The U.S. delegation was led by Ambassador W. Averell Harriman. The 14 nations signed the Declaration on the Neutrality of Laos on 23 July 1962, which reestablished Laos as a neutral state and created a tripartite government representing the Pathet Lao, the neutralists, and the rightists. During the meeting, Secretary of State Dean Rusk and Harriman shook Chen Yi's hand, and had brief exchanges. For a recent article on the Laotian Crisis, see Kochavi, "Limited Accommodation, Perpetuated Conflict," 95–135. The Laotian Crisis was also discussed at the Warsaw talks between the Chinese and U.S. ambassadors, but not as a main issue.

41. See FRUS, 1961–63, 22: 51–52, 231–33, 332–33, 363–65, 405–7.

42. See, for example, FRUS, 1961–63, 22: 25–26, 213–14, 216–17. There were never any official offers made by the United States government, although there continued to be discussions with U.S. representatives in Warsaw about presenting the idea in a "low key" way that would not make it seem like a propaganda ploy. Ibid., 231–33.

43. Rusk to Beam, 4 March 1961, FRUS, 1961–63, 22: 22–25.

44. Beam to the Department of State, 29 June 1961, ibid., 22: 86.

45. Important question resolution: the admission of the PRC to the UN requires a two-thirds majority at the UN General Assembly. It was sponsored by New Zealand with U.S. instigation. See Tian Jin and Yu, Zhongguo Zai Lianheguo, 30.

46. Rusk to Beam, 13 August 1961, FRUS, 1961–63, 22: 120–22.

47. Beam to the Department of State, 2 September 1961, ibid., 130–33.

48. Niu Dayong, "Sino-American Ambassadorial Talks," 450.

49. ZHJH, 86–87.

50. Ibid., 88–89.

51. Ibid., and Cabot to the Department of State, 23 June 1962, FRUS, 1961–63, 22: 273–75. Wang's attitude in this discussion is that if the PRC attacks Taiwan, it is internal matter, but if Jiang attacks the mainland, it is international matter. Wang told Cabot, "should an attack occur the US would certainly be held responsible for it, and in that event it would no longer be a matter concerning Chiang Kai-shek and Taiwan, but one which would involve China and the US." See "A Résumé of Warsaw Talks," box 2187, RG 59, p.163. There is a discrepancy between Cabot's report to the State Department and Wang's memoir account. Wang noted, "At the time of his departure, Cabot even told me that the US and China should take concerted action to stop Jiang in event of his attack on mainland." See ZHJH, 90. This could not be confirmed in Cabot's report.

52. ZHJH, 90.

53. On 4 September 1958, the PRC government declared that the extent of its territorial waters was 12 nautical miles. China lodged the first "serious warning" against U.S. intrusion into its territorial water on 7 September. Over the years, China kept an account of these warnings. By late 1971, the Chinese government had lodged 476 serious warnings against U.S. intrusions into its territorial waters and sky. Many of these intrusions were U.S. reconnaissance flights. There were incidents in which U.S. combat aircraft conducting operations against North Vietnam either strayed into China or strayed

too close to the Chinese coast, and were shot down by Chinese aircraft. Most of these Chinese "warnings" were reiterated at the Warsaw talks. See ZRGW57, 428; Li Changjiu and Shi, *Zhongmei Guanxi Erbainian*, 195.

54. Cabot to the Department of State, 20 September 1962, *FRUS, 1961–63*, 22: 318–20.

55. *MZZ49*, 2: 1227.

56. *DZJJG* 1: 368.

57. *ZEN49*, 2: 507–508; Telegram from the Consulate General at Singapore to the Department of State, 13 November 1962, *FRUS,, 1961–63*, 22: 324 n. 2.

58. Bowles to Kennedy (GRC Operation against the Mainland), 8 June 1962, box 2150, Central Decimal File, 1960–1963, RG 59.

59. Letter from President Kennedy to President Chiang, 11 April 1963, *FRUS, 1961–63*, 22: 359–62.

60. Memorandum of Conversation: United States Relations with the Republic of China, 11 September 1963, Ibid., 386–92.

61. Cabot to the Department of State, 17 May 1962, *FRUS, 1961–63*, 22: 225–26.

62. A limited ban prohibited tests in the atmosphere, in outer space, and beneath the surface of the seas, tentatively signed by the three nuclear powers—the U.S., the UK, and the USSR on 25 July 1963.

63. "Chinese Government Statement on the Partial Test-Ban Treaty, July 31, 1963" in *Peking Review*, no. 31, 2 August 1963, pp. 7–8, cited in MacFarquhar, *Sino-American Relations*, 198–200.

64. ZEWW, 543 n. 259.

65. Cabot to the Department of State, 7 August 1963, *FRUS, 1961–63*, 22: 378–82.

66. *Public Papers of the Presidents, John F Kennedy, 1963*, 320.

67. "A Résumé of the Warsaw Talks," box 2187, RG 59, p. 175.

68. Cabot to the Department of State, 11 September 1963, *FRUS, 1961–63*, 22: 392–95.

69. Ibid.

70. Ibid.

71. CIA Memorandum, The North Vietnamese Crisis, 6 August 1964, box 48, National Security File (NSF)/Vietnam, LBJPL.

72. Whiting, *Chinese Calculus of Deterrence*, 175.

73. James C. Thomson to Chester Cooper of the NSC staff, 10 February 1965, *FRUS, 1964–68*, 2: 228–29.

74. Ball comment at White House meeting, 10 February 1965, cited in ibid., 222.

75. Briefing Paper Prepared by the Office of National Estimate, 11 June 1965, ibid., 766–68.

76. McNamara to Johnson, 7 December 1965, ibid., 619.

77. Memorandum for the Record (Meeting of an Executive Group of the National Security Council, 16 October 1964), *FRUS, 1964–68*, 30: 108–09.

78. Joint Chiefs of Staff to Secretary of Defense McNamara, 16 January 1965, ibid., 144–46.

79. Schoenbaum, *Waging Peace and War*, 454; Zeiler, *Dean Rusk*, 99–100.

80. China, Long Range Study, vol. 1, June 1966, pp. 191–94, box 245, National Security Files/China File: China, LBJPL.

81. CIA, Communist Intentions in Vietnam, 29 July 1966, box 239, National Security File (NSF)/Vietnam, LBJPL. China's bottom line was that it would intervene "if North Vietnam were invaded or if the collapse of the Communist regime seemed likely." But the reality was that internal disarray during the Cultural Revolution made it less likely that China would enter the war in Vietnam. At least, the onset of the Cultural Revolution severely curtailed China's ability to influence outside events. China's

capability may not have matched its rhetoric. As the worst-case scenario never happened, it was impossible to reach a definitive conclusion. As the historian Chen Jian shows, as the suspicion and friction between the Chinese and the Vietnamese over issues such as the role of Chinese troops in Vietnam, and Vietnamese closer ties with Moscow than Beijing, widened from late 1965 on, the Chinese became less enthusiastic about entering into a full-scale war with the U.S. on North Vietnam's behalf. See Chen Jian, *Mao's China and the Cold War*, 229–35.

82. "Historical Reports Relating to Diplomacy during the Lyndon Johnson Administration, 1963–1969," Office of the Executive Secretariat, box 4, RG 59.

83. Foot, "Redefinitions," 277–79.

84. Steele, *American People and China*, 102.

85. See Iriye, *U.S. Policy toward China*. James Thomson's 15 March 1966 report on the Hearings is in *FRUS, 1964–68*, 30: 274–75; and further discussion of the need for the administration to embrace "containment without isolation," in Harriman to Moyers, 3 June 1966, ibid., 318–19.

86. Foot, "Redefinitions," 279.

87. Ibid.

88. Editorial Note: President Johnson discussed U.S. policy in Asia, 12 July 1966, *FRUS, 1964–68*, 30: 356.

89. "Historical Reports Relating to Diplomacy . . . , 1963–1969," box 4, RG 59.

90. Reischauer to the Department of State, 11 August 1966, *FRUS, 1964–68*, 30: 366–72.

91. "Historical Reports Relating to Diplomacy . . . , 1963–1969," box 4, RG 59.

92. MacFarquhar, *Sino-American Relations*, 235–40.

93. In the spring and early summer of 1962, Wang Jiaxiang, the head of the CCP's International Liaison Department, submitted to the party's top leadership a series of reports on international affairs. Wang was soon denounced as advocating a revisionist line — "three reconciliations and one reduction," that is to reconcile with the imperialists, the reactionaries, and the revisionists, and to reduce assistance to the struggle of the peoples of Asia, Africa, and Latin America. For details on this event, see Xu Zehao, *Wang Jiaxiang Zhuan*, 556–68; Wang, *Wang Jiaxiang Xuanji*, 444–60. Many scholars argue that Wang Jiaxiang "directed his criticism at erroneous foreign propaganda and at Mao Zedong." See Li Jie, "Changes in China's Domestic Situation in the 1960s and Sino-U.S. Relations," 510. Some contend that Wang was challenging Mao and charting a different foreign policy. For example, Chen Jian writes, "Mao's wrecking of the Sino-Soviet relationship did not happen without challenge within the CCP leadership." Chen then mentions Wang Jiaxiang's reports as evidence. See Chen Jian and Yang Kuisong, "Chinese Politics and the Collapse of the Sino-Soviet Alliance," 276; Chen Jian, *Mao's China and The Cold War*, 83. Many Western scholars accept these arguments. I disagree and believe that the word "challenge" is overstated. Indeed, Wang Jiaxiang was only making suggestions. After the Zunyi Conference of 1935, Wang never attempted to "challenge" Mao. He was only trying to be a useful adviser to Mao. Once Wang learned that Mao didn't like his idea, he hurried to make self-criticism and gave up without a fight.

94. Mao Zedong's talk with V.G. Wilcox, the general secretary of the New Zealand Communist Party, 22 May 1963, in Bo, *Ruogan Zhongda Juece yu Shijian de Huigu*, 2: 1154.

95. Jiang Changbin and Ross, *Cong Duizhi Zouxiang Huanhe*, 267–68.

96. See Wang Yongqin, "Chronicle of Sino-American-Soviet Relations," no. 4 (1997): 113.

97. ZNP, 1949–1976, 2: 676.

98. Foot, *Practice of Power*, 187.

99. "Historical Reports Relating to Diplomacy . . . , 1963–1969," box 4, RG 59.
100. See "A Résumé of Warsaw Talks," box 2187, RG 59.
101. Cabot to the Department of State, 25 November 1964, *FRUS, 1964–68*, 30: 134–35.
102. "A Résumé of the Warsaw Talks," box 2187, RG 59, p.194.
103. Ibid.
104. Cabot to the Department of State, 26 November 1964, *FRUS, 1964–68*, 30: 135–37.
105. Wang Guoquan, "My Tenure as Ambassador," 2: 152–53.
106. "A Résumé of the Warsaw Talks," box 2187, RG 59, p.194.
107. Ibid., 196.
108. *Peking Review*, no. 21, 20 May 1966, 17.
109. *Department of State Bulletin*, v. 54, no. 1406 (6 June 1966): 884–85.
110. Gronouski to the Department of State, 25 May 1966, *FRUS, 1964–68*, 30: 314–17.
111. "Exposing New US Fraud over Nuclear Weapons" by Observer, *Peking Review*, no. 26, 24 June 1966, 27–28.
112. Thomson to Bundy, 5 August 1964, *FRUS, 1964–68*, 30: 75–76.
113. Cabot to the Department of State, 23 September 1964, *FRUS, 1964–68*, 30: 99–100.
114. Cabot to the Department of State, 24 September 1964, ibid., 102–104.
115. Cabot to the Department of State, 24 February 1965, ibid., 148–50; "A Résumé of the Warsaw Talks," box 2187, RG 59, p. 195.
116. Cabot to the Department of State, 21 April 1965, *FRUS, 1964–68*, 30: 165–66.
117. ZEN49, 2: 723; ZEWHD, 445. On 10 April 1966, in a meeting with Pakistani journalists, Zhou Enlai openly stated China's four-point policy toward the U.S., which was published in *Peking Review*, no. 20, on 13 May 1966. Roderick MacFarquhar argued that China's decision to publish the four-point statement was because "the Chinese may have felt there was some possibility of an American pre-emptive strike against their nuclear installations." See MacFarquhar, *Sino-American Relations*, 214, 226.
118. Ironically, Washington's decision to postpone Ayub Khan's visit resulted from uneasiness with Pakistan's increasingly close relationship with China, particularly with the remarks about Vietnam Ayub Khan made in Beijing in early March. See McMahon, *Cold War on the Periphery*, 318–24.
119. Zhou Enlai conveyed China's four-point policy to the United States through Tanzania president Julius Nyerere on 6 June and the Zambia government delegation on 20 August 1965. See ZEN49, 2: 736; ZEWHD, 474. On 31 May 1965, PRC foreign minister Chen Yi summoned British chargé d'affaires Donald C. Hopson in Beijing and asked him to transmit China's four-point message to Washington. London quickly delivered Chen Yi's message to Washington. See Chen Jian, *Mao's China and the Cold War*, 217.
120. ZEWW, 460 n.
121. Gronouski to the Department of State, 25 May 1966, *FRUS, 1964–68*, 30: 314–17.
122. Gronouski to the Department of State, 7 September 1966, ibid., 383.
123. Ibid.
124. "A Résumé of the Warsaw Talks," p. 211, box 2187, RG 59. Gronouski to the Department of State, 9 September 1966, *FRUS, 1964–68*, 30: 386–87.
125. Bundy to Ball, 4 December 1965, *FRUS, 1964–68*, 30: 228–30.
126. Ibid.
127. Wang Guoquan, "My Tenure as Ambassador," 155.
128. Letter from the Representative to the United Nations (Goldberg) to President Johnson, 28 April 1966; Rostow to Johnson, 30 April 1966, *FRUS, 1964–68*, 30: 293–96. By 1965, the Johnson administration came to believe that the Albanian resolution would gain a simple majority in 1966. In a meeting with Dean Rusk, William Bundy, Joseph Sisco (the assistant secretary of state for international organizations), and Arthur Goldberg rec-

ommended that "Washington support countries such as Canada who were ready to argue openly for two Chinas at the 1966 UN General Assembly session." See in Foot, *Practice of Power*, 43.

129. Thomson to Rostow, 4 August 1966, *FRUS, 1964–68*, 30: 364–66.

130. Bundy to Rusk, 13 May 1966, ibid., 299–300.

131. Bundy to Rusk, 20 May 1966, ibid., 306–308.

132. Gronouski to the Department of State, 25 January 1967, ibid., 509–512.

133. Thomson, "On the Making of U.S. China Policy," 233.

134. Bundy to Ball, 4 December 1965, *FRUS, 1964–68*, 30: 228–30.

135. Gronouski to the Department of State, 16 December 1965, ibid., 232–34.

136. Wang Guoquan, "My Tenure as Ambassador," 153–54.

137. "Historical Reports Relating to Diplomacy . . . 1963–1969," box 4, RG 59.

138. Gronouski to the Department of State, 25 May 1966, *FRUS, 1964–68*, 30: 314–17.

139. For example, see Alfred Jenkins to Rostow, 16 September 1966, ibid., 388–89.

140. Steven M. Goldstein made a similar observation in his "Dialogue of the Deaf?" 231.

141. Rusk to Gronouski (Guidance for 133rd Meeting), 29 May 1967, *FRUS, 1964–68*, 30: 574–79.

142. Bundy to Rusk (Instructions for 132nd Warsaw Talks), 30 December 1966, ibid., 492–93.

143. Between 1965 and 1968, Beijing strongly opposed peace talks between Hanoi and Washington. See Zhai, *China and the Vietnam War*, 157.

144. Rusk to Gronouski (Guidance for 132nd Meeting), 3 January 1967, *FRUS, 1964–68*, 30: 498.

145. John M. Cabot had spoken of the educational function in 1965. See "Cabot to Bundy, September 16, 1965" in ibid., 206; Alfred Jenkins suggested the use of the Warsaw talks as an educational platform in "Paper Prepared by Alfred Jenkins, February 22, 1968," in ibid., 658; Walt Rostow highlighted "Warsaw as an Education Forum" for President Johnson's attention in "Rostow to Johnson, 24 February 1968," in ibid., 665.

146. "Paper Prepared by Alfred Jenkins, 9 October 1968," ibid., 713.

147. Goldstein, "Dialogue of the Deaf?" 232.

148. William Bundy and Alfred Jenkins brought together these themes in the following memos: see *FRUS, 1964–68*, 30: 645–59, 709–18.

149. Rostow to President Johnson (Recommended Change in Treasury Regulations on the Trade of U.S. Subsidiaries Abroad with China), 6 January 1969, ibid., 729–30.

150. From May to August 1967, the Foreign Ministry didn't function normally due to the assault from the "rebel faction." All leading cadres, including Foreign Minister Chen Yi, were under fire, and were not allowed to work. China's relations with many countries deteriorated. The office of the British chargé d'affaires in Beijing was set on fire on 22 August 1967. After this incident, Zhou Enlai, with Mao's support, regained control over foreign affairs. For a Chinese version of this period of history, see Jin Ge, "The Beginning and End of 'Seizing Power' in the Foreign Ministry," 207–43.

151. Since 130th meeting, on 25 May 1966, the formal sessions were followed by informal discussions at the Chinese Embassy between the American and Chinese advisers and interpreters. At these meetings, the two sides discussed the points in the formal talks that required clarification, as well as interpreting problems. The atmosphere was relaxed and cordial. As the interval between the talks grew longer, the channel between the embassies in Warsaw was used increasingly to pass messages of interest between the two governments. See "Historical Reports Relating to Diplomacy . . . 1963–1969," box 4, RG 59.

152. Rusk to Gronouski (134th Ambassadorial-level US-ChiCom Meeting), 4 January

1968, *FRUS, 1964–68*, 30: 624–29; Luo, "The Beginning of the Thawing of Sino-American Relations," 23–24.

153. Gronouski to the Department of State, *FRUS, 1964–68*, 30: 630–32.

154. See Editorial Note, ibid., 676–77.

155. Luo, "The Beginning of the Thawing of Sino-American Relations," 24.

156. Tucker, *China Confidential*, 201.

157. Ibid.

158. "Outgoing Telegram, Department of State," 14 April 1966, box 2025, Central Foreign Policy Files, 1964–66, Political and Defense, RG 59.

159. "Paper Prepared by Alfred Jenkins, 9 October 1968," *FRUS, 1964–68*, 30: 709.

160. *ZHJH*, 93.

161. Steven Goldstein suggests this point in his article. See Goldstein, "Dialogue of the Deaf?" 236.

162. Thomson, "On the Making of U.S. China Policy."

163. Goldstein, "Dialogue of the Deaf?" 236. Henry Kissinger later argued that the Geneva/Warsaw talks were of little value. He wrote in his memoirs that these meetings were "sterile" and "could not point to a single accomplishment." See Kissinger, *White House Years*, 684. Kissinger's depiction of Nixon's opening up to China as a revolutionary reversal of Cold War policy contradicts the historical record.

6. Entering a New Era

1. Nixon first used the term in his acceptance speech at the Republican convention in Miami Beach, Florida, on 8 August 1968. He claimed that "we are entering an era of negotiation" in his inaugural address on 20 January 1969. See Editorial Note in *FRUS, 1969–76*, 1: 49 and 53.

2. Gaddis, *Strategies of Containment*, 284–87.

3. Recounted in Freeman, "The Process of Rapprochement," 2.

4. Hersh, *Price of Power*, 357.

5. Li Ke and Hao, *Wenhua Dageming Zhong de Renmin Jiefangjun*, 249–51.

6. Yang Kuisong, "From the Zhenbao Island Clashes to Sino-American Rapprochement," 7–8; Xu Yan, "The Sino-Soviet Border Clashes of 1969," 6–10.

7. Kissinger recorded in his memoirs that in August 1969, a Soviet diplomat in Washington inquired about "what the U.S. reaction would be to a Soviet attack on Chinese nuclear facilities." See Kissinger, *White House Years*, 183. See also discussions in Yang Kuisong, "From the Zhenbao Island Clashes to Sino-American Rapprochement," 12. In the latter half of the year, the Western press also reported rumors of Soviet plans to strike at China's nuclear base.

8. All Chinese ambassadors, except Huang Hua in Egypt, were recalled to take part in the Cultural Revolution.

9. Gao, *Wannian Zhou Enlai*, 407.

10. Xiong, *Wo de Qingbao yu Waijiao Shengya*, 166. Xiong, a senior intelligence and foreign service officer, was appointed as assistant to the marshals' study group. Xiong's account was more reliable than other Chinese sources. The marshals' first meeting was on 7 June 1969. According to Chinese scholar Wang Yongqin, Mao first instructed the four marshals to study the international situation on 19 February. Mao again asked the four marshals to research international issues on 22 March and 19 April. See Wang, "Chronicle of Sino-American-Soviet Relations," no. 4 (1997): 118–19 and 121.

11. Xiong, *Wo de Qingbao yu Waijiao Shengya*, 166.

12. Xu Yan, "Sino-Soviet Border Clashes of 1969," 10; Yang Kuisong, "From the Zhenbao Island Clashes to Sino-American Rapprochement," 11–19.

13. The CCP Central Committee and the Administrative Group of the CMC, "Report on Measures Needed to Be Taken to Enhance Air Defense," 27 August 1969, CCA, cited from Yang, "The Sino-Soviet Border Clash of 1969," 36–37.

14. See "The CCP Central Committee's Order for General Mobilization in Border Provinces and Regions," 28 August 1969, CWIHPB, no. 11 (Winter 1998): 168–69.

15. Xiong, Wo de Qingbao yu Waijiao Shengya, 184–86.

16. Ibid., 187.

17. Gao, Wannian Zhou Enlai, 408. In the West, there has been speculation that opposition to Mao-Zhou's efforts to reach out to the United States existed within Chinese leadership in late 1960s and early 1970s. During the Mao-Nixon summit in February 1972, Mao intentionally threw out this claim. Mao told Nixon on 21 February, "In our country also there is a reactionary group which is opposed to our contact with you. The result was that they got on an airplane and fled abroad." See "Memorandum of Conversation (Mao and Nixon), 21 February 1972," box 91, NSCF, NPMP. Henry Kissinger reported in his memoirs that Lin Biao, then China's defense minister and Mao's designated successor, was opposed to China's rapprochement with the United States. See Kissinger, White House Years, 696–97. This allegation has been continuously disseminated in Western writings. See Garver, China's Decision for Rapprochement with the United States, 134–37; Foot, Practice of Power, 105; Ross, Negotiating Cooperation, 27; Bundy, A Tangled Web, 109, 165. Most recently, Mann, About Face, 26; and Kimball, Nixon's Vietnam War, 261. Robert Garson claimed that it was Mao's wife, Jiang Qing, the leader of the radicals, who was against rapprochement with the United States. See Garson, United States and China since 1949, 123. However, no Chinese document has surfaced to confirm these hypotheses. All available Chinese sources indicate that Mao and Zhou were in total control of China's foreign policy decision-making and that Lin Biao had virtually no interest in foreign policy.

In this book, I utilize the term "ultra-leftist," referring to those who clung to Mao's revolutionary line in words and were inertial to changes in Chinese politics during the Cultural Revolution. These people were static but not resistant to Mao's instructions, especially regarding China's U.S. policy. The "ultra-leftists" may include Lin Biao and his clique, radical leaders such as Mao's wife Jiang Qing, Kang Sheng, Chen Boda, and other officials from different central ministries. These "leftist" leaders had made their political rise during the Cultural Revolution due to their radical views and loyalty to Mao. At times, they might not be aware of Mao's true intention and were reluctant to make an abrupt change of attitude toward the number-one enemy, the United States. It was unlikely that they would oppose Mao's decisions as their political fortune depended on Mao's patronage. Thus, although they were strong supporters of the Cultural Revolution, and were not in favor of improving relations with the U.S., they made no open opposition to Mao's decision to reach a rapprochement with the United States.

18. Chen Jian contends that the geopolitics-centered interpretation alone does not fully reveal the complicated reasons behind Mao's decision to improve relations with the United States. In order to achieve a better understanding of the issue, he places the Sino-American rapprochement in the context of the fading status of Mao's continuous revolution. He points out that the Sino-American rapprochement came at a time when the Cultural Revolution and the more general enterprise of Mao's continuous revolution had been declining. See Chen Jian, Mao's China and the Cold War, 239. This author argues that many factors contribute to U.S.-China rapprochement. The decade-long Sino-American talks, China as a nuclear power, the U.S. quagmire in Vietnam, and

Nixon's personal background and initiatives all facilitated the rapprochement process. Evelyn Goh's study shows that "the ideas of reconciliation with China were already being propagated and debated within official circles in the United States during the 1960s." See Goh, *Constructing the U.S. Rapprochement with China*, especially conclusion.

19. See Deborah and Gerald Strober's interviews with Alexander Haig and H. R. Haldeman in Strober, *Nixon Presidency*, 130.

20. William Bundy argues that "a new relationship with China was far from being a top priority from the start" in the Nixon administration. See Bundy, *Tangled Web*, 100.

21. Walters, *Silent Missions*, 525.

22. Nixon, *Memoirs of Richard Nixon*, 257.

23. Haldeman, *Ends of Power*, 91.

24. Anna Chennault was at this time the nominal head of the China Lobby, which had links with Taiwan and strongly opposed any change in U.S. policy toward mainland China.

25. Strober and Strober, *Nixon Presidency*, 130.

26. The above paragraph is based on Tucker, *China Confidential*, 219–20; idem, *Taiwan, Hong Kong, and the United States*, 98–99.

27. Nixon, *Memoirs of Richard Nixon*, 373–74.

28. See Editorial Note in *FRUS, 1969–72*, 65.

29. In February 1969, Beijing cancelled the 135th ambassadorial meeting that had been scheduled for 20 February 1969 as Washington provided asylum to Liao Heshu, the Chinese chargé d'affaires in Netherlands, who defected to the West early in the month.

30. *Renmin Ribao*, 28 January 1969. For the English text of the essay, see *Peking Review*, 31 January 1969, 7–10. Chen Jian notes there were subtle changes in Mao's attitude toward Nixon from the beginning of the new administration. Mao ordered the publication of Nixon's inaugural address to show that he had noticed Nixon's message that "the United States was willing to develop relations with all countries in the world." See Chen Jian, *Mao's China and the Cold War*, 238–39.

31. United Press International, dispatch from Hong Kong, 1 March 1969.

32. *Renmin Ribao*, 25 April 1969.

33. Tyler, *Great Wall*, 58.

34. Ibid., 62.

35. Ibid., 63.

36. "U.S. China policy 1969–72," Tab 3, folder 3, box 86, NSCF (HAK Office Files).

37. "U.S. China policy 1969–72," Tab 4, folder 1, box 86, NSCF.

38. Xiong, *Wo de Qingbao yu Waijiao Shengya*, 178–79.

39. "U.S. China policy 1969–72," Tab 1, folder 1, box 86, NSCF. NSSM was published on 5 February 1969.

40. Phillips, "Nixon's China Initiative," 132.

41. "US China Policy and Nuclear Planning Group Issues," May 15, 1969, H-111, SRG Minutes 1969, NSC Institutional Files, box 373, NPMP; Also see Editorial Note in *FRUS, 1969–76*, 1: 81; Kissinger, *White House Years*, 182.

42. Hersh, *Price of Power*, 358.

43. See Editorial Note in *FRUS, 1969–76*, 1: 92; Holdridge, *Crossing the Divide*, 31. In his memoirs, Nixon notes that the doctrine he announced on Guam was misinterpreted by some as signaling a U.S. withdrawal from Asia, as well as other parts of the world. In his view, "the Nixon Doctrine was not a formula for getting America out of Asia, but one that provided the only sound basis for America's staying in and continuing to play a responsible role in helping non-communist nations and neutrals as well as our Asian allies to defend their independence." See Nixon, *Memoirs of Richard Nixon*, 395.

44. Burr, "Sino-American Relations," 85. Also see Bundy, *Tangled Web*, 105.

45. Kissinger, *White House Years*, 180–81. See also Aijazuddin, *From a Head, Through a Head, To a Head*. Pakistan was an ideal message bearer. It maintained good relations with China and the United States. Nixon told the Pakistani president that "the US should not be party to any arrangements designed to isolate China. He asked President Yahya to convey his feeling to the Chinese at the highest level." See Editorial Note in *FRUS, 1969–76*, 1: 97.

46. "U.S. China policy 1969–72," Tab 5, folder 1, box 86, NSCF. The Rogers speech came as a surprise to Nixon and Kissinger, who had not cleared it and preferred to conduct their China opening in secret. Early on 29 April 1969, at the annual luncheon of the Associated Press in New York City, Rogers expressed the Nixon administration's desire for improved relations with China. He declared that the United States "will take initiatives to reestablish more normal relations with Communist China." See Editorial Note in *FRUS, 1969–76*, 1: 78.

47. "Address before the National Press Club, Canberra, Australia, August 8," *Department of State Bulletin*, v. 61, no. 1575 (1 September 1969): 179–80.

48. Kissinger, *White House Years*, 182.

49. Garthoff, *Détente and Confrontation*, 219. Steven Phillips contends that China policy was closely held and the full NSC met only once to discuss this topic. No decisions were reached at the 14 August 1969 meeting, but Nixon's handwritten notes of a briefing he received provide insight into the president's understandings of the PRC. See Phillips, "Nixon's China Initiative," 132.

50. See Whiting, "Sino-American Détente," 336; Holdridge, *Crossing the Divide*, 35.

51. Western media suspected that Kosygin planned to meet with Zhou Enlai at Ho Chi Minh's funeral in early September of 1969. Zhou led a Chinese delegation to condole Ho's death, arriving on 4 September and leaving the same day. Thus, Zhou intentionally avoided meeting with Kosygin in Hanoi. Chinese sources denied such a speculation. After arriving at Hanoi on 6 September, through the Chinese embassy in Vietnam, Kosygin asked to meet with Zhou Enlai in Beijing on his way to Moscow. However, Kosygin was not able to receive China's invitation until he was already at Dushanbe, Tadzhikistan Republic, USSR, on 11 September. See ZEZ, 2: 1083; ZRGW57, 274.

52. Gao, *Wannian Zhou Enlai*, 411. The Sino-Soviet border negotiations, which started on 20 October 1969, continued, with a few interruptions, right up to the end of the 1980s. Beijing attempted to create the impression that should the U.S. remain uncompromising in its negotiation with the PRC, there might be at any moment a breakthrough in relations with the Soviet Union. See Elizavetin, "Kosygin-Zhou Talks at Beijing Airport," 52–54.

53. During his August 1969 around-the-world trip, Nixon informed the leaders of Romania and Pakistan of his interests in improved relations with the PRC. In the late summer and fall of that year, Pakistani President Yahya Khan offered to play an active role in rapprochement. In the Pakistani channel, Nixon and Kissinger had found a secret avenue for communication that bypassed the Department of State. In December, the Pakistani ambassador to the United States, Agha Hilaly, transmitted the first direct message from the PRC. Hilaly reported that PRC leaders had released two detained Americans and were willing to renew the Warsaw talks without preconditions, and Kissinger replied that the United States was interested in improving relations. See Phillips, "Nixon's China Initiative," 135.

54. CIA Intelligence Memorandum, "Signs of Life in Chinese Foreign Policy," 11 April 1970, copy at NS Archive, cited in Burr, "Sino-American Relations," 97.

55. Xue, *Dangdai Zhongguo Waijiao*, 219. See also "Stoessel to Secretary of State," 3

December 1969, pp. 23–28, Subject-Numeric files, 1967–1969, POL-US, RG 59. Stoessel mentioned in the telegram that the Chinese diplomat he tried to approach was Lei Yang, Chinese chargé d'affaires to Poland, but actually, it was Li Juqing, the Chinese embassy's second secretary; the interpreter was Jing Zhicheng. Also see Luo, "My Years in Poland," 179–80. Zong, "Textual Research into Some Facts of Chinese Diplomatic History,"103–109. Kissinger was not satisfied with Stoessel's procrastination, and had to send Stoessel three cables and warn him, "Either you do it or we will get someone who will." Stoessel's version was that he had been unable to approach the Chinese official privately at any party or diplomatic reception that fall and winter. See Hersh, *Price of Power*, 359. The question remained. Why didn't the United States make use of the exiting second-secretary level contact to notify Beijing of Washington's interest in serious talks? A plausible answer might be that the Chinese didn't regard the contact very highly.

56. ZEZ, 2: 1087.

57. ZEN49, 3: 336; ZEZ, 2: 1088. See also Kissinger, *White House Years*, 188.

58. Interview with CCP historians, January 2002.

59. Ibid.

60. Qian, "The Beginning of the Renewal of Sino-American Warsaw Talks."

61. Luo, "My Years in Poland," 181. "Telegram, Stoessel to the Secretary of State, 8 January 1970," Subject-Numeric files, 1970–73, Pol Chicom US, RG 59. Two points should be noted here. First, in the past, the ambassadorial talks had been held in a meeting place arranged by the Polish government; this time, the Americans, obviously for the purpose of maintaining secrecy, proposed to move meetings to the two embassies, to which the Chinese agreed immediately. Two informal meetings were held in the respective embassies in Warsaw on 11 December 1969 and 8 January 1970. Stoessel was invited to the Chinese embassy for tea and to arrive at the front door on 11 December. It was designed to send a clear signal to the Soviets. Second, as China did not have an ambassador in Poland at the time since mid-1967, the last two meetings of the ambassadorial talks were held between Chinese chargé d'affaires Lei Yang and U.S. Ambassador Stoessel.

62. Green, *War and Peace with China*, 110.

63. ZEN49, 3: 344.

64. Zhou Enlai's Talk with Khwaja Mohammad Kaiser, Pakistan's ambassador to China, 22 January 1970. Cited in Ross and Jiang, *Re-examining the Cold War*, 337.

65. Stoessel-Lei Talks, Report of 135th Meeting, 20 January 1970, and Memorandum for the President, Guidance for Sino-U.S. Ambassadorial Meeting, box 2187, Pol-Chicom US, RG 59.

66. Ibid.

67. Since the early days of the Sino-American ambassadorial talks in September 1955, the Chinese government had been proposing a ministerial-level talk between the two sides. The American side insisted on the Chinese releasing all American citizens before dealing with other issues.

68. Stoessel-Lei Talks, Report of 135th Meeting, 20 January 1970, and Memorandum for the President, Guidance for Sino-U.S. Ambassadorial Meeting, box 2187, Pol-Chicom US, RG 59. It is also worth noting that after their formal meeting, Stoessel and Lei Yang adjourned to another room and met less formally. See Freeman, "The Process of Rapprochement," 2.

69. See Nixon, *U.S. Foreign Policy for the 1970s*, 140–42.

70. Gao, *Wannian Zhou Enlai*, 415.

71. ZEN49, 3: 348; ZEZ, 2: 1089. Zhou Enlai made a key change in the statement's wording. The original text prepared by the Foreign Ministry reads that the Chinese government "will *consider receiving*" the American official. Zhou changed "will consider

receiving" to "will receive." Next to the change, the premier added: "Considering that at the 135th meeting [the meeting held on 20 January 1970], our side had already mentioned that we are willing to consider [receiving the American official] or [making the contact] through other channels, and the American side also mentioned at the last meeting that [they will send an envoy] to Beijing for direct discussion, if we still use 'will consider,' it is too light a statement, therefore I changed it to 'will receive.' This is still lighter than 'will welcome,' but it is more substantial than 'will consider.'" In order to pacify the ultra-leftists, after getting Mao's permission for the change, Zhou immediately wrote to Kang Sheng, one of the major figures of the ultra-leftists, explaining why he made such a change. See "Zhou Enlai's Letter to Kang Sheng, 13 February 1970," cited from Gao, *Wannian Zhou Enlai*, 416.

72. Gong, *Kuayue Honggou*, 50–51; see also Stoessel-Lei Talks, Report of 136th Meeting, 20 February 1970, box 2188, Pol Chicom-US, RG 59.

73. Stoessel-Lei Talks, Report of 136th Meeting, 20 February 1970, box 2188, Pol Chicom US, RG 59. Author's emphasis.

74. The wording in the Shanghai Communiqué goes as follows: "it will progressively reduce its forces and military installations on Taiwan as the tension in the area diminishes." See Harding, *Fragile Relationship*, Appendix B, 373–77.

75. See Ross, *Negotiating Cooperation*, 34. Robert Ross interviews U.S. government officials.

76. Gaddis, *Strategies of Containment*, 303. Foreign Service officers in the State Department, such as Marshall Green, were sensitive to the effect of these talks with China on East Asian nations' morale and confidence in America as they had cast their lot with American policy in their relations with China over the years. The State Department wanted to go slowly and take careful account of East Asian reactions, not least in Japan. See Bundy, *Tangled Web*, 107.

77. Refer to trade, travel, and prisoners.

78. Kissinger, *White House Years*, 690–91. Marshall Green argued that Kissinger distorted the State Department's views. Green said, "I remember very well that Henry sent over and asked our views on this, for whatever they were worth. One of the things that I mentioned to him was that I trusted, before we were committed to a high-level meeting, one of our high-level people would have some advance indication that it would result in something that was constructive. Nothing would be worse than to go out there and then get slapped in the face. It would be the end of all that we hoped to achieve in our U.S.-China relations. . . . Kissinger implies that we were throwing cold water. It was not true at all. All we were saying is that we didn't know all of the pieces in the puzzle." See Tucker, *China Confidential*, 239–40.

79. "A Higher-Level Sino-US Meeting in Peking," 5 March 1970, box 2188, POL Com US, RG 59.

80. Hersh, *Price of Power*, 361.

81. Bundy, *Tangled Web*, 107.

82. The Chinese rejected the U.S. proposal to meet on 1–3 April. Then the U.S. turned down the Chinese suggestion for a meeting on 15 April. See "Next Warsaw Meeting, Paul H. Kreisberg to Marshall Green," 22 April 1970, box 2188, POL Com US, RG 59.

83. Kissinger, *White House Years*, 692.

84. ZEN49, 3: 372.

85. Mann, *About Face*, 25.

86. *Renmin Ribao*, 11 July 1970. At the same time, Beijing announced that another American, Hugh Redmond, who had been imprisoned since 1954, had committed suicide three months earlier.

87. The United States withdrew from Cambodia on 30 June 1970. See Kissinger, *White House Years*, 516.

88. One Chinese source claims that Zhou Enlai carefully directed all. He even intervened over the size of the photo that was to be published in *Renmin Ribao*, which served as a model for all other major Chinese newspapers to follow. See Yang Mingwei and Chen, *Zhou Enlai Waijiao Fengyun*, 243. Other historians disputed this point. Zong Daoyi argued that there was no proof that Zhou personally intervened over the size of the picture. See Zong, "The Textual Research into Some Facts of Chinese Diplomatic History," 103–14. Unfortunately, Nixon and Kissinger missed the significance of the Chinese gesture. See Kissinger, *White House Years*, 698; MZZ49, 2: 1628. Snow had been a friend of Mao and the Chinese Communists since the mid-1930s, when he visited the Chinese Communist base areas in northern Shaanxi province and interviewed Mao and many other CCP leaders. His highly acclaimed book, *Red Star over China*, published in 1938, helped create a positive image of the Chinese Communist movement both within and outside China.

89. Chen Jian, *Mao's China and the Cold War*, 256.

90. Kissinger records, "I came to understand that Mao intended to symbolize that American relations now had his personal attention, but it was by then a purely academic insight: we had missed the point when it mattered." See Kissinger, *White House Years*, 699. The White House rejected Allen Whiting's offer to interrogate Snow on the ground that Snow had often gone to China and was unreliable.

91. Since early October 1970, Snow had been waiting to interview the chairman. On 5 November, he had a lengthy interview with Zhou Enlai, which focused on international issues. Then, several times he thought he was to meet the chairman soon, but the meeting was postponed repeatedly.

92. Minutes, interview with Edgar Snow, 18 December 1970, *JYMZW*, 13: 166–68.

93. See Nixon, *Memoirs of Richard Nixon*, 547.

94. I am grateful to William Burr for reminding me of this point. Edgar Snow, "A Conversation with Mao Tse-tung," *Life* 70 (30 April 1971): 46–48. Kissinger pointed out in his memoirs, "We did not learn of the interview until several months later." See Kissinger, *White House Years*, 702–703.

95. Holdridge, *Crossing the Divide*, 47.

96. *Time*, 5 October 1970.

97. Memorandum of Conversation (Kissinger and Zhou Enlai), July 9, 1971, box 1032, NSCF.

98. Green, Holdridge, and Stoke, *War and Peace with China*, 115.

99. Nixon, *Memoirs of Richard Nixon*, 546.

100. Hersh, *Price of Power*, 365.

101. "Memorandum of Conversation: Meeting between the President and Pakistan President Yahya," 25 October 1970, folder 2, box 1031, NSCF.

102. A copy of the message dictated by Ambassador Hilaly to Kissinger is in folder 2, box 1031, NSCF.

103. Kissinger, *White House Years*, 701.

104. Henry Kissinger to the President, "Conversation with Ambassador Bogdan," 11 January 1971, folder 2, box 1031, NSCF.

105. Ibid.

106. "Did Chou Enlai tell Edgar Snow anything new about Taiwan?" 4 January 1971, box 2188, POL Com US, RG 59.

107. POLO I, "Briefing Book for the President" (Taiwan), July 1971, p. 1, box 1032, NSCF.

108. The original of the reply was given to Ambassador Hilaly for delivery to President Yahya Khan. A copy of it is at folder 2, box 1031, NSCF.

109. "Foreign Policy Report," folder 1, box 86, NSCF (HAK Office files).

110. "U.S. China policy 1969–72," p. 3, folder 1, box 86. Earlier, on 21 July 1969, the U.S. State Department announced that it was relaxing restrictions on American citizens traveling to China. Tourists were permitted to bring back $100 worth of Chinese goods.

111. Xue, *Dangdai Zhongguo Waijiao*, 220.

112. "Instruction from Mao to Zhou Enlai," 15 March 1971, cited in Gao, *Wannian Zhou Enlai*, 430; Qian, *Xiaoqiu Zhuandong Daqiu*, 140.

113. Qian, *Xiaoqiu Zhuandong Daqiu*, 214–16; Gao, *Wannian Zhou Enlai*, 430.

114. Gao, *Wannian Zhou Enlai*, 430.

115. Qian, *Xiaoqiu Zhuandong Daqiu*, 267–68.

116. Huang Hua was then China's ambassador to Canada. Zhang Wenjin was director-general, Western European and American Department, the Foreign Ministry. He had been a close assistant of Zhou dating back to the Marshall Mission in 1946.

117. Qian, *Xiaoqiu Zhuandong Daqiu*, 236; Xu Dashen, *Zhonghua Renmin Gongheguo Shilu*, 3: 698–99.

118. Solomon, *Chinese Negotiating Behavior*, 30.

119. The Chinese television commentator's opening remarks at the matches, which emphasized that "for a long time, friendship has existed between the Chinese and American peoples" and that "the visit by the American table tennis team will enhance such friendship," were carefully examined and revised by Zhou Enlai himself. See Qian, *Pingpang Waijiao Shimo*, 268–71.

120. Minutes, Zhou Enlai, "Conversations with the American Table Tennis Delegation," 14 April 1971, in ZEWW, 469–75. The Chinese media reported the meeting extensively. See, for example, *Renmin Ribao*, 15 April 1971, front page, where the quote can be found.

121. "U.S. China policy 1969–72," Tab 23, folder 1, box 86, NSCF.

122. Kissinger, *White House Years*, 710.

123. "Message from Premier Chou Enlai," 21 April 1971 (Delivered to Dr. Kissinger–6:15 P.M., April 27, 1971), folder 2, box 1031, NSCF. It was Mao who believed that America's special envoy should come to Beijing publicly. The chairman, in reviewing the message, commented: "If they want to come, they should come in the open light. Why should they hide the[ir] head and pull in the[ir] tail?" See Wei, "Inside Stories of Kissinger's Secret Visit to China," 36.

124. "Extract of MEMCOM dated May 5, 1971," folder 2, box 1031, NSCF.

125. Nixon, *Memoirs of Richard Nixon*, 549–50. Nixon toyed with Kissinger over the choice of the emissary for a few days. Such names as Nelson Rockefeller, David Bruce, Elliot Richardson, and George Bush, then U.S. ambassador to the United Nations, were bandied. See also "Record of Nixon-Kissinger Telephone Conversation Discussing Zhou's Message and Possible Envoys to China, 27 April 1971," box 1031, NSCF.

126. This message is in folder 2, box 1031, NSCF.

127. Gong, *Kuayue Honggou*, 97–98.

128. Mann, *About Face*, 28.

129. Gaddis, *Strategies of Containment*, 306.

130. ZEN49, 3: 458; ZEZ, 2: 1096.

131. Yang Mingwei and Chen, *Zhou Enlai Waijiao Fengyun*, 247–48.

132. "The Central Committee Politburo's Report on the Sino-American Meeting" (drafted by Zhou Enlai), 26 May 1971, quoted from Gong, *Kuayue Honggou*, 103–104; Also ZEZ, 2: 1096–97, and ZEN49, 3: 458–59.

133. Gong, *Kuayue Honggou*, 104.

134. Gong, "Chinese Decision-Making and the Thawing of U.S.-China Relations," 697.

135. Gong, *Kuayue Honggou*, 105–106. According to the Chinese record, some Politburo members had concerns about the new U.S.-China contact. They raised a series of questions. Some believed that the talks between China and the United States were unusual and might have negative effects upon the spirit for struggle on the part of the American people. Some asked whether or not the Sino-American talks would have a negative impact upon the anti-American war in Indochina and the peace talks in Paris. Some asked if talks could be a trick of Nixon and Kissinger. See Xu Dashen, *Zhonghua Renmin Gongheguo Shilu*, 3: 713–14.

136. ZEZ, 2: 1096; ZEN49, 3: 458–59; MZZ49, 2: 1633.

137. Gong, *Kuayue Honggou*, 107.

138. "Text of Note Handed to HAK by Hilaly, 8:30 P.M., June 2, 1971," folder 2, box 1031, NSCF.

139. Kissinger, *White House Years*, 727.

140. Nixon, *Memoirs of Richard Nixon*, 552.

7. Breaking the Ice

1. Holdridge, *Crossing the Divide*, 45.

2. The briefing book for Kissinger's secret visit to Beijing is declassified at NA. It is in the form of "Briefing Book for the President," July 1971, in box 1032, NSCF. Also see Holdridge, *Crossing the Divide*, 45.

3. Kissinger, *White House Years*, 730–31.

4. "Briefing Book for the President," July 1971, pp. 3–5 (Scope Paper), box 1032, NSCF.

5. Ibid., 5–6.

6. Ibid., 7.

7. "Briefing Book for the President," July 1971, p. 6, box 1032, NSCF.

8. "Meeting between President, Dr. Kissinger, and General Haig, Thursday, July 1, Oval Office," 1 July 1971, box 1036, NSCF (China General, July–October 1971).

9. "Nixon handwritten note," July 1971, in POLO 1 ("Briefing Book for the President," July 1971), folder 1, box 1032, NSCF.

10. "Meeting between President, Dr. Kissinger, and General Haig, Thursday, July 1, Oval Office," 1 July 1971, box 1036, NSCF.

11. Tao, *Zhongmei Guanxishi*, 536.

12. ZEZ, 2: 1097.

13. Tang, "A Mysterious Mission," 4: 39.

14. Gong, *Kuayue Honggou*, 108.

15. Zhang Ying, *Sui Zhang Wenjin Chushi Meiguo*, 33–34; idem, "Random Recollection of Premier Zhou's Later Years," 375–76. Also Wang Xiangtong, *Wode Zhangfu Ji Chaozhu*, 83–84.

16. ZEN49, 3: 467.

17. Holdridge, *Crossing the Divide*, 50.

18. See Su, *Meiguo Duihua Zhengce Yu Taiwan Wenti*, 370. Also see Kissinger, *White House Years*, 741.

19. Holdridge, *Crossing the Divide*, 53.

20. Transcripts of the meetings are now available in box 1032, NSCF.

21. Speech, Zhou Enlai, "Explaining the Sino-American Communiqué," 3 March 1972, CCA (an excerpt of the speech is published in ZEN49, 3: 515); Kissinger, *White House Years*, 745.

22. Xiong Xianghui was then appointed as Zhou's special assistant.

23. Memorandum of Conversation (Kissinger and Zhou Enlai), July 9, 1971. p. 6, box 1032, NSCF.

24. Ibid.

25. Kissinger to the President, "My Talks with Chou En-lai," July 14, 1971, p. 12, box 1032, NSCF.

26. Memorandum of Conversation (Kissinger and Zhou Enlai), July 9, pp. 11–15 and July 10 (Afternoon), 1971, p. 15, box 1032, NSCF. Also see Xiong, *Wo de Qingbao yu Waijiao Shengya*, 337. John Holdridge noted in his memoirs that Zhou was satisfied with Kissinger's presentation. See Holdridge, *Crossing the Divide*, 57–58. He recorded, "Zhou's response was immediate: 'Good,' he said, 'these talks may now proceed.'" This could not be found in the "Memorandum of Conversation, July 9, 1971." The transcripts of the Memcons indicate the assurance was made rather late after extensive give-and-take between Kissinger and Zhou Enlai.

27. Memorandum of Conversation (Kissinger and Zhou Enlai), July 9, 1971, p. 15, box 1032, NSCF.

28. Ibid., p. 14. Also see Memorandum of Conversation (Kissinger and Zhou Enlai), July 10 (Afternoon), 1971, p. 5, box 1032, NSCF.

29. Memorandum of Conversation (Kissinger and Zhou Enlai), July 10 (Afternoon), 1971, pp. 3–20, box 1032, NSCF.

30. Memorandum of Conversation (Kissinger and Zhou Enlai), July 10 (Evening), 1971, p.2, box 1032, NSCF. Ambassador Stoessel already told the Chinese at the last two Warsaw talks in early 1970.

31. Memorandum of Conversation (Kissinger and Zhou Enlai), July 10 (Afternoon), 1971, p. 14, box 1032, NSCF.

32. Memorandum of Conversation (Kissinger and Zhou Enlai), July 9, 1971, pp. 17–35, box 1032, NSCF.

33. This was a lie. According to Chinese sources, China had sent military advisers to North Vietnam since 1950. When war escalated in Vietnam in the 1960s, China dispatched a total number of 320,000 engineering and antiaircraft artillery forces to North Vietnam between 1965 and 1973. See Jiang Ying, "Conflict and Restraint," 275.

34. Memorandum of Conversation (Kissinger and Zhou Enlai), July 9, 1971, pp. 17–35, box 1032, NSCF.

35. Kissinger to the President, "My Talks with Chou Enlai," 14 July 1971, and Memorandum of Conversation (Kissinger and Zhou Enlai), 9–11 July 1971, box 1032, NSCF; see also Wei, "Inside Stories of Kissinger's Secret Visit to China," 40–41.

36. President Nixon's Kansas City Remarks, July 6, 1971, folder 1, box 86 (Country Files-Far East), NSCF.

37. Nixon, *Memoirs of Richard Nixon*, 552–53; Kissinger, *White House Years*, 748–49.

38. Wei, "Inside Stories of Kissinger's Secret Visit to China," 40–41.

39. Chen Jian, *Mao's China and the Cold War*, 267–68.

40. Wei, "Inside Stories of Kissinger's Secret Visit to China," 42.

41. Memorandum of Conversation (Kissinger and Zhou Enlai), 10 July 1971 (12:10–6:00 P.M.), pp.7–8, box 1032, NSCF.

42. Memorandum of Conversation (Kissinger and Zhou Enlai), July 9, 1971, pp.35–45, box 1032, NSCF.

43. Ibid., pp. 35–38.

44. Memorandum of Conversation (Kissinger and Zhou Enlai), 10 July 1971 (12:10–6:00 P.M.), box 1032, NSCF. Also see Kissinger, *White House Years*, 750; Wei, "Inside Stories of Kissinger's Secret Visit to China," 42–43; Green, *War and Peace with China*, 125.

45. Chen Jian, *Mao's China and the Cold War*, 268.

46. Memorandum of Conversation (Kissinger and Zhou Enlai), July 9, 1971, pp. 3, 9–12, and 14, box 1032, NSCF.

47. In his memoirs, Kissinger mentioned that Zhou was hosting the reception for the North Korean leader Kim Il-sung. Actually, the guest was Kim Jung-rin, a politburo member and secretary of the Korean Workers' Party. See also ZEWHD, 596; Wei, "Inside Stories of Kissinger's Secret Visit to China," 43.

48. Wei, "Inside Stories of Kissinger's Secret Visit to China," 43–44. Kissinger, not knowing why Huang did not show up on time, mentioned in his memoirs: "We never found out whether it was a deliberate tactic to unsettle us, whether there was a Politburo meeting, whether Mao insisted on reviewing the talks, or whether, as was most likely, we faced a combination of all these." See Kissinger, *White House Years*, 751. In actuality, Huang was at Mao's home waiting for the chairman's instructions as Mao was sleeping. According to Kissinger, Huang Hua and Zhang Wenjin failed to appear at the scheduled time, and at about 10:45 P.M. he was told that Chinese drafters would not arrive until 9:00 the next morning. Kissinger complained to Chinese protocol officials that as the president's representative, he should have a precise meeting time from the Chinese, and they could not keep him on the standby. Then Zhou Enlai appeared at about 11:15 P.M. and said Chinese drafters would arrive shortly. See Kissinger to the President, "My Talks with Chou En-lai," July 14, 1971, p. 9, box 1032, NSCF. (Wei Shiyan indicated in his article that Zhou arrived at 10:15 P.M. See Wei, p. 44.)

49. Memorandum of Conversation (Kissinger and Chinese officials), July 11, 1971, box 1032, NSCF. Also see Wei, "Inside Stories of Kissinger's Secret Visit to China," 44–45; Kissinger, *White House Years*, 752–53. According to a Chinese account, Kissinger only added "with pleasure" to describe that "President Nixon has accepted the invitation."

50. Holdridge, *Crossing the Divide*, 62.

51. See Kissinger to the President, "My Talks with Chou En-lai," p. 10, box 1032, NSCF.

52. Memorandum of Conversation (Kissinger and Zhou Enlai), July 10 (Afternoon), 1971, p. 2, box 1032, NSCF.

53. In 1967, Defense Secretary Robert McNamara asked his assistant Leslie Gelb to compile a documentary history of the American involvement in Vietnam. *Pentagon Papers*, which emerged from this study, concluded that U.S. leaders since Franklin Roosevelt had deceived the public into supporting an unwinnable war. In June 1971, Daniel Ellsberg, a former Pentagon analyst, turned over this classified national security document to the *New York Times*. *Anderson Papers*: starting from 13 December 1971, columnist Jack Anderson began to publish NSC documents that showed the U.S. support for Pakistan in the December 1971 war with India.

54. Memorandum of Conversation (Kissinger and Zhou Enlai), July 10 (Evening), 1971, p. 2, box 1032, NSCF.

55. Walters, *Silent Missions*, 527–29. Cao, "Recalling the Secret 'Paris Channel,'" 2: 48–49.

56. Kissinger, *White House Years*, 765–66.

57. Cao, "Recalling the Secret 'Paris Channel,'" 49.

58. Ibid., 50. Kissinger secretly met and talked with Ambassador Huang Zhen on 25 July, 16 August, and 13 September 1971.

59. Winston Lord, Memorandum for Henry Kissinger, "July 26 Meeting with Chinese

Ambassador in Paris," 30 July 1971, Policy Planning Council, Director's file (Winston Lord), box 330, RG 59.

60. "Memorandum for Kissinger from Kennedy/Lord," 13 November 1971, Director's file (Winston Lord), box 330, RG 59.

61. The United Nations accepted the PRC into the organization on 26 October 1971, twenty-two years after the founding of the People's Republic. The Chinese Nationalist government in Taiwan withdrew from it.

62. "Memorandum for Kissinger from Kennedy/Lord," 13 November 1971, Director's file (Winston Lord), box 330, RG 59.

63. Kissinger, *White House Years*, 768–69.

64. Larry, *No Peace, No Honor*, 74.

65. Kissinger, *White House Years*, 768–69; Walters, *Silent Missions*, 529–30.

66. Kissinger, *White House Years*, 768.

67. Ibid., 768.

68. Hersh, *Price of Power*, 376.

69. Kissinger, *White House Years*, 747. Kissinger covered up in another way: he (and later Nixon) had no American interpreters present for any of their private talks with the Chinese leaders—a practice they also used in their talks with the Soviet Union.

70. "General Haig to General Walters," box 330, POL Chicom US, RG 59.

71. Cao, "Recalling the Secret 'Paris Channel,'" 51.

72. Wei, "Kissinger's Second Trip to China," 59.

73. Kissinger, *White House Years*, 775.

74. Ibid., 776.

75. "A Strong Weapon to Unite the People and Defeat the Enemy—Study 'On Policy,'" in *Renmin Ribao*, 16 August 1971.

76. The document, dated 21 July 1971, is apparently authentic. See Chao, "The Change in Peiping's Foreign Policy."

77. Wang Nianyi, *Da Dongluan de Niandai*, 415–33. There are two recent books on the Lin Biao incident, which shed new light on this mystery. Jin Qiu, who is the daughter of General Wu Faxian (former commander of the Chinese air force and one of the generals accused of plotting against Mao), challenges Beijing's official account of the Lin Biao Incident. Jin suggests that policy differences between Mao and Lin went back to the Great Leap Forward, and became a bit sharper with Lin's efforts to keep the PLA out of the Cultural Revolution. She points out that Lin Liguo, the son of Lin Biao, was not able to implement his unsophisticated plan to assassinate Mao and that Lin Biao himself was never prepared to challenge Mao's authority, let alone to kill him. Jin Qiu argues that Lin Biao's flight from Beijing on 13 September 1971 was "accidental" resulting from his fear of Mao's purge. See Jin, *Culture of Power*, esp. chapter 7 and conclusion. Frederick C. Teiwes and Warren Sun argue that "Lin Biao was tragically entrapped by his political system and political culture . . . a victim who could not escape Mao's increasingly unpredictable demands." See Teiwes and Sun, *Tragedy of Lin Biao*, 166–67.

78. Gao, *Wannian Zhou Enlai*, 427–28; Chen Jian, *Mao's China and the Cold War*, 270.

79. Gao, *Wannian Zhou Enlai*, 442.

80. Ibid., 441.

81. Holdridge, *Crossing the Divide*, 70–71.

82. Wei, "Kissinger's Second Trip to China," 62.

83. The announced interim visit was four days in Beijing. Kissinger said on 5 October 1971 that he would be in Beijing for four days. See "Ziegler announces forthcoming HAK interim trip to Peking," Tab 41. After he returned from China, journalists asked

Kissinger why he stayed two extra days in Beijing. Kissinger answered, "Why did we stay not two days longer, but one day longer than we had planned. The tentative plan was to leave the morning of the 25th, Peking time, but, of course, before we left we had no detailed knowledge of how long the discussions, specially the technical discussions, would take; you know, many nuts and bolts questions of telephone service and all this sort of paraphernalia which I did not even understand. So, there was a specific requirement of having these finished." Kissinger left Beijing at 10:30 A.M. on 26 October 1971. See "HAK gives background briefing on interim trip, says trip will be after Jan. 1, denies impact on Chirep vote," Tab 46, in folder 1, box 86, NSCF.

84. *ZEWHDJ*, 608–609. For Kissinger's report on the trip, as transmitted to the State Department, see "Alexander Haig to Theodore Eliot," 28 January 1972, Top Secret Subject-Numeric Files, 1970–73, POL 7, Kissinger, RG 59.

85. Kissinger, *White House Years*, 779.

86. Holdridge, *Crossing the Divide*, 68.

87. POLO II—Transcript of Meeting (October 22, 1971, 4:15–8:28 P.M.), p.40, folder 2, box 1034, NSCF.

88. Wei, "Kissinger's Second Trip to China," 68.

89. Ibid., 66–67; Kissinger, *White House Years*, 781.

90. POLO II—Transcript of Meeting (October 22, 1971, 4:15–8:28 P.M.), p.11, folder 2, box 1034, NSCF.

91. Wei, "Kissinger's Second Trip to China," 68–69.

92. Ibid., 67.

93. Chen Jian, *Mao's China and the Cold War*, 272.

94. Kissinger, *White House Years*, 782.

95. Ibid.

96. Tucker, *China Confidential*, 256. Wei, "Kissinger's Second Trip to China," 69.

97. Wei, "Kissinger's Second Trip to China," 69.

98. POLO II—Transcript of Meeting (October 25, 1971, 10:12–11:00 A.M.), pp.1–2, box 1034, NSCF.

99. POLO II—Transcript of Meeting (October 26, 1971, 5:30–8:10 A.M.), p. 2, box 1034, NSCF.

100. Ibid., p. 2.

101. Ibid., p. 9.

102. POLO II—Transcript of Meeting (October 26, 1971, 5:30–8:10 A.M.), p. 27. Also Tab B final agreed tentative draft, folder 4, box 1035, NSCF. The underlined portion is the Chinese formulation that the U.S. side had termed unacceptable. The italic part is also changed in the Shanghai Communiqué.

103. Ibid., 14.

104. Ibid., 15.

105. Ibid.

106. See, for example, editorial essay, "The Tide of History Cannot Be Stopped," *Renmin Ribao*, 28 October 1971.

107. Tucker, *China Confidential*, 264. There was much guessing among journalists on the effect of Kissinger's second trip to Beijing on the UN vote. For example, Seymour M. Hersh wrote, "Photographs of his sight-seeing in Peking made page one in New York and obviously affected the UN delegates, who voted on October 25 to seat China." He went further to say that China's satisfaction at its adroit handling of the Nixon administration was made clear in September 1971 by Huang Hua, who had aided Zhou Enlai in his negotiations with Kissinger. "The Americans say they are going to step down from some of their high responsibilities in Asia," Huang told the journalist

Wilfred Burchett. "We are happy to provide a small stool for them." See Hersh, *Price of Power*, 378.

108. See "HAK gives background briefing on interim trip, says trip will be after Jan. 1, denies impact on Chirep vote." Tab 46, p. 6, in folder 1, box 86, NSCF.

109. Ibid., p. 6. Tab 46, box 86, NSCF.

110. Green et al., *War and Peace with China*, 128.

111. When General Haig and his advance team first arrived in Shanghai, they were treated very coolly because Haig failed to return a toast at the welcome party, hosted by radical Shanghai leaders. Only with Zhou Enlai's direct intervention, with Mao's consent, did Shanghai leaders change their attitude toward the American in the last few hours of their stay in Shanghai. Interview with Zhang Hanzhi, interpreter for American advance team. See *Nixon's China Game* in http:www.pbs.org/wgbh/amex/china/filmmore/reference/interview/.

112. Tian and Wang, *Lao Waijiaoguan Huiyi Zhou Enlai*, 100–101, Wei, "The Course of Haig's Advance Team to China to Prepare for Nixon's Visit to China," 3: 76; Kissinger, *White House Years*, 1050.

113. Top Secret, Haig to Walters, 17 November 1971, POL Chicom US, box 330, RG 59.Wei, "The Course of Haig's Advance Team to China to Prepare for Nixon's Visit to China," 3: 76.

114. "Walters's report regarding his meeting with the Chinese," 18 November 1971, POL Chicom US, box 330, RG 59.

115. Wei, "The Course of Haig's Advance Team to China to Prepare for Nixon's Visit to China," 3: 72.

116. Ibid.

117. Haig trip-memcoms, 7 January 1972 (11:45 P.M.), p. 5, box 1037, NSCF.

118. Haig trip-memcoms, 3 January 1972 (Midnight), pp.1–8, box 1037, NSCF; Wei, "The Course of Haig's Advance Team to China to Prepare for Nixon's Visit to China," 3: 73; Kissinger, *White House Years*, 1051.

119. Kissinger's Memorandum for the President, "Briefing Papers for the China Trip (Taiwan)," p.11, folder 4, box 847, NSCF.

120. Haig trip-memcoms, 7 January 1972 (11:45 P.M.), p. 5, box 1037, NSCF.

121. Haig trip-memcoms, 3 January 1972 (Midnight), p. 3, box 1037, NSCF.

122. Wei, "The Course of Haig's Advance Team to China to Prepare for Nixon's Visit to China," 3: 78–79.

123. Ibid., 79.

124. Haig trip-memcoms, 7 January 1972 (11:45 P.M.), p. 4, box 1037, NSCF. Also Minutes, Zhou Enlai's conversations with Alexander Haig, 6 January 1971, quoted from ZEZ, 2: 1104–1105.

125. Haig trip-memcoms, 3 January 1972 (Midnight), p. 13, box 1037, NSCF. Wei, "The Course of Haig's Advance Team to China to Prepare for Nixon's Visit to China," 3: 71–82.

126. Ross, *Negotiating Cooperation*, 49. Ross's account was based on his interview with Haig.

127. Hersh, *Price of Power*, 442. Hersh's account was based on his interview with North Vietnamese deputy foreign minister Nguyen Co Thach in Hanoi in August 1979. Thach had been present with Pham Van Dong in Beijing in November 1971.

128. Wei, "The Course of Haig's Advance Team to China to Prepare for Nixon's Visit to China," 3: 75.

129. Vernon A. Walters, "39th Meeting with the Chinese in Paris on 6 February 1972," POL Chicom US, box 330, RG 59.

130. The failed effort to arrange for Le Duc Tho to meet with the American officials

on Chinese soil is mentioned briefly in the memoirs of Vernon Walters. "We had asked them whether there would be any possibility of President Nixon seeing Le Duc Tho, who would be in Peking around the time." Walters records, "They [Chinese officials] said it was none of their business, and they would not arrange the meeting." See Walters, *Silent Missions*, 546. This differs from his reports to the NSC (in which Walters claims that the U.S. wants the Chinese to help to arrange a meeting between Kissinger and Le Duc Tho). See Vernon A. Walters, "39th Meeting with the Chinese in Paris, 6 February 1972," and "41st Meeting with the Chinese in Paris, 11 February 1972," POL Chicom US, box 330, RG 59.

131. Walters, "41st Meeting with the Chinese in Paris, 11 February 1972," POL Chicom US, box 330, RG 59.

132. Nixon's handwritten notes, 15 February 1972, folder 1, box 7, WHSF, NPMP.

133. Ross, *Negotiating Cooperation*, 45.

134. Nixon, *U.S. Foreign Policy for the 1970s: The Emerging Structure of Peace*, 3: 26–37.

135. The Quadripartite Agreement on Berlin was signed on 3 September 1971, by the Soviet Union, the United States, Great Britain, and France. See Dobrynin, *In Confidence*, 233. For a discussion of the significance of this agreement to the Soviet leadership, see Gates, *From the Shadows*, 44.

136. Mr. and Mrs. Strober's interview with Winston Lord in Strober, *Nixon Presidency*, 130.

137. Years later, Vietnamese leaders accused the Chinese of "selling out" and "betraying" Vietnam in order to come to a rapprochement with the U.S. They alleged that the Chinese tried to prevent them from uniting the country and to force them to recognize the puppet regime in the South. See Memorandum of Conversation (Li Xiannian and Pham Van Dong, 10 September 1977). Cited in Shen Zhihua and Li, "Sino-U.S. Reconciliation and China's Vietnam Policy," 99. Some historians seem to echo this point. See Pollack, "The Opening to America," 469–74. From the declassified Memorandum of Kissinger and Zhou talks, we can see this accusation is groundless. It goes contrary to Chinese philosophical belief and "principled stand." In traditional Chinese culture, friendships among peoples and nations are valued. To sell out the interests of friends is despised. This author's interview with Chinese Party historians, January 2002.

138. In the wake of Kissinger's secret visit to Beijing, a North Vietnam party paper, *Nhan Dan* (People's Daily) carried an editorial titled "'The Nixon Doctrine' Is Bound to Failure." After reading the piece, on 20 July 1971, Zhou Enlai wrote to Zhang Chunqiao and Yao Wenyuan, two party officials in charge of propaganda, that "the editorial reveals the apprehension and estimation of the Vietnamese comrades. I think the whole text can be published. Do not only publish excerpts from it." In this way, Zhou continued, China could demonstrate its "attitude of being open and aboveboard. The progress of the events will prove that China under Chairman Mao's leadership has always supported the resistance war of the people of the three Indochinese countries to the end." Zhang Chunqiao, however, opposed the idea of publishing the Vietnamese commentary in China, so the *Nhan Dan* editorial was not made available to the Chinese public. Evidently Zhang was afraid of the negative impact the Vietnamese article might have on the Chinese. See ZEN49, 3: 469–70. Hersh, *Price of Power*, 375–76. Shen Zhihua and Li, "Sino-U.S. Reconciliation and China's Vietnam Policy," 103.

139. These assurances could be summarized as the following six points. First, the U.S. would not seek a "two Chinas" or a "one China, one Taiwan" policy; second, the U.S. would not support the Taiwan independence movement, which was growing in strength on the island; third, U.S. would not permit Japanese troops to move into Taiwan; fourth, the U.S. would not support any Nationalist military action against the

mainland; fifth, the U.S. would withdraw its troops from Taiwan as tension in the area eased; sixth, the normalization of U.S.-China relations would come in the first two years of Nixon's second term. See Memorandum of Conversation (Kissinger and Zhou Enlai), July 9, 1971, box 1032, NSCF.

140. Patrick Tyler makes this argument, "These private declarations were a nod to reality, but they also marked the repudiation of the long-standing American policy that the status of Taiwan was 'yet to be determined.'" See Tyler, *A Great Wall*, 99.

141. Kissinger, *White House Years*, 720.

142. "US Strategy in Current Sino-US Talks," 6 February 1970, box 2187, Pol Chicom US, RG 59.

143. "Briefing Book for the President (Taiwan)," July 1971, p. 6, box 1032, NSCF.

144. Memorandum of Conversation (Kissinger and Zhou Enlai), July 9, 1971, pp. 10–14, box 1032, NSCF.

145. Haldeman, *Haldeman Diaries*, 319.

146. These positions were also not Kissinger's impromptu invention. It is in the briefing book. Kissinger took the advice of his staff. See POLO I, "Briefing Book for the President" (Scope Paper), July 1971, p. 8, box 1032, NSCF.

147. Ibid.

8. Summit Talks

1. Nixon, *Memoirs of Richard Nixon*, 580.

2. *New York Times*, 20 February 1972.

3. Nixon, *Memoirs of Richard Nixon*, 559.

4. "Bipartisan Leadership Meeting," 17 February 1972, President's Handwriting Series, box 16, WHSF. The U.S. did not insist on any precondition, such as the nonuse of force toward Taiwan, for the summit. Neither did the PRC insist on immediate settlement of the Taiwan question.

5. Nixon, *Memoirs of Richard Nixon*, 557–58.

6. The question mark is Nixon's. He apparently wasn't sure exactly how much the United States wanted or could expect from China regarding Indochina.

7. Nixon's notes, 16 February 1972, folder 1, box 7, WHSF.

8. "The President Briefing Paper for the China Trip," Indochina-Vietnam, pp. 7–11, folder 4, box 847, NSCF.

9. Tucker, *China Confidential*, 268.

10. Kissinger's Memorandum for the President, "Your Encounter with the Chinese," 5 February 1972, p.1, folder 2, box 91, NSCF.

11. Ibid., p. 7.

12. Kissinger's Memorandum for the President, "Meeting with Mao Tse-Tung," 15 February 1972, p. 1, folder 2, box 847, NSCF.

13. See Editorial Note in *FRUS*, 1969–76, 1: 359.

14. Kissinger's Memorandum for the President, "Mao, Chou and the Chinese Litmus Test," 19 February 1972, p. 1, folder 2, box 847, NSCF.

15. Ibid.

16. Ibid., Nixon's notes, WHSF.

17. Kissinger's Memorandum for the President, "Meeting with Mao Tse-Tung," 15 February 1972, p. 17, folder 2, box 847, NSCF.

18. Ibid.

19. Nixon, *Memoirs of Richard Nixon*, 560.

20. Nixon's notes, 16 February 1972, folder 1, box 7, WHSF.

21. See Kissinger Memorandum for the President, "Your Encounter with the Chinese," 5 February 1972, p. 3, folder 4, box 91, and "Mao, Chou, and the Chinese Litmus Test," 19 February 1972, folder 2, box 847, HAK Office Files, NSCF. Underline is in the original text.

22. Mann, *About Face*, 14.

23. Nixon-Chou Talks (General/US-PRC Relations, 22 February 1972), p. 13, box 848, NSCF.

24. *ZEN49*, 3: 498.

25. *ZEN49*, 3: 511–12.

26. Nixon wanted his gesture to symbolize the beginning of a new relationship between the two countries, just as Dulles's insult to Zhou Enlai marked the era of animosity toward the People's Republic of China. The story that Dulles refused to shake Zhou Enlai's extended hand at the Geneva Conference in 1954 has been widely told. Nevertheless, Ambassador Wang Bingnan claimed in his memoirs that the handshaking incident never happened. See *ZHJH*, 21–22. Xu Jingli, deputy director of Foreign Ministry Archives, claims that he has checked all the newly declassified Chinese diplomatic files, and concludes that this is a purely fabricated story. See Xu Jingli, *Jiemi Zhongguo Waijiao Dang'an*, 276–79. But according to Chinese scholar Jia Qingguo's interview with Ambassador U. Alexis Johnson on 31 July 1986, Johnson said he personally witnessed the incident. See Ross and Jiang, *Re-examining the Cold War*, 427 n. 6. Johnson's memoirs also recorded that during a break in the first session, Dulles entered the lounge and Zhou, who was already there, walked across the room "with a broad smile and his usual air of urbane familiarity." Zhou extended his arm. Dulles, noting the "press photographers poised" for a story, quickly turned his back. See Johnson, *Right Hand of Power*, 204.

27. Gao, *Wannian Zhou Enlai*, 396–97.

28. Nixon, *Memoirs of Richard Nixon*, 559; Kissinger, *White House Years*, 1054–55; Wei, "President Nixon's Trip to China," 85.

29. Nixon, *The Memoirs of Richard Nixon*, 560; Wei, "President Nixon's Trip to China," 85. What Zhou wanted to stress was that there were no formal diplomatic relations and no direct high-level contact between the two sides since late 1946 after General Marshall's failure to mediate the Chinese civil war.

30. Kissinger, *White House Years*, 1054; Holdridge, *Crossing the Divide*, 82.

31. Wei, "President Nixon's Trip to China," 83–85.

32. Tucker, *China Confidential*, 270.

33. Nixon, *Memoirs of Richard Nixon*, 560.

34. *MZZ49*, 2: 1635–36; "Memorandum of Conversation: Mao and Nixon, 21 February 1972," p. 1, box 91, NSCF. Kissinger and Winston Lord were present during Mao-Nixon meeting. Nixon did not ask his secretary of state, William Rogers, to come with him. Lord was there as note-taker.

35. Wei, "President Nixon's Trip to China," 86.

36. Xiong, *Wo de Qingbao yu Waijiao Shengya*, 254.

37. Chen Jian, *Mao's China and the Cold War*, 273.

38. Xiong, *Wo de Qingbao yu Waijiao Shengya*, 254.

39. Chen Jian, *Mao's China and the Cold War*, 273.

40. Transcript of Mao Zedong's Conversation with Nixon, 21 February 1972, cited *MZZ49*, 2: 1638. For an English version of the conversation, see "Memorandum of Conversation: Mao and Nixon, 21 February 1972," p. 10, box 91, NSCF.

41. For Mao's health during this period and its implications for the Nixon visit, see Li Zhisui, *Private Life of Chairman Mao*, 553–65. Kissinger mistakenly believed that

Mao had suffered a series of strokes before the meetings. See Kissinger, *White House Years*, 1061.

42. He, "Mao's Most Respected Enemy," 143.

43. "Memorandum of Conversation: Mao and Nixon, 21 February 1972" p. 8, box 91, NSCF. Also see Burr, *Kissinger Transcripts*, 64.

44. Nixon, *Memoirs of Richard Nixon*, 563.

45. Burr, *Kissinger Transcripts*, 59.

46. "Memorandum of Conversation: Mao and Nixon, 21 February 1972," p. 10, box 91, NSCF; Burr, *Kissinger Transcript*, 65.

47. Kissinger's Memorandum for the President, "Your Encounter with the Chinese," 5 February 1972, p. 2, folder 2, box 91, NSCF.

48. "Premier Chou En-lai's Toast at the Banquet in Honor of President Nixon," folder 10, box 72, President's Personal Files, WHSF. Also see Kissinger, *White House Years*, 1069.

49. "President Nixon's Toast, Peking, China, 21 February 1972," folder 10, box 72, President's Personal Files, WHSF. Nixon, *Memoirs of Richard Nixon*, 564.

50. Wei, "President Nixon's Trip to China," 89–90; Holdridge, *Crossing the Divide*, 87–88.

51. Wei, "President Nixon's Trip to China," 91; Holdridge, *Crossing the Divide*, 88. With Zhou Enlai's collaboration, Kissinger skillfully kept Secretary of State Rogers out of communiqué drafting.

52. Wei, "President Nixon's Trip to China," 91.

53. Ibid., 94.

54. Tucker, *China Confidential*, 273.

55. Wei, "President Nixon's Trip to China," 89–90.

56. Nixon-Chou Talks (Soviet Union, 22 February 1972), 2–3, folder 6, box 848, NSCF.

57. Nixon-Chou Talks (General/US-PRC Relations, 22 February 1972), p.13, box 848, NSCF.

58. The last portion was declassified in December 2003.

59. Nixon's notes, 23 February 1972, folder 1, box 7, President's Personal Files, WHSF.

60. Nixon-Chou Talks (Indochina, 22 February 1972), p. 27, folder 6, box 848, NSCF.

61. Nixon's notes, "First Private Meeting," WHSF.

62. Memorandum for the President, "Subject: Policy toward Taiwan," 2 February 1972, folder 2, box 88, NSCF.

63. "The President Briefing Paper for the China Trip," Taiwan, p. 4, folder 4, box 847, NSCF.

64. Nixon's notes, 22 February 1972, folder 1, box 7, WHSF. Also Wei, "President Nixon's Trip to China," 89–90.

65. Nixon-Chou Talks (Taiwan, 22 February 1972), p. 5, folder 6, box 848, NSCF.

66. Ibid., p. 6.

67. ZRGW70, 364.

68. Nixon-Chou Talks (Taiwan, 24 February 1972), box 848, NSCF.

69. Ibid., p. 9.

70. Ibid., p. 6. Also ZRGW70, 364.

71. ZRGW70, 364.

72. Nixon-Chou Talks (Taiwan, 24 February 1972), pp. 9–10, box 848, NSCF.

73. Ibid., p. 6.

74. Ibid., p. 10.

75. Ibid., pp.10–11.

76. Ibid., p. 7.

77. Nixon's notes, 22 February 1972, folder 1, box 7, WHSF. Also Wei, "President Nixon's Trip to China," 89–90.

78. ZRGW70, 364.

79. Ibid. Also Nixon-Chou Talks (Indochina, 28 February 1972), pp. 8–9, folder 6, box 848, NSCF.

80. Wei, "Inside Stories of Kissinger's Secret Visit to China," p. 41. "The President Briefing Paper for the China Trip," Indochina-Vietnam, p. 1, folder 4, box 847, NSCF.

81. Nixon-Chou Talks (Indochina, 22 February 1972), p. 25, NSCF.

82. Mann, *About Face*, 45. Also see Nixon notes, 22 February 1972, WHSF. Nixon-Chou Talks (Indochina, 22 February 1972), p. 21, folder 6, box 848, NSCF; Kissinger, *White House Years*, 568.

83. Nixon notes, 22 February 1972, WHSF; Nixon-Chou Talks (Indochina, 22 February 1972), p. 20, box 848, NSCF.

84. Nixon-Chou Talks (Indochina, 22 February 1972), p. 22, box 848, NSCF.

85. Ibid., p. 25.

86. Mann, *About Face*, 45.

87. Nixon's notes, 22 February 1972, box 72, Presidential Personal Files, WHSF.

88. Ibid. Also Nixon-Chou Talks (Indochina, 22 February 1972), p. 22, folder 6, box 848, NSCF.

89. Nixon-Chou Talks (Indochina, 24 February 1972), p. 16, and Nixon-Chou Talks (Indochina, 28 February 1972), pp. 8, 10, box 848, NSCF.

90. Nixon-Chou Talks (Indochina, 24 February 1972), pp.17, 19, box 848, NSCF.

91. Kissinger, *White House Years*, 1087.

92. Nixon-Chou Talks (Soviet Union, 22 February 1972), p.10, box 848, NSCF.

93. Qiao (Guanhua)-Kissinger Talks (23 February 1972, 9:35 a.m.–12:34 P.M.), box 92, HAK Office Files, NSCF.

94. "Nixon's notes, 22 February 1972," folder 1, box 7, President's Personal Files, WHSF. On the previous day, Nixon and Zhou Enlai had held one "plenary" session, which Rogers and other State Department officials were permitted to attend. The private sessions included Kissinger, but not the State Department officials.

95. "The President Briefing Paper for the China Trip," the Soviet Union, pp. 5, 7, folder 4, box 847, NSCF.

96. Nixon-Chou Talks (Soviet Union, 23 February 1972), pp. 21, 36–39, folder 6, box 848, NSCF.

97. Ibid., pp. 3, 20.

98. Nixon's notes, 22 February 1972, folder 1, box 7, President's Personal Files, WHSF.

99. "The President Briefing Paper for the China Trip," South Asia, p. 7, folder 4, box 847, NSCF.

100. Nixon-Chou Talks (South Asia, 23 February 1972), pp.9–11, folder 6, box 848, NSCF. Nixon told Zhou he had a problem with regard to military assistance as the U.S. Congress and the public opposed military assistance to Pakistan.

101. "The President Briefing Paper for the China Trip," Japan, p. 3, folder 4, box 847, NSCF.

102. Nixon's notes, 16 February 1972, folder 1, box 7, President's Personal Files, WHSF.

103. Nixon's notes, 15 February 1972; Nixon-Chou Talks (23 February 1972, 2:00–6:00 P.M.), box 87, President's Office Files, WHSF.

104. Nixon's notes, 15 February 1972, WHSF.

105. Nixon's notes, 16 February 1972, WHSF.

106. Nixon's notes, 22 February 1972, "First Private Meeting," folder 1, box 7, President's Office Files, WHSF.

107. Nixon-Chou Talks (23 February 1972, 2:00–6:00 P.M.), box 87, President's Office Files, WHSF.

108. Nixon-Chou Talks (24 February 1972, 5:15–8:05 P.M.), box 87, WHSF.

109. Qiao (Guanhua)-Kissinger Talks (24 February 1972, 9:59 A.M.–12:42 P.M.), p. 13, in "Dr. Kissinger's Meetings in the PRC during the Presidential Visit, 1972," box 92, NSCF. Also see Burr, *Kissinger Transcripts*, 66.

110. Li Lianqing, *Waijiao Yingcai Qiao Guanhua*, 192.

111. Gong, *Kuayue Honggou*, 103.

112. Qiao-Kissinger Talks (24 February 1972, 9:59 A.M.–12:42 P.M.), p. 21, box 92, NSCF. Also Solomon, *Chinese Negotiating Behavior*, 145; Wei, "President Nixon's Trip to China," 95.

113. Qiao-Kissinger Talks (24 February 1972, 9:59–12:42 P.M.), p. 17, box 92, NSCF.

114. Ibid., pp. 17–18.

115. Qiao-Kissinger Talks (24 February 1972, 3:30–3:45 P.M.), p. 2. Also see Li Lianqing, *Waijiao Yingcai Qiao Guanhua*, 192.

116. Qiao-Kissinger Talks (25 February 1972, 2:35–2:45 P.M.), p. 1, box 92, NSCF. Kissinger, *White House Years*, 1077–78; Li Jian, *Diaoyutai Guoshi Fengyun*, 745–46.

117. Qiao-Kissinger Talks (25 February 1972, 12:50–1:15 A.M.), box 92, NSCF. "Taiwan is a province of China" is used in the Chinese version. There is a certain level of ambiguity in the U.S. posture toward Taiwan.

118. "Progress made in the Communiqué during the President's visit," folder 2, box 88, NSCF. Also Qiao-Kissinger Talks (25 February 1972, 12:50–1:15 A.M.), p. 3, box 92, NSCF; and Wei, "President Nixon's Trip to China," 94–95.

119. "Progress made in the Communiqué during the President's visit," folder 2, box 88, NSCF.

120. Nixon, *Memoirs of Richard Nixon*, 571.

121. Kissinger, *Years of Upheaval*, 47.

122. In his speech at the National Press Club in January 1950, when talking about the U.S. defense perimeter in Asia, Secretary of State Dean Acheson excluded Korea and Taiwan. Critics later charged this was a major cause for North Korea's attack of South Korea.

123. Green, *War and Peace with China*, 145–46. Tucker, *China Confidential*, 275.

124. Ross, *Negotiating Cooperation*, 48.

125. Hong Wen, *Hezuo Huanshi Duikang*, 3: 955. Qiao-Kissinger Talks (26 February 1972, 10:20–1:40 A.M.), p. 9, box 92, NSCF.

126. Hong Wen, *Hezuo Huanshi Duikang*, 3: 955–57; Kissinger, *White House Years*, 1083–84.

127. Qiao-Kissinger Talks (26–27 February 1972, 10:20–1:40 A.M.), p. 4, box 92, NSCF.

128. Hong Wen, *Hezuo Huanshi Duikang*, 3: 953; Kissinger, *White House Years*, 1083. John Holdridge and Winston Lord also mentioned this point, but recorded it as follows: "in the section dealing with Taiwan, spoke of all 'people' on either side of the Taiwan Strait regarding Taiwan as part of China. State objected to the word 'people,' maintaining that the inhabitants of Taiwan who looked upon the island as their home regardless of the point of origin in China of their ancestors, and who regarded themselves as 'Taiwanese,' would not necessarily agree that Taiwan was part of China. Satisfactory substitute wording was found by changing the word 'people' to 'Chinese.'" See Green, *War and Peace with China*, 145–46. Holdridge, *Crossing the Divide*, 93; Tucker, *China*

Confidential, 275. The final text read: "The United States acknowledged that *all Chinese* on either side of the Taiwan Strait maintain there is but one China and that Taiwan is part of China. The United States Government does not challenge that position."

129. Holdridge, *Crossing the Divide*, 95; Kissinger, *White House Years*, 1084.

130. Garthoff, *Détente and Confrontation*, 272.

131. Harding, *A Fragile Relationship*, Appendix B, The Shanghai Communiqué, 376.

132. "The President Briefing Paper for the China Trip," the Soviet Union, pp. 5–7, folder 4, box 847, NSCF.

133. Nixon, *Memoirs of Richard Nixon*, 568.

134. Shen Zhihua, "Sino-American Rapprochement and China's Vietnam Policy," 239.

135. Nixon-Chou Talks (Indochina, 28 February 1972), p. 9, folder 6, box 848, NSCF.

136. Nixon, *Memoirs of Richard Nixon*, 565.

137. Hanhimaki, *Flawed Architect*, 200.

138. "Introductory Remarks (Re China)," 17 February 1972, President's Handwriting Series, box 16, President's Office Files, WHSF.

139. "CCP Central Committee: 'Notice on the Joint Sino-American Communiqué, March 7, 1972," cited in Gong, *Kuayue Honggou*, 182.

140. Kissinger's Memorandum for the President, "Your Encounter with the Chinese," 5 February 1972, p. 6, folder 2, box 91, NSCF.

141. Qiao-Kissinger Talks, (27 February 1972, 11:30 A.M.–1:55 P.M.), p. 4, box 92, NSCF.

142. Even Charles Freeman, who was Nixon's interpreter during the China trip and annoyed at Nixon for excluding him as interpreter from the summit talks, admitted that Rogers was not a highly intellectual man. He recalled that Rogers tried to explain the game of golf to Ji Pengfei. As Ji knew nothing about golf or Rogers's great golf hero Sam Snead, "I could see this was disastrous, but had to go along with it." It was "the most ridiculous moment of my life as an interpreter," recalled Freeman years later. See Tucker, *China Confidential*, 270.

9. Conclusion

1. Hunt, *Genesis of Chinese Communist Foreign Policy*, 215.

2. Zhongyang Tongzhangbu he Zhongyang Dang'anguan, comp., *Zhonggong Zhongyang Jiefang Zhanzheng Shiqi Tongyi Zhanxian Wenjian Xuanbian*, 161; ZZWX, 14: 430.

3. Mao Zedong, "We should gradually and completely destroy imperialist control power in China," 5 March 1949, in *MZWW*, 79.

4. Mao Zedong, "The Chinese people are willing to cooperate with people all over the world," 15 June 1949, *MZWW*, 91.

5. Hunt, *Genesis of Chinese Communist Foreign Policy*, 215.

6. "United States Policy toward the PRC, 1949–1969," p. 98, box 8, RG 59.

7. NSC-48/5, "United States Objectives, Policies and Courses of Action in Asia," *FRUS, 1951*, 6: 35, 37.

8. Thomson, "On the Making of U.S. China Policy," 230.

9. Thomson, "Dragon under Glass: Time for a New China Policy."

10. Snyder, Bruck, and Sapin, "The Decision-making Approach to the Study of International Politics," 203.

11. Robinson, "Chinese Foreign Policy from the 1940s to the 1990s," 562.

12. Lu Ning, *Dynamics of Foreign-policy Decision-making in China*, 161–62.

13. Scholars have more solid proof that Lin Biao differed with Mao on sending Chinese troops to Korea in 1950 and refused to lead the Chinese People's Volunteers. Lei Yingfu, a military aide to Mao and Zhou during the Korean War, recalled in his memoir that Lin Biao figured very prominently in arguing against China's involvement in the Korean War at a conference of senior leaders on 6 October 1950. Lin said "Fight, fight. We have been fighting over several decades in the past. . . . People now want peace. It is utterly against the people's will to engage in more fighting. [Our] nation has just liberated, the domestic economy is a great mess, the army's equipment is still to be updated. . . . How can we afford more warfare? Besides, we could be pretty confident fighting the Guomindang, yet to fight the modern American [army] equipped with atom bombs [is quite another matter]. Are we [really] capable? In my view the Party Center should consider the matter carefully and adopt a safe approach." See Lei, *Tongshuaibu Canmou de Zhuihuai*, 169–70.

14. Cited from Hamrin, "Elite Politics and the Development of China's Foreign Relations," 83.

15. After the Korean War, Dulles convinced Eisenhower that the best strategy to facilitate the inevitable split between China and the Soviet Union was "to keep pressure on Communist China and make its way difficult so long as it is in partnership with Soviet Russia." See Gaddis, *United States and the End of the Cold War*, 74–75.

16. Thomson, "On the Making of U.S. China Policy," 233–37.

17. Bundy, *Tangled Web*, 104.

18. Six Americans remained in China at the closing of the Warsaw talks in February 1970: Bishop James Walsh, Hugh Redmond, John Downey, Richard Fecteau, Robert Flynn, and Philip Smith. Hugh Redmond died in China in April 1970. The Chinese released Bishop James Walsh in July 1970. Richard Fecteau was released in 1971. The remaining three were released in March 1973.

19. Hamrin, "Elite Politics and the Development of China's Foreign Relations," 73.

20. Hunt, *Genesis of Chinese Communist Foreign Policy*, 28.

21. Mao Zedong, "From now on, the Chinese people stand up," MZW, 5: 343–44.

22. Zhang Baijia, "Zhou Enlai—The Shaper and Founder of China's Diplomacy," 80.

23. ZEWW, 61–62.

24. Ikle, *How Nations Negotiate*, 145.

25. Ibid., 123; Blaker, *Japanese International Negotiating Style*, 102.

26. Johnson to Secretary of State, 12 August 1955, FRUS, 1955–57, 3: *Supplement*.

27. Kissinger, *White House Years*, 1054.

28. Ikle, *How Nations Negotiate*, 145.

29. Thomson, "On the Making of U.S. China Policy," 243.

30. Ikle, *How Nations Negotiate*, 160.

31. Kissinger, *White House Years*, 745.

32. Ibid., 746.

33. Ibid., 747.

34. "Background Briefing, July 16, 1971," folder 1, box 86, NSCF.

35. Nixon, *Memoirs of Richard Nixon*, 571–72.

36. Ibid., 577.

37. Iriye, "Culture and International History," 215.

38. Lewicki, Saunders, and Minton, *Essentials of Negotiation*, 183.

39. Fairbank, *China Perceived*, 96.

40. Zhang Shu Guang, *Economic Cold War*, 270.

41. Levine, "Perception and Ideology in Chinese Foreign Policy," 30.

42. Zhang Shu Guang, *Economic Cold War*, 273–74.

43. Iriye, "Introduction: The Korean War in the Domestic Context," 1–3.

44. Starkey, Boyer, and Wilkenfeld, *Negotiating a Complex World*, 65.

45. Kinhide, "The Cultural Premises of Japanese Diplomacy," 45–46.

46. Zartman and Berman, *Practical Negotiator*, 144.

47. Raymond Cohen, *Negotiating across Cultures*, 219.

48. Johnson, *Right Hand of Power*, 262.

49. Young, *Negotiating with the Chinese Communists*, 371.

50. Kissinger, *White House Years*, 1056.

51. E.g., Solomon, *Chinese Negotiating Behavior*, 71; Young, *Negotiating with the Chinese Communists*; Wilhelm, *Chinese at the Negotiating Table*.

52. In June 1972, China gave two giant pandas to the United States after Nixon's trip to China. These two pandas—Ling-Ling (a female) and Xing-Xing [Hsing-Hsing] (a male)—were kept at the National Zoological Park in Washington, D.C. Ling-Ling died in 1992, and Xing-Xing died in 1999.

53. Fairbank, *China Perceived*, 110.

BIBLIOGRAPHY

Chinese-language Sources

Archives
PRC *Waijiao Dang'an* [Diplomatic Files, Foreign Ministry Archives, the People's Republic of China]. Beijing.

Newspapers, Magazines, and Journals
Bainianchao [Hundred-year Tide]. Beijing.
Dangdai Zhongguoshi Yanjiu [Contemporary China History Studies]. Beijing.
Dangde Wenxian [Party Historical Documents]. Beijing.
Dangshi Bolan [Well-read in Party History]. Beijing.
Dangshi Yanjiu Ziliao [Materials on Party History Research]. Beijing.
Dongbei Ribao [Northeast Daily]. Shenyang.
Lishi Yanjiu [Historical Studies]. Beijing.
Meiguo Yanjiu [American Studies]. Beijing.
Renmin Ribao [People's Daily]. Beijing.
Renwu [Biographical Studies]. Beijing.
Waijiao Xueyuan Xuebao [Journal of Foreign Affairs College]. Beijing.
Xinhua Yuebao [New China Monthly]. Beijing.
Zhonggong Dangshi Yanjiu [Studies of CCP History]. Beijing.
Zhonggong Dangshi Ziliao [Materials on CCP History]. Beijing.

Books, Articles, and Other Documents
Bo Yibo. *Ruogan Zhongda Juece yu Shijian de Huiyi* [Reflections on Some Major Policy-making Decisions and Events]. 2 vols. Beijing: Zhongyang Dangxiao Chubanshe, 1991.
Cao Guisheng. "Recalling the Secret 'Paris Channel' between China and the United States." In *Xin Zhongguo Waijiao Fengyun*, ed. Pei Jianzhang, 2: 46–56.
Chai Chengwen. "The Decision-making Path Taken by Mao Zedong and Zhou Enlai in Leading the Armistice Negotiations during the Korean War." *Dangdai Zhongguoshi Yanjiu*, no. 6 (2000): 10–21.
———. "Material on the Formation and Evolution of the Leading Group for the Korean War Armistice Negotiations." *Dangdai Zhongguoshi Yanjiu*, no. 6 (2000): 22–24.
Chai Chengwen and Zhao Yongtian. *Banmendian Tanpan* [The Panmunjom Negotiations]. Beijing: Jiefangjun Chubanshe, 1989.

——. *Kangmei Yuanchao Jishi* [A Factual Record of the War to Resist America and Assist Korea]. Beijing: Jiefangjun Chubanshe, 1987.

Chen Dunde. *Mao Zedong-Nikesen Zai 1972* [Mao Zedong and Nixon in 1972]. Beijing: Kunlun Chubanshe, 1988.

Chen Guangxiang. "Why Didn't the PLA Liberate Shanghai Immediately after Crossing the Yangzi?" *Dangshi Yanjiu Ziliao*, no. 178 (May 1992).

Cheng Yunxing. *Fengyun Teshi—Lao Waijiaojia Wang Bingnan* [Special Envoy of the Time: Senior Diplomat Wang Bingnan]. Beijing: Zhongguo Wennian Chubanshe, 2001.

Chinese Academy of Military Sciences, ed. *Zhongguo Renmin Zhiyuanjun Kangmei Yuanchao Zhan Shi* [The War History of the Chinese People's Volunteers in the War to Resist U.S. Aggression and Assist Korea]. Beijing: Junshi Kexue Chubanshe, 1988.

Chiu Hongdah and Ren Xiaoqi, eds. *Zhonggong Tanpan Celue Yanjiu* [Research on CCP Negotiation Strategy]. Taibei: Lianhe Baoshe, 1987.

Dai Chaowu. "The Development of China's Nuclear Weapon and the Rupture of Sino-Soviet Relations (1954–1962)." *Dangdai Zhongguoshi Yanjiu*, no. 3 (2001): 76–85.

Dangdai Zhongguo [China Today] Series. *Kangmei Yuanchao Zhanzheng* [The War to Resist U.S. Aggression and Aid Korea]. Beijing: Zhongguo Shehui Kexue Chubanshe, 1990.

Du Ping. *Zai Zhiyuanjun Zongbu* [At CPV Headquarters: Memoirs of Du Ping]. Beijing: Jiefangjun Chubanshe, 1989.

Editorial Division of Shijie Zhishi, ed. *Taiwan Wenti Wenjian Huibian* [A Collection of Materials Concerning the Taiwan Issue]. Beijing: Shijie Zhishi Chubanshe, 1957.

——. *Zhongmei Guanxi Ziliao Huibian* [Documentary Collection on Sino-American Relations]. Vol. 1 (part 1). Beijing: Shijie Zhishi Chubanshe, 1957.

——. *Zhongmei Guanxi Ziliao Huibian* [Documentary Collection on Sino-American Relations]. Vol. 2 (part 2). Beijing: Shijie Zhishi Chubanshe, 1961.

——. *Zhonghua Renmin Gongheguo Duiwai Guanxi Wenjianji: 1949–1950* [A Collection of Documents of Foreign Relations of the PRC]. Vol. 1. Beijing: Shijie Zhishi Chubanshe, 1957.

——. *Zhonghua Renmin Gongheguo Duiwai Guanxi Wenjianji: 1951–1953* [A Collection of Documents of Foreign Relations of the PRC]. Vol. 2. Beijing: Shijie Zhishi Chubanshe, 1958.

Gao Wenqian. *Wannian Zhou Enlai* [Zhou Enlai's Later Years]. Hong Kong: Mirror Books, 2003.

Gong Li. "Chinese Decision-Making and the Thawing of U.S.-China Relations." In *Cong Duizhi Zouxiang Huanhe*, ed. Jiang and Ross, 670–718.

——. *Kuayue Honggou: 1969–1979 nian Zhongmei Guanxi de Yanbian* [Across the Chasm: The Evolution of China–U.S. Relations, 1969–1979]. Zhengzhou: Henan Renmin Chubanshe, 1992.

Guoji Zhanlue Xuehui [Foundation for International Strategic Studies], comp. *Huanqiu Tongci Liangre—Yidai Lingxiumen de Guoji Zhanlue Sixiang* [It Is the Same Temperature around the Globe: The International Strategic Thoughts of a Generation of Chinese Leaders]. Beijing: Zhongyang Wenxian Chubanshe, 1993.

Han Huaizhi and Tan Jingqiao, chief eds. *Dangdai Zhongguo Jundui de Junshi Gongzuo* [The Military Affairs of the Contemporary Chinese Army]. 2 vols. Beijing: Zhongguo Shehui Kexue Chubanshe, 1989.

Han Xu et al. "The Envoy Who Paved the Way for Sino-American Normalization." In

Jiangjun, Waijiaojia, Yishujia: Huang Zhen Jinian Wenji [General, Diplomat, Artist: Collected Works in Memory of Huang Zhen], ed. Yao Zhongming, Xia Wushen, and Pei Jianzhang. Beijing: Jiefangjun Chubanshe, 1992.

Hao Yufan. "Observing the Policy-making Process of American Government from Its Decision on Using Force against the Chinese Nuclear Facilities." *Zhonggong Dangshi Yanjiu*, no. 3 (2001): 40–45.

He Di. "The Development of the CCP's Policy toward the United States, 1945–49." *Lishi Yanjiu* (June 1987): 15–33.

Hong Wen, ed. *Hezuo Huanshi Duikang—Jiedu Zhongmei Fenghui* [Cooperation or Confrontation: Decoding Sino-American Summit]. Beijing: Jincheng Chubanshe, 1998.

Hong Xuezhi. *Kangmei Yuanchao Zhanzheng Huiyi* [Recollections of the War to Resist U.S. Aggression and Assist Korea]. Beijing: Jiefangjun Wenyi Chubanshe, 1990.

Hu Qiaomu. *Hu Qiaomu Huiyi Mao Zedong* [Hu Qiaomu's Recollections of Mao Zedong]. Beijing: Renmin Chubanshe, 1994.

Huang Hua. "My Contacts with John Leighton Stuart in the Early Days after the Liberation of Nanjing." In *Xinzhongguo Waijiao Fengyun*, ed. Pei Jianzhang, 1: 22–31.

Ji Chaozhu. *Cong "Yang Wawa" dao Waijiaoguan: Ji Chaozhu Koushushi* [From "Doll" to Diplomat: Ji Chaozhu's Oral History]. Beijing: Beijing Daxue Chubanshe, 2000.

Jia Qingguo. *Wei Shixian de Hejie: Zhongmei Guanxi de Gehe yu Weiji* [The Unrealized Rapprochement: Estrangements and Crises in Sino-American Relations]. Beijing: Wenhua Yishu Chubanshe, 1998.

Jiang Changbin and Robert Ross, chief eds. *Cong Duizhi Zouxiang Huanhe—Lengzhan Shiqi de Zhongmei Guanxi Zai Tantao* [From Confrontation to Détente: Re-examining Sino-American Relations during the Cold War]. Beijing: Shijie Zhishi Chubanshe, 2000.

Jiang Ying. "Conflict and Restraint: Sino-American Relations during the Vietnam War." In *Cong Duizhi Zouxiang Huanhe*, ed. Jiang and Ross, 257–96.

Jin Chongji, chief ed. *Liu Shaoqi Zhuan* [A Biography of Liu Shaoqi]. Beijing: Zhongyang Wenxian Chubanshe, 1998.

——*Zhou Enlai Zhuan, 1949–1976* [A Biography of Zhou Enlai, 1949–1976]. 2 vols. Beijing: Zhongyang Wenxian Chubanshe, 1998.

Jin Chongji et al. *Zhou Enlai Nianpu, 1898–1949* [The Chronicle of Zhou Enlai, 1898–1949]. Beijing: Zhongyang Wenxian and Renmin Chubanshe, 1989.

——. *Zhou Enlai Zhuan, 1898–1949* [A Biography of Zhou Enlai, 1898–1949]. 2 vols. Beijing: Zhongyang Wenxian Chubanshe, 1998.

Jin Ge. "The Beginning and End of 'Seizing Power' in the Foreign Ministry." In *Zhou Enlai De Zuihou Suiyue, 1966–1976* [Zhou Enlai's Last Years, 1966–1976], ed. An Jianshe. Beijing: Zhongyang Wenxian Chubanshe, 1995, 207–43.

Kang Jie. *Waijiao Douzhi Renwu* [Wise Diplomatic Personages]. Xi'an: Taibai Wenyi Chubanshe, 1995.

Lei Yingfu et al. *Tongshuaibu Canmou de Zhuihuai* [Recollections of the Headquarters Staff]. Jiangsu: Jiangsu Wenyi Chubanshe, 1994.

Li Changjiu and Shi Lujia, eds. *Zhongmei Guanxi Erbainian* [Two Hundred Years of Sino-American Relations]. Beijing: Xinhua Chubanshe, 1984.

Li Danhui. "38th Parallel and 17th Parallel: A Comparative Study of the Information Exchanges between China and the United States during the Korean and Vietnam Wars." *Zhonggong Dangshi Yanjiu*, no. 3 (2001): 32–39.

———, ed. *Zhongguo yu Yinduzhina Zhanzheng* [China and the Indochina War]. Hong Kong: Cosmos Books LTD, 2000.

Li Jian, ed. *Diaoyutai Guoshi Fengyun* [Winds and Clouds of State Affairs at *Diaoyutai*]. Xi'an: Taibai Wenyi Chubanshe, 1995.

Li Jie. "Changes in China's Domestic Situation in the 1960s and Sino-U.S. Relations." In *Cong Duizhi Zouxiang Huanhe*, ed. Jiang Changbin and Ross, 491–537.

Li Ke and Hao Shengzhang. *Wenhua Dageming Zhong de Renmin Jiefangjun* [The People's Liberation Army during the Cultural Revolution]. Beijing: Zhonggong Dangshi Ziliao Chubanshe, 1989.

Li Lianqing. *Da Waijiaojia Zhou Enlai* [Great Diplomat Zhou Enlai]. 5 vols. Hong Kong: Cosmos Books LTD, 1994–2001.

———. *Waijiao Yingcai Qiao Guanhua* [Qiao Guanhua: Diplomatic Genius]. Nanjing: Jiangsu Renmin Chubanshe, 2000.

Li Ping et al. *Zhou Enlai Nianpu, 1949–1976* [The Chronicle of Zhou Enlai, 1949–1976]. 3 vols. Beijing: Zhongyang Wenxian and Renmin Chubanshe, 1997.

Li Rui. "Random Notes on the Takeover of Shenyang." *Zhonggong Dangshi Ziliao*, 40 (February 1992).

Liao Xinwen, "Historical Review of Mao Zedong's Decision to Bombard Jinmen in 1958." *Dangde Wenxian*, no. 1 (1994): 31–36.

Lin Ke, Xu Tao, and Wu Xujun. *Lishi de Zhenshi—Mao Zedong Shenbian Gongzuo Renyuan de Zhengyan* [The True Life of Mao Zedong: Eyewitness Accounts by Mao's Staff]. Hong Kong: Liwen Chubanshe, 1995.

Liu Jianfei. *Diren, Pengyou Huanshi Huoban—Zhongmeiri Zhanlue Guanxi Yanbian (1899–1999)* [Enemies, Friends or Partners: Evolution of Chinese-American-Japanese Strategic Relations, 1899–1999]. Beijing: Zhongyang Wenxian Chubanshe, 2000.

Lu Jianhong. *Zonghong Baihe Yufengyun—Zhou Enlai de Tanpan Yishu* [Maneuvering Diplomatic Winds and Clouds: Zhou Enlai's Negotiating Style]. Beijing: Zhongyang Wenxian Chubanshe, 1997.

Lu Zhikong. *Waijiao Jubo* [Diplomatic Authority]. Zhengzhou: Henan Renmin Chubanshe, 1989.

Luo Yisu. "The Beginning of the Thawing of Sino-American Relations in 1970s—Recollection of the Last Two Sino-American Ambassadorial Talks." *Waijiao Xueyuan Xuebao* [Journal of Foreign Affairs College], no. 4 (2000): 23–26.

———. "My Years in Poland." In *Dangdai Zhongguo Shijie Waijiao Shengya*, ed. Wang Taiping, 4: 165–84.

Mao Zedong. *Jianguo Yilai Mao Zedong Wengao* [Mao Zedong's Manuscripts since the Founding of the PRC]. 15 vols. Beijing: Zhongyang Wenxian Chubanshe, 1987–99.

———. *Mao Zedong Junshi Wenji* [A Collection of Mao Zedong's Military Papers]. 6 vols. Beijing: Junshi Kexue Chubanshe, 1993.

———. *Mao Zedong Junshi Wenxuan—Neibuban* [Selected Military Works of Mao Zedong: Internal Edition]. Beijing: Zhanshi Chubanshe, 1981.

———. *Mao Zedong Shuxin Xuanji* [Selected Correspondence of Mao Zedong]. Beijing: Renmin Chubanshe, 1983.

———. *Mao Zedong Waijiao Wenxuan* [Selected Diplomatic Papers of Mao Zedong]. Beijing: Shijie Zhishi Chubanshe, 1994.

———. *Mao Zedong Wenji* [A Collection of Mao Zedong's Papers]. 8 vols. Beijing: Renmin Chubanshe, 1993–2000.

———. *Mao Zedong Xuanji* [Selected Works of Mao Zedong]. 5 vols. Beijing: Renmin Chubanshe, 1965 and 1977.

Mao Zedong Yijiusanliunian Tong Sinuo de Tanhua [Conversations between Mao Zedong and Edgar Snow in 1936]. Beijing: Renmin Chubanshe, 1980.

Nie Rongzhen. *Nie Rongzhen Huiyilu* [Nie Rongzhen Memoirs]. Beijing: Jiefangjun
Chubanshe, 1984.

Niu Dayong. "Crossing a River in the Same Boat or Sharing the Same Bed but Dream-
ing Different Dreams—Inside Stories of the Relationship between Kennedy
and Jiang Jieshi." *Bainianchao*, no. 1 (2001): 13–19.

———. "The Dream of 'Returning to the Mainland' and U.S. 'Controlling' Policy—
Inside Stories of the Relationship between Kennedy and Jiang Jieshi." *Bainianchao*, no. 5 (2001): 46–56.

———. "Sino-American Ambassadorial Talks, 1961–1963." In *Lengzhan Yu Zhongguo*,
ed. Zhang and Niu, 436–61.

———. "A Disharmonious Episode at the United Nations—Inside Stories of the Relationship between Kennedy and Jiang Jieshi." *Bainianchao*, no. 4 (2001): 12–22.

———. "Wind and Rain in Tranquility—Inside Stories of the Relationship between
Kennedy and Jiang Jieshi." *Bainianchao*, no. 2 (2001): 18–24.

Niu Jun. *Cong Heerli dao Maxieer: Meiguo Tiaoting Guogong Maodun Shimo* [From
Hurley to Marshall: American Mediation of the GMD-CCP Conflict]. Fuzhou:
Fujian Renmin Chubanshe, 1988.

———. *Cong Yan'an Zouxiang Shijie: Zhongguo Gongchandang Duiwei Guanxi de
Qiyuan* [Marching from Yan'an into the World: The Origins of the CCP's Foreign Relations]. Fuzhou: Fujian Renmin Chubanshe, 1992.

———. "The Evolution of New China's Diplomacy and its Main Characteristics." *Lishi
Yanjiu*, no. 5 (1999): 23–42.

———. "On the Historical Background of the Change of Chinese Policy towards the
U.S. in 1960s." *Dangdai Zhongguoshi Yanjiu*, no. 1 (2000): 52–65.

Pan Jia et al. *Zhongguo Lingdaoren yu Waiguo Zhengyao Huitan Jishi* [Memorandum
of Conversations between Chinese Leaders and Foreign Political Dignitaries].
Changsha: Hunan Renmin Chubanshe, 2001.

Pang Xianzhi, chief ed. *Mao Zedong Nianpu, 1893–1949* [The Chronicle of Mao Zedong, 1893–1949]. 3 vols. Beijing: Zhongyang Wenxian and Renmin Chubanshe, 1993.

Pang Xianzhi and Jin Chongji, chief eds. *Mao Zedong Zhuan, 1949–1976* [A Biography
of Mao Zedong, 1949–1976]. 2 vols. Beijing: Zhongyang Wenxian Chubanshe,
2003.

Pei Jianzhang, chief ed. *Dangdai Zhongguo Shijie Waijiao Shengya* [Diplomatic Careers of Contemporary Chinese Envoys]. Vols. 1–2. Beijing: Shijie Zhishi Chubanshe, 1995.

———, chief ed. *Mao Zedong Waijiao Sixiang Yanjiu* [Research on Mao Zedong's Diplomatic Thought]. Beijing: Shijie Zhishi Chubanshe, 1994.

———, chief ed. *Xin Zhongguo Waijiao Fengyun* [Winds and Clouds in New China's
Diplomacy]. Vols. 1–3. Beijing: Shijie Zhishi Chubanshe, 1990–94.

———, chief ed. *Yanjiu Zhou Enlai—Waijiao Sixiang yu Shijian* [Studying Zhou Enlai:
His Diplomatic Thought and Practice]. Beijing: Shijie Zhishi Chubanshe, 1989.

———, chief ed. *Zhonghua Renmin Gongheguo Waijiaoshi, 1949–1956* [A Diplomatic
History of the People's Republic of China, 1949–1956]. Beijing: Shijie Zhishi
Chubanshe, 1994.

Pei Jianzhang and Feng Yaoyuan, eds. *Zhou Enlai Waijiao Huodong Dashiji, 1949–1975*
[Chronology of Zhou Enlai's Diplomatic Activities, 1949–1975]. Beijing: Shijie
Zhishi Chubanshe, 1993.

Pei Monong. *Zhou Enlai yu Xin Zhongguo Waijiao* [Zhou Enlai and New China's Di-
  plomacy]. Beijing: Zhongyang Dangxiao Chubanshe, 2002.
Peng Dehuai. *Peng Dehuai Junshi Wenxuan* [Selected Military Papers of Peng De-
  huai]. Beijing: Zhongyang Wenxian Chubanshe, 1988.
———. *Peng Dehuai Zishu* [The Autobiographical Notes of Peng Dehuai]. Beijing:
  Renmin Chubanshe, 1981.
Qi Dexue. *Chaoxian Zhanzheng Juece Neimu* [Inside Stories of Decision-making during the Korean War]. Shenyang: Liaoning Daxue Chubanshe, 1991.
———. *Juren de Jiaoliang: Kangmei Yuanchao Gaoceng Juece he Zhidao* [Contest be-
  tween Giants: High-level Decision-making and Guidance during the War to Re-
  sist the U. S. and Assist Korea]. Beijing: Zhongyang Dangxiao Chubanshe, 1999.
Qian Jiang. "The Beginning of the Renewal of Sino-American Warsaw Talks." *Bai-
  nianchao*, no. 3 (2000).
———. "An Important Turning Point at Geneva Conference." *Bainianchao*, no. 10
  (2000): 27–32.
———. *Pingpang Waijiao Shimo* [Ping-Pong Diplomacy: The Beginning and the End].
  Beijing: Dongfang Chubanshe. 1987.
———. *Xiaoqiu Zhuandong Daqiu: Pingpang Waijiao Muhou* [Little Ball Moves Big
  Ball: Behind Ping-Pong Diplomacy]. Beijing: Dongfang Chubanshe. 1997.
Qing Shi. "Inside Stories of the Korean Armistice: Secret from Russian Archives." *Bai-
  nianchao*, no. 3 (1997): 44–56.
Qu Aiguo. "On the War to Resist U.S. Aggression and Assist Korea—An Interview with
  Cencral Chai Chengwen." *Renwu*, no. 5 (1992): 5–50.
Shen Zhihua. "Ending the Korean War—Political Considerations of Sino-Soviet
  Leaders." In *Lengzhan yu Zhongguo*, ed. Zhang and Niu, 182–215.
———. *Mao Zedong, Sidalin yu Chaoxian Zhanzheng* [Mao Zedong, Stalin, and the
  Korean War]. Guangzhou: Guangdong Renmin Chubanshe, 2003.
———. *Mao Zedong, Sidalin yu Hanzhan* [Mao Zedong, Stalin, and the Korean War].
  Hong Kong: Cosmos Books LTD, 1998.
———. "Sino-American Rapprochement and China's Vietnam Policy: 1968–1973." In
  Zhongguo yu Yinduzhina Zhanzheng, ed. Li Danhui, 221–50.
———. *Zhongsu Tongmeng yu Chaoxian Zhanzheng Yanjiu* [Studies on the Sino-Soviet
  Alliance and the Korean War]. Guilin: Guangxi Shida Chubanshe, 1999.
Shen Zhihua and Li Danhui. "Sino-U.S. Reconciliation and China's Vietnam Policy
  (1971–1973)." *Meiguo Yanjiu*, no. 1 (2000): 98–116.
Shen Zonghong and Meng Zhaohui, chief eds., *Zhongguo Renmin Zhiyuanjun Kang-
  mei Yuanchao Zhanshi* [History of the Chinese People's Volunteers' War to Re-
  sist the United States and Assist Korea]. Beijing: Junshi Kexue Chubanshe, 1988.
Shi Zhe. *Feng yu Gu* [Peaks and Valleys]. Beijing: Hongqi Chubanshe, 1992.
———. "With Chairman Mao in the Soviet Union." *Renwu* (May 1988): 3–24.
———. *Zai Lishi Juren Shenbian: Shi Zhe Huiyilu* [Together with Historical Giants: Shi
  Zhe Memoirs]. Beijing: Zhongyang Wenxian Chubanshe, 1991.
Su Ge. *Meiguo Duihua Zhengce yu Taiwan Wenti* [American China Policy and the
  Taiwan Issue]. Beijing: Shijie Zhishi Chubanshe, 1998.
Tang Longbin. "A Mysterious Mission—Receiving Kissinger's Secret China Visit." In
  Xin Zhongguo Waijiao Fengyun, ed.Yu Wuzhen, 4: 35–47.
Tao Wenzhao. "President Truman's China Policy and General Marshall's Mission to
  China." *Lishi Yanjiu* (January 1986): 40–48.
———, chief ed. *Zhong Mei Guanxi Shi, 1949–1972* [PRC-USA Relations, 1949–1972].
  Shanghai: Shanghai Renmin Chubanshe, 1999.

Tian Jin and Yu Mengjia. *Zhongguo Zai Lianheguo—Gongtong Dizhao Meihao de Shijie* [China at the United Nations—To Create a Better World Together]. Beijing: Shijie Zhishi Chubanshe, 1999.

Tian Zengpei and Wang Taiping, eds. *Lao Waijiaoguan Huiyi Zhou Enlai* [Senior Diplomats' Remembrance of Zhou Enlai]. Beijing: Shijie Zhishi Chubanshe, 1998.

Wan Xian et al. *Zhongguo Bainian Waijiao Fengyunlu* [Winds and Clouds of a Hundred Years of Chinese Diplomacy]. 3 vols. Shenyang: Shenyang Chubanshe, 1995.

Wang Bingnan. *Zhongmei Huitan Jiunian Huigu* [Nine Years of Sino-American Talks: A Retrospect]. Beijing: Shijie Zhishi Chubanshe, 1985.

Wang De. "Mao Zedong and Zhou Enlai Wanted to Visit the United States in 1944–45." *Mao Zedong Sixiang Yanjiu* [Studies of Mao Zedong Thought] (February 1982): 7–11.

Wang Fan. "Behind 'The Thawing' That Shocked the World: Reception and Guarding Work during Nixon's Trip to China—Recollections of Wu Jiecheng, Deputy Head of the Central Security Guards Regiment." *Dangshi Bolan* (September 2001): 11–24; (November 2001): 34–39.

Wang Funian. "A Summary of the Negotiations on the Korean Cease-fire." *Dangshi Yanjiu Ziliao* (June 1983): 2–12.

Wang Guoquan. "My Tenure as Ambassador." In *Dangdai Zhongguo Shijie Waijiao Shengya*, ed. Pei Jianzhang, 2: 141–66.

Wang Jianwei. "The U.S. Policy toward China, 1948–50." *Lishi Yanjiu* (November 1986): 34–45.

Wang Jiaxiang. *Wang Jiaxiang Xuanji* [Selected Works of Wang Jiaxiang]. Beijing: Renmin Chubanshe, 1989.

Wang Li and Qiu Shengyun. "Historical Exploit: Zhou Enlai and the Process of Opening the Door of Sino-American Relations." In *Yanjiu Zhou Enlai*, ed. Pei Jianzhang, 202–11.

Wang Nianyi. *Da Dongluan de Niandai* [Years of Great Upheaval]. Zheng Zhou: Henan Renmin Chubanshe, 1988.

Wang Taiping, chief ed. *Dangdai Zhongguo Shijie Waijiao Shengya* [Diplomatic Careers of Contemporary Chinese Envoys]. Vols. 4–5. Beijing: Shijie Zhishi Chubanshe, 1996–97.

——, chief ed. *Zhonghua Renmin Gongheguo Waijiaoshi, 1957–1969* [A Diplomatic History of the People's Republic of China, 1957–1969]. Beijing: Shijie Zhishi Chubanshe, 1998.

——, chief ed. *Zhonghua Renmin Gongheguo Waijiaoshi, 1970–1978* [A Diplomatic History of the People's Republic of China, 1970–1978]. Beijing: Shijie Zhishi Chubanshe, 1999.

Wang Xiangtong. *Wode Zhangfu Jichaozhu—44 nian de Waijiao Shengya* [My Husband Jichaozhu: Forty-four Years of Diplomatic Service]. Taiyuan: Shanxi Jiaoyu Chubanshe, 1997.

Wang Yan, chief ed. *Peng Dehuai Nianpu* [A Chronological Record of Peng Dehuai]. Beijing: Renmin Chubanshe, 1998.

Wang Yongqin. "Chronicle of Sino-American-Soviet Relations, 1966–1976," *Dangdai Zhongguoshi Yanjiu*, no. 4 (1997): 112–26; no. 5 (1997): 110–26; no. 6 (1997): 143–56; no. 1 (1998): 103–21.

Wei Shiyan. "Inside Stories of Kissinger's Secret Visit to China." In *Xin Zhongguo Waijiao Fengyun*, ed. Pei Jianzhang, 2: 33–45.

——. "Kissinger's Second Trip to China." In *Xin Zhongguo Waijiao Fengyun*, ed. Pei Jianzhang, 3: 59–70.

———. "President Nixon's Trip to China." In *Xin Zhongguo Waijiao Fengyun*, ed. Pei Jianzhang, 3: 83–96.

———. "The Course of Haig's Advance Team to China in Preparation for Nixon's Visit to China." In *Xin Zhongguo Waijiao Fengyun*, ed. Pei Jianzhang, 3: 71–82.

Wu Lengxi. *Shinian Lunzhan* [Ten Years of Wars of Words]. 2 vols. Beijing: Zhongyang Dangxiao Chubanshe, 1999.

———. *Yi Maozhuxi—Wo Qinzi Jingli de Ruogan Zhongda Lishi Shijian Pianduan* [Recollections of Chairman Mao: My Personal Experience of Several Important Historical Events]. Beijing: Xinhua Chubanshe, 1995.

Wu Xiuquan. *Zai Waijiaobu Banian de Jingli, January 1950–October 1958* [My Eight Years in the Foreign Ministry: January 1950–October 1958]. Beijing: Shijie Zhishi Chubanshe, 1983.

Xie Li. "An Analysis of Zhou Enlai's Diplomatic Strategy toward the Capitalist Countries in Europe." In *Yanjiu Zhou Enlai*, ed. Pei Jianzhang, 239–45.

Xie Yixian. *Waijiao Zhihui yu Moulue: Xin Zhongguo Waijiao Lilun he Yuanze* [Diplomatic Wisdom and Strategy: New China's Foreign Policy Theory and Principles]. Zhengzhou: Henan Renmin Chubanshe, 1993.

Xiong Xianghui. "Prelude to Opening Sino-American Relations: Research and Proposals of the Four Veteran Marshals Regarding the International Situation in 1969." In *Xin Zhongguo Waijiao Fengyun*, ed. Yu Wuzhen, 4: 7–34.

———. *Wo de Qingbao yu Waijiao Shengya* [My Career in Intelligence and Diplomacy]. Beijing: Zhongyang Dangxiao Chubanshe, 1999.

Xu Dashen, chief ed. *Zhonghua Renmin Gongheguo Shilu* [A Factual Record of the People's Republic of China]. Changchun: Jilin Renmin Chubanshe, 1994.

Xu Jingli. *Jiemi Zhongguo Waijiao Dang'an* [Declassifying Chinese Diplomatic Files]. Beijing: Zhongguo Dang'an Chubanshe, 2005.

———. *Lingqi Luzao: Jueqi Juren de Waijiao Fanglue* [Building a New Kitchen: Diplomatic Strategies of the Rising Giant]. Beijing: Shijie Zhishi Chubanshe, 1998.

Xu Yan. *Diyici Jiaoliang: Kangmei Yuanchao Zhanzheng de Lishi Huigu yu Fansi* [The First Encounter: A Historical Retrospect and Reflections on the War to Resist U.S. Aggression and Assist Korea]. Beijing: Zhongguo Guangbo Dianshi Chubanshe, 1990.

———. "The Sino-Soviet Border Clashes of 1969." *Dangshi Yanjiu Ziliao*, no. 5 (1994): 2–13.

Xu Zehao. *Wang Jiaxiang Zhuan* [Biography of Wang Jiaxiang]. Beijing: Dangdai Zhongguo Chubanshe, 1996.

Xue Mouhong, chief ed. *Dangdai Zhongguo Waijiao* [Contemporary Chinese Diplomacy]. Beijing: Zhongguo Shehui Kexue Chubanshe, 1988.

Yang Kuisong. "From the Zhenbao Island Clashes to Sino-American Rapprochement." *Dangshi Yanjiu Ziliao*, no. 12 (1997): 5–19.

———. "The Origins of Soviet-U.S. Cold War and Its Impact on Chinese Revolution." *Lishi Yanjiu*, no. 5 (1999): 5–22.

———. "The Ward Case and the Shaping of New China's American Policy." *Lishi Yanjiu*, no. 5 (1994): 104–18.

Yang Mingwei and Chen Yangyong. *Zhou Enlai Waijiao Fengyun* [Diplomatic Winds and Clouds of Zhou Enlai]. Beijing: Jiefangjun Wenyi Chubanshe, 1995.

Yao Xu. *Cong Yalujiang dao Banmendian* [From the Yalu River to Panmunjom]. Beijing: Renmin Chubanshe, 1985.

———. "Peng Dehuai's Great Contribution to the War to Resist the United States and Assist Korea." *Dangshi Yanjiu Ziliao* (January 1982): 2–12.

——. "The Wisdom of Deciding to Resist the United States and Assist Korea." *Dangshi Yanjiu Ziliao* (October 1980): 5–14.

Yao Zhongming et al. *Jiangjun, Waijiaojia, Yishujia: Huang Zhen Jinian Wenji* [General, Diplomat, and Artist: Essays in Memory of Huang Zhen]. Beijing: Jiefangjun Chubanshe, 1992.

Ye Fei. *Ye Fei Huiyilu* [Ye Fei's Memoirs]. Beijing: Jiefangjun Chubanshe, 1988.

Yu Huamin. "The Secret Contact between the U.S. and Chinese Communists Shortly before the Founding of New China." *Bainianchao*, no. 11 (2001): 19–25; no. 12 (2001): 27–33.

Yu Wuzhen, chief ed. *Dangdai Zhongguo Shijie Waijiao Shengya* [Diplomatic Careers of Contemporary Chinese Envoys]. Vol. 3. Beijing: Shijie Zhishi Chubanshe, 1996.

——, chief ed. *Xin Zhongguo Waijiao Fengyun* [Winds and Clouds in New China's Diplomacy]. Vol. 4. Beijing: Shijie Zhishi Chubanshe, 1996.

Zhang Baijia. "The Policies of the GMD and the CCP toward the United States, 1937–45." *Lishi Yanjiu* (June 1987): 3–14.

——. "Zhou Enlai and China's Entry into the International Political Arena." *Zhonggong Dangshi Yanjiu*, no. 1 (1998): 36–45.

Zhang Baijia and Jia Qingguo. "The Steering Wheel, Shock Absorber and Surveying Instrument in Antagonism: Sino-American Ambassadorial Talks Seen from the Chinese Perspective." In *Cong Duizhi Zouxiang Huanhe*, ed. Jiang and Ross, 169–94.

Zhang Baijia and Niu Jun, eds. *Lengzhan Yu Zhongguo* [The Cold War and China]. Beijing: Shijie Zhishi Chubanshe, 2002.

Zhang Dongyue. "General Deng Hua in the War of Resisting the U.S. and Assisting Korea." *Bainianchao*, no. 9 (2001): 39–43.

Zhang Hanzhi. *Wo yu Qiao Guanhua* [Qiao Guanhua and I]. Beijing: Zhongguo Qingnian Chubanshe, 1994.

Zhang Shu Guang. "American Strategic Thinking and Decision-making in China Policy: A General Consideration." *Shanghai Shehui Kexueyuan Xueshu Jikan* [Shanghai Academy of Social Sciences Academic Quarterly], no. 2 (2001): 91–100.

——. *Meiguo Duihua Zhanlue Kaolei yu Juece* [U.S. Strategic Thinking and Policymaking toward China]. Shanghai: Shanghai Waiyu Jiaoyu Chubanshe, 2002.

Zhang Ying. "Random Recollection of Premier Zhou's Later Years." In *Lao Waijiaoguan Huiyi Zhou Enlai*, ed. Tian and Wang, 374–83.

——. *Sui Zhang Wenjin Chushi Meiguo: Dashi Furen Jishi* [Serving in the United States with Zhang Wenjin: An Account of an Ambassador's Life]. Beijing: Shijie Zhishi Chubanshe, 1996.

Zhang Zhirong. *Zhou Enlai yu Waijiao Buzhang Men* [Zhong Enlai and Foreign Ministers]. Beijing: Zhongyang Dangxiao Chubanshe, 1999.

Zheng Derong, Shao Pengwen, Zhu Yang, and Gu Min. eds. *Xin Zhongguo Jishi, 1949–1984* [Records of New China, 1949–1984]. Jilin: Dongbei Shifan Daxue Chubanshe, 1986.

Zhonggong Zhongyang Dangxiao Jiaoyanshi [Teaching and Research Section on Party History, Central Party School], ed. *Zhonggong Dangshi Cankao Ziliao* [Reference Materials on the History of the Chinese Communist Party]. Beijing: Renmin Chubanshe, 1980.

Zhonggong Zhongyang Wenxian Yanjiushi [CCP Central Archives and Manuscript Division], comp. *Jianguo Yilai Zhongyao Wenxian Xuanbian* [A Selection of Significant Documents since the Founding of the PRC]. 20 vols. Beijing: Zhongyang Wenxian Chubanshe, 1992.

Zhongyang Dang'anguan, comp. *Zhonggong Zhongyang Wenjian Huibian: 1954* [A Collection of CCP Central Committee Documents, 1954]. Beijing: Shijie Zhishi Chubanshe, 1956.

———. *Zhonggong Zhongyang Wenjian Xuanji* [Selected CCP Central Committee Documents]. 18 vols. Beijing: Zhonggong Zhongyang Dangxiao Chubanshe, 1989–92.

Zhongyang Tongzhanbu he Zhongyang Dang'anguan, comp. *Zhonggong Zhongyang Jiefang Zhanzheng Shiqi Tongyi Zhanxian Wenjian Xuanbian* [A Selection of Documents on the CCP Central Committee's United Front during the Liberation War], "internal circulation." Beijing: Zhongyang Dang'an Chubanshe, 1988.

Zhou Enlai. *Zhou Enlai Junshi Wenxuan* [Selected Military Papers of Zhou Enlai]. Beijing: Renmin Chubanshe, 1997.

———. *Zhou Enlai Tongyi Zhanxian Wenxuan* [Selected Works by Zhou Enlai on the United Front]. Beijing: Renmin Chubanshe, 1984.

———. *Zhou Enlai Waijiao Wenxuan* [Selected Diplomatic Papers of Zhou Enlai]. Beijing: Zhongyang Wenxian Chubanshe, 1990.

———. *Zhou Enlai Xuanji* [Selected Works of Zhou Enlai]. 2 vols. Beijing: Renmin Chubanshe, 1984.

Zhu Yuanshi. "Liu Shaoqi's Secret Visit to the Soviet Union in 1949." *Dangde Wenxian*, no. 3 (1991): 74–80.

Zi Zhongyun. *Meiguo Duihua Zhengce de Yuanqi yu Fazhan, 1945–1950* [The Origins and Evolution of U.S. Policy toward China, 1945–1950]. Chongqing: Chongqing Chubanshe, 1987.

———. "U.S. Policy toward Taiwan around the Founding of the PRC." *Guoji Wenti Yanjiu* [Studies of International Affairs] (March 1982): 34–42.

Zong Daoyi. "The Textual Research into Some Facts of Chinese Diplomatic History." *Dangdai Zhongguoshi Yanjiu*, no. 6 (1997): 103–14; no. 3 (2001): 95–102.

Materials in English

Archives

Franklin Delano Roosevelt Library—Hyde Park, New York.
Lyndon B. Johnson Library—Austin, Texas.
———. Lyndon Johnson Papers (National Security Files).
U.S. National Archives—College Park, Maryland.
———. Record Group 59: Records of Department of State.
Decimal Files, 1955–63.
Subject-Numeric Files, 1963–73.
Records of Policy Planning Council, Director's Files (Winston Lord), 1969–73.
Records of Office of Chinese Affairs.
Records of Office of Intelligence and Research.
———. The Nixon Presidential Materials Project (NPMP).
National Security Council Files (NSCF).
For the President's Files (Winston Lord)—China Trip/Vietnam.
For the President's Files—China/Vietnam Negotiations.
HAK Office Files.
White House Central Files, Subject Files.
White House Special Files (WHSF).
President's Office Files-President's Handwriting Series.
President's Personal Files.

——. Record Group 263: Records of Central Intelligence Agency. National Intelligence Estimates Concerning the Soviet Union, 1950–61.

——. Record Group 218: Records of the Joint Chiefs of Staff.

——. Record Group 273: Records of the National Security Council.

Government Documents

Eisenhower, Dwight D. *Public Papers of the Presidents of the United States: Dwight D. Eisenhower, 1953–1961.* Washington, D.C.: U.S. Government Printing Office, 1960–61.

Hermes, Walter G. *Truce Tent and Fighting Front.* Washington, D.C.: Government Printing Office, 1966.

Johnson, Lyndon B. *Public Papers of the Presidents of the United States: Lyndon B. Johnson, 1963–1969.* Washington D.C.: U.S. Government Printing Office, 1965–69.

Kennedy, John F. *Public Papers of the Presidents of the United States: John F. Kennedy, 1961–1963.* Washington D.C.: U.S. Government Printing Office, 1962–64.

Nixon, Richard. *Public Papers of the Presidents of the United States: Richard M. Nixon, 1969–1974.* Washington, D.C.: U.S. Government Printing Office, 1970–75.

——. *U.S. Foreign Policy for the 1970s: A New Strategy for Peace* (A Report to the Congress, 18 February 1970). Washington D.C.: U.S. Government Printing Office, 1970.

——. *U.S. Foreign Policy for the 1970s: The Emerging Structure of Peace* (A Report to Congress, 9 February 1972). Washington, D.C.: U.S. Government Printing Office, 1972.

Pentagon Papers (Gravel Edition). Boston: Beacon Press, 1971.

Truman, Harry S. *Public Papers of the Presidents of the United States: Harry S. Truman, 1945–1953.* Washington, D.C.: U.S. Government Printing Office, 1961–66.

U.S. Congress. Senate. Committee on Foreign Relations. *The United States and the Korean Problem, Document, 1943–1953.* 83rd Congress, 1st session, 1953. Washington, D.C.: Government Printing Office, 1953.

——. Senate. Sub-Committee on National Security and International Operations. *Peking's Approach to Negotiation.* Washington, D.C.: Government Printing Office, 1969.

U.S. Department of State. *Department of State Bulletin.* Washington, D.C.: Government Printing Office, 1950–72.

——. *Foreign Relations of the United States.* Washington, D.C.: Government Printing Office.

    1948, vol. 8: *The Far East: China.* 1973.
    1949, vol. 8: *The Far East: China.* 1978.
    1949, vol. 9: *The Far East: China.* 1974.
    1950, vol. 7: *Korea.* 1976.
    1951, vol. 1: *National Security.* 1979.
    1951, vol. 6: *Asia and the Pacific* (two parts). 1977.
    1951, vol. 7: *Korea and China* (two parts). 1983.
    1952–54, vol. 3: *United Nations Affairs.* 1979.
    1952–54, vol. 12: *East Asia and the Pacific* (two parts).
      —Part 1, 1984.
      —Part 2, 1987.
    1952–54, vol. 14: *China and Japan* (two parts). 1985.
    1952–54, vol. 15: *Korea* (two parts). 1984.
    1952–54, vol. 16: *The Geneva Conference.* 1981.

1955–57, vol. 2: *China*. 1986.
1955–57, vol. 3: *China*. 1986.
1955–57, vol. 3: *China* (Microfiche Supplement). 1987.
1958–60, vol. 19: *China*. 1996.
1958–60, vol. 19: *China* (Microfiche Supplement). 1996.
1961–63, vol. 5: *Soviet Union*. 1998.
1961–63, vol. 8: *National Security Policy*. 1996.
1961–63, vol. 22: *Northeast Asia*. 1996.
1964–68, vol. 2: *Vietnam* (January–June, 1965). 1996.
1964–68, vol. 30: *China*. 1998.
1969–76, vol. 1: *Foundations of Foreign Policy, 1969–1972*. 2003.

Newspapers and Magazines

The New York Times. New York.
Peking Review. Beijing.
People's China. Beijing.

Books and Articles

Accinelli, Robert. *Crisis and Commitment: United States Policy toward Taiwan, 1950–1955*. Chapel Hill: University of North Carolina Press, 1996.
Acheson, Dean. *Present at the Creation: My Years in the State Department*. New York: W. W. Norton, 1969.
Aijazuddin, F. S. *From a Head, Through a Head, To a Head: The Secret Channel between the U.S. and China through Pakistan*. Oxford: Oxford University Press, 2000.
Avruch, Kevin. *Culture and Conflict Resolution*. Washington D.C.: United States Institute of Peace Press, 1998.
Bacchus, Wilfred. "The Relationship between Combat and Peace Negotiations: Fighting While Talking in Korea, 1951–53." *Orbis* 17 (Summer 1973): 547–74.
Bailey, Sydney D. *How Wars End: The United Nations and the Termination of Armed Conflict: 1946–1964*. Oxford: Clarendon Press, 1982.
———. *The Korean Armistice*. New York: St. Martin's Press, 1992.
Barnett, A. Doak. *The Making of Foreign Policy in China: Structure and Process*. Boulder, Colo.: Westview Press, 1985.
Barrett, David D. *Dixie Mission: The United States Army Observer Group in Yenan, 1944*. Berkeley: Center for China Studies, University of California-Berkeley, 1970.
Beam, Jacob D. *Multiple Exposure: An American Ambassador's Unique Perspective on East-West Issues*. New York: W. W. Norton, 1978.
Berman, Larry. *No Peace, No Honor: Nixon, Kissinger, and the Betrayal in Vietnam*. New York: Free Press, 2001.
Bernstein, Barton. "The Origins of America's Commitment in Korea." *Foreign Service Journal* 55 (March, 1978): 10–13, 34.
———. "The Struggle over the Korean Armistice: Prisoners of Repatriation?" In *Child of Conflict: the Korean-American Relationship, 1943–1953*. ed. Bruce Cumings. Seattle: University of Washington Press, 1983, 261–307.
———. "Syngman Rhee: The Pawn as Rook: The Struggle to End the Korean War." *Bulletin of Concerned Asian Scholars* 10 (Jan.–Feb. 1978): 38–47.
———. "Truman's Secret Thoughts on Ending the Korean War." *Foreign Service Journal* 57 (November 1980): 31–33, 44.
Blaker, Michael. *Japanese International Negotiating Style*. New York: Columbia University Press, 1977.

Blaker, Michael, Pal Giarra, and Ezra Vogel. *Case Studies in Japanese Negotiating Behavior*. Washington, D.C.: United States Institute of Peace Press, 2001.

Bland, Larry I., ed., *George C. Marshall's Mediation Mission to China*. Lexington, Va.: George C. Marshall Foundation, 1998.

Blum, Robert M. *Drawing the Line: The Origins of the American Containment Policy in East Asia*. New York: W. W. Norton, 1982.

Borg, Dorothy, and Waldo Heinrichs, eds. *Uncertain Years: Chinese-American Relations, 1947–1950*. New York: Columbia University Press, 1980.

Buhite, Russell D. *Soviet-American Relations in Asia, 1945–1954*. Norman: University Press of Oklahoma, 1981.

Bundy, William. *A Tangled Web: The Making of Foreign Policy in the Nixon Presidency*. New York: Hill and Wang, 1998.

Burr, William. *The Kissinger Transcripts: The Top Secret Talks with Beijing and Moscow*. New York: W. W. Norton, 1998.

———. "Sino-American Relations, 1969: Sino-Soviet Border Conflict and Steps toward Rapprochement." *Cold War History* 1, no. 3 (April 2001): 73–112.

Burr, William, and Jeffrey T. Richelson. "Whether to 'Strangle the Baby in the Cradle': The United States and the Chinese Nuclear Program, 1960–64." *International Security* 25, no. 3 (Winter 2000/01): 54–99.

Carter, Carolle J. *Mission to Yenan: American Liaison with the Chinese Communists 1944–1947*. Kentucky: University of Kentucky Press, 1997.

Chang, Gordon H. *Friends and Enemies: The United States, China, and the Soviet Union, 1948–1972*. Stanford, Calif.: Stanford University Press, 1990.

Chang, Gordon H., and He Di. "The Absence of War in the U.S.-China Confrontation over Quemoy and Matsu in 1954–1955: Contingency, Luck, Deterrence?" *American Historical Review* 98 (December 1993): 1502–23.

Chang, Jaw-Ling Joanne. *Peking's Negotiating Style, A Case Study of U.S.-PRC Normalization*. Baltimore: UM Law School, Occasional Papers/Reprints Series in Contemporary Asian Studies, no. 5 (1985): 1–22.

———. *United States–China Normalization: An Evaluation of Foreign Policy Decision Making*. Monograph Series in World Affairs, vol. 22. Denver, Colo.: Graduate School of International Studies, University of Denver, 1986.

Chao Ch'un-shan. "The Change in Peiping's Foreign Policy as Viewed from the Line Adapted by the CCP." *East Asia Quarterly* (Taiwan) 5 (October 1973).

Chen Jian. "All under Heaven Is Great Chaos: Beijing, the Sino-Soviet Border Clashes, and the Turn toward Sino-American Rapprochement, 1968–1969." CWIHPB, no. 11 (Winter 1998–99): 155–75.

———. "China's Changing Aims during the Korean War." *The Journal of American-East Asian Relations* 1 (Spring 1992): 8–41.

———. *China's Road to the Korean War: the Making of the Sino-American Confrontation*. New York: Columbia University Press, 1994.

———. *Mao's China and The Cold War*. Chapel Hill: University of North Carolina Press, 2001.

———. "The Myth of America's 'Lost Chance' in China: A Chinese Perspective in Light of New Evidence." *Diplomatic History* 21, no. 1 (Winter 1997): 77–86.

———. "The Sino-Soviet Alliance and China's Entry into the Korean War." CWIHP *Working Paper*, no. 1. Washington, D.C.: Woodrow Wilson Center, December 1991.

———. "The Ward Case and the Emergence of Sino-American Confrontation, 1948–1950." *Australian Journal of Chinese Affairs*, no. 30 (July 1993): 149–70.

Chen Jian and Yang Kuisong, "Chinese Politics and the Collapse of the Sino-Soviet Alliance." In *Brothers in Arms*, ed. Westad, 246–94.

Chen Xiaolu. "China's Policy toward the United States, 1949–1955." In *Sino-American Relations, 1945–1955*, ed. Harding and Yuan, 184–97.

Christensen, Thomas. "A Lost Chance for What? Rethinking the Origins of U.S.-PRC Confrontation." *Journal of American-East Asian Relations*, no. 4 (Fall 1995): 249–78.

———. *Useful Adversaries: Grand Strategy, Domestic Mobilization, and Sino-American Conflict, 1947–1958*. Princeton, N.J.: Princeton University Press, 1996.

———. "US-Japan Relations and China's Strategic Thinking 1948–51." *Harvard University Asia Center*, Triangular Relations Conference, http://www.fas.harvard.edu/~asiactr/TR_Christensen.htm.

Clark, Mark W. *From the Danube to the Yalu*. New York: Harper and Brothers, 1954.

Cohen, Raymond. *Negotiating across Cultures: International Communication in an Interdependent World*. Washington D.C.: U.S. Institute of Peace Press, 1997.

Cohen, Warren I. "Acheson, His Advisers, and China, 1949–1950." In *Uncertain Years*, ed. Borg and Heinrichs, 13–52.

———. "American Perceptions of China." In *Dragon and Eagle*, ed. Oksenberg and Oxnam, 54–86.

———. "Conversations with Chinese Friends: Zhou Enlai's Associates Reflect on Chinese-American Relations in the 1940s and the Korean War." *Diplomatic History* 11, no. 3 (Summer 1987): 283–89.

———. "Domestic Factors Affecting US Policy toward Asia 1947 and 1971–1973." *Harvard University Asia Center*, Triangular Relations Conference, http://www.fas.harvard.edu/~asiactr/TR_Cohen.htm.

———. "Symposium: Rethinking the Lost Chance in China—Introduction: Was there a 'Lost Chance' in China?" *Diplomatic History* 21, no. 1 (Winter 1997): 71–75.

Dean, Arthur H. "What It's Like to Negotiate with the Chinese." *New York Times Magazine* (30 October 1966): 44–45.

Deardorff, A. V. "The General Validity of the Law of Comparative Advantage." *Journal of Political Economy* 88, no. 5 (1980): 941–57.

Dobrynin, Anatoly F. *In Confidence: Moscow's Ambassador to America's Six Cold War Presidents (1962–1986)*. New York: Times Books, 1995.

Downs, Chuck. *Over the Line: North Korea's Negotiating Strategy*. Washington, D.C.: American Enterprise Institute Press, 1999.

Eisenhower, Dwight D. *The White House Years*. Vol. 1: *Mandate for Change, 1953–1956*. Garden City, N.Y.: Doubleday, 1963.

———. *The White House Years*. Vol. 2: *Waging Peace, 1957–1961*. Garden City, N.Y.: Doubleday, 1965.

Elizavetin, Alexei. "Kosygin-Zhou Talks at Beijing Airport." *Far Eastern Affairs*, no. 1–3 (1993): 52–65.

Esherick, Joseph W., ed. *Lost Chance in China: The World War II Dispatches of John S. Service*. New York: Random House, 1974.

Fairbank, John K. *China Perceived: Images and Policies in Chinese-American Relations*. New York: Random House, 1976.

Faure, Guy Oliver, and Jeffrey Z. Rubin, eds. *Culture and Negotiation: The Resolution of Water Disputes*. Thousand Oaks, Calif: Sage, 1993.

Fisher, Glen. *International Negotiation: A Cross-Cultural Perspective*. Yarmouth, Me.: Intercultural Press, 1980.

———. *Mindsets: The Role of Culture and Perception in International Relations*. Yarmouth, Me.: Intercultural Press Inc., 1988.

Foot, Rosemary. "Nuclear Coercion and the Ending of the Korean Conflict." *International Security* 13, no. 3 (Winter 1988/89): 92–112.

———. *The Practice of Power: U.S. Relations with China since 1949.* Oxford: Clarendon Press, 1997.

———. "Redefinitions: The Domestic Context of America's China Policy in the 1960s." In *Re-examining the Cold War*, ed. Ross and Jiang, 262–87.

———. *A Substitute for Victory: The Politics of Peacemaking at the Korean Armistice Talks.* Ithaca, N.Y.: Cornell University Press, 1990.

———. *The Wrong War: American Policy and the Dimensions of the Korean Conflict, 1950–53.* Ithaca, N.Y.: Cornell University Press, 1985.

Freeman, Charles, Jr. "Is Diplomacy Really a Profession?" *Foreign Service Journal* (March 1995): 17–21.

———. "The Process of Rapprochement: Achievements and Problems." In *Sino-American Normalization and Its Policy Implications*, ed. Gene T. Hsiao and Michael Witunski. New York: Praeger, 1983, 1–27.

Gaddis, John Lewis. "The American 'Wedge' Strategy, 1949–1955." In *Sino-American Relations, 1945–1955*, ed. Harding and Yuan, 157–83.

———. "Dividing Adversaries: The United States and International Communism, 1945–1958." In Gaddis, *The Long Peace: Inquiry into the History of the Cold War.* New York: Oxford University Press, 1987, 147–94.

———. "New Conceptual Approaches to the Study of American Foreign Relations: Interdisciplinary Perspectives." *Diplomatic History* 14, no. 3 (Summer 1990): 405–23.

———. "The Strategic Perspective: The Rise and Fall of the 'Defense Perimeter' Concept, 1949–1951." In *Uncertain Years*, ed. Borg and Heinrichs, 61–118.

———. *Strategies of Containment: A Critical Appraisal of Postwar American National Security Policy.* New York: Oxford University Press, 1982.

———. *The United States and the End of the Cold War: Implications, Reconsiderations, Provocations.* New York: Oxford University Press, 1992.

Garson, Robert. *The United States and China since 1949.* Teaneck, N.J.: Fairleigh Dickinson University Press, 1994.

Garthoff, Raymond L. *Détente and Confrontation, American-Soviet Relations from Nixon to Reagan.* Rev. ed. Washington, D.C.: Brookings Institution, 1994.

Garver, John. *China's Decision for Rapprochement with the United States, 1969–1971.* Boulder, Colo.: Westview Press, 1982.

———. *Foreign Relations of the People's Republic of China.* Upper Saddle River, N.J.: Prentice Hall, 1993.

———. "Little Chance: Revolutions and Ideologies." *Diplomatic History* 21, no. 1 (Winter 1997): 87–94.

Gates, Robert M. *From the Shadows: The Ultimate Insider's Story of Five Presidents and How They Won the Cold War.* New York: Simon and Schuster, 1997.

Gittings, John. "Talks, Bomb, and Germs: Another Look at the Korean War." *Journal of Contemporary Asia* (November 1975): 205–17.

Goh, Evelyn. *Constructing the U.S. Rapprochement with China, 1961–1974: From "Red Menace" to "Tacit Ally."* New York: Columbia University Press, 2005.

Goldstein, Steven M. "Dialogue of the Deaf? The Sino-American Ambassadorial-Level Talks, 1955–1970." In *Re-examining the Cold War*, ed. Ross and Jiang, 200–237.

Goncharov, Sergei. "Stalin's Dialogues with Mao Zedong: I. V. Kovalev Answers Questions of Sinologist S. N. Goncharov." *Journal of Northeast Asian Studies* 10, no. 4 (Winter 1991–92): 43–76.

Goncharov, Sergei, John W. Lewis, and Xue Litai. *Uncertain Partners: Stalin, Mao, and the Korean War.* Stanford, Calif.: Stanford University Press, 1993.

Goodman, Allan E. *Negotiating While Fighting: The Diary of Admiral C. Turner Joy at the Korean Armistice Conference.* Stanford, Calif.: Hoover Institution Press, 1978.

Goodwin, Deborah, ed. *Negotiation in International Conflict: Understanding Persuasion.* London: Frank Cass, 2001.

Gordon, Leonard H. "U.S. Opposition to the Use of Force in the Taiwan Straits, 1954–1962." *Journal of American History* 72 (December 1985): 578–646.

Green, Marshall, John H. Holdridge, and William N. Stoke. *War and Peace with China: First-hand Experiences in the Foreign Service of the United States.* Bethesda, Md.: Dacor Press, 1994.

Haldeman, H. R. *The Haldeman Diaries: Inside the Nixon White House.* New York: G. P. Putman's Sons, 1994.

Haldeman, H. R., with Joseph DiMona. *The Ends of Power.* New York: Times Books, 1978.

Hamrin, Carol Lee. "Elite Politics and the Development of China's Foreign Relations." In *Chinese Foreign Policy*, ed. Robinson and Shambaugh, 70–114.

Hanhimaki, Jussi M. *The Flawed Architect: Henry Kissinger and American Foreign Policy.* New York: Oxford University Press, 2004.

Harding, Harry. *A Fragile Relationship: The United States and China since 1972.* Washington, D.C.: Brookings Institution, 1992.

Harding, Harry, and Yuan Ming, eds. *Sino-American Relations, 1945–1955: A Joint Reassessment of a Critical Decade.* Wilmington, Del.: Scholarly Resources, 1989.

He, Di. "The Evolution of the Chinese Communist Party's Policy toward the United States, 1944–1949." In *Sino-American Relations, 1945–1955*, ed. Harding and Yuan, 31–50.

———. "The Evolution of the People's Republic of China's Policy toward the Offshore Islands." In *The Great Powers in East Asia 1953–1960*, ed. Warren Cohen and Akira Iriye. New York: Columbia University Press, 1990, 222–45.

———. "The Most Respected Enemy: Mao Zedong's Perception of the United States." *China Quarterly* 137 (March 1994): 144–58.

Hersh, Seymour M. *The Price of Power: Kissinger in the Nixon White House.* New York: Summit Books, 1983.

Hilsman, Roger. *To Move a Nation: The Politics of Foreign Policy in the Administration of John F. Kennedy.* Garden City, N.Y.: Doubleday, 1967.

Holdridge, John H. *Crossing the Divide: An Insider's Account of the Normalization of U.S.–China Relations.* Lanham, Md.: Rowman and Littlefield, 1997.

Hunt, Michael H. *The Genesis of Chinese Communist Foreign Policy.* New York: Columbia University Press, 1996.

Hunt, Michael H., and Odd Arne Westad. "The Chinese Communist Party and International Affairs: A Field Report on New Historical Sources and Old Research Problems." *China Quarterly* 122 (June 1990): 258–72.

Hunt, Michael H., and Niu Jun, eds. *Toward a History of Chinese Communist Foreign Relations, 1920s–1960s: Personalities and Interpretive Approaches.* Washington, D.C.: Woodrow Wilson Centers, 1995.

Ikenberry, G. John. *American Foreign Policy: Theoretical Essay.* 2nd ed. New York: HarperCollins, 1996.

Ikle, Fred Charles. *How Nations Negotiate.* New York: Harper and Row, 1964.

Immerman, Richard H. "The United States and the Geneva Conferences of 1954: A New Look." *Diplomatic History* 14, no. 1 (Winter 1990): 43–66.

Iriye, Akira. *Cultural Internationalism and World Order*. Baltimore, Md.: John Hopkins University Press, 1997.

——. "Culture and International History." In *Explaining the History of American Foreign Relations*, ed. Michael Hogan and Thomas G. Paterson. New York: Cambridge University Press, 1991, 214–25.

——. "Introduction: The Korean War in the Domestic Context." *Journal of American-East Asian Relations* 2, no. 1 (Spring 1993): 1–3.

——, ed. *U.S. Policy toward China: Testimony Taken from the Senate Foreign Relations Committee Hearings, 1966*. Boston: Little, Brown, 1968.

Jervis, Robert, and Jack Snyder, eds. *Dominoes and Bandwagons: Strategic Beliefs and Great Power Competition in the Eurasian Rimland*. New York: Oxford University Press, 1991.

Jin Qiu. *The Culture of Power: The Lin Biao Incident in the Cultural Revolution*. Stanford, Calif.: Stanford University Press, 1999.

Johnson, U. Alexis, with Jef Olivarius McAllister. *The Right Hand of Power*. Upper Saddle River, N.J.: Prentice Hall, 1984.

Johnston, Alastair Iain. *Cultural Realism: Strategic Culture and Grand Strategy in Chinese History*. Princeton, N.J.: Princeton University Press, 1995.

Joy, C. Turner. *How Communists Negotiate*. New York: Macmillan, 1955.

Kaufman, Burton I. *The Korean Conflict*. Westport, Conn.: Greenwood Press, 1999.

——. *The Korean War: Challenges in Crisis, Credibility, and Command*. Philadelphia: Temple University Press, 1986.

Keith, Ronald. *The Diplomacy of Zhou Enlai*. New York: St. Martin's Press, 1989.

Kenen, Peter B., et al. *The International Economy*. 4th ed. New York: Cambridge University Press, 2000.

Kennan, George F. *American Diplomacy*. Expanded Ed. Chicago: University of Chicago Press, 1984.

——. (Mr. X), "The Sources of Soviet Conduct." *Foreign Affairs* 25, no. 4 (July 1947): 566–82.

Kimball, Jeffrey. *Nixon's Vietnam War*. Lawrence: University Press of Kansas, 1998.

Kissinger, Henry. *Diplomacy*. New York: Simon and Schuster, 1994.

——. *The White House Years*. Boston: Little, Brown, 1979.

——. *Years of Upheaval*. Boston: Little, Brown, 1982.

Kochavi, Noam. *A Conflict Perpetuated: China Policy during the Kennedy Years*. Westport, Conn.: Praeger, 2002.

——. "Limited Accommodation, Perpetuated Conflict: Kennedy, China, and the Laos Crisis, 1961–1963." *Diplomatic History* 26, no. 1 (Winter 2002): 95–135.

Koen, Ross Y. *The China Lobby in American Politics*. New York: Octagon Books, 1974.

Kreisberg, Paul H. "China's Negotiating Behavior." In *Chinese Foreign Policy*, ed. Robinson and Shambaugh, 453–77.

Kuznitz, Leonard A. *Public Opinion and Foreign Policy: America's China Policy, 1949–1979*. Westport, Conn.: Greenwood Press, 1984.

Lall, Arthur. *How Communist China Negotiates*. New York: Columbia University Press, 1968.

Lavin, Franklin L. "Negotiating with the Chinese." *Foreign Affairs* 73, no. 4 (July/August 1994): 16–22.

Levine, Steven I. "Perception and Ideology in Chinese Foreign Policy." In *Chinese Foreign Policy*, ed. Robinson and Shambaugh, 30–46.

Lewicki, Roy J., David M. Saunders, and John W. Minton. *Essentials of Negotiation*. 2nd ed. Boston: Irwin/McGraw-Hill, 2001.

Lewis, John Wilson, and Xue Litai. *China Builds the Bomb*. Stanford, Calif.: Stanford University Press, 1988.

Li Zhisui. *The Private Life of Chairman Mao*. New York: Random House, 1994.

Lippmann, Walter. *The Cold War, a Study in U.S. Foreign Policy*. New York: Harper and Row, 1972.

Liu Xiaohong. *Chinese Ambassadors: The Rise of Diplomatic Professionalism since 1949*. Seattle: University of Washington Press, 2001.

Logevall, Fredrik. "Bernath Lecture: A Critique of Containment." *Diplomatic History* 28, no. 4 (September 2004): 473–99.

Lu Ning. *The Dynamics of Foreign Policy Decision-making in China*. 2nd ed. Boulder, Colo. Westview Press, 2000.

MacFarquhar, Roderick, documented and introduced. *Sino-American Relations, 1949–71*. Newton Abbot, UK: David and Charles, 1972.

Mann, James. *About Face: A History of America's Curious Relationship with China*. New York: Alfred A. Knopf, 1999.

Martin, Edwin W. *Divided Counsel: The Anglo-American Response to Communist Victory in China*. Lexington: University Press of Kentucky, 1986.

Mayers, David A. *Cracking the Monolith: U.S. Policy against the Sino-Soviet Alliance, 1949–1955*. Baton Rouge: Louisiana State University Press, 1986.

McMahon, Robert. *The Cold War on the Periphery*. New York: Columbia University Press, 1996.

Moise, Edwin E. *Modern China, A History*. New York: Longman, 1994.

Mushakōji Kinhide. "The Cultural Premises of Japanese Diplomacy." In *The Silent Power: Japan's Identity and World Role*, ed. Japan Center for International Exchange. Tokyo: Simul Press, 1976.

Nakajima Mineo. "Foreign Relations: From the Korean War to the Bandung Line." In *Cambridge History of China*. Vol. 14: *The People's Republic, Part I: The Emergence of Revolutionary China, 1949–1965*, ed. Roderick MacFarquhar, John Fairbank, and Denis Twitchett. Cambridge: Cambridge University Press, 1991, 259–92.

Nelson, Keith L. *The Making of Détente: Soviet-American Relations in the Shadow of Vietnam*. Baltimore: Johns Hopkins University Press, 1995.

Niu Jun. "1962: The Eve of the Left Turn in China's Foreign Policy." CWIHP *Working Paper*, no. 48. Washington, D.C.: Woodrow Wilson Center, October 2005.

———. "On The Internally-oriented Characteristic of China's Diplomacy from 1945 to 1955." *Harvard University Asia Center*, Triangular Relations Conference, http://www.fas.harvard.edu/~asiactr/TR_Niu.htm.

———. "The Origins of the Sino-Soviet Alliance." In *Brothers in Arms*, ed. Odd A. Westad, 47–89.

Nixon, Richard. "Asia after Vietnam." *Foreign Affairs* 46, no. 1 (October 1967): 111–25.

———. *The Memoirs of Richard Nixon*. New York: Grosset and Dunlap, 1978.

Oksenberg, Michel, and Robert B. Oxnam, eds. *Dragon and Eagle, United States–China Relations: Past and Future*. New York: Basic Books, 1978.

Peng Dehuai. *Memoirs of a Chinese Marshal: The Autobiographical Notes of Peng Dehuai*. Peking: Foreign Language Press, 1984.

Phillips, Steven. "Nixon's China Initiative, 1969–1972." In *Documenting Diplomacy in the 21st Century*. Washington, D.C.: United States Department of State, 2001, 130–46.

Pillar, Paul R. *Negotiating Peace: War Termination as a Bargaining Process*. Princeton, N.J.: Princeton University Press, 1983.

Pollack, Jonathan D. "The Opening to America." In *Cambridge History of China*. Vol.

15: *The People's Republic, Part 2: Revolutions within the Chinese Revolution, 1966–1982*, ed. Roderick MacFarquhar, John Fairbank, and Denis Twitchett. Cambridge: Cambridge University Press, 1991, 402–74.

Porter, Brian. *Britain and the Rise of Communist China*. London: Oxford University Press, 1967.

Pye, Lucian. *Chinese Negotiating Style, Commercial Approaches and Cultural Principles*. New York: Quorum Books, 1992.

Rees, David. *Korea: The Limited War*. New York: St. Martin's Press, 1964.

Rhode, Grant, and Reid Whitlock, eds. *Treaties of the People's Republic of China, 1949–1978*. Boulder, Colo.: Westview Press, 1980.

Robinson, Thomas. "Chinese Foreign Policy from the 1940s to the 1990s." In *Chinese Foreign Policy*, ed. Robinson and Shambaugh, 555–602.

Robinson, Thomas, and David Shambaugh, eds. *Chinese Foreign Policy: Theory and Practice*. Oxford: Clarendon Press, 1994.

Romberg, Alan D. *Rein in at the Brink of the Precipice: American Policy toward Taiwan and U.S.-PRC Relations*. Washington, D.C.: Henry L. Stimson Center, 2003.

Ross, Robert S. *Negotiating Cooperation: The United States and China, 1969–1989*. Stanford, Calif.: Stanford University Press, 1995.

Ross, Robert S., and Jiang Changbin, eds. *Re-examining the Cold War: U.S.-China Diplomacy, 1954–1973*. Cambridge: Harvard University Press, 2001.

Salisbury, Harrison E. *The New Emperors: China in the Era of Mao and Deng*. Boston: Little, Brown, 1992.

Schecter, Jerrold L. *Russian Negotiating Behavior: Continuity and Transition*. Washington, D.C.: United States Institute of Peace Press, 1998.

Schoenbaum, Thomas J. *Waging Peace and War: Dean Rusk in the Truman, Kennedy, and Johnson Years*. New York: Simon and Schuster, 1988.

Service, John S. *The Amerasia Papers: Some Problems in the History of US-China Relations*. Berkeley: Center for Chinese Studies, University of California, 1971.

Shambaugh, David. *Beautiful Imperialism: China Perceives America, 1972–1990*. Princeton, N.J.: Princeton University Press, 1991.

Shaw, Yu-Ming. *An American Missionary in China, John Leighton Stuart and Chinese-American Relations*. Cambridge: Harvard University Press, 1992.

———. "John Leighton Stuart and U.S.–Chinese Communist Rapprochement in 1949: Was There Another 'Lost Chance in China'?" *China Quarterly* 89 (March 1982): 74–96.

Shen Zhihua. "The Discrepancy between the Russian and Chinese Versions of Mao's 2 October 1950 Message to Stalin on Chinese Entry into the Korean War: A Chinese Scholar's Reply." CWIHPB, nos. 8–9 (Winter 1996–Spring 1997): 237–42.

———. "Sino-North Korean Conflict and its Resolution during the Korean War." CWIHPB, nos. 14–15 (Winter 2003–Spring 2004): 9–24.

Sheng, Michael M. *Battling Western Imperialism: Mao, Stalin, and the United States*. Princeton, N.J.: Princeton University Press, 1997.

Shenkar, Oded, and Simcha Ronen. "The Cultural Context of Negotiations: The Implications of Chinese International Norms." *Journal of Applied Behavioral Science* 23, no. 2 (1987): 263–75.

Short, Philip. *Mao: A Life*. New York: Henry Holt, 1999.

Simmons, Robert R. *The Strained Alliance: Peking, Pyongyang, Moscow, and the Politics of the Korean Civil War*. New York: Free Press, 1975.

Snow, Edgar. "A Conversation with Mao Tse-tung." *Life* 70 (30 April 1971): 46–48.

———. *Red Star over China*. New York: Random House, 1938.

Snyder, Richard C., H. W. Bruck, and Burton Sapin. "The Decision-making Approach to the Study of International Politics." In *International Politics and Foreign Policy: a Reader in Research and Theory*, ed. James N. Rosenau. New York: Free Press, 1969, 199–206.

Snyder, Scott. *Negotiating on the Edge: North Korean Negotiating Behavior.* Washington, D.C.: United States Institute of Peace Press, 1999.

Solomon, Richard H. "China: Friendship and Obligation in Chinese Negotiating Style." In *National Negotiation Styles*, ed. Binnendijk Hans. Washington, D.C.: Department of State Publication, 1987, 1–16.

———. *Chinese Negotiating Behavior: Pursuing Interests through "Old Friends."* Washington, D.C.: United States Institute of Peace Press, 1999.

Spence, Jonathan D. *The Search for Modern China.* New York: W. W. Norton, 1991.

Stairs, Denis. *The Diplomacy of Constraint: Canada, the Korean War, and the United States.* Toronto: University of Toronto Press, 1974.

Starkey, Brigid, Mark A. Boyer, and Jonathan Wilkenfeld. *Negotiating a Complex World.* Lanham, Md.: Rowman and Littlefield, 1999.

Steele, Archibald T. *The American People and China.* New York: McGraw-Hill, 1966.

Stevenson, Adlai E. "Putting First Things First: A Democratic View." *Foreign Affairs* 38, no.1 (January 1960): 191–208.

Stewart, Sally, and Charles F. Keown. "Talking with the Dragon: Negotiating in the People's Republic of China." *Columbia Journal of World Business* (Autumn 1989): 68–72.

Strober, Deborah H., and Gerald S. Strober. *The Nixon Presidency: An Oral History of the Era.* Washington, D.C.: Brassey's, 2003.

Stuart, John Leighton. *Fifty Years in China.* New York: Random House, 1954.

———. *John Leighton Stuart's Diary.* Palo Alto, Calif.: Yenching University Alumni Association of USA, 1980.

Stueck, William W., Jr. *The Korean War: An International History.* Princeton, N.J.: Princeton University Press, 1995.

———. *Rethinking the Korean War–A New Diplomatic and Strategic History.* Princeton, N.J.: Princeton University Press, 2002.

———. *The Road to Confrontation: American Policy toward China and Korea, 1947–1950.* Chapel Hill: University of North Carolina Press, 1981.

Suh Dae-Sook. *Kim Il Sung: The North Korean Leader.* New York: Columbia University Press, 1988.

Teiwes, Frederick C. *Politics at Mao's Court: Gao Gang and Party Factionalism in the Early 1950s.* New York: M. E. Sharpe, 1990.

Teiwes, Frederick C., and Warren Sun. *The Tragedy of Lin Biao: Riding the Tiger during the Cultural Revolution, 1966–1971.* Honolulu: University of Hawai'i Press, 1996.

Terri, Ross. *Mao Zedong: A Biography.* Rev. ed. Stanford, Calif.: Stanford University Press, 2000.

Thomson, James C. "Dragon under Glass: Time for a New China Policy." *Atlantic Monthly Group* (October 1967). *Atlantic on line:* http://www.theatlantic.com/unbound/flashbks/china/thomson1.htm

———. "On the Making of U.S. China Policy, 1961–9: A Study in Bureaucratic Politics." *China Quarterly* 50 (April–June 1972): 220–43.

Tsou Tang. *America's Failure in China, 1941–1950.* 2 vols. Chicago: University of Chicago Press, 1963.

Tu Wei-ming. "Chinese Perceptions of America." In *Dragon and Eagle*, ed. Oksenberg and Oxnam, 87–106.

Tucker, Nancy B. *Patterns in the Dust: Chinese-American Relations and the Recognition Controversy, 1949–1950*. New York: Columbia University Press, 1983.

———. *Uncertain Friendships: Taiwan, Hong Kong and the United States, 1945–1992*. New York: Twayne Publishers, 1994.

———, ed. *China Confidential: American Diplomats and Sino-American Relations, 1945–1996*. New York: Columbia University Press, 2001.

Tyler, Patrick. *A Great Wall, Six Presidents and China: An Investigative History*. New York: Public Affairs, 1999.

Van Slyke, Lyman P., ed. *The China White Paper, August 1949*. Stanford, Calif.: Stanford University Press, 1967.

Vatcher, William H., Jr. *Panmunjom: The Story of the Korean Military Armistice Negotiations*. New York: Frederick A. Praeger, 1958.

Walt, Stephen M. *The Origins of Alliances*. Ithaca, N.Y.: Cornell University Press, 1987.

Walters, Vernon. *Silent Missions*. Garden City: N.Y.: Doubleday, 1978.

Weathersby, Kathryn. "New Findings on the Korean War." CWIHPB, no. 3 (Fall 1993): 1, 14–18.

———. "New Russian Documents on the Korean War." CWIHPB, nos. 6–7 (Winter 1995/96): 30–41.

———. "Soviet Aims in Korea and the Origins of the Korean War." CWIHP *Working Paper*, no. 8, November 1993.

———. "The Soviet Role in the Early Phase of the Korean War: New Documentary Evidence." *Journal of American-East Asian Relations* 3 (Winter 1994): 1–33.

———. "Stalin, Mao and the End of the Korean War." In *Brothers in Arms*, ed. Odd A. Westad, 90–116.

Westad, Odd Arne, ed. *Brothers in Arms: The Rise and Fall of the Sino-Soviet Alliance, 1945–1963*. Stanford, Calif.: Stanford University Press, 1998.

———. *Cold War and Revolution: Soviet–American Rivalry and the Origins of the Chinese Civil War*. New York: Columbia University Press, 1993.

———. "Losses, Chances, and Myths: The United States and the Creation of the Sino-Soviet Alliance, 1945–1950." *Diplomatic History* 21, no. 1 (Winter 1997): 105–15.

Whalen, Richard. *Drawing the Line: The Korean War, 1950–1953*. Boston: Little, Brown, 1990.

Whiting, Allen S. *China Crosses the Yalu: The Decisions to Enter the Korean War*. New York: Macmillan, 1960.

———. *The Chinese Calculus of Deterrence*. Ann Arbor: University of Michigan Press, 1975.

———. "Quemoy 1958: Mao's Miscalculations." *China Quarterly* 63 (September 1975): 263–70.

———. "Sino-American Détente." Review of *The Ends of Power*, by H. R. Haldeman; *The White House Years*, by Henry Kissinger; and *The Memoirs of Richard M. Nixon*, by Richard M. Nixon. *China Quarterly* 82 (June 1980): 334–41.

Wilhelm, Alfred D., Jr. *The Chinese at the Negotiating Table: Style and Characteristics*. Washington, D.C.: National Defense University, 1994.

Xia Yafeng. "Negotiating at Cross-Purposes: Sino-American Ambassadorial Talks, 1961–1968." *Diplomacy and Statecraft* 16, no. 2 (June 2005): 297–329.

———. "The Taiwan Issue in Sino-U.S. Rapprochement Negotiations." In *Taiwan in The Twenty-First Century*, ed. Xiaobing Li and Zuohong Pan. Lanham, Md.: University Press of America, 2003, 281–317.

———. "Vietnam for Taiwan? A Reappraisal of Nixon-Zhou Enlai Negotiation on

Shanghai Communiqué." *American Review of China Studies* 3, no. 1 (Spring 2002), 35–55.

Yan Xuetong. "Conditions for Chinese-U.S. Strategic Cooperation." *Harvard University Asia Center*, Triangular Relations Conference, http://www.fas.harvard.edu/~asiactr/TR_Yan.htm.

Yang Kuisong. "The Sino-Soviet Border Clash of 1969: From Zhenbao Island to Sino-American Rapprochement." *Cold War History* 1, no. 1 (August 2000): 21–52.

———. "The Soviet Factor and the CCP's Policy toward the United States in the 1940s." *Chinese Historian* 5, no. 1 (Spring 1992): 17–34.

Young, Kenneth T. *Negotiating with the Chinese Communists: The United States Experience, 1953–1967*. New York: McGraw-Hill Book Company, 1968.

Zartman, I. William, and Maureen R. Berman. *The Practical Negotiator*. New Haven: Yale University Press, 1982.

Zeiler, Thomas W. *Dean Rusk: Defending the American Mission Abroad*. Wilmington, Del.: Scholarly Resource, 2000.

Zhai Qiang. "China and the Geneva Conference of 1954." *China Quarterly* 129 (March 1992): 103–22.

———. *China and the Vietnam War*. Chapel Hill: University of North Carolina Press, 2000.

———. *The Dragon, the Lion, and the Eagle: Chinese-Britain-American Relations, 1949–1958*. Kent, Ohio: Kent University Press, 1994.

Zhang Baijia. "Zhou Enlai—The Shaper and Founder of China's Diplomacy." In *Toward a History of Chinese Communist Foreign Relations*, ed. Hunt and Niu, 67–88.

Zhang Shu Guang. "China's Strategic Culture and Cold War Confrontations." In *Reviewing the Cold War: Approaches, Interpretations, Theory*, ed. Odd Arne Westad. London: Frank Cass, 2000, 258–80.

———. *Deterrence and Strategic Culture: Chinese-American Confrontations, 1949–1958*. Ithaca, N.Y.: Cornell University Press, 1992.

———. *Economic Cold War: America's Embargo against China and the Sino-Soviet Alliance, 1949–1963*. Washington, D.C.: Woodrow Wilson Center Press and Stanford, Calif.: Stanford University Press, 2001.

———. "In the Shadow of Mao: Zhou Enlai and New China's Diplomacy." In *The Diplomats 1939–1979*, ed. Gordon A. Craig and Francis L. Loewenheim. Princeton, N.J.: Princeton University Press, 1994, 337–70.

———. *Mao's Military Romanticism: China and the Korean War, 1950–53*. Lawrence: University Press of Kansas, 1995.

———. "Preparedness Eliminates Mishaps: The CCP's Security Concerns in 1949–1950 and the Origins of the Sino-American Confrontation." *Journal of American-East Asian Relations* 1 (Spring 1992): 42–72.

Zhang Shu Guang, and Chen Jian, eds. *Chinese Communist Foreign Policy and the Cold War in Asia: New Documentary Evidence, 1944–1950*. Chicago: Imprint Publications, 1996.

INDEX

Italicized page numbers refer to illustrations.

ABOUT THE AUTHOR

Yafeng Xia is Assistant Professor of East Asian and Diplomatic History at Long Island University, Brooklyn. During the 1990s, he was in the Chinese Foreign Service, including a three-year tenure at the Chinese Embassy in Washington, D.C.

CPSIA information can be obtained at www.ICGtesting.com
Printed in the USA
BVOW06*1530031115

425419BV00011B/59/P